高等学校新形态规划教材

大学生安全防卫学双语教程

Bilingual Course on Security and Defense for College Students

王　成　杨默衍　葛小雨　编著

西北工业大学出版社

西　安

【内容简介】 本教程特色在于将大学生的安全观念、防卫技能和体育品德三项安全素养的培养，贯穿渗透于安全理论篇和格斗技术篇两大模块，引导大学生从安全观念、安全理论、品德教育和防卫技能四个方面，达到能够自我识别安全风险、自我应对安全险情、自我保护人身安全的目的。

本教程将理论与实践相结合，安全健康与自卫防身相结合，构建大学生安全教育的新体系与自卫防身课程教学的新模式，营造新时代大学生安全生态环境。

【Introduction】 The characteristic of this course is to cultivate the security concepts, defense skills, and sports ethics of college students, which are integrated into the two major parts of Security Theory education and Combat Techniques. From four aspects: security concepts, security theories, moral education, and defense skills, it guides college students to identify security risks, respond to unsafe situations, and protect personal security.

Combining theory with practice, combining security and health with self-defense skills, the course constructs a new system of security education for college students and a new model of self-defense course teaching, creating a safe ecological environment for college students in the new era.

图书在版编目（CIP）数据

大学生安全防卫学双语教程 ：汉英对照 / 王成，杨默衍，葛小雨编著. -- 西安 ：西北工业大学出版社，2024.11. -- ISBN 978-7-5612-9611-0

Ⅰ . G645.5；G852.4

中国国家版本馆CIP数据核字第2024ED0182号

DAXUESHENG ANQUAN FANGWEIXUE SHUANGYU JIAOCHENG

大 学 生 安 全 防 卫 学 双 语 教 程

王成 杨默衍 葛小雨 编著

责任编辑：隋秀娟 张英哥		策划编辑：杨 军	
责任校对：朱辰浩		装帧设计：高永斌 董晓伟	

出版发行：西北工业大学出版社

通信地址：西安市友谊西路 127 号　　邮编：710072

电　　话：(029) 88491757，88493844

网　　址：www.nwpup.com

印 刷 者：西安浩轩印务有限公司

开　　本：787 mm×1 092 mm　　　1/16

印　　张：21.75

字　　数：487 千字

版　　次：2024 年 11 月第 1 版　　2024 年 11 月第 1 次印刷

书　　号：ISBN 978-7-5612-9611-0

定　　价：88.00 元

安全防卫教育为学生平安保驾护航

（代序）

随着社会的快速发展、科技的飞速进步与生活方式的转变，现代社会的安全问题也愈加复杂。作为一门涉及人身安全、公共安全和社会稳定的重要学科，安全防卫教育在全球范围内得到了越来越多的关注，并逐渐从传统的自卫技能训练转向了更加综合性的危机应对、心理调适、法律保障等领域。

大学生群体正处于成长的关键阶段，面临着诸多安全威胁，包括校园欺凌、交通事故、消防安全等等。学会更好地保护自己以应对突发事件，成为了当代大学生的必备素质。为帮助大学生系统地掌握应对现代社会各种安全威胁的知识，使其具备必要的安全防护能力，西北工业大学王成教授等多位在安全防卫学领域具有一定理论基础和丰富实践经验的专家学者组建了编写团队，共同完成了《大学生安全防卫学双语教程》的编写工作。

《大学生安全防卫学双语教程》涵盖大学生安全防卫学的基本理论、基本的防卫技能、危机应对、急救知识及法律常识等内容。该书尤其注重使用简明易懂的语言，介绍真实案例和实践技巧，有较强的实践指导作用。《大学生安全防卫学双语教程》具有双语教学的特点：不仅为大学生提供了中文讲解，还配有英文翻译，帮助学生在学习安全防卫知识的同时提升英语水平和跨文化沟通能力。该书的双语特质不仅适应国内学生的需求，更具国际视野。

总之，《大学生安全防卫学双语教程》应时而生，选题独到，编写思路新颖，兼具科普性、实操性和国际性。希望该书的出版能帮助大学生安全教育的发展开辟新路径，从而构建更加安全和谐的社会环境。

当然，作为一种新的尝试，该书还有许多方面不够完善。"大学生安全防卫学"这一提法是否妥当，还须商榷。万事开头难，感谢王成教授及其团队勇敢地迈出了关键一步。期待更多学者关注新时代大学生安全防卫学，关注安全教育。

教育部基础教育教学指导委员会安全教育专业委员会副主任委员

教育部高等学校教育学类教学指导委员会委员

山西师范大学教育学部副部长、教授、博士生导师

2024 年 8 月 18 日

前　　言

随着教育理念的不断更新和教育改革的深入推进，安全教育逐渐成为教育体系中的重要组成部分。2018 年《教育部办公厅关于防范学生溺水事故的预警通知》（教督厅函〔2018〕4 号）提出"坚持预防为主，进一步加强防溺水安全教育"。2019 年出台的《教育部等五部门关于完善安全事故处理机制维护学校教育教学秩序的意见》（教政法〔2019〕11 号）指出要"着重加强学校安全事故预防"。2020 年教育部印发的《大中小学国家安全教育指导纲要》指出，维护好社会治安和公共卫生等方面是社会和谐稳定的基础，应加强学生面临群体性事件、暴力恐怖活动、新型违法犯罪等威胁的应对能力。每份文件的修订、完善和细化，都是生活实例的映照。为此，应警钟长鸣，防微杜渐，掐断影响生命安全的引线。

本教程秉持理论与实践并进的原则，从精神和物质两个层面切入，以提高个体的生命安全意识、危险识别意识和自我保护能力。具体而言，本教程主要分为安全理论和格斗技术两个篇章。

安全理论篇主要围绕影响个人生命安全的两个重要因素——意外事故和刑事犯罪。安全理论篇的学习，使大家明白遇到火灾、溺水、运动损伤等事故时如何施救、自救，以及如何预防；遇见各类刑事案件时，如何不战而屈人之兵以及如何防患于未然。

格斗技术篇则是针对遇见暴力刑事犯罪案件避无可避，采取格斗策略时所需学会的具身技能展开。内容参考武术散打、擒拿、综合格斗等多个项目，以帮助学生应对不同场景、不同特点的刑事犯罪。

另外，本教程为了让大家更直观地感受各类刑事犯罪对社会、家庭及个人带来的危害影响，以及格斗技能的具体使用方法，在相应章节插入了生动的案例参考和动作的应用说明。读者可扫描章节最后的二维码，观看相关微课视频；同时也可登陆西北工业大学出版社官方网站查看本教程的教学课件、考试习题及答案讲解。

总之，安全防卫教育不仅仅是知识的传授，更是意识的培养和能力的提升。希望通过本教程的学习，能够唤醒大家对自身安全的重视。安全无小事，每个社会公民都应当具备基本的防卫技能和应急处置能力，以保障自身的安全与健康。

本教程的编写分工如下。王成：教程的总体规划，章节设置，知识点安排；教案的总体设计；视频录制；等等。杨默衍：教程撰写，包括文字、图片、表格等的制作；视频的技术动作指导、视频录制；等等。葛小雨：教程的翻译、校对；视频录制；等等。

本教程的编写得到了各界专家学者的鼎力支持，在此，笔者向所有参与撰写和审核的老师、同学以及相关单位表示衷心的感谢。同时，也诚挚地期盼广大读者能够对本教程提出宝贵意见，以便在今后的修订和完善中加以改进。

希望本教程能够成为大学生安全教育的重要参考资料，为培养具有高度安全意识和防卫能力的新时代大学生贡献一份力量。愿每一位读者都能从本教程中受益，提高自身的安全防卫意识和能力，共同建设更加安全和谐的社会环境和校园环境。

编著者

2024 年 6 月

Preface

With the continuous updating of educational concepts and the deepening of educational reform，security education has gradually become an important component of the education system. The Early Warning Notice on Preventing Student Drowning Accidents issued by the General Office of the Ministry of Education in 2018 proposed to "prioritize prevention and further strengthen drowning security education". The Opinions on Improving the Mechanism for Handling Security Accidents and Maintaining the Order of School Education and Teaching issued in 2019 pointed out that "emphasis should be placed on strengthening the prevention of school security accidents". The Guidelines for National Security Education in Primary，Secondary and Primary Schools issued by the Ministry of Education in 2020 pointed out that social security and public health protection are the foundation of social harmony and stability，students should enhance their ability to face threats such as group incidents，violent terrorist activities，and new types of illegal activities. The revision，improvement，and refinement of each document are reflected by real-life examples. Therefore，the alarm bell should always ring，prevention measures should be taken，and any leads that may affect life security should be cut off.

This course adheres to the principle of combining theory and practice，and approaches from both spiritual and material levels to enhance individuals' awareness of life security，danger identification，and self-protection ability. Specifically，this course is mainly divided into two Parts: Security Theory and Combat Techniques.

The Security Theory Part mainly focuses on two important factors that affect personal life security—accidents and criminal offenses. Through the study of security theory，students will understand how to rescue others，self-rescue，and prevent accidents such as fires，drowning，and sports injuries; and when encountering various criminal cases，how to defeat others without fighting，and how to prevent them before they occur.

The fighting skills section is aimed at the embodied skills that need to be learned when adopting fighting strategies in cases where violent criminal offenses are unavoidable. The content covers multiple martial arts such as Sanda，grappling，and comprehensive combat，in order to help everyone cope with crimes in different scenes and characteristics.

In addition，since this course aims to provide a more direct understanding of the harmful effects of various criminal offenses on society，families，and individuals，as well as to illustrate the specific use of combat skills，vivid case references and action application references have been inserted in the corresponding chapters. The QR codes placed in the end of relative chapters can be scanned to watch videos. Meanwhile, the official website of Northwestern Polytechnical University Press provides courseware, tests and answers for readers.

In short，security and defense education is not only about imparting knowledge，but also about cultivating awareness and enhancing abilities. I hope that through the study of this course，we can awaken everyone's awareness of their own security. Security is no small matter，and every citizen in society should have basic defense skills and emergency response capabilities to ensure their own security and health.

The compilation of this course consists of the following work. Wang Cheng: Overall planning of the course, arrangement of chapters and knowledge points; overall design of lessons; video recording, etc. Yang Moyan: Overall writing, including the production of text, images, tables, etc; techniques and action guidance in video recording, etc. Ge Xiaoyu: Overall translation and proofreading of the course; video recording, etc.

The compilation of this course has received strong support from experts and scholars from all walks of life. We would like to express our sincere gratitude to all the teachers，students，and relevant units who participated in the compilation and review. At the same time，we sincerely hope that readers can provide valuable feedback on this course，so that we can make improvements in future revisions and modification.

I hope this course can function as an important reference material for security education for college students，and contribute to cultivating new era college students with high security awareness and defense ability. May every reader benefit from this course，enhance their awareness and ability of security and defense，and work together to build safer and more harmonious social and campus environments.

Authors

2024.6

目　　录 | CONTENTS

第一部分　安全理论篇　Part I　Security Theory

第二部分　格斗技术篇　PART II　Combat Techniques

第一部分 安全理论篇

PART Ⅰ Security Theory

第一章
大学生安全防卫学简介

Chapter 1
Introduction to Security Education and Defense Studies

第一节
大学生安全防卫学概述

Section 1
Overview of Security Education and Defense Studies for College Students

一、大学生安全防卫学相关概念

1. Concepts Related to Security Education and Defense Studies

（一）"安全"的概念界定

《说文解字》载："安，静也。"《尔雅》载："安，定也。"引申之意为心神的宁静和安定。此外，《左传·襄公十一年》道"心安而不惧，形劳而不倦"；《易·系辞下》言"是故君子安而不忘危"；《前汉·贾谊传》载"置之安处则安，置之危处则危"，将"安"与"危"相对立。为此，"安"的本意即无危为安，临危不惧。

《说文解字》中的"全"有两种写法，一为"全"，释为"完也，从人，从工"。段玉裁注，"从工者，如巧者之制造必完好也。"二写作"全"，释为"篆文全从玉，纯玉曰全"。不论是从人，还是从玉，其核心本意指代完整、全部、纯粹，即无损为全。

(1) Definition of the Concept of "Security"

Origin of Chinese Characters says: "Security is a kind of peace. " While *Erya* records: "Security is a kind of stable life. " The extended meaning is tranquility and stability of the mind. In addition, the *Zuo's Commentary* states: "The heart is at ease but not afraid, and the fatigue is tireless." The *Yi* states: "A wise person is safe and never forgets danger." The *Book of Han* records that "If you place it in a safe place, it is safe; if you place it in a dangerous place, it is dangerous", opposing "security" and "danger". Therefore, the original meaning of "security" is to be safe without danger, fearless without danger.

There are two ways to write " 全 " in *Origin of Chinese Characters*, one is " 全 ", which is interpreted as "perfect things are divided into two parts: people and work." Duan Yucai noted, "The work means that those who are skilled in craftsmanship must have their manufacturing in good condition." The other writing is " 全 ", which means "seal script with jade, pure jade is called Quan". Whether it is from people or from jade, its core original meaning refers to completeness, fullness, purity, and integrity and undamaged is considered complete.

综上，安全即指不受威胁，没有危险、危害、损失。但学界对于安全概念的定义仍存在主客观二元论和客观论的争辩。主客观二元论认为安全就是客观上不存在威胁，主观上不存在恐惧；客观论则认为安全就是没有危险、不受威胁的客观状态。本教程更倾向于主客观二元论的观点。

（二）"防卫"的概念界定

"防，堤也。"本义为堤坝。《周礼·稻人》曰："以防止水。"以此为点，词义可延伸至戒备与守卫之义。正如《左忠毅公逸事》所载，"逆阉防伺甚严，虽家仆不得近。"表示防备甚严，即使家仆都不能接近。

卫，同衞。《说文解字》载："卫，宿卫也。"即住宿于值勤地，整夜守卫。《玉篇》曰："卫护也。"《战国策·赵策》言："以卫王宫。"另外，在甲骨文中，卫字的字形就是四足环绕城邑之形，表达对于城邑的护卫。由以上可知，"卫"的本意为保护和守护。

将防与卫联合使用可见宋朝秦观的《东城被盗得世字》。文中载道："野人无机心，触事少防卫。"质朴的村民缺少狡诈诡变的心，遇事常疏于防备。综上，防卫指防御和保卫的活动或措施。

In summary, security refers to not being threatened, without danger, harm, or loss. However, there is still a debate in the academic community about the definition of security concept between subjective and objective dualism and objectivity. The dualism of subject and object holds that Security is an objective state where there is no threat objectively and no fear subjectively. Objectively speaking, Security is an objective state where there is no danger and no threat. This course tends to lean towards a dualistic perspective of subjectivity and objectivity.

(2) Definition of the Concept of "Defense"

"Fang" means a type of dam. The *Rites of the Zhou*, a classical book in ancient China states: "Fang means to prevent water from stopping." Based on this, the meaning of the word can be extended to mean vigilance and guarding. As recorded in "The Story of Duke Zuo Zhongyi", "Rebel and eunuchs in ancient China are very guarded against other people, even domestic servants cannot approach them" expresses that is our defensive attitude towards others.

According to the *Origin of Chinese Characters*, "Wei" means staying at the duty station and guarding all night. *The Jade Chapter* says: "Wei" is a type of guard and protect." *Intrigues of the Warring States* states: "To guard the palace." In addition, in oracle bone inscriptions, the shape of the character "Wei" is the shape of a city surrounded by four legs, expressing the protection of the city. From the above, it can be inferred that the original meaning of "Wei" is to protect and guard.

The combination of "Fang" and "Wei" can be seen in the book of Qin Guan "The World's Character of Dongcheng Stolen" during the Song Dynasty. In the text, it is said: "Wild people have no intention and are less guarded in case of trouble." Rustic villagers lack a cunning heart, and often neglect to be prepared in case of trouble. In summary, defense refers to the activities or measures of defense.

（三）安全防卫学的概念界定

根据不同安全对象可分为国家安全、社会安全、个人安全。从问题层面看，可分为文化安全、生命安全、信息安全等。随着社会的发展、制度的变革，安全的内涵与外延也在不断发展。但其最初的发生学本源指向的是生命，因为生存权或生命权是人赖以生存和发展的前提。从马斯洛的需求理论而言，生命属于生理需求，是其他需求的基底，只有具备生存权才能谈种族延续，论社会发展。另外，只有公民具备安全，才有社会安全和国家安全。为此，生命安全是其他安全的基础，否则如无源之水，无本之木。安全防卫则是指为了生命安全免受不法侵害而采取的制止不法侵害的行为或措施。

本教程未使用"自卫"一词。主要是由于自卫仅凸显了个人层面的安全，缺少公共社会安全以及国家安全的广阔视角。为此，本教程使用"防卫"一词，强调个人安全防卫应上升至社会和国家安全防卫。两者互为根本，无数个体汇聚，铸造国家护盾，国家安全又为个人的安全提供保护网。

安全防卫学是一门实用科学，它是综合了犯罪学中的原理与知识，司法系统与警方的犯罪统计数据与案例，以及各种拳术中的实用格斗技巧而形成一套独立的

(3) Definition of the Concept of Security and Defense Studies

According to the different objects of security, it can be divided into national security, social security, and personal security. From a problem perspective, it can be divided into cultural security, life security, information security, etc. The connotation and extension of security are constantly expanding and developing with the development of social and institutional changes. But its initial genetic origin pointed to life, because the right to survival or the right to life is a prerequisite for human survival and development. From Maslow's theory of needs, life belongs to physiological needs and is the foundation of other needs. Only with the right to survival can we talk about racial continuity and social development. Only citizens with security can have social and national security. Therefore, life security is the foundation of other security, otherwise like water without a source, there is no foundation. Security defense refers to the actions or measures taken to prevent illegal infringement in order to ensure the security of life.

The term "self-defense" is not used in this course, mainly because self-defense only highlights the personal level of security and is in lack of a broad perspective on public social security and national security. Therefore, this course uses the term "defense" and emphasizes that personal security defense should be elevated to social and national security defense, both of which are fundamental to each other. Countless individuals gather to forge a national shield, and national security provides a protective net for individual security.

Security and defense is a practical science that integrates the principles and knowledge of criminology, crime statistics and cases from the judicial system and police, as well as practical combat techniques in various martial arts, to form an independent system of security

安全自卫防身学体系。安全防卫学不仅研究、发展及检验对付暴力犯罪的理论、策略、技术及仪器设备，而且设计各种相关实用课程并向广大人民群众推广，以提高人民群众的防身意识，让人民群众学会防身的策略与技能。

and self-defense. Security and self-defense studies not only focus on researching, developing, and testing theories, strategies, techniques, and equipment for dealing with violent crimes, but also on researching and designing various practical courses and help them promoting them to the general public, in order to enhance their self-defense awareness and help them learn self-defense strategies and skills.

二、安全防卫学的目的与意义

2. The Purpose and Significance of Security and Defense Studies

（一）安全防卫学的目的

大学生安全防卫课程的主要目的是培育和增强大学生的生命意识、安全防卫意识和国家安全意识。生命意识是基础，只有尊重生命、爱护生命才能做到爱自己、爱父母、爱他人，建构和谐的社会环境。安全防卫意识是重点。在当下的社会生活中，无时无刻都有面临着各类风险的可能性，只有具备基本的自我防范意识和处理能力，才能预防危险，降低风险，并在面对危及生命的应激刺激时不惊慌失措。国防安全意识是核心。没有国家的强大作为护盾，就谈不上个人的安稳生活。为此，安全防卫的主要目的有：①让学生熟悉常见事故以及各类暴力的理论预防知识，掌握各类格斗技能，保护自己从各类意外事故和伤害事件中安全脱身；②通过个人层面的安全防卫，间接提高国家安全防卫意识；③以各类生动的实例为引，使学生明白生命的脆弱与宝贵。

(1) The Purpose of Security and Defense Studies

The main purpose of college student security and defense courses is to cultivate and enhance their awareness of life, security and defense, and national security. Life consciousness is the foundation. Only by respecting and caring for life can we love ourselves, parents, and others, and build a harmonious social environment. Security and defense awareness is the key. In today's social life, we are constantly faced with the possibility of various risks. Only with basic self-protection awareness and processing ability can we prevent danger, reduce the possibility of risks, and not panic when facing life-threatening stress stimuli. National defense and security awareness is the core. Without the strength of a country as a shield, there is no way for an individual to live a stable life. The main purpose of security defense is first, to familiarize students with the theoretical prevention knowledge of common accidents and various forms of violence, master various combat skills, and protect themselves from accidents and injuries. Second, through personal level security defense, indirectly enhance national awareness. Third, use various vivid examples as a guide, help students understand the fragility and value of life.

（二）安全防卫学的意义

2010 年 7 月 29 日正式公布实施的《国家中长期教育改革和发展规划纲要》指出"要重视安全教育、生命教育、国防教育和可持续发展教育"。安全防卫学秉持以人为本，以安全为要，以生命至上为原则，培育学生的个人以及国家安全意识，促进可持续性发展。

1. 强化生命安全教育

现代社会生活的主旋律是"效率"。人们很难停止脚步，让心灵休憩与停顿。许多年轻人熬夜的本质原因是只有夜晚才属于自己，白天则顶着学业、就业、生活"三座大山"，身心压力剧增，导致许多大学生出现"生命的困顿"，表现为陷入严重的郁闷、无聊、纠结、"活得很累"等状态。严重者则发展到网瘾、自闭、斗殴、自残；再严重者就沦入到吸毒、自杀、伤害他人的种种困境之中①。

此外，在科学主义的工具理性主导下，天平逐渐向科学性知识倾斜，导致人文性生命教育不足。学生习得了很多理论公式，却仍无法解出生命的价值和生活的意义。由此，一方面会导致部分大学生轻生，另一方面会造成校园欺凌问题。主要原因是大学生对生命缺少尊重和敬畏。只有

(2) The Significance of Security and Defense Studies

The National Medium and Long Term Education Reform and Development Plan Outline, officially announced and implemented on July 29, 2010, pointed out that "we should attach importance to security education, life education, national defense education, and sustainable development education". The security and defense course adheres to the principle of putting people first, prioritizing security, and putting life first. It can cultivate students' awareness of personal and national security awareness, and promote sustainable development.

1) Strengthen Life Security Education

The main theme of modern social life is "efficiency". It is difficult for people to stop their steps and let their minds rest and pause. The fundamental reason why many young people stay up late is that only the night belongs to them, while the day is burdened by "the three mountains" of academic research, job hunting, and life stress. The increased physical and mental pressure has led to many college students experiencing "life difficulties", manifested as serious depression, boredom, entanglement, and "living very tired". Severe cases may develop into internet addiction, autism, fighting with others, and self harm; the most serious cases fall into various difficulties such as drug use, suicide, and harming others.

In addition, under the horizon of instrumental rationality of scientism,balance gradually leans towards scientific knowledge, leading to insufficient humanistic life education. Students have learned many theories, but still cannot see the value and meaning of life. As a result, on the one hand, it will lead to the phenomenon of some college students committing suicide, and on the other hand, it will cause the problem of violence on university campuses. The main reason is that college students lack respect and reverence for life. Only by

---

① 郑晓江. 生命困顿于生命教育 [J]. 南昌大学学报（人文社会科学版）,2012,43(2):48-54.

使学生树立正确的生命观、生存观和生活观才能根绝此问题。

安全教育的本质是生命教育。本教材从安全理论与防卫技能两个方面入手，以案例为支撑，通过生命教育、生存教育和生活教育三个层面的内容，提高个体的生命意识和生存能力，并贯彻于日常生活中。让学生学会尊重生命、珍惜生命、了解生命的可贵，促进学生积极主动、健康地发展生命，提升生命的质量，实现生命的意义和价值。

2. 培育国家安全意识

当下世界经济格局正处于剧烈变化中，地区、国家间的摩擦不断。如2020年中印边境地区爆发的大规模肢体冲突事件、2022年的俄乌冲突、2023年的巴以冲突、缅甸内战都印证此点。根据马克思的辩证唯物观可知，联系是普遍的，没有孤立存在的事物。"家国"亦是如此，没有强大的国家作为支撑，何来家庭与个人的幸福美满；没有无数个体的支撑，又何来强大的国家。在国家冲突中，个体利益的实现是建立在国家集体利益实现的基础之上的，缺乏国家的支持与保护，个体生活的方方面面都会受到波及与影响。

家国同构。中华民族共同体意识和爱国精神是每位公民应具备的素养，国家安全意识是每位公民应具备的使命。国家的自主

enabling students to establish correct views on life, survival, and living can this problem be eradicated.

The essence of security education is life education. This course, starting from two aspects—Security Theory and Combat Techniques, is supported by cases. Through the content of life education, survival education, and life education, people's awareness and ability to survive are improved, and this concept is implemented in daily life. Enable students to learn to respect life, cherish life, understand the value of life, promote active and healthy development of life, improve the quality of life, realize the meaning and value of life, and raise awareness of security education.

2) Cultivate National Security Awareness

The current global economic landscape is undergoing drastic changes, with constant friction between regions and countries. The large-scale physical conflicts that erupted in the China-India border area in 2020, the Russia-Ukraine conflict in 2022, the Israeli Palestinian Conflict in 2023, and the Burmese Civil War all confirm this point. According to Marx's dialectical materialism, connection is universal and there are no isolated things. The same goes for "family and country". Without the support of a strong country, there can be no happiness for families and individuals. Without the support of countless individuals, there can be no strong country. In national conflicts, the realization of individual interests is based on the realization of national collective interests. Without the support and protection of the state, all aspects of individual life will be affected.

Family and country are isomorphic. The sense of community and patriotism of the Chinese nation are qualities that every citizen should possess. National security awareness is a mission that every citizen should possess. The autonomy

权是个人的财产权、生命权、健康权得以保证的前提。换言之，抽象的国家概念需要具体的个体谱写与照亮。

3. 提高安全意识与能力

国家为了治理社会不良风气，保证社会治安稳定以及群众安居乐业，分别于1983年、1996年以及2001年进行了三次"严打"，使社会风气得以拨乱反正，使盗窃团伙、抢劫团伙及黑恶势力得以有效肃清和整治。社会属性是人的类属性，阶级性是人的本质特征之一。随着社会的发展，人类物质和精神文明水平得以显著提升，但人的欲壑难填。正如马克思在《资本论》中所说，有50%的利润，资本就能铤而走险；有100%的利润，资本就敢践踏一切人间法律；有300%的利润，资本就敢犯任何罪行。国家统计局发布的《中国统计年鉴2023》显示2022年受理故意伤害案件10万多起，殴打他人案件约219.5万起，杀人案件5 000多起，强奸案件3.9万多起。可见，危险仍是存在的。当个体的各类需求无法通过正当的手段满足时，就可能采取不当的方法。

另外，在日常生活中，除了各类刑事犯罪外，人们还面临各类更迭的病毒、各式各样的疾病，以及始料未及的事故等危险因素。换言之，"世界是精彩的，社会是复杂

of a country is a prerequisite for ensuring individual property rights, life rights, and health rights. In other words, abstract national concepts require concrete individual composition and illumination.

3) Improve Security Awareness and Capabilities

In order to regulate the negative social atmosphere, ensure social security and stability, and the well-being of the people, the country implemented three severe crackdowns in 1983, 1996, and 2001, respectively. This allowed the social atmosphere to be rectified, and theft, robbery, and evil forces to be effectively eradicated and rectified. Sociality is a human attribute, and class nature is one of the essential characteristics of human beings. Even though material and spiritual civilization can be significantly improved with the development of society, human desires also increase accordingly. As Marx said in *Das kapital*, capital holders can take risks for 50% profit; For the sake of 100% profit, capital holders dare to trample on all human laws. When there is a 300% profit, capital holders dare to commit any crime. Therefore, the danger still exists. According to the *2023 China Statistical Yearbook* released by the National Bureau of Statistics, there were over 100,000 cases of intentional injury, about 2.195 million cases of assault, over 5,000 cases of murder, and over 39,000 cases of rape accepted in 2022. When an individual's various needs cannot be met through legitimate means, inappropriate measures will be taken.

In addition, in daily life, in addition to various criminal offenses, we also face various changing viruses, diseases, and unexpected accidents, which are all dangerous factors. In other words, "The world is wonderful, society is complex, and danger exists." Violent crimes are ubiquitous, accidents

的, 危险是存在的。"暴力犯罪无所不在, 意外无时不在。安全防卫学意在从安全知识与格斗技术两个方面引入, 帮助大家建立形成和掌握安全意识与能力, 降低各类危险发生的概率。

are always present. Security and defense studies aim to be introduced to people through Security Theory and Combat Techniques to help people establish and master security awareness and abilities, and reduce the probability of various dangers occurring.

三、安全防卫学的特征

3. The Characteristics of Security and Defense Studies

（一）防御性与被动性

影响个人生命安全的"三座大山"有意外事故、疾病和暴力犯罪。即使遵守交通规则, 依然有概率遇见酒驾; 即使做好各类防御措施, 但诱发疾病的因素千万种, 也只能做到降低发病概率; 即使不主动招惹他人, 依然可能成为歹徒的犯罪实施对象, 正所谓"匹夫无罪, 怀璧其罪"。因此, 对于个体而言都是被动地预防和防卫。

（二）不可预知性

从暴力犯罪的角度看, 自卫者与歹徒之间的较量是一场不对等、不公平的战争, 受害者在明处, 而歹徒却在暗处。人们无法提前预知歹徒是谁, 歹徒的攻击目标是谁、想干什么及在何时何地, 如何作案。

在日常生活中, 各类媒体平台常常会报道犯罪的案例及各类事故的新闻。作为旁观者, 可能没有丝毫触动, 且很快就将其抛诸脑后, 认为发生在自己身上的

(1) Defensive and Passive Nature

"The three mountains" that affect personal security include accidents, illnesses, and violent crimes. Even if traffic regulations are followed, there is still a chance of encountering drunk driving; even with various protection measures in place, there are millions of factors that can trigger diseases, and the probability can only be reduced; even if you do not actively provoke others, you may still become the target of criminals. As the saying goes, "a man is innocent, but he is guilty of stashing precious jade". Therefore, for individuals, it is passive prevention and defense that they take.

(2) Unpredictability

From the perspective of violent crimes, the conflict between self-defenders and criminals is an unequal and unfair war, where the victims are in the open while the criminals are in the dark. People cannot predict in advance who the culprit is, who the target is, what they want to do, when, where, and how they will commit the crime, so prevention is still difficult.

In daily life, various media platforms often report on crime cases and news about various accidents. As observers, we may not have been touched at all and quickly forget. We might believe that the probability of crimes happening to ourselves is very low. However, it is only when one

概率很低，直至成为事实的受害者，才感到后悔、懂得学习自卫防身的重要性、明白安全知识的重要性。

人们不能只从自己的经历中去学习，有些事做错了可以重来，而预防暴力犯罪与各类事故是不可以把希望寄托于获得第二次机会上的。应从别人的惨痛经验教训中学会预防并保护自己，未雨绸缪，才是智者。

（三）残酷性

2023 年，我国全年出生人口 902 万人，出生率为 6.4%，死亡人口为 1 110 万人，死亡率为 7.9%，死亡人数远大于出生人口数，数字的背后是无数条鲜活生命的逝去，也折射出生命的脆弱与死亡的残酷。疾病、事故以及犯罪等不仅给人们的生命财产安全以及社会经济造成极大的威胁与破坏，还为其家人的心灵蒙上阴影。

（四）复杂性

导致意外事故的因素有个人的不安全行为、物的不安全状态、管理制度的缺陷与不足，以及环境不安定因素；导致个人实施犯罪行为的因素有社会因素、心理因素以及生理因素等；导致疾病的因素有遗传、环境以及生活方式等。维护生命安全好比一场战争，又好比一场体育比赛，参赛者的准备程度、智力水平、技术水平、身体条件，以及特定的场

becomes a victim of crimes that one feels regretful, understands the importance of learning self-defense, and understands the importance of security knowledge.

People cannot just learn from their own experiences. Some things can be redone when they are wrong, while preventing violent crime and various accidents cannot rely on a second opportunity for hope. Learning to prevent and protect oneself from the painful experiences and lessons of others is the wise way.

(3) Cruelty

In 2023, China had a total birth population of 9.02 million, with a birth rate of 6.4%, and a death population of 11.10 million, with a death rate of 7.9%. The number of deaths far exceeded the number of births, and behind the numbers were countless lives lost, reflecting the fragility and cruelty of life. Diseases, accidents, and crimes not only pose great threats and damages to people's lives, property, and socio-economic security, but also cast a shadow over the hearts of their families.

(4) Complexity

The factors that lead to accidents include personal unsafe behavior, unsafe conditions of objects, deficiencies in management systems, and unstable environmental factors; the factors that lead to individuals committing criminal acts include social, psychological, and physiological factors; factors that can cause diseases include genetics, environment, and lifestyle. It's like a war or a sports match concerning life security protection, the level of preparation, intelligence, technical skills, physical conditions, as well as specific occasions and circumstances will have a significant impact on the outcome. In short, there are many factors that

合与具体情况都将对胜负产生重大影响。简言之，影响生命安全的因素有很多，但我们要尽量把握可控因素，预防不可控因素。例如，个人的不安全行为完全在自我控制范围内，对于不可控的因素，例如环境等，则应尽量去避免。

affect life security, but we should try to grasp controllable factors and prevent uncontrollable factors. For example, if an individual's unsafe behavior is completely within his self-control range, we should try to avoid uncontrollable factors such as the environment.

第二节
安全防卫学的发展与现状

Section 2
Development and Current State of Security and Defense Studies

一、自卫防身课程的发展

弗洛伊德认为本能是推动个体行为的内在动力。人类最基本的本能包括生的本能和死亡本能（攻击本能）两类。其中生的本能包括性欲本能和个体生存本能。

自我防卫就是人类在物竞天择的自然法则下、生存的本能驱使下，在与自然界的斗争过程中产生的。自卫的攻击方式随着生产力的变革以及不断的战争活动更新迭代。各类冷兵器虽不断推陈出新，但"个人徒手格斗"是贯穿历史长河的关键词，徒手对抗是器械类技术的基础，器械类技术是徒手对抗的延伸。

秦汉时期防身自卫术被称作"拨乱手搏"，比赛形式较为正规。该时期武术攻防格斗术也有了很大的发展。汉代手搏也

1. The Development of Self-defense Courses

Freud believed that instinct is the intrinsic driving force behind individual behavior. The most basic instincts of human beings include two types: the instinct to live and the instinct to die (attack instinct). The innate instincts include sexual desire instincts and individual survival instincts.

Self-defense is the process of human struggle against nature, driven by the laws of natural selection and the instinct for survival. The attack methods of self-defense have evolved and iterated with the changes in productivity and continuous warfare activities. Although various types of cold weapons are constantly being innovated, "individual unarmed combat" is a key word that runs through history. Unarmed combat is the foundation of equipment technology, and equipment technology is an extension of unarmed confrontation.

During the Qin and Han dynasties, self-defense techniques were known as "chaotic hand fights", and the competition format was relatively formal. Martial arts, such as offensive and defensive fighting, also developed greatly.

叫"弃""卞"。擂台竞技在唐代更加广泛，手搏、角抵备受重视，比赛几乎形成制度。到宋代，手搏术作为强身健体、活动筋骨的主要手段，在民间广为流行。清代出现了许多民间练武团体，如"社""馆"等组织，各馆之间经常比武较量，切磋武艺，所以"打擂"在民间广为流行①。

但自卫防身术的提出与体系建成则源于欧美国家，主要是由于影响社会安全的危险因素——暴力犯罪起数不断上升。有暴力就有对立词：防暴力——自卫。对此，美国于1880年前后针对有关自卫的法律条文进行了讨论。1905年首本有关安全自卫防身的专著问世，主要内容是教授人们如何通过拳击格斗的技能满足自卫的需求。1940年左右出版的相关著作将主要内容从拳击格斗更改为柔道，教导人们如何防范暴力犯罪及学习柔道和柔术以自卫。1960年至1970年的十年间，有关安全自卫的书籍逐步增多，但大部分仍停留于教导人们用各种拳术自卫。直至20世纪80年代，安全自卫不再局限于格斗技术，而是增加了如何防范及脱逃的内容。从1990年以后，安全自卫面

During the Han Dynasty, hand wrestling was also known as "Qi" or "Bian". Arena competition became more widespread in the Tang Dynasty, with hand wrestling and corner kicks being highly valued, and competitions almost forming a system. In the Song Dynasty, hand wrestling was widely popular among the people as the main means of strengthening the body and activating muscles and bones. In the Qing Dynasty, many folk martial arts training groups emerged, such as "Martial Community" and " Martial Arts School". Each School often competed and exchanged martial arts skills, so "to join an open competition" was widely popular among the people.

But the proposal and construction of self-defense techniques as a system originated from European and American countries, mainly due to the increasing risk factors affecting social security—violent crime. Where there is violence, there is opposition. Therefore prevention of violence means self-defense. In response to this, the United States discussed legal provisions related to self-defense around 1880. The first monograph on security and self-defense was published in 1905. The main content is to teach people how to meet their self-defense needs through boxing and fighting skills. The related works published around 1940 changed the content from boxing and fighting to judo, teaching people how to prevent violent crime and learn judo and jujutsu for self-defense. During the decade from 1960 to 1970, there was a gradual increase in books on security and self-defense, but most of them remained focused on teaching people how to use various martial arts to defend themselves. Until the 1980s, security and self-defense were no longer limited to combat techniques, but added content on how to prevent and escape. Since 1990, the group and content of security and self-defense

① 罗斌 . 自我防卫术技击应用研究 [J]. 体育文化导刊 ,2015(12):79-83.

向的群体与内容更加多元和多样，上至老人，下至妇女儿童及特殊群体。尤其是女性受暴案件屡见不鲜。许多女性自我保护意识差、身体素质差、应变能力欠缺，使其在面对暴力突发事件时常表现得束手无策。因此，推广和普及女子防身术，提高女性的防卫意识，加强女性应变技能，对维护女性安全和社会稳定具有重大意义。因此，自卫防身术还有"女子防身术"的别称。

我国系统宣传和教授防身自卫的课程起步较晚，通过查阅文献资料能够了解到女子防身术课程最早于1988年在江苏公安专科院校开设，自此，我国关于防身术的研究拉开序幕。1999年，北京体育大学面向北京市学院路地区15所高校大学生推出"自卫防身术"课程。2002年，北京大学开设"安全教育与自卫防身"课程。同年，在教育部主办的全国280所重点大学体育部长培训班上，北京大学陈工教授介绍并呼吁开展自卫防身学课程。目前"自卫防身课程"已在全国多所高校开设，并逐渐走进中小学课堂。

have become more diverse, from the elderly to women and children as well as special groups. Especially, cases of female becoming violence victims are not uncommon. Many women have poor self-defense awareness, physical fitness, and adaptability, making them often helpless in the face of violent emergencies. Therefore, promoting and popularizing women's self-defense techniques, enhancing women's defense awareness, and strengthening women's adaptability skills are of great significance for maintaining women's security and social stability. For this reason, self-defense courses also have the name "women's self-defense techniques".

The promotion and teaching of self-defense courses in China started relatively late. According to literature research, women's self-defense courses were first established in Jiangsu Public Security Vocational College in 1988. Since then, research on self-defense in China has begun. In 1999, Beijing Sport University launched the "Self-defense Techniques" course for 15 university students in the Xueyuan Road area of Beijing. In 2002, Peking University offered a course on "Security Education and Self-defense". In the same year, Professor Chen Gong from Peking University introduced and called for the development of self-defense and self-defense courses at the training course for sports ministers from 280 key universities nationwide, sponsored by the Ministry of Education. At present, the "Self-defense Course" has been offered in many universities across the country and gradually entered the classrooms of primary and secondary school students.

二、自卫防身课程现状

（一）理论与实践背离

理论来源于实践，同时，实践又不断促进理论的螺旋上升和发展，构成互为支撑的统一体。从自卫防身课程的发展脉络可知，我国在推广自卫防身课程或女子防身术时，大多将聚焦点置于"防身"二字，"重技术、轻理论"，突出的是具身层面的技术，注重教授学生面对肢体冲突等情况时如何化解与自保，但缺少理论层面的安全预防教育。

具体而言，主要表现在以下方面。首先，我国防身课程主要是以某类搏击项目为中介，如摔跤、跆拳道、武术等，缺乏系统的内容整合。其次，教学内容缺少使用的场景介绍，导致学生难以灵活、综合运用于实际情境中。最后，自卫防身的预防对象是暴力犯罪，应与犯罪学领域相结合，强化对"防患于未然"犯罪预防理念教育，即对自卫防身的预防意识、理念、方式，灵活机动的躲避、脱身、对峙谈判的技巧教育，在实施正当防卫时，在法律上度的把握，以及暴力犯罪人的心理特征等的综合教育。但现实教育仍有提升空间。因此，总的来说，我国自卫防身术的技术、理念总体尚处于萌芽阶段。

2. The Current State of Self-defense Courses

(1) Deviation Between Theory and Practice

Theory originates from practice, and at the same time, practice continuously promotes the spiral rise and development of theory, forming a mutually supportive unity. From the development of self-defense courses, it can be seen that in China, when promoting self-defense courses or women's self-defense techniques, the focus is mostly on the word "self-defense", "emphasizing technology over theory", highlighting the embodied level of technology, emphasizing teaching students how to resolve and protect themselves when facing physical conflicts and other situations.

Specifically, this is mainly reflected in the following aspects. First, self-defense courses in our country mainly serve as intermediaries for certain types of combat projects, such as wrestling, taekwondo, martial arts, etc., lacking a systematic content system. Second, the content lacks a scenario introduction for use, resulting in students being unable to apply it comprehensively in practical situations. Third, self-defense against violent crimes should be combined with criminology, and strengthen the education of students on crime prevention in advance. This includes education on self-defense prevention awareness, concepts, and methods, flexible avoidance, escape, and confrontation or negotiation skills, as well as comprehensive education on the legal degree of legitimate defense in implementing self-defense and the psychological characteristics of violent criminals. But for education in reality, there is still room for progress. Therefore, overall, the technology and concept of self-defense in China are still in the embryonic stage.

（二）缺乏全面的安全教育内容

安全教育一直是我国教育体系中的"重点问题"，以1992年国家教育委员会颁布的《普通高校学生安全教育及管理暂行规定》为标志，该文件要求学校各部门和有关群众团体或组织要相互配合，普及安全知识，增强学生的安全意识和法治观念，提高防范能力，如防火、防盗、防破坏、防意外伤害等。2002年教育部颁布实施的《学生伤害事故处理办法》规定，学校应当对在校学生进行必要的安全教育和自护自救教育。2007年《中小学公共安全教育指导纲要》指明对中小学生的公共安全教育主要包括社会安全、自然灾害安全和网络信息安全等六大模块的教育内容。2010—2016年国家又围绕消防安全、网络安全、毒品预防、法制安全和国防安全等若干教育主题，陆续颁布《关于加强中小学消防安全宣传教育工作的通知》《教育部、司法部、中央综治办、共青团中央关于进一步加强青少年学生法制教育的若干意见》《青少年法治教育大纲》《教育部办公厅关于深入开展首个全民国家安全教育日活动的通知》等政策文件，2018年又出台了《教育部关于加强大中小学国家安全教育的实施意见》《教育部办公厅关于防范学生溺水事故的预警通知》，各个文件的发布都诠释了安

(2) Lack of Comprehensive Security Education Content

Security education has always been a "key issue" in China's education system. It is marked by the Interim Regulations on Security Education and Management of Ordinary College Students issued by the National Education Commission in 1992, which requires all departments and relevant mass organizations of schools to cooperate with each other, popularize security knowledge, enhance students' security awareness and legal awareness, and improve prevention capabilities, such as fire prevention, theft prevention, damage prevention, and accidental injury prevention. In 2002, the Ministry of Education issued and implemented the Measures for Handling Student Injury Accidents, which stipulated that schools should provide necessary security education and self-protection and self-rescue education to students on campus. In 2007, the Guidelines for Public Security Education in Primary and Secondary Schools specified the education content for six major modules of social security, natural disaster security, and network information security for primary and secondary school students. From 2010 to 2016, our country issued the Notice on Strengthening Fire Security Propaganda and Education in Primary and Secondary Schools around several educational themes such as fire security, network security, drug prevention, legal security, and issued other national documents such as Several Opinions on Further Strengthening Legal Education for Youth Students, Outline of Legal Education for Youth, and Notice on Deepening the First National Security Education Day for All were issued. In 2018, Implementation Opinions on Strengthening National Security Education in Primary, Secondary, and Primary Schools and Early Warning Notice on Preventing Student Drowning Accidents were also issued. The release of various documents demonstrates the importance of

全教育的重要性。

自卫防身是安全教育的重要有机组成部分。自卫防身不仅仅是教导个体在面临暴力刑事犯罪时，如被袭击或避无可避时，保护自己的搏击技术，还应包括消防、溺水等公共安全领域事故的预防。此外，随着我国通过各类举措打击和肃清暴力犯罪，暴力犯罪的起数正不断下降；然而，与暴力犯罪相对应的智力犯罪——诈骗，正成为新的焦点。自卫防身教育者应以点带面，承担起安全教育的责任。

security education.

Self-defense is an important organic component of security education. Self-defense is not only a combat technique that individuals use to protect themselves when facing violent criminal offenses, such as being attacked or finding no escape, but also preventive knowledge of public security, including fire and drowning. With the crackdown and elimination of violent crimes and the deepening reform of legal regulations in our country, the number of violent crimes is constantly decreasing. On the other hand, the intellectual crime corresponding to violent crimes—fraud—is becoming a new black spot. Self-defense educators should take on the responsibility of security education from point to surface.

第三节
大学生安全防卫学的研究内容

Section 3
Research Content of Security and Defense Studies for College Students

人一生最重要的财富便是生命，如图 1-1 所示，人的一生有各种追求，如同用阿拉伯数字书写 "1,000,000"，六个 "0" 分别代表家庭、金钱、学业、事业及自我价值实现等，而如果没有代表生命的 "1"，则所有的 "0" 都毫无意义。没有健康的生命作为载体，上述所有的追求都不复存在。正如毛主席所言："体者，载知识之车而寓道德之舍也。""无体是无德智也。" 没有身体作为前提，一切皆为虚妄。毁灭生命与健康的因素看似成千上万，实际归纳

The most important wealth for people is their life. As shown in the following figure, a person's life has various pursuits, just like writing one million in Arabic numerals (Figure 1-1). The six zeros represent family, wealth, education, career, and self realization, respectively. If there is no "1" representing life, all "0" are meaningless. Without a healthy life as a carrier, all the above pursuits no longer exist. As Chairman Mao once said, "The body is the vehicle of knowledge, the sacrifice of morality." "The absence of the body is for the sake of virtue and knowledge." Without a body as a prerequisite, everything is illusory. There may seem to be thousands of factors that can destroy life and health, but in reality, there are only three (see Figure 1-2).

下来却只有三种，如图 1-2 所示。

1, 000, 000

生命/健康　　　　　学业　事业　金钱　　　　　家庭　朋友　自我价值实现

图 1-1　没有生命就没有一切　Without life, there is nothing

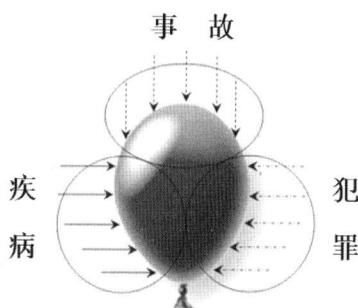

图 1-2　毁灭生命与健康的三大因素　Three major factors that destroy life and health

1. 各类事故

事故包括交通事故（车祸、空难、沉船）、运动事故、自然灾害（地震、火灾、洪水、龙卷风）、食物中毒、医疗事故、建筑事故等。任何事故人们都有概率碰上，且任何一个事故都可轻而易举地毁灭一个人的生命与健康。

2. 各类疾病

人体有运动系统、神经系统、内分泌系统、循环系统、呼吸系统、消化系统、泌尿系统、免疫系统，以及生殖系统九大系统。各系统间协调配合，使人体各种复杂的生命活动能够正常进行。与此同时，作为一个有机系统的整体，任何部分出现问题，都会影响整体的功能运行，导致系统机

1) Various Accidents

Accidents include traffic accidents (car accidents, air accidents, sunken ships), sports accidents, natural disasters (earthquakes, fires, floods, tornadoes), food poisoning, medical accidents, construction accidents, etc. These accidents could happen to anyone. Any of these accidents can easily destroy a person's life and health.

2) Various Diseases

The human body consists of nine major systems: motor system, nervous system, endocrine system, circulatory system, respiratory system, digestive system, urinary system, immune system and reproductive system. Coordination is conducted among various systems to enable the normal functioning of various complex life activities in the human body. At the same time, human body is an organic system as a whole, any partial problem will affect the overall functional operation, leading to disorder

能的失序和紊乱，严重时可失去生命或健康。根据世界卫生组织的数据，2001 年非传染性疾病死亡人数占全球死亡人数的 61%（3 100 万），2019 年增长到 74%（4 100 万）。《2022 年我国卫生健康事业发展统计公报》显示，2022 年全国甲乙类传染性疾病（除新冠病毒感染外）报告发病 243.1 万例，死亡 2.2 万人。

3. 暴力犯罪

暴力犯罪包括故意杀人、故意伤害致人重伤或死亡、强奸、抢劫、贩毒、放火、爆炸、投毒等，此类暴力犯罪的受害者，轻则受伤残疾，重则失去生命。

上述三个因素是危害人类生命安全的重要原因。人类为保证自身的生命安全，必须学会预防和应付此类不稳定因素。虽常言道："生命无常，世事难料。"但在具备安全常识的前提下，人们依然能够将遇害概率或伤害降至最低。各类事故很多，本教程针对大学生日常生活中常见的水、火，以及运动事故。一方面，水火无情，但与日常生活紧密相伴。另一方面，在"全民健身"的倡议下，人人都需要锻炼，但是锻炼往往伴随着拉伤、扭伤等运动损伤问题。另外，在当下，我国虽已是世界最安全的国家之一，但有群体就会有摩擦和冲突，打架斗殴等伤害类事件也就不可避

of systemic functions, and in severe cases, threatening individual life or health. According to data from the World Health Organization, non-communicable disease deaths accounted for 61% (31 million) of global deaths in 2001, and increased to 74% (41 million) in 2019. According to the *2022 Statistical Bulletin of Health Development in China*, in 2022, there are 2.431 million cases and 22,000 deaths of Class A and B infectious diseases (except for coronavirus infection).

3) Violent Crimes

This includes homicide, intentional injury causing serious injury or death, rape, robbery, drug trafficking, arson, explosion, drug poisoning, etc. Victims of such violent crimes can be injured or disabled, and in severe cases, lose their lives.

In summary, the three categories are important factors that endanger human life security. To ensure their own life security, humans must learn to prevent and deal with such factors. As the saying goes, "Life is impermanent, things are unpredictable." But with security knowledge, we can still minimize the probability of suffering crimes or harm. There are many types of accidents, and this course focuses on water, fire, and sports accidents that college students often encounter in their daily lives. On the one hand, the ruthlessness and cruelty of water and fire are closely intertwined with daily life. On the other hand, under the initiative of "extensive fitness-for-all activities", everyone needs to exercise, but exercise is accompanied by sports injuries such as strains and sprains. In addition, in the current era, although China is already one of the safest countries in the world, there will always be friction and conflicts among groups. Injuries such as fights are inevitable. Therefore, how to prevent and avoid various risks, and how to use self-

免。为此，如何预防和规避各类风险，怎样运用自卫技术保护自己是安身立命之本。

影响生命健康的其中一座大山——疾病，属于医学研究的范畴，本教程不做阐释，大家可查阅相关书籍，根据各类传染性疾病和非传染性疾病的特征做好防护工作。简言之，安全自卫学主要研究如何防范及应对各类事故和犯罪。

defense techniques to protect oneself are the foundation of survival.

Diseases, one of the major mountains that affects life and health, falls within the scope of medical book research. This course does not provide any explanation. Students can refer to relevant books and take preventive measures based on the characteristics of various infectious and non communicable diseases. In short, security and self-defense studies mainly focus on two key elements: how to prevent and respond to various accidents and crimes.

思考一

1. 大学生安全防卫学的定义是什么？

2. 大学生安全防卫学的目的与意义是什么？

3. 大学生安全防卫学的特征有哪些？

4. 大学生安全防卫学的研究内容包括什么？

Reflection 1

1. What is the definition of security and defense studies for college students?

2. What is the purpose and significance of security and defense studies for college students?

3. What are the characteristics of security and defense studies among college students?

4. What are the research content of college student security and defense studies?

第一章微课视频

第二章
常见事故预防与控制

Chapter 2
Prevention and Control of Common Accidents

事故指发生于预期之外的，造成人身伤害、财产或经济损失的事件。本章的事故主要指意外事故，即个体的行为虽然在客观上造成了损害结果，但并非出于行为人的主观意愿，而是出于不能预见的原因。

意外事故包括交通安全、自然灾害、食品安全、实验室安全等多种类型，覆盖人们日常生活的方方面面。人们无时无刻不面临着意外，只是概率上的大小不同。当个体能识别危险信号，具备对各类事故的安全防范意识与应对能力时，可降低意外事故发生的概率。

人们日常生活中最常接触和不能离开的就是水与火。水是生命之源：地球71%是由水覆盖的，人体的70%是由水组成的。火是文明之光：照明、热能、冶炼以及食物烹饪等等都离不开火。但水与火为人类生活带来便利的同时，也将危险带至人们身旁，稍有不慎，就将带来巨大的伤亡和经济损失。此外，随着体教融合与全民健身的政策推进、体育设施的不断完善，人们对于生命质量要求的不断提高，"体育"成为社交与休闲的重要方式，而与其

Accidents refer to events that cause personal injury, property damage, or economic losses beyond expectations. In this chapter, accidents mainly refer to unforeseen accidents, where the individual's actions objectively result in damage, but not intentionally. These accidents occur due to unforeseeable reasons.

Accidents include various types such as traffic security, natural disasters, food security, laboratory security, etc., covering all aspects of people's daily lives. People face accidents all the time, just the difference in probability. When individuals are able to recognize danger signals and have security awareness and response measures for various accidents, the possibility of accidents occurring can be reduced.

The most frequently encountered and inseparable things in people's daily lives are water and fire. Water is the source of life, 71% of the Earth is covered by water, and 70% of the human body is composed of water. Fire is the light of civilization. Lighting, thermal energy, smelting, and food cooking all rely on fire. But while water and fire bring convenience to human life, they also carry danger with them. A slight mistake can bring huge casualties and economic losses. In addition, with the integration of sports and education and the promotion of national fitness policies, the continuous improvement of sports facilities, and the increasing demand for quality of life, "sports" have become an important way of socializing and leisure, and frequent sports accidents continue to occur.

常伴的运动事故也不断上演。

　　为此，本章主要阐述三个方面的内容：涉火安全、涉水安全、运动安全。在此基础上，介绍基础生命支持的心肺复苏技术，以提高危及生命时刻的生存率。

Therefore, this chapter mainly elaborates on three aspects: fire security, water security, and sports security. And on this basis, this chapter will introduce the cardiopulmonary resuscitation technology supported by Basic Life Support to improve the survival rate at life-threatening moments.

第一节
涉火安全

Section 1
Fire Security

　　根据国家消防救援局 2023 年上半年发布的数据，全国共接报火灾 55 万起，死亡 959 人，受伤 1 311 人，直接财产损失 39.4 亿元，与 2022 年同期相比，火灾起数和受伤人数分别上升 19.9% 和 9.3%。为此，我们一定要提高对火的重视程度，切不可视为儿戏。本节将先阐明燃烧的基本条件和充分条件，并依据因病施症的思路，介绍各类火灾的预防和控制。

According to data released by the National Fire Rescue Bureau for the first half of 2023, there were 550,000 reported fires nationwide, resulting in 959 deaths, 1,311 injuries, and direct property losses of 3.94 billion yuan. Compared with the same period in 2022, the number of incidents and casualties increased by 19.9% and 9.3%, respectively. Therefore, we must pay attention to fire and not treat them casually. This section will first explain the basic and sufficient conditions of combustion. Following the logic of diagnosing and treating diseases, it will then introduce the prevention and control of various types of fires.

一、燃烧的概述

1. Overview of Combustion

　　着火即燃烧，指燃烧物与氧化剂作用发生的放热反应，具有化学反应、放热、发光三个特征，三者缺一不可。如电灯泡虽然具备发热和发光两个特征，但缺少化学反应，生石灰遇水发生了化学反应并释放了大量的热能，但没有产生光能，故都无法称之为燃烧。

Fire is combustion, which refers to the exothermic reaction between the combustion material and the oxidant. It has three characteristics: chemical reaction, exothermic reaction, and luminescence, all of which are indispensable. Although electric light bulbs have the characteristics of heating and emitting light, they lack chemical reactions; Quicklime undergoes a chemical reaction with water and releases a large amount of heat energy, but does not produce light energy, so it cannot be called combustion.

（一）燃烧的基本条件

燃烧的三个基本特征是化学反应、放热和放光，但产生燃烧的条件是什么？答案是"可燃物、助燃物、引火源"。与燃烧的特征一样，燃烧产生的三要素也必须同时具备、相互作用，任何要素的缺失都不会产生燃烧。

1. 可燃物

可燃烧物指能与空气中的氧气或其他氧化剂发生化学反应的物质，如木制物品，汽油、纸张、氢、硫等。可燃物是发生燃烧的内因和基本条件。根据燃烧物的不同形态可分为气体燃烧、液体燃烧、固体燃烧三类。三者之中，气体最易燃烧且速度快，其次是液体燃烧，最后是固体燃烧。

2. 助燃物

助燃物也称氧化剂，指能与可燃物发生氧化反应的物质。通常所言的氧化剂主要指存在于空气中的氧气，以及能够提供氧气的含氧化合物和氯气等。

3. 引火源

引火源是为可燃物与助燃物提供燃烧反应的能量来源。一般分为直接火源与间接火源两大类。直接火源包括明火（炉火、摩擦的火花、烛火等）、电弧和电火花（电器设备、电器线路）、雷击三种。间接火源包括高温（高

(1) Basic Conditions for Combustion

The three basic characteristics of combustion are chemical reaction, heat release, and light emission. But what are the conditions for combustion to occur? The answer is "combustible material, oxidizer, and ignition source". Similar to the characteristics of combustion, these three elements of combustion must be present simultaneously and interact with one another. The absence of any element will prevent combustion.

1) Combustible Material

Combustible materials are substances that can create chemical reactions with oxygen in the air or other oxidizers. Examples include wooden items, gasoline, paper, hydrogen, sulfur, etc. Combustible materials are the internal factors and basic conditions for combustion. Depending on the form of the combustible material, combustion can be classified into three types: gas combustion, liquid combustion, and solid combustion. Among these, gases are the most easily combustible and have a faster combustion rate, followed by liquid and solid combustion.

2) Combustion Aids

The combustion aids, also known as a combustion-supporting substance, refers to a material that can create oxidation reactions with combustible materials. Commonly referred to as oxidizers are oxygen present in the air, and oxygen-containing compounds and chlorine that can provide oxygen.

3) The Ignition Source

The ignition source provides the energy for the combustion reaction between the combustible material and the combustion aids. It is generally divided into two categories: direct ignition sources and indirect ignition sources. Direct ignition sources include open flames (stove fire, friction sparks, candle flames, etc.), arcs and sparks (electrical equipment, electrical circuits), and lightning. Indirect ignition sources

温加热、烘焙，设备故障发热等）、自燃起火（可燃物与氧化剂接触起火等）两种。

（二）燃烧的充分条件

常言道，"不能抛开剂量谈毒性。"燃烧亦是如此。即使具备燃烧的基本条件，燃烧仍不会发生，还需各要素达到燃烧水平。换言之，燃烧的产生要在满足基本条件的基础上，满足充分条件。具体为：

1. 可燃物浓度

可燃气体或可燃液体的蒸气必须与空气混合达到一定的比例才会燃烧或爆炸，不同可燃气体可燃浓度的界值不尽相同，如甲烷的可燃浓度为 5% ～ 15%，乙烷为 3% ～ 9.5%，丙烷为 2.4% ～ 9.5%，氢气为 4% ～ 75%。当可燃物气体的比例低于或高于边界值时都不会发生燃烧。

2. 氧化剂浓度

不同的可燃物发生燃烧都有最低的含氧量要求，低于这个界值，即使具备燃烧的基本条件仍不会发生燃烧。如汽油的最低含氧量要求为 14%，煤油为 15%，乙醚为 12%。

3. 火源能量

不同可燃物发生燃烧，具有固定的最低能量要求。如汽油的最小点火能量剂量为 0.2 mL，乙醚（5.1%）为 0.19 mL。

include high temperatures (high-temperature heating, baking, equipment malfunctions generating heat, etc.) and spontaneous combustion (contact between combustible material and oxidizer causing ignition).

(2) Sufficient Conditions for Combustion

As the saying goes, "Toxicity cannot be discussed without considering the dose." The same applies to combustion. Even if the basic conditions for combustion are met, combustion will not occur unless each element meets the demand. In other words, the occurrence of combustion, based on meeting the basic conditions, requires the fulfillment of sufficient conditions. Specifically:

1) Combustible Concentration

Combustible gases or vapors must mix with air in a certain proportion to ignite or explode. The threshold values for the combustible concentration vary for different combustible gases. For example, the combustible concentration of methane is 5%–15%, ethane is 3%–9.5%, propane is 2.4%–9.5%, and hydrogen is 4%–75%. Combustion will not occur if the combustible gas ratio is below or above the boundary value.

2) Oxidizer Concentration

Different combustible materials have minimum oxygen requirements for combustion. Below this threshold, combustion will not occur even if the basic conditions for combustion are met. For example, gasoline requires a minimum oxygen content of 14%, kerosene is 15%, and ether is 12%.

3) Ignition Energy

Different combustible materials have fixed minimum energy requirements for combustion. For instance, the minimum ignition energy for gasoline is 0.2 mL, and for ether (5.1%), it is 0.19 mL.

二、灭火的措施

燃烧的产生和持续是基于燃烧的基本条件和充分条件的。而灭火的措施就是破坏燃烧条件，使燃烧反应终止。灭火的措施主要包括冷却、窒息、隔离三种。

（一）冷却法

通过将可燃物的温度降到燃点以下，可以停止燃烧。对于一般固体物质的火灾，主要是通过冷却作用，用水扑灭。水具有较大的热容量和很高的汽化热值，在灭火过程中，水能大量吸收热量，使燃烧物的温度迅速降低，从而使火焰熄灭。

（二）窒息法

燃烧需要在特定的氧气浓度以上才能进行，低于这个浓度，燃烧就无法维持。通常情况下，当氧气浓度低于15%时，燃烧无法继续。窒息灭火法通过阻止空气流入燃烧区域或用不燃烧的气体稀释空气，从而使燃烧物得不到足够的氧气而熄灭。例如，使用泡沫灭火器喷射出特定物质覆盖燃烧物表面，油锅着火时立即盖上锅盖，或者用湿棉被或沙土覆盖燃烧物表面，等等。

具体而言，窒息灭火有两种方法。第一种是阻止氧气流入燃烧区。第二种是通过稀释方法降

2. Fire Extinguishing Measures

The generation and sustenance of combustion are based on the basic and sufficient conditions for combustion. Fire extinguishing measures aim to disrupt the conditions for combustion, thereby terminating the combustion reaction. The primary methods of fire extinguishing include cooling, smothering, and isolation.

(1) Cooling Method

By lowering the temperature of combustible materials below the ignition point, combustion can be stopped. For fires involving general solid materials, they are mainly extinguished through cooling and water use. Water has a large heat capacity and high heat of vaporization. During the fire extinguishing process, water can absorb a large amount of heat, causing the temperature of the combustion material to rapidly decrease, thereby extinguishing the flame.

(2) Smothering Method

Combustion requires a minimum oxygen concentration to occur, and below this level, combustion cannot sustain. Normally, combustion cannot continue when the oxygen concentration is below 15%. The smothering fire extinguishing method prevents air from flowing into the combustion area or dilutes the air with non combustible gas, thereby preventing the combustion material from receiving sufficient oxygen and extinguishing it. For example, use a foam fire extinguisher to cover the surface of the combustor. When the oil pan catches fire, immediately cover the lid of the pan, or use a wet quilt or sand to cover the surface of the combustor.

Specifically, there are two methods for smothering fire extinguishing. The first method is to prevent oxygen from flowing in the space. The second method is to reduce oxygen concentration

低氧浓度，如通入二氧化碳、氮气或蒸气，这种方法多用于密闭或半密闭空间。如果条件允许，还可以使用水淹法进行窒息灭火。

（三）隔离法

在燃烧的三要素中，可燃物是燃烧的主要条件。将已着火物体与附近的可燃物隔离，就可中止燃烧。隔离的方法有两种：第一种是将可燃物与氧气和热隔离；第二种是将可燃物与火焰和氧气隔离。

三、学校消防安全预防

燃烧产生的要素为可燃物、助燃物及引火源。可燃物及助燃物（氧气）在日常生活中是客观存在的，绝大多数可燃物即使暴露在空气中，若没有引火源的作用，火灾亦不会发生。从此角度而言，学校消防安全预防的实质就是控制和消除引火源。学校的场景包括宿舍、教室、实验室及图书馆等。基于四类情景，在学校中我们应做到如下几点。

（1）严禁在宿舍内使用卡式炉、酒精炉、电热炉等大功率电器和假冒劣质电器产品。

（2）切勿在宿舍内私拉电线，接移动插座和（或）将电源连接线或插板放在床上；勿在电线和灯管等设备上搭挂衣物。

through dilution using non-combustible gases, such as carbon dioxide, nitrogen, or steam, which is often used in enclosed or semi-enclosed spaces. If conditions permit, the water flooding method can also be used for smothering fire extinguishing.

(3) Isolation Method

Among the three elements of combustion, combustible material is a primary condition for combustion. By isolating the ignited object from nearby combustible materials, combustion can be halted. There are two isolation methods. The first involves isolating combustible material from oxygen and heat. The second involves isolating combustible material from flames and oxygen.

3. School Fire Security Prevention

The elements produced by combustion are combustible materials, combustion aids, and ignition sources. Combustibles and combustion aids (oxygen) objectively exist in daily life. Even if the vast majority of combustibles are exposed in the air, without the action of a fire source, fires will not occur. From this perspective, the essence of school fire security prevention is to control and eliminate ignition sources. Schools include scenarios such as dormitories, classrooms, laboratories, and libraries. Based on these four types of scenarios, we should meet the following demands.

① It is strictly prohibited to use high-power electrical appliances such as butane gas stoves, alcohol stoves, electric stoves, and counterfeit low-quality electrical products in the dormitory.

② Do not privately pull electrical wires and mobile sockets in the dormitory, or place power connection wires or plug boards on the bed; do not hang clothes on equipment such as wires and lamps.

（3）勿使用不合规格或破损的插板、插头或连接转换线；不将大功率电器集中于一个插座，应做到专插专用，否则容易造成电流过载，出现短路和跳闸，导致爆炸，引起火灾。

（4）切勿在宿舍、教室、实验室等场所吸烟、乱扔烟头、玩火和焚烧物品。

（5）勿在宿舍使用蜡烛看书，不要将台灯靠近枕头和被子，尽量不使用蚊香，使用时，应与可燃物隔离。

（6）当离开宿舍、实验室及教室时，最后一人必须确保所有电源关闭。

（7）勿将易燃、易爆物品带到宿舍、教室、实验室和图书馆等区域。

（8）保证宿舍楼内消防设备的正常使用，不占用和堵塞疏散通道；留意宿舍、教室、实验室及图书馆等区域内的消防器材位置，并熟悉使用方法；熟悉安全出口的位置和疏散通道的方向，学会疏散逃生。

四、火场自救

（一）熟悉建筑结构，把握生命通道

楼梯、疏散通道、安全出口或直通室外地平面的门等都是火灾发生时最重要的逃生通道。因此，

③ Do not use non-standard or damaged plug boards, plugs, or connecting conversion cables; do not concentrate high-power electrical appliances in one socket. It should be dedicated for specific insertion, otherwise it is easy to cause current overload, short circuit and tripping, leading to explosion and fire.

④ Do not smoke, litter cigarette butts, play with fire, or burn items in dormitories, classrooms, laboratories, and other places.

⑤ Do not use candles to read books in the dormitory, do not place desk lamps near pillows and blankets, try to not use mosquito coils, and isolate them from combustible materials when using.

⑥ When leaving the dormitory, laboratory, and classroom, the last person must ensure that all power is turned off.

⑦ Do not bring flammable and explosive materials to areas such as dormitories, classrooms, laboratories, and libraries.

⑧ Ensure that the fire-fighting equipment in the dormitory building does not occupy or block evacuation routes; pay attention to the location of fire-fighting equipment in areas such as dormitories, classrooms, laboratories, and libraries, and be familiar with the usage methods; familiarize oneself with the location of fire exits and the direction of evacuation routes, and learn how to evacuate and escape.

4. Self-Rescue in a Fire Incident

(1) Master the Fire Escape Route

Stairs, evacuation routes, fire exits, or doors that directly lead to outdoor surfaces are the most important escape routes in the event of a fire. Therefore, whether in familiar areas such

无论是在熟悉的区域，如住宿区、教学区或办公区，还是在陌生的场所，如电影院、酒店等，首先要做的就是熟悉安全出口、疏散通道和楼梯等生命通道的位置。

（二）防微杜渐，扑灭雏火

当火灾发生时，如果火势不大，并且身边有灭火器、消防栓等器具，应在确保自身安全的前提下，按照灭火方法迅速控制火源，切勿惊慌失措。另外，谨慎开门窗，以免错过最佳扑救时机，使小火演变成大火，造成更大的危害。

（三）勿恋财物，迅速逃离

火灾的发展过程分为点燃、扩散、成长和衰退四个阶段。当火势从点燃阶段进入扩散阶段时，应迅速逃离，因为普通房间起火，3 min 内火焰就会蔓延至整个房间，且烟气中含有致命毒气。因此，切勿贪恋财物，避免延误逃生时机。另外，穿过浓烟时要尽量贴近地面前进，有条件的话用湿毛巾捂住口鼻，迅速逃离，避免大声呼喊求救，以防吸入一氧化碳。逃生时切勿乘坐电梯，不清楚火源位置时不要乱跑，以免使自己陷入更大的危险。

（四）身上着火，切莫慌乱

身处火场时，若身上着火，千万不要惊慌失措、东奔西跑或胡乱拍打。奔跑时产生的风会使火势加剧，并可能将火源带到其他可燃物旁，导致更大的火灾。

as accommodation, teaching, or office areas, or in unfamiliar places such as cinemas, hotels, etc., the first thing to do is to familiarize oneself with the location of fire exits, evacuation routes, stairs, and other vital passages.

(2) Prevent and Extinguish Small Fires

When a fire occurs, if the fire is not severe and there are fire extinguishers, hydrants, and other equipment nearby, the fire source should be quickly controlled according to the fire extinguishing methods while ensuring personal security, and do not panic. In addition, be cautious when opening doors and windows to avoid missing the best time to extinguish a small fire and turning it into a large one, causing greater harm.

(3) Leave the Property, and Quickly Escape

The development process of fires can be divided into four stages: ignition, diffusion, growth, and decline. When the fire enters the spreading stage from the ignition stage, one should quickly escape, because if a normal room catches fire, the flames will spread to the entire room within 3 minutes, and the smoke contains deadly toxic gases. Therefore, do not be greedy for property and avoid missing the escape opportunity. In addition, when passing through thick smoke, try to move as close to the ground as possible. If possible, cover your mouth and nose with a damp towel, quickly escape, and avoid shouting for help to prevent inhaling carbon monoxide. Do not take the elevator during evacuation, and do not run around without knowing the location of the fire source to avoid putting yourself in greater danger.

(4) Do Not Panic if Fire on Your Body

When in a fire scene, if your body catches fire, do not panic, run around or slap randomly. The wind generated during running can exacerbate the fire and potentially bring the ignition source to other combustible materials, leading to larger fires. Therefore, if there is a fire, the first thing

因此，若身上着火，首先应尽快脱掉衣物。如果无法及时脱掉衣物，应在没有可燃物的地面上打滚，以扑灭身上的火苗。如果有人在场，可以用麻袋、毯子等包裹着火的人，或向其身上浇水，或者帮助撕掉着火的衣物。切勿直接用灭火器喷射着火的人，以免灭火剂中的药剂引起伤口感染。

（五）因地制宜，及时转移

火灾发生时，如果安全出口和疏散通道无法通行，应迅速从着火房间转移到未着火房间。一楼着火时，可以从窗户跳出；二楼着火时，可以双手抓住窗户或阳台边缘，慢慢将双脚向下滑离；三楼及以上着火时，可以先将棉被等软物扔到楼下缓冲，然后再设法逃生。

（六）利用工具，及时逃生

身处火场时，若逃生通道被烟火封堵，可通过消防专用绳、梯子等工具从阳台将自己吊到地面或下层阳台、窗户逃生。无消防专用绳时可用衣物、被单等做绳子，逃生时必须保证重量能承受。有能力的人可利用房间外墙壁上的供水管道逃生。

（七）灵活躲藏，等待救援

发生火灾后，在无法逃离火场的情况下，可以选择躲藏在不易受高温影响并且有直通外界空气的通道，例如阳台、天台、平屋顶等地方，或者选择清空的仓库、

to do is to take off your clothes as soon as possible. If you are unable to take off your clothes in a timely manner, you should roll on the ground without combustible materials to extinguish the flames on your body. If someone is present, you can wrap the person on fire with a burlap, blanket, or water them, or help to tear off the burning clothes. Do not directly use a fire extinguisher to spray people on fire, as the chemicals in the extinguishing agent may cause wound infections.

(5) Adapt to Local Conditions and Escape

When a fire occurs, if the fire exits and evacuation routes are impassable, it is necessary to quickly transfer from the burning room to the non-burning room. When the first floor catches fire, you can jump out of the window; when the second floor catches fire, you can grab the window or balcony edge with both hands and slowly slide your feet down and escape. When there is a fire on the third floor or higher, you can first throw soft items like blankets down to cushion the fall, and then attempt to escape.

(6) Make Full Use of Tools to Escape

When in a fire, if the escape route is blocked by fires, you can use firefighting ropes, ladders, and other tools to lift yourself from the balcony to the ground or lower-floor balcony or window to escape. When there is no firefighting rope, clothes, sheets, etc., can be used as ropes. When escaping, it must be able to withstand it. People with conditions can use the water supply pipeline on the outer wall of the room to escape.

(7) Flexible Hiding and Waiting for Rescue

Catching a fire, if it is impossible to escape from the fire, you can choose to hide in places that are not easily affected by high temperatures and have direct access to the outside air, such as balconies, rooftops, flat roofs, or choose to hide in empty warehouses, smoke-proof stairs,

防烟楼梯等少有可燃物的地方。切忌躲藏在床底、衣柜等密闭空间，因为此类地方不仅危险，且不易被消防人员发现。

（八）正确报警

身陷火海，无处逃生时，应设法向外面的人求助，并向消防人员报警。主要方法包括以下几种。

（1）发声。站在阳台或趴在外窗呼喊。

（2）发光。可将点燃的木条、蜡烛、打火机、手电筒、应急灯具等发光物品伸出屋外挥动。

（3）扔物品。不断向有人的地方扔出书本、文具等物品。

（4）通断电灯。在室内有电的情况下，不断打开和关闭电灯，引起抢救人员的注意。

（5）打电话。在电话或手机完好的情况下，拨打亲人电话或直接拨打 119。

（6）挥动衣物。用木条、竹竿等挂上鲜艳的衣物、窗帘等伸出屋外摆动，引起营救人员的注意。

and other places with few combustibles. Avoid hiding in enclosed spaces such as beds and wardrobes, as such places are not only dangerous but also less likely to be detected by firefighters.

(8) Report Fire Alarm Correctly

Trapped in a sea of fire with nowhere to escape, one should seek help from people outside and report the fire. Main methods include the following ones.

① Shout for help. Stand on the balcony or lying outside the window shouting.

② Make things glow. Light-emitting items such as lit wooden candles, lighters, flashlights, emergency lighting fixtures, etc. can be swung deep outside the house.

③ Throw items. Continuously throw books, stationery, and other items into occupied areas.

④ Turn on and off the lights. Continuously turn on and off the lights indoors to attract the attention of rescue personnel.

⑤ Make a phone call. When the phone or mobile phone is in good condition, dial the phone number of a loved one or directly call 119.

⑥ Wave your clothes. Hang bright-colored clothes or curtains with wooden strips, bamboo poles, etc., and swing them outside to attract the attention of rescue personnel.

第二节
涉水安全

Section 2
Water Security

世界卫生组织 2024 年的最新数据指出，全球每年因溺水死亡的人数约为 23.5 万。在我国，每年约有 5.7 万人死于溺水，其中少

The World Health Organization reports that in 2024, approximately 235,000 people die from drowning globally every year. In China, about 57,000 people die from drowning annually, with children and adolescents accounting for 56%

年儿童溺水死亡人数占 56%。《中国青少年儿童伤害现状回顾报告》显示，2010—2015 年，溺水已成为 0～19 岁青少年儿童死亡的重要原因。为了强化和提高公众预防溺水意识，第七十五届联合国大会于 2021 年 4 月 28 日通过首个全球预防溺水决议，并将每年 7 月 25 日定为"世界预防溺水日"。

无论是从公共安全层面还是个人安全防卫层面，在下水前掌握溺水的预防措施及下水遇险后的自救方法都非常重要。如此做，不仅能够让他人成功帮助你，你也能对他人施以援手。

一、水灾自救

水灾常发生在台风季和汛期，后者主要指江河中由于流域内季节性降水、融冰、化雪等引起的定时性水位上涨的时期。我国汛期主要是由于夏季暴雨和秋季连绵阴雨造成的。汛期是一年中降水量最大的时期，容易引起洪涝灾害。由大降雨导致的洪涝又有间接引发滑坡、增加电击的可能性。应急管理部发布的 2022 年全国自然灾害基本情况数据显示，2022 年我国共发生 38 次区域性暴雨，全国 28 个省份的 626 条河流发生超警戒以上洪水，大江大河共发生 10 次编号洪水。另外，7 月—8 月辽河流域发生了较为严重的洪

of the total drowning deaths. According to the *China Youth and Children Injury Status Review Report* drowning became an important cause of death among children and adolescents aged 0–19 from 2010 to 2015. To strengthen public awareness and prevention of drowning, the 75th United Nations General Assembly passed the first-ever global drowning prevention resolution on April 28, 2021, designating July 25 as "World Drowning Prevention Day".

Mastering the preventive measures before entering the water and the self-rescue methods in case of drowning danger are crucial from both public security and personal security perspectives. This knowledge not only enables others to assist you successfully but also allows you to lend a helping hand to others.

1. Self-Rescue in Water Disasters

Water disasters often occur during typhoons and flood seasons, the latter primarily referring to periods when river levels rise periodically due to seasonal precipitation, ice melting, and snow melting in the watershed. In China, flood seasons are mainly caused by heavy summer rains and continuous autumn rainfall. The flood season is the period with the highest precipitation during the year, making it prone to flooding disasters. Heavy rainfall can indirectly trigger landslides and increase the likelihood of electric shocks. According to the 2022 basic data on natural disasters released by the Ministry of Emergency Management, China experienced 38 regional heavy rainfalls in 2022. Floods exceeding warning levels occurred in 626 rivers across 28 provinces, and major rivers experienced 10 numbered floods. Additionally, serious flood disasters occurred in the Liao River Basin in July and August, resulting in significant

涝灾害。四川、青海等局地突发山洪灾害造成较大人员伤亡。全年洪涝灾害共造成 3 385 万人次受灾，因灾死亡失踪 171 人，直接经济损失 1 289 亿元。此外，全国共发生滑坡、崩塌、泥石流等地质灾害 5 659 起，以中小型为主，主要集中在中南、华南、西南等地。

综上，汛期内由于暴雨天气导致的降雨量增加，造成的危险场景包括洪涝、雷击、泥石流和滑坡等。为此，应熟知降水量的级别和标准（见表 2-1），并根据级别的不同，提前建立预警信号，做好相应对策。

【案例一　河南"7·20 特大暴雨灾害"】2021 年 7 月 17 日—23 日，河南省遭遇历史罕见的特大暴雨，引发了严重的洪涝

casualties due to flash floods in specific areas of Sichuan and Qinghai. Throughout the year, floods affected 33.85 million people, causing 171 deaths and disappearances and direct economic losses of 128.9 billion yuan. Moreover, the country experienced 5,659 geological disasters in medium and small scales such as landslides, collapses, and debris flows, mainly concentrated in central-southern, southern, and southwestern regions.

In summary, during the flood season, increased rainfall due to heavy rain poses various risks, including flooding, lightning, debris flows, and landslides. Therefore, it is essential to be familiar with rainfall levels and standards (see Table 2-1) and establish early warning signals and corresponding strategies based on different levels.

[Case 1　"Extremely heavy rainstorm disaster on July 20" in Henan Province]　From July 17 to 23, 2021, Henan Province encountered a rare extremely heavy rainstorm, which caused serious floods. Especially on July 20, Zhengzhou City

表 2-1　暴雨等级预警表　Rainstorm Level Warning Table

级别 Level	标准 Criteria
蓝色预警 Blue Warning	12 小时内降雨量将达 50 毫米以上，或者已达 50 毫米以上且降雨可能持续 Rainfall is expected to reach or exceed 50 millimeters within the next 12 hours, or it has already reached 50 millimeters with the possibility of continuation.
黄色预警 Yellow Warning	6 小时内降雨量将达 50 毫米以上，或者已达 50 毫米以上且降雨可能持续 Rainfall is expected to reach or exceed 50 millimeters within the next 6 hours, or it has already reached 50 millimeters with the possibility of continuation.
橙色预警 Orange Warning	3 小时内降雨量将达 50 毫米以上，或者已达 50 毫米以上且降雨可能持续 Rainfall is expected to reach or exceed 50 millimeters within the next 3 hours, or it has already reached 50 millimeters with the possibility of continuation.
红色预警 Red Warning	3 小时内降雨量将达 100 毫米以上，或者已达 100 毫米以上且降雨可能持续 Rainfall is expected to reach or exceed 100 millimeters within the next 3 hours, or it has already reached 100 millimeters with the possibility of continuation.

灾害，尤其是在 7 月 20 日，郑州市遭受了重大的人员伤亡和财产损失。这场灾害导致河南省 150 个县（市、区）的 1 478.6 万人受灾，造成 398 人死亡或失踪，其中郑州市 380 人，占全省的 95.5%。灾害直接导致了经济损失达到 1 200.6 亿元，其中郑州市的损失达到 409 亿元，占全省的 34.1%。

一般所指的水灾，以洪涝灾害为主。洪涝，指因大雨、暴雨或持续降雨造成低洼地区淹没、渍水的现象。洪涝可分为河流洪水，湖泊洪水和风暴洪水等。其中河流洪水依照成因不同，又可分为暴雨洪水、山洪、融雪洪水、冰凌洪水和溃坝洪水等几种类型。遇到洪涝时应做到以下几点（可参考案例三）。

（一）注意信息播报，冷静撤离

根据电视和广播等提供的洪水信息、住所位置和房屋结构，冷静选择撤离位置。若来不及撤离，应秉持"人往高处走，水往低处流"的原则，选择稳固的高地，如山坡和结构牢固的楼房上层，避免盲目撤离。

（二）通信畅通，寻求救援

保持通信畅通。被洪水包围时，要尽快与当地政府相关部门取得联系，报告自己的方位和险情，积极寻求救援。

suffered heavy casualties and property losses. The disaster caused 14.786 million people in 150 counties (cities, districts) suffering, and 398 people were killed or missing, of which 380 are in Zhengzhou City, accounting for 95.5% of the province. The disaster directly caused economic losses of 120.06 billion yuan, of which 40.9 billion yuan was in Zhengzhou City, accounting for 34.1% of the province.

Floods are generally referred to as the main type of water disaster. Flooding refers to the phenomenon of low-lying areas being submerged or waterlogged due to heavy rain, torrential rain, or continuous rainfall. Flooding can be classified into river floods, lake floods, storm surges, etc. Among them, river floods can be further categorized into various types based on their causes: rainstorm floods, flash floods, snowmelt floods, ice floods, and dam-break floods. When encountering floods, one should do the following.

(1) Pay Attention to Information Broadcasts and Evacuate Calmly

Based on flood information provided by television and radio, and considering the location and structure of residences, calmly choose evacuation locations. If there is not enough time to evacuate, adhere to the principle of "people move to higher ground, and water flows to lower ground", selecting stable high ground such as hillsides and upper floors of structurally sound buildings, avoiding blind evacuation.

(2) Maintain Communication and Seek Rescue

Keep communication channels open. If surrounded by floods, promptly contact local government authorities, report your location and the situation, and actively seek rescue.

（三）远离危险区域

强降雨天气不要进入地下室、地铁和隧道等危险区域；远离高压线、高压电塔等有供电危险标志的区域，防止触电。

（四）选择正确逃生行为

切勿游泳逃生，不要攀爬至带电的电线杆、铁塔，远离倾斜电杆和电线断头。若被卷入洪水中，尽可能抓住固定的或能漂浮的东西，寻找机会逃生。

（五）注意黑井

城市内涝达到一定程度时，因部分地区地下管道压力增大，会将马路上的井盖冲走，行人一旦掉落到黑井之中，就有可能有生命危险。为此，若房屋结构稳定，应尽量非必要不出门。一定要出门时，不要光脚或穿拖鞋；行走时，最好在手里握一根竹竿探路，同时动作要慢，通过对路面两边栅栏、隔离带和路灯高度的观察，评估水的深度。

（六）食品安全

洪涝灾害发生后，容易引发各类传染病疫情，如肠道传染病、呼吸道传染病及自然疫源性疾病等。主要的传染病风险来自饮用水设施和死水的污染。因此，为了防范传染病的发生，需要备足速食、饮用水和日用品，避免喝生水或来源不明的水，尽量选择煮沸后的水。食物必须彻底煮熟，不能食用被洪水浸泡过的食

(3) Stay Away from Danger Zones

During heavy rainfall, avoid entering basements, subways, tunnels, or other hazardous areas. Keep away from areas with high-voltage lines, power towers, and other areas with signs of electrical danger to prevent electrical shock.

(4) Follow Correct Evacuation Procedures

Do not attempt to swim to escape and avoid climbing onto electrified poles, iron towers, and stay away from leaning utility poles and broken power lines. If caught in floodwaters, try to grab onto something stable or buoyant and look for opportunities to escape.

(5) Beware of Open Well

When urban waterlogging reaches a certain level, the pressure of underground pipelines in some areas increases, which will wash away the well covers on the road. Once pedestrians fall into the black well, it may cause life-threatening situations. Therefore, if the structure of the house is stable, it is advisable to avoid going out unless it is necessary. Be sure not to go barefoot or wear slippers when going out; when walking, it is best to hold a bamboo pole in your hand to explore the road, while moving slowly and adjusting at any time. By observing the height of the fence on both sides of the road, the isolation strip, and the street lights, evaluate the depth of the water.

(6) Ensure Food Security

After a flood disaster occurs, it is easy to trigger various infectious disease outbreaks, such as intestinal infectious diseases, respiratory infectious diseases, and natural source diseases. The main risk of infectious diseases comes from pollution of drinking water facilities and stagnant water. Therefore, in order to prevent the occurrence of infectious diseases, it is necessary to prepare enough fast food, drinking water, and daily necessities, avoid drinking raw water or water from unknown sources, and choose boiled water. Food must be thoroughly cooked, and food soaked in floods cannot be used.

物，也不能用被污染的水或来源不明的水清洗蔬菜水果。切忌食用病死、毒死或死因不明的家畜、家禽、鱼虾。

（七）创伤处理

如在大雨中有被刮破出现流血的情况，脱离污染环境后要按住伤口，用流动的清水冲洗伤口周围。若条件受限应尽量用干净布料摁住伤口，止血后包扎。

（八）雷雨天注意事项

雷雨天气时，最好把家用电器的电源切断，不要接打固定电话；远离带电设备，不要接触天线、煤气管道、铁丝网、金属窗、建筑物外墙等；不要赤脚站在泥地或水泥地上，防止触电；不要靠近树、电线杆和广告牌，防止雷电，例如案例二。

【案例二　雨后电击】2018年6月8日晚，广东省佛山市禅城区一对母女在公交站触电身亡，且同天下午，广州机场路南云西街路口浸水的绿化带附近一名男子疑似触电倒地身亡。地区供电局工作人员现场勘查发现，两起事故皆是事故人员雨后趟水，公交站台广告牌漏电所致。

【案例三　水灾自救】2021年7月，暴雨狂袭郑州。一位女子带着儿子和女儿驾车行驶在回家的路上时，被水位及膝的洪水冲到道路正中，车辆既无法继续行

Vegetables and fruits cannot be washed with contaminated water or water from unknown sources. Avoid consuming livestock, poultry, fish, and shrimp that have died from illness, poisoning, or unknown causes.

(7) Wound Management

If injured and bled during heavy rain, wash the surroundings of the wound with flowing clean water after leaving the contaminated environment. Use clean fabric to apply pressure to the wound area and stop bleeding after finding a clean cloth if conditions constrained.

(8) Precautions during Thunderstorms

In thunderstorm weather, it is advisable to disconnect the power supply of household appliances and avoid using landline telephones. Stay away from charged equipment, do not touch antennas, gas pipelines, wire mesh, metal windows, exterior walls of buildings, etc. Do not stand barefoot on muddy or concrete ground to prevent electrical conductivity. Avoid approaching trees, utility poles, and billboards to prevent lightning strikes(see Case 2).

[Case 2　Electric shock after rain] On the evening of June 8, 2018, a mother and daughter in Chancheng District, Foshan City, Guangdong Province, were electrocuted to death at a bus stop. In the afternoon of the same day, a man near the flooded green belt at the intersection of Guangzhou Airport Road and Nanyun West Street was suspected to have been electrocuted and fell to the ground. Staff from the regional power supply bureau conducted on-site inspections and found that both accidents were caused by water splashing after rain and electric leakage from bus stop billboards.

[Case 3　Self-rescue from flood] In July 2021, rainstorm hit Zhengzhou. A woman with her son and daughter was driving home when she was hit by a knee-high flood and it hit them to the center of the road. The car was unable to continue driving and the doors could not be opened.

驶，车门也无法打开。车外迅速上涨的洪水加剧了孩子们的恐慌。女子首先安抚好孩子们的情绪，随后立即拨通报警电话。但信号线路已堵塞，电话没打通。面对此突发事件，女子让自己保持冷静，随后确认周边信息，并根据位置定位，在网上寻求帮助。女子首先通过外卖和点评软件搜索，找到附近一家便利店老板的电话，打通后，请求对方去车里救人。与此同时，女子还发布朋友圈叙述情况，请求在车子附近的人帮忙营救。便利店老板接到了女子的求救电话，但他当时在几千米之外的地方抢险救人。于是他立即拨打便利店旁边的宾馆电话，把救人任务传递下去。宾馆大堂两位小伙接到便利店老板的消息，展开救援。两位小伙涉水而行翻越护栏。试图敲开天窗，但是无果。同时，面馆老板也听到了外边的呼救声，操起家里的大铁锤，冲入风雨中。面馆老板先用铁锤在汽车的后挡风玻璃上凿出一个小洞，而后绕到汽车的左后方，对着车窗猛砸了三下。车窗碎裂，母子三人最终得以被营救出来。

二、溺水后的自救与施救

溺水指大量水或其他液体被吸入肺内，导致人体进入缺氧窒息的状态。进入血液循环的水引

The rapidly rising flood outside the car intensified the children's panic. The woman first calmed the children's emotions and immediately dialed the alarm number. But the signal is blocked and the phone loses connection. Faced with this unexpected event, the woman first keeps herself calm, then confirms the surrounding information and seeks help online based on location. The woman first searched through a food delivery and review App to find the phone number of a nearby convenience store owner. At the phone call, she asked the owner for help. At the same time, the woman is still narrating the situation on her social media and seeking help from people near the car to rescue her. The convenience store owner received the call from this woman, but he was rescuing someone else from a few kilometers away. So he immediately dialed the hotel number next to the convenience store and passed on the rescue mission. Two young men in the hotel lobby received a message from the convenience store owner. They waded through the water and climbed over the guardrail, attempting to open the skylight, but to no avail. At the same time, the noodle shop owner also heard the cries for help outside, grabbed the big hammer at home, and rushed into the wind and rain. The noodle shop owner first chiseled a small hole in the rear windshield of the car with a hammer, then went around to the left rear of the car and smashed it three times against the window. The car window shattered, and the mother and her children were ultimately rescued.

2. Self-Rescue and Rescue after Drowning

Drowning refers to a state where a large amount of water or other liquid is inhaled into the lungs, leading to oxygen deficiency and suffocation in the human body. The ingestion of

起血液渗透压改变、电解质紊乱和组织损害，最后造成呼吸停止和心脏停搏而死亡。

教育部每年都会发布关于溺水安全教育等主题内容。在汛期，溺水事故进入高发期，要切实强化溺水预防工作，保障生命安全。世界卫生组织发布的《全球溺水报告：预防一个主要杀手》指出，溺水是全世界各区域儿童和青年的十大主要死因之一。全球每年约有37.2万人溺亡，我国每年约有5.9万人死于溺水，其中未成年人占据95%以上。近年来，溺水成为我国儿童意外伤害致死事故的"头号杀手"。溺水事件中，溺亡率高达89%。乡村是溺水事件的高发场所，留守青少年是高发人群。从性别看，超八成溺水青少年为男性。尤其是暑期，防溺水成为青少年安全教育的首要话题，但年年发布预警，年年有溺水事件发生，其根本原因是家长和孩子有认识误区。

相比于城市，河道、水库、池塘、水坝等易发生溺水的水域更加广泛地分布于乡村。而且，乡村水域的复杂程度远高于城镇水域，相应的防护措施也更为薄弱，这些造成将近70%的溺水意外发生在乡村。

water affects blood osmotic pressure, electrolyte balance, and causes tissue damage, ultimately resulting in respiratory failure and cardiac arrest leading to death.

Every year, the Ministry of Education issues content related to drowning security education, emphasizing the high incidence of drowning accidents during the flood season. Practical measures need to be taken to strengthen drowning prevention efforts and ensure the security of lives. The World Health Organization's report titled *Global Drowning Report: Preventing a Leading Killer* points out that drowning is one of the top ten leading causes of death for children and youth worldwide. Globally, about 372,000 people drown each year, with approximately 59,000 annual drowning deaths in China, where minors account for over 95%. In recent years, drowning has become the "number one killer" in accidental deaths among Chinese children, with an 89% fatality rate in drowning incidents. Rural areas are hotspots for drowning incidents, and left-behind children are a vulnerable population. In terms of gender, over 80% of drowning incidents involve male adolescents. As the summer vacation approaches, preventing drowning becomes a primary topic in youth security education. However, despite annual warnings, drowning incidents persist, primarily due to misconceptions held by parents and children.

In comparison to urban areas, water bodies prone to drowning incidents, such as rivers, reservoirs, ponds, and dams, are more widely distributed in rural settings. Moreover, rural-area waters are more complex than those in cities, with correspondingly weaker protective measures. As a result, nearly 70% of drowning incidents occur in rural areas.

（一）溺水自救与预防

1. 冷静应对，保存体力

即使不会游泳，人在水中也是可以漂浮的，落水后人体会随着水的浮力不断起伏。为此，要保持镇定，不要在水中胡乱扑腾，保持体力，可采用"抱膝式"和"仰漂式"两个自救动作。

采用抱膝式时，双手抱住膝盖，低头成蜷缩状，人体会慢慢上浮，当感觉背部离开水面时，迅速向下推水，同时抬头换气，然后下沉恢复抱膝状态。循环往复，以确保自身的正常呼吸，延长自救时间。

仰漂式指让身体的脸部口、鼻部分浮出水面，其余的部位则在水面下，维持浮力。首先将双手放于水中，人往后仰，保持口鼻浮出水面进行缓慢换气。当下沉时闭上嘴巴，鼻子出气，微微推水，等待上浮。切记不能将手上举或挣扎，以免使身体下沉。

2. 减少负担，利用工具

落水后，应及时甩掉身上鞋子和口袋里的重物，如钥匙、手机、皮带等。寻找一切可以利用的漂浮物或可增加浮力的东西进行自救，如身边的木板、矿泉水瓶、空的塑料袋、泡沫箱子、外套、裤子、救生圈等，此类物品都能产生一定的浮力，给予更多的漂浮时间。另外，使用外套衣服或裤子时，将袖口打结浮力更佳。

(1) Self-Rescue and Prevention of Drowning

1) Stay Calm, Conserve Energy

In water, even non-swimmers can float, as the human body moves with the buoyancy of water. Therefore, it is essential to remain calm, avoid frantic movements, conserve energy, and employ two self-rescue positions: the fetal position and the back float.

In the fetal position, clasp your knees with both hands, lower your head into a curled position, allowing the body to gradually float upward. When you feel your back above the water surface, quickly push down, simultaneously lift your head for breathing, then sink back into the fetal position, repeating this cycle to ensure normal breathing and extend the self-rescue time.

The back float involves keeping the face, mouth, and nose above the water surface while the rest of the body remains submerged, maintaining buoyancy. Begin by placing both hands in the water, tilting your body backward, keeping your mouth and nose above the water for slow breathing. When submerging, close your mouth, exhale through your nose, slightly push the water, and wait to float up. Avoid raising or struggling with your hands, as it may cause the body to sink.

2) Reduce Burden, Utilize Tools

After falling into the water, promptly discard shoes and heavy items in pockets, including keys, phones, belts, and others. Look for floating objects capable of providing additional buoyancy for self-rescue, such as nearby planks, mineral water bottles, empty plastic bags, foam boxes, jackets, pants, life buoys, etc. These items generate buoyancy, offering more time to stay afloat. When using jackets or pants, tying knots at the cuffs enhances buoyancy.

3. 节省体力，有效呼救

当周围没人的时候要保存体力，进行有频率的呼救即可，不要一直呼救，否则容易造成体力不支下沉。当周围有人的时候，尽力发出声响或呼救，引起他人注意。

4. 配合施救，减少反抗

若有人跳水施救，溺水者要尽量放松，让自己保持冷静，等待救援人员施救。同时应仰卧水面，配合施救者，由施救者将自己拖拽到安全地带。不可紧紧抱住施救者挣扎或用力拉扯。否则，可能造成两人同时丧命。

5. 肌肉痉挛，反向拉伸

若手指抽筋，则可将手握拳，然后用力张开，迅速反复做多次。若是小腿或脚趾抽筋，先吸一口气，仰浮于水上，用抽筋肢体对侧的手握住抽筋肢体的脚趾，用力向身体方向拉，同时用同侧的手掌压在抽筋肢体的膝盖上，帮助抽筋腿伸直或膝关节伸直，脚尖回勾，保持状态 10 s，重复动作直至恢复。

6. 无人区域，不可前往

大部分的溺水都发生在无人看管的水库、河沟、池塘等水域。一些水域表面看起来清浅，水流不快，但实际上水底情况复杂，往往是到了水中才发现危险。另外，在开放性水域中人体表面热量流失很快，入水前的体表温度是 35℃，短短半分钟可能就降到

3) Save Energy and Effectively Call for Help

When no one is around, conserve energy by periodically calling for help instead of continuous shouting, as continuous shouting may lead to exhaustion and sinking. When others are present, make efforts to create sound or call for help to attract attention.

4) Cooperate with Rescue Efforts to Reduce Resistance

If someone jumps in to rescue, relax and remain calm, awaiting rescue personnel. Lie on your back, allowing the rescuer to drag you to a safe area. Do not tightly cling to the rescuer, struggle, or pull forcefully, as it may lead to a simultaneous tragic outcome for both.

5) Do Reverse Stretching When Muscle Spasms

If fingers cramp, make a fist, then forcefully open it, repeating several times. For leg or toe cramps, take a deep breath, float on your back in the water, use the hand on the opposite side to grasp the toes of the cramped leg, pull towards the body, simultaneously pressing the hand on the same side against the knee joint, assisting in straightening the cramped leg or knee joint. Hold for ten seconds, repeat until recover.

6) Avoid Swimming in Unattended Water Areas

Most drowning incidents occur in unattended water bodies such as reservoirs, ditches, ponds, etc. Some water surfaces may appear shallow with slow currents, but the underwater conditions are complex, often leading to danger only after entering the water. Moreover, in open water, body heat is rapidly lost. The surface temperature before entering the water is 35 degrees, in just half a minute, it may drop to 30 degrees, making cramps and fatigue likely to occur. With

只有 30℃，在此情况下容易发生疲劳甚至抽筋的情况，又无人看管，很难得到救援。为此，一定不要去没有人看管和缺少安全设施的地方游泳。

（二）溺水施救

人民网舆情数据中心公布的《2022 中国青少年防溺水大数据报告》指出，多人溺水现象频发，往往是一人发生溺水，多人营救导致的。为此，掌握足够的救援知识和相应的能力至关重要。

（1）发现有人溺水要马上拨打 120 电话，随后再进入急救工作。

（2）若施救者水性不佳或不熟悉水域情况，万不可贸然下水，否则不但无法营救成功，还可能搭上自己的性命。

（3）施救者应尽快找到周围可取的漂浮物，抛给落水者。若无法找到，施救者可以脱下长裤，在水中浸泡，扎紧裤管充气后，再扎紧裤腰，抛给落水者。

（4）施救者下水后不要从落水者的正面靠近，应该从后面或侧面包抄施救，以仰泳的方法把落水者带到安全处。

（5）在救助过程中，一定要使落水者露出水面，保证其顺利呼吸，减轻落水者的危机感和恐惧感。

（6）救援时，最好将落水者向上托出水面的同时，自己主动下沉。落水者一旦呼吸到空气就不会拼命抓紧，此时施救者再伺

no one around to supervise, it is hard to receive rescue. Therefore, avoid swimming in unattended areas without security facilities.

(2) Drowning Rescue

The *2022 China Youth Drowning Prevention Big Data Report* released by the People's Daily Online Public Opinion Data Center indicates that incidents of multiple drownings often result from attempts to rescue a single drowning individual. Therefore, having sufficient rescue knowledge and skills is crucial.

① If someone is found drowning, immediately shout for help and call 120, then swiftly engage in aid after making the call.

② If the rescuer is weak in swimming or unfamiliar with the water conditions, they should not rashly enter the water. Doing so not only jeopardizes the rescue attempt but may also risk their own life.

③ Rescuers should quickly find any available floating objects in the vicinity and throw them to the person in distress. If none are found, rescuers can take off long pants, immerse them in water, inflate the pant legs, tighten them, and throw them to the drowning person.

④ Rescuers entering the water should avoid approaching the drowning individual from the front. Instead, approach from behind or the side, bring the drowning person to safety in backstroke.

⑤ During the rescue process, it is necessary to keep the drowning person above the water surface, ensure their smooth breathing, and reduce their sense of crisis and fear.

⑥ When rescuing, it is best to lift the drowning person above the water while actively sinking. Once a drowning person breathes in the air, they will not grab tightly, and then the rescuer can wait for an opportunity to

机完成救助。

（7）若溺水者口鼻有淤泥和杂草等，应首先清除。

（8）若溺水者已昏迷，呼吸很微弱或停止，做完上述处理后，应进行人工呼吸。

（三）溺水预防措施

1. 了解机体状态

患有心脏病、高血压、癫痫病、肺结核、中耳炎、皮肤病、严重沙眼的人群，处在月经期的女性，以及各类具有传染病的群体都不宜下水游泳。

2. 做好热身活动

人体的温度一般比水温高，在未做热水活动的情况下，忽然下水会导致皮肤受到刺激，使得肌肉产生强烈收缩，发生肌肉痉挛等问题，进而可能导致溺水事故。

3. 注意天气状态

雷雨天气在水中，容易被雷击中；若遇狂风时，强风可导致强劲的洋流和离岸流，把游泳者带离安全区域。另外，高温、寒冷及多雾等极端天气中，紫外线强辐射、能见度降低等情况的发生都会严重危害到个人安全。

complete the rescue.

⑦ If the drowning person has mud and weeds in their mouth and nose, they should be removed first.

⑧ If the drowning person is unconscious, breathing is weak or stops, artificial respiration should be performed after completing the above treatment.

(3) Drowning Prevention Measure

1) Understand Body Conditions

Individuals with heart disease, hypertension, epilepsy, tuberculosis, otitis media, skin diseases, severe trachoma, and various infectious diseases are not suitable for swimming. Women in menstruation should also avoid swimming.

2) Warm up Properly

Since the human body generally has a higher temperature than the water, sudden immersion without warm-up activities can stimulate the skin, causing muscles to contract intensely, leading to cramps and potential drowning accidents.

3) Monitor Weather Conditions

Thunderstorm weather in water makes it easy to be struck by lightning; When encountering strong winds, strong winds can cause strong ocean currents and offshore currents, taking swimmers away from safe areas. In addition, extreme weather conditions such as high temperature, cold, and foggy weather can seriously endanger personal security due to strong UV radiation and reduced visibility.

第三节
运动安全

Section 3
Physical Security

运动安全指个体在运动过程中应注意的安全事项和应具备的安全意识。具体指体育过程中发生的机械性和物理性的伤害，即运动损伤。根据国务院下发的《全民健身计划（2021—2025年）》所提供的数据，到2025年，经常参加体育锻炼人数比例达到38.5%，大约5.39亿人次。值得关注的是，随着运动人口数大幅提升，如何避免运动伤害和急救也成为了一个重点话题。《2009—2014健身行业产值规模》表明，经常运动的人运动损伤率达到85%以上，据此推算到2025年，出现运动损伤的人数将达4.58亿之多。为此，了解运动过程中的注意事项以及出现运动损伤等意外的处理方法非常重要。

本节首先从整体层面介绍运动软组织损伤处理的一般性原则，然后具体介绍常见运动损伤类型的处理方法，最后从运动损伤预防的角度介绍运动前应该做的措施、运动中应注意的事项。

Physical security refers to the security precautions and awareness that individuals should pay attention to during exercise. Specifically, it refers to mechanical and physical injuries that occur during the sports process, namely sports injuries. According to the data provided by the *National Fitness Plan (2021-2025)* issued by the State Council, by 2025, the proportion of people who regularly participate in physical exercise will reach 38.5%, approximately 539 million people. It is worth noting that with the significant increase in the number of exercising people, how to avoid sports injuries and provide first aid has become a key topic. According to the *2009-2014 Fitness Industry Output Scale*, the sports injury rate of people who exercise regularly reaches over 85%. Based on this, it is estimated that by 2025, the number of people who experience sports injuries will reach 458 million. Therefore, it is very important to understand the precautions during exercise and the handling methods for accidents such as sports injuries.

This section first introduces the general principles of handling soft tissue sports injuries from a holistic perspective, then specifically introduces the methods of handling commonly occurring types of sports injuries. Finally, from the perspective of sports injury prevention, it introduces the measures that should be taken before exercise and the precautions that should be taken during exercise.

一、运动软组织损伤处理的一般性原则

软组织与硬组织——骨骼相对应。软组织损伤指在运动过程中，人体的肌肉、肌腱、韧带、关节囊、滑膜囊、神经、血管等组织受到撞击、牵张、扭转、压迫等引起的损伤。常见的软组织损伤有肌肉拉伤、韧带扭伤、挫伤、撞伤、肌腱炎、滑膜炎等。

运动损伤处理的原则经历了传统的 RICE 原则[①]、PRICE 原则[②]、POLICE 原则[③]，再到 2019 年《英国运动医学期刊》（*British Journal of Sports Medicine*，BJSM）新推出的急性和亚急性软组织损伤处理的 PEACE&LOVE 原则。值得注意的是，相较于以往的原则，PEACE&LOVE 原则取消了"ICE——冰敷"。其认为冰敷虽有能降低组织温度、抑制炎症反应、减少局部肿胀和患肢疼痛的作用，但由于组织的愈合修复需要病理性的发炎反应，过度压抑发炎反应，反而会延缓组织清除坏死细胞的速率，影响组织的重建愈合速率[④]。但部分观点认为，受伤后

1. General Principles for Managing Soft Tissue Injuries

Soft tissue corresponds to hard tissue—bones. Soft tissue injury refers to the damage caused to the muscles, tendons, ligaments, joint capsules, synovial capsules, nerves, blood vessels, and other tissues of the human body during exercise by means of impact, tension, torsion, compression, etc. Common soft tissue injuries include muscle strain, ligament sprain, contusion, collision, tendonitis, synovitis, etc.

The principles of sports injury management have gone through the traditional RICE principle, PRIME principle, POLICE principle, and then the PEACE&LOVE principle for acute and subacute soft tissue injury management, which was newly introduced in the *British Journal of Sports Medicine* (BJSM) in 2019. It is worth noting that compared to previous principles, the PEACE&LOVE principle eliminates the previous "ICE—ice compress" and believes that although ice compress can decrease tissue temperature, inhibit inflammatory reactions, reduce local swelling and limb pain, the healing and repair of tissues require pathological inflammatory reactions. Excessive suppression of inflammatory reactions can actually delay the rate of tissue clearance of necrotic cells, affecting the rate of tissue reconstruction and healing. However, some views suggest that after injury, there is no need to completely cancel ice therapy, as although ice therapy cannot promote healing, it

---

① RICE 原则，即处理急性软组织损伤的基本原则，包括四个步骤：休息（Rest）、冰敷（Ice）、加压包扎（Compression）、抬高患肢（Elevation）。

② PRICE 原则，在 RICE 原则的基础上增加了保护（Protection）。

③ POLICE 原则，用 OL（Optimal Loading，适当负重）代替了 PRICE 原则中的 R。

④ ALEXANDER J, ALLAN D R, RHODES D D. Cryotherapy in sport: a warm reception for the translation of evidence into applied practice[J]. Res sports med, 2021, 10:1-4.

无需完全取消冰敷，因为冰敷虽无法促进愈合，但能抑制出血、减少肿痛，只需注意冰敷频率，保持在 1～2 次即可。

（一）急性软组织损伤处理原则

急性期即炎症反应期，持续时间为 3～5 天，主要表现为炎症体征，如疼痛、肿胀、红肿、发热和功能受限。PEACE 指软组织损伤的"急性期"应遵循的原则，主要强调重视自愈能力，减少过度医疗。PEACE 分别指保护患肢（Protection）、抬高患肢（Elevation）、避免使用抗炎药（Avoid anti-inflammatories）、加压（Compression）和认知教育（Education）。具体操作如下。

1. P——保护患肢

在运动过程中出现急性运动软组织损伤后，应采取相应的制动措施，限制运动 1～3 天，避免受伤的肌肉纤维被再次拉长，造成二次伤害。

2. E——抬高患肢

将患肢抬至高于心脏的位置，有利于促使间质液流出组织，并促进血液循环，减轻肿胀反应。

3. A——避免使用抗炎药

损伤后急性期内应避免使用抗炎药物治疗。软组织损伤的病理病程可分为炎症期、增生期/肉芽期和重塑期三个时期，炎症期作为康复的第一步，在无并发症情况下可持续约 72 小时。炎

can inhibit bleeding and reduce swelling and pain. Only pay attention to the frequency of ice therapy and maintain 1–2 times.

(1) Principles of Acute Soft Tissue Injury Management

The acute phase, also known as the inflammatory response phase, lasts for 3–5 days and is mainly characterized by inflammatory signs such as pain, swelling, redness, fever, and limited function. PEACE refers to the principles that should be followed during the acute phase of soft tissue injury, mainly emphasizing the importance of self-healing ability and reducing excessive medical treatment. PEACE refers to Protection, Elevation, Avoid anti-inflammatories, Compression and Education. The specific operation is as follows.

1) P—Protection

After acute sports soft tissue injury occurs during exercise, corresponding measures should be taken to limit exercise for 1–3 days, prevent the injured muscle fibers from being stretched again, and avoid secondary injury.

2) E—Elevation

Lifting the affected limb above the heart is beneficial for promoting interstitial fluid to flow out of the tissue, promoting blood circulation, and reducing swelling reactions.

3) A—Avoid Anti-inflammatories

Anti-inflammatories should be avoided during the acute phase after injury. The pathological course of soft tissue injury can be divided into three stages: inflammation, proliferation/granulation, and remodeling. Inflammation, as the first step of rehabilitation, can last for about 72 hours without complications. Inflammation is a defensive defense of the body

症是机体对刺激的一种防御性防御，若盲目使用抗炎药物可能会抑制软组织愈合的进程，延缓软组织修复。

4. C——加压

使用绷带或贴扎等方式，给予受伤部位外部压力，可以限制关节内水肿和组织出血。

5. E——认知教育

在治疗师或医生的帮助下对患者进行认知教育，让患者了解损伤的原因、损伤的情况、治疗方式对康复的益处，使患者主动参与康复训练。

（二）亚急性软组织损伤处理原则

亚急性期在急性期之后。该时期炎症消失，组织开始修复，脆弱的胶原组织纤维在损伤处形成瘢痕组织，持续时间为3天～6周。LOVE原则是亚急性期应秉持的原则，强调使患者保持积极心态，尽快进行康复训练。LOVE分别指适宜的负荷（Load）、乐观的心理状态（Optimism）、促进血液循环（Vascularization）、运动训练（Exercise）。具体操作如下。

1. L——适宜负荷

LOVE原则的L和以往提出的POLICE原则中的OL一致，指的均是康复训练的适宜负荷。该步骤强调软组织损伤恢复期应鼓励患者在不加重病情、不产生疼痛的情况下，主动参与活动训练，这

against stimulation. Blindly using anti-inflammatories may inhibit the process of soft tissue healing and delay soft tissue repair.

4) C—Compression

Using bandages to apply external pressure to the injured area can limit joint edema and tissue bleeding.

5) E—Education

It refers to providing cognitive education to patients with the help of therapists or doctors, enabling them to understand the causes, conditions, and benefits of treatment for rehabilitation, and encouraging them to actively participate in rehabilitation training.

(2) Principles of Management for Subacute Soft Tissue Injury

The subacute phase occurs after the acute phase, during which inflammation disappears and tissue begins to repair. Fragile collagen fibers form scar tissue at the site of injury, lasting for 3 days to 6 weeks. The LOVE principle is a principle that should be upheld during the subacute phase, emphasizing patients maintaining a positive attitude and conducting rehabilitation training as soon as possible. LOVE refers to Load, Optimism, Vascularization, and Exercise. The specific operation is as follows.

1) L—Load

The L in LOVE principle and the OL in previously proposed POLICE principle both refer to the appropriate load for rehabilitation training. This step suggests that during the recovery period of soft tissue injuries, patients should be encouraged to actively participate in activity training without worsening the condition or causing pain, which will greatly

将有助于患者肉骨骼的康复。

2. O——乐观的心理状态

康复不仅仅是身体上的康复，心理的康复同样重要。忧郁、恐惧等负面心理可能会影响复原。

3. V——促进血液循环

急性期之后的有氧心肺运动能促进血液循环，加快新陈代谢，增加损伤部位营养物质的供应及有害物质或代谢废物的排出，促进组织愈合修复。有氧运动要根据机体的恢复情况，建议遵循从低等强度到中等强度的有氧运动处方要求，安排适合的有氧运动方式（如步行、八段锦等，强度必须达最大心率 60%）。

4. E——运动训练

软组织损伤后，长期制动或卧床会引起肌力下降、关节活动范围减小、感觉减弱等问题，进而影响患者日后肢体功能的恢复。因此，损伤后在不加重患者病情、不引起剧烈疼痛的情况下，早期活动有助于运动能力、肌肉力量和本体感觉的维持和恢复，在亚急性期进行运动训练可以确保功能得到最佳恢复，减少复发性损伤及避免留下后遗症。

二、常见运动损伤的处理

常见的运动损伤的类型主要有皮肤擦伤、划伤，挫伤，肌肉拉伤，关节扭伤，关节脱臼及骨折等。

contribute to the recovery of musculoskeletal patients.

2) O—Optimism

Rehabilitation is not only physical, but also psychological. Negative emotions such as depression and fear may affect recovery.

3) V—Vascularization

Aerobic cardiopulmonary exercise after the acute phase can promote blood circulation, accelerate metabolic capacity, increase the supply of nutrients to the injured area, eliminate harmful substances or metabolic waste, and promote tissue healing and repair. Aerobic exercise should be based on the recovery of the body, and it is recommended to follow the requirements of aerobic exercise prescription from low to moderate intensity, and arrange suitable aerobic exercise methods (such as walking, Baduanjin, etc., the intensity must reach 60% of a maximum heart rate).

4) E—Exercise

After soft tissue injury, long-term immobilization or bed rest can cause problems such as decreased muscle strength, reduced joint range of motion, and weakened sensation, which in turn affects the patient's future recovery of limb function. Therefore, early activity after injury can help maintain and recover motor ability, muscle strength, and proprioception without exacerbating the patient's condition or causing severe pain. Exercise training during the subacute phase can ensure optimal functional recovery, reduce recurrent injuries and avoid sequelae.

2. Treatment of Common Sports Injuries

Common sports injuries include skin abrasion, contusions, sprains, muscle strains, joint dislocation and fractures.

（一）皮肤擦伤、划伤

擦伤是钝性物与皮肤表层摩擦而造成的以表皮剥脱为主要改变的损伤，是开放伤中最轻的一类创伤。最常见的为跑步重心不稳摔倒而导致的皮肤擦伤。

处理方法：如擦伤部位较浅，只需涂红药水即可。但是当擦伤创面较脏或有渗血时，应用生理盐水清创后再涂上红药水或紫药水。

（二）挫伤

挫伤是指由于钝性的暴力作用于身体的表面，未造成皮肤的破裂，但损伤了皮下组织、肌肉和血管。运动过程中常见的挫伤原因包括器械撞击和人与人之间的碰撞。如在团体对抗球类项目中（足球、篮球等运动），在对抗或抢球过程中发生碰撞。

症状：挫伤通常肉眼可见，局部有淤血、青紫、肿胀，有明显的触痛和压痛。

处理方法：在遵循PEACE&LOVE原则的基础上，局部冷敷，用冷水袋、专用的冰敷袋或冷饮敷在挫伤部位的表面，冷敷时间大概为 $10 \sim 20$ min。在24 h 内冷敷或加压包扎，72 h 后理疗或热敷。需要注意的是，24 h 后即刻热敷可能会引起组织重新肿胀。

（三）肌肉拉伤

肌肉拉伤是指肌肉在运动过程中因过度收缩或牵拉，超过肌

(1) Skin Abrasion and Scratches

Skin abrasion results from friction between blunt objects and the skin, causing superficial damage with the main alteration being epidermal abrasion. It is the mildest type of trauma among open wounds. The most common type is skin abrasions caused by falls of unstable running center of gravity.

Treatment: If the abrasion is shallow, applying red medicine is sufficient. However, for dirty or bleeding abrasions, cleaning with saline is necessary before applying red or purple medicine.

(2) Contusions

A contusion is caused by blunt violence acting on the surface of the body, causing no skin rupture, but damaging subcutaneous tissue, muscles, and blood vessels. Common contusions reasons during exercise include instrument impacts and collisions between people. In team sports such as football and basketball, collisions occur during the process of confrontation or grabbing the ball.

Symptoms: Contusions are visible, showing local bruising, discoloration, swelling, and noticeable tenderness and pain.

Treatment: Following the principles of PEACE&LOVE, apply local cold compression using ice packs, specialized cold packs, or chilled compresses for approximately 10–20 minutes. Cold compression or pressure bandaging can be applied within 24 hours, and after 72 hours, physiotherapy or warm compresses can be considered. Be cautious as immediate warm compresses within 24 hours may cause tissue reswelling.

(3) Muscle Strain

Muscle strain occurs when a muscle undergoes excessive contraction or stretching beyond its capacity

肉承受能力而引起的损伤。根据肌肉损伤的程度可分为三级。一级（轻度）为不明显的肌肉拉伤；二级（中度）为部分肌肉断裂；三级（严重）为完全断裂。常见的例子包括因跳跃或快速转身时脚踝位置不稳导致的韧带过度拉伸或撕裂。

症状：肌肉拉伤后，拉伤部位剧痛，用手可摸到因肌肉紧张形成的索条状硬块，触疼明显，局部肿胀或皮下出血，活动明显受到限制。

处理方法：具体见挫伤的处理方法。若是重度拉伤应立即送医院进行治疗。另外，肌肉拉伤后不可进行肌肉拉伸以及肌肉的过度按摩。

（四）关节扭伤

关节扭伤是指四肢关节或躯体部位的软组织（如肌肉、肌腱、韧带等）损伤，而无骨折、脱臼、皮肉破损等。

症状：关节扭伤多为运动时不稳向一侧倾斜或踩在他人足上或高低不平的地面上面受伤，伤后局部能力立即丧失，有明显的肿胀和疼痛等症状。

处理方法：见挫伤的处理方法。

（五）关节脱臼

关节脱臼又称关节脱位，指因外力作用使关节面失去正常的连接。关节脱位可分为全脱位和半脱位两种。

during movement, resulting in injury. It can be categorized into three degrees of severity: mild, moderate, and severe. Common examples include excessive stretching or tearing of ligaments due to unstable ankle position during jumping or rapid turning.

Symptoms: After muscle strain, there is intense pain at the affected site, palpable muscle tension forming a cord-like lump, noticeable tenderness, localized swelling, or subcutaneous bleeding, and significant restriction of movement.

Treatment: Follow the treatment methods for contusions. Patients with severe strains should be promptly taken to the hospital for treatment. Additionally, avoid muscle stretching and excessive massage after muscle strain.

(4) Joint Sprain

A sprain refers to damage to the soft tissues (muscles, tendons, ligaments, etc.) around joints or body parts without fractures, dislocations, or skin damage.

Symptoms: Joint sprains often occur when instability during movement leads to injury, causing immediate loss of function, noticeable swelling, and pain.

Treatment: Follow the treatment methods for contusions.

(5) Joint Dislocation

Joint dislocation, also known as dislocation, occurs when external force disrupts the normal connection of joint surfaces. Dislocations can be complete or partial.

症状：关节脱位后常出现畸形，有局部疼痛和关节肿胀，失去正常活动能力。

处理方法：用长度和宽度相称的夹板固定伤肢。若没有夹板，可将伤肢固定在自己的躯干或健肢上，防止震动，随后及时送医院治疗。切不可随意做整复手术，避免增加伤害。

（六）骨折

骨折是骨骼受到极度应力（张力、压缩、弯曲、旋转及剪切）和应变的结果。

症状：主动和被动活动疼痛；肿胀及畸形；压痛和叩击痛；出现骨擦音。

处理方法：若运动中发生骨折应立即制动休息，固定包扎并及时就医。骨折后继续运动会导致不适症状加重。另外，为了维持骨折部位的稳定性，避免损伤程度进一步加重，可就地取材，选择硬木板、树枝、绷带等物品，对骨折部位进行固定包扎，同时还要观察局部情况，如果有出血现象，还需要给予按压止血。通过上述方式处理之后如果还能够活动，可自行到就近的医院骨科就诊；若无法活动可以寻求周围人的帮助或拨打120急救电话。由医生根据骨折的严重程度给予手法复位或切开复位，必要时用石膏或夹板固定。

Symptoms: After joint dislocation, deformity, local pain, and joint swelling are commonly seen, accompanied by a loss of normal mobility.

Treatment: Immobilize the injured limb with a splint of appropriate size. If a splint is not available, secure the injured limb to the trunk or the unaffected limb to prevent vibration. Seek medical treatment promptly, avoiding unnecessary attempts at resetting to prevent further harm.

(6) Fracture

A fracture is the result of extreme stress and strain on the bones (tension, compression, bending, rotation, and shearing).

Symptoms: Active and passive movement causes pain; swelling and deformity; tenderness and percussion pain; crepitation.

Treatment: If a fracture occurs during exercise, immediately immobilize and rest, and seek medical attention promptly. Continuing to exercise after a fracture will worsen symptoms. Use locally available materials, such as wooden boards, branches, or bandages, to fix and bandage the fractured area. Observe the local situation; if there is bleeding, provide compression to stop bleeding. After these initial measures, if you can still move, seek medical attention at the nearest orthopedic hospital; if unable to move, seek help from nearby individuals or call emergency services (e.g., 120) for medical assistance. Depending on the severity of the fracture, the doctor may use manual reduction or surgical reduction and may apply a cast or splint as needed.

三、运动损伤的预防措施

运动过程中发生损伤的诱因包括：心理层面的情绪不稳定，获胜动机过强，生理层面的活动不充分，在身心疲惫的状态下运动，认知层面的安全知识与意识不足等多个方面。现就运动损伤的主要原因进行分析，并提供相应的预防措施，以期引起警觉，防止运动损伤的发生。

（一）做好热身活动

热身活动可提高中枢神经系统的兴奋性，加强呼吸系统和心血管系统的机能，提高肌肉的弹性和力量，加大关节活动幅度。而不做热身活动，肌肉的黏滞性将增强，使肌肉僵硬。同时，各脏器由于生理惰性，无法调整至运动状态，将降低运动表现，增大发生运动损伤的可能。

（二）注意休息，保持较好的运动状态

在以"内卷"为标签的当下，不管是学生、老师，还是其他行业的工作者都承受着学业、科研、工作等相关 KPI（key performance indicator，关键绩效指标）和其他指标的重压，导致身心长期处于疲惫状态，加之熬夜等不良习惯引起睡眠不充足。在此状态下，进行体育运动时，肌肉力量、动作的准确性和身体的协调性显著下降，警觉性和注意力减退，反

3. Prevention Measures for Sports Injuries

The causes of injury during exercise include: emotional instability at the psychological level; strong motivation to win; insufficient physiological activities; exercise in a state of physical and mental fatigue; other aspects such as insufficient security knowledge and awareness at the cognitive level. This part analyzes the main causes of sports injuries and provides corresponding preventive measures to raise awareness and prevent the occurrence of sports injuries.

(1) Effective Warm-up Activities

Engaging in warm-up activities enhances the excitability of the central nervous system, improves respiratory and cardiovascular system functions, increases muscle elasticity and strength, and expands joint range of motion. Skipping warm-ups causes muscle viscosity and stiffness. Without proper warm-up, physiological inertia prevents organs from adjusting to the exercise state, reducing performance and increasing the likelihood of sports injuries.

(2) Adequate Rest for Maintaining Optimal Physical Condition

In the current era labeled as "involution", whether it is students, teachers, or other professionals, they are all under the heavy pressure of academic and research related KPIs and other indicators, leading to long-term physical and mental fatigue. In addition, inadequate sleep is caused by bad habits such as staying up late. In this state, when engaging in sports, muscle strength, accuracy of movements, and coordination of the body significantly decrease, alertness and attention decrease, reaction is slow, and it is difficult to participate in vigorous exercise or practice movements, which can easily lead to injuries.

应迟钝，此时若参加剧烈运动或练习较难动作，易导致损伤发生。

（三）保持注意力集中

许多人喜欢运动时佩戴耳机听音乐或故事。在一般的周期性运动中，如慢跑、蹬自行车出现损伤的概率较小。但当开始复杂的运动时则会出现很大问题，由于注意力不集中，未聚焦于动作本身，就会出现损伤。因此，当进行高负荷、动作较为复杂的动作时，应保持注意力集中，关注动作本身。

（四）科学训练

个人应根据身体状态和需求有针对性地选择运动项目，配以适宜的运动强度和运动量。例如长时间未进行体育活动，身体状态不佳，就应该从小运动量的活动开始，如慢跑、蹬自行车等。切勿进行中长跑或高强度对抗比赛。若过于疲惫，就应适当休息，莫强行进行高强度训练。此外，求胜动机不要太强，莫要过于情绪化，头脑发热，做超出能力的动作。

（五）穿着适宜的运动服装

运动时，应身穿合身的运动服装和运动鞋。不合身的服装会限制和影响运动过程中的肢体伸展，尤其不能穿牛仔裤和皮鞋运动。不合脚的鞋可能导致落脚感不对，导致扭伤等运动损伤的发生。

（六）不在恶劣条件下运动

极端恶劣的环境条件会给心

(3) Stay Focused

Many individuals prefer to wear headphones and listen to music or stories during exercise. While the probability of injury is relatively low during regular cyclic exercises like jogging or cycling, more complex activities can pose significant problems due to lack of concentration. Therefore, when performing high-load or complex movements, maintaining focused on the activity itself is crucial.

(4) Scientific Training

Individuals should choose sports activities tailored to their physical conditions and needs, accompanied by appropriate exercise intensity and volume. For those who have been inactive for an extended period, starting with low-intensity activities such as jogging or cycling is advisable. Avoid engaging in long-distance running or high-intensity competitive games. If excessively fatigued, take adequate breaks and avoid taking high-intensity training. Additionally, it's crucial not to have an overly strong motivation for victory.

(5) Appropriate Sports Attire

Wearing well-fitted sportswear and sports shoes is essential during exercise. Ill-fitting clothing can restrict and affect the stretching of limbs during movement, especially wearing denim pants and leather shoes for exercise. Inappropriate sports shoes may result in improper foot placement, leading to sprains and other injuries.

(6) Avoid Exercise in Harsh Conditions

Extremely harsh environmental conditions exert

血管系统造成很大的压力。恶劣环境主要包括高温、低温和空气污染等天气。此时，应选择适宜项目在室内锻炼。

（七）注意运动场地

运动时，应检查场地是否平整；健身或需使用器械时，应提前检查器械是否有瑕疵或故障。若居家运动，空间相对有限的情况下要综合考虑周围环境。

（八）寻求辅助支持，提高自我保护能力

在健身房等环境锻炼，若增加的负荷重量超出自身能力时，应在他人辅助下进行，切勿逞强。

第四节
心肺复苏技术

心肺复苏（Cardio Pulmonary Resuscitation, CPR）是心肺复苏技术的简称，是针对心脏和呼吸骤停的急症患者采取的抢救关键措施。若在患者的心脏和呼吸骤停的 4～6 min 内未采取任何措施，脑部会因为缺氧出现不可逆的脑细胞损伤，超过 10 min 会直接造成不可复原的死亡。CPR 的目的是恢复患者的自主呼吸和自主循环。《中国心脏骤停与心肺复苏报告 (2022 年版)》显示我国院外心脏骤停发病率约为 10 万分之 97.1。

significant stress on the cardiovascular system. Harsh conditions include high temperatures, low temperatures, and air pollution. It is advisable to choose suitable activities to exercise indoors.

(7) Check Exercise Facilities

Before engaging in physical activities, check whether the exercise area is even. For fitness or equipment-based exercises, inspect for defects and malfunctions. When exercising at home with limited space, consider the overall environment.

(8) Seek Auxiliary Assistance to Improve Self-Protective Abilities

In gym or similar settings, when increasing weight loads, ensure there is supervision and assistance from others. Avoid overexertion.

Section 4
Cardiopulmonary Resuscitation Techniques

CPR is the abbreviation for cardio-pulmonary resuscitation techniques, which are critical measures taken for patients suffering from sudden cardiac and respiratory arrest. If no measures are taken within 4−6 minutes after the onset of cardiac and respiratory arrest, the brain will suffer from irreversible damage due to hypoxia, and irreversible death will occur within 10 minutes. The purpose of CPR is to restore the patient's spontaneous breathing and circulation. The *Chinese Cardiac Arrest and CPR Report (2022 Edition)* shows that the incidence of out-of-hospital cardiac arrest in our country is about 97.1/100,000.

一、心肺复苏技术运用场景

心肺复苏技术运用的常见场景包括触电、溺水、窒息、呼吸道疾病中的支气管堵塞和心血管疾病中的心肌梗死等情况导致的"三无"状态，即无呼吸、无心跳、无意识。"三无"的确认可通过对患者两侧的肩膀轻拍并大声呼喊进行。此外，通过观察胸廓是否有起伏、感觉是否有鼻息、聆听是否有呼吸音，确认心跳和呼吸状态。

二、心肺复苏操作

心肺复苏技术包括中有四个关键步骤，分别是开放气道（Airway）、人工呼吸（Breathing）、胸外按压（Compression）和电除颤（Defibrillation），即 A—B—C—D。若身边有 D——除颤器（Automated External Defibrillator, AED），应尽早使用。其他三个关键步骤在 2010 年以前采用的是 A—B—C 顺序，此后，将顺序改为 C—A—B。顺序的更改更加强调胸外按压的质量和重要性：以足够的速率和幅度进行按压，保证每次按压后胸廓完全回弹，尽可能减少按压中断并避免过度通气。若患者未有好转应持续循环 C—A—B 过程 5 组。具体操作如下。

1. Application Scenarios of Cardiopulmonary Resuscitation Technology

Common application situations include electric shock, drowning, suffocation, bronchial obstruction in respiratory diseases, and myocardial infarction in cardiovascular diseases, leading to a state of "three nos". Namely, no breathing, no heartbeat, and no consciousness. The confirmation of "three nos" can be achieved by lightly tapping and shouting on both sides of the patient's shoulders to confirm their state of consciousness. In addition, by observing whether there is any fluctuation in the chest, feeling nasal breathing, and listening for breathing sounds, the heartbeat and breathing status can be confirmed.

2. CPR Operations

CPR techniques include four key steps: Airway, Breathing, Compression, and Defibrillation, that is, A–B–C–D. Before 2010, the sequence was A–B–C, and since then, the sequence has been changed to C–A–B. The change in sequence emphasizes the quality and importance of chest compression: to perform compressions at an adequate rate and amplitude, ensuring complete chest recoil after each compression, minimizing interruptions in compression, and avoiding hyperventilation. If there is no improvement in the patient's condition, continue the C–A–B process for 5 cycles. If there is a D (AED) available, it should be used as soon as possible. The specific operation is as follows.

（一）确认环境安全，确认患者意识状态

1. 确认环境安全

发现有人晕倒时，首先观察四周安全，做好自身保护，例如在公路中是否会出现过往车辆。

2. 判断患者意识

快步走到患者身体右侧，双膝跪地，双手轻轻拍打患者肩膀呼喊患者，"先生 / 女士你怎么了，还好吗？"观察其是否有反应，若无反应，开始下一步。

（二）呼救并获取 AED

如果患者无意识，立即向周围人求助，拨打急救电话 120，并取来 AED。呼救时，首先表明自身身份，其次求助周围群体，应指明求助对象的特征，避免旁观者效应。例如"穿黑夹克的男士请帮我拨打 120""穿白裙子的女士请帮助我取一下附近的 AED"。

（三）确认呼吸与脉搏

呼救后，应立即对患者的呼吸与脉搏进行判断检查，如果患者还有心跳和呼吸，心肺复苏反而会增加室颤的风险。呼吸与脉搏的观察与判断应同时进行，并通过口述"1 001，1 002……"计时。呼吸与脉搏的判断应在 10 s 内完成。若判断患者无脉搏和自主呼吸则进行下一步。

1. 颈动脉搏动观察

颈动脉位于气管与胸锁乳突肌的沟内。具体来说，将食指与中

(1) Confirm the Security of the Environment and the Patient's Consciousness State

1) Confirm the Security of the Environment

When you discover someone has fainted, the first step is to observe the surroundings for security and protect yourself, for example, whether there will be passing vehicles on the road.

2) Confirm the Patient's Consciousness State

Quickly walk to the patient's right side, crouch on your knees, and gently pat the patient's shoulders while calling out, "Sir/Madam, how are you doing, are you okay?" wait for any response. If there is no response, proceed to the next step.

(2) Seek Help and Obtain an AED

If the patient is unconscious, immediately ask for help from people around, call the emergency number 120, and retrieve an AED. When calling for help, first indicate your own identity, then ask for help from the surrounding crowd, specifying the characteristics of the person you need help from to avoid bystander effect, for example, "The man in the black jacket, please call 120 for me," or "The lady in the white skirt, please help me retrieve the nearby AED."

(3) Confirm Breathing and Pulse

After seeking help, you should immediately check the patient's breathing and pulse. If the patient still has heartbeats and breathing, CPR can actually increase the risk of ventricular fibrillation. The observation and judgment of breathing and pulse should be done simultaneously, and you can count aloud from 1,001, 1,002... to time it. The judgment of breathing and pulse should be completed within 10 seconds. If there is no pulse and spontaneous breathing, proceed to the next step.

1) Carotid Artery Pulse Observation

The carotid artery is located in the groove between the trachea and the sternocleidomastoid muscle. Specifically, place

指的指腹放置于气管正中（男性可触及喉结），并向一旁滑移 2 ～ 3 cm 即可观察患者脉搏跳动情况。

2. 自主呼吸判断

呼吸的判断可通过两种方式进行。一是通过将面部贴近患者的口鼻部，感受患者的呼吸气流。二是观察患者的胸的起伏情况。

（四）胸外按压

确认为"三无"状态，则进行胸外按压。

实施胸外按压过程中，应始终观察患者的面部，从而判断胸外按压对患者的效果。

1. 按压位置

按压位置位于两乳头的连接的中间点，若遇到老年女性则应通过"划肋弓法"，在剑突上方两横指位置按压。

2. 按压手势

按压时，十指相扣，掌心翘起（不能让手指全部接触患者的胸部，这样会导致身体进一步前移，增加肋骨骨折的风险性），上身前倾，腕、肘、肩伸直成一条直线，以髋关节为支点，利用身体的重量垂直向下用力。

3. 按压频率与深度

按压深度为 5 ～ 6 cm，按压频率为 100 ～ 120 次 /min。按压深度不足时，血液将无法供应至大脑。因此相较于血液供应不足导致的大脑缺血，肋骨等问题则不足为虑。

the fingertips of your index and middle fingers on the midline of the trachea (for males, you can feel the larynx), and slide them outward 2–3 centimeters to observe the patient's pulse.

2) Assessment of Spontaneous Breathing

Breathing can be assessed through two methods. One is to bring your face close to the patient's mouth and nose to feel the patient's breath. The other is to observe the rise and fall of the patient's chest.

(4) Chest Compressions

When the patient is confirmed "three nos", chest compression should be implemented immediately.

During chest compressions, you should always observe the patient's face to assess the effectiveness of the compressions.

1) Compression Position

The pressing position is located at the midpoint of the connection between the two nipples. If encountering elderly women, you should use the "rib arch technique" and place the two horizontal fingers above the xiphoid process to compress.

2) Compression Technique

When compressing, the fingers should be interlocked, the palms should be raised (do not let the fingers fully contact the patient's chest, as this can cause the body to shift further forward and increase the risk of rib fractures), the upper body should be leaning forward, and the wrists, elbows, and shoulders should be straight, forming a straight line, using the hip joint as the pivot, applying vertical force downward with the weight of the body.

3) Compression Frequency and Depth

The compression depth should be 5–6 centimeters, and the compression frequency should be 100–120 compressions per minute. Insufficient depth can prevent blood supply to the brain. Thus, compared to brain ischemia caused by inadequate blood supply, issues such as rib fractures are of secondary concern.

（五）开放气道

检查患者口腔内有无异物，若存在痰液等分泌物，需用食指与中指呈 C 形将异物取出和清除。开放气道可使用仰头抬颌法。仰头仰颌法是临床上心肺复苏中最常见的一个开放气道的方法，操作如下：一手将小鱼际部位置于患者前额并下压，使患者处于后仰状态，另一手的食指与中指置于下颌骨近下颏或下颌角处，抬起下颌，但要注意不要压迫病人气管。

（六）人工呼吸

放置呼吸膜，左手捏住患者鼻翼两侧（手呈 "OK" 状），正常吸气，口唇包住患者口唇，缓缓吹起，并观察胸廓起伏变化，松开左手手指 2 s 后，再次送气。按压与通气按照 30 ∶ 2 的比率进行。

（七）效果评价

心肺复苏的首要目的就是使患者恢复自主呼吸和心跳。如何判断心肺复苏实施的效果，是否需要继续进行呼吸支持，可参考如下指标。

1. 脉搏和呼吸

心肺复苏过程颈动脉搏动，且停止按压后脉搏仍然跳动，说明患者自主心跳已恢复。

2. 神志与自主呼吸

如自主呼吸微弱，仍需呼吸支持；如患者恢复正常呼吸或大

(5) Open the Airway

Check the patient's mouth for any objects or secretions such as phlegm. If there are any, use your index and middle fingers in a C-shape to remove and clear the obstructions. The airway can be opened using the head tilt-jaw lift technique. This is the most common method of opening the airway during cardiopulmonary resuscitation in clinical practice. The operation is as follows: One hand places the little finger area on the patient's forehead and presses down to put the patient in a backward tilted position; with the other hand, the index and middle fingers are placed near the chin or angle of the mandible, lifting the jaw but being careful not to press on the patient's trachea.

(6) Artificial Respiration

Place the breathing barrier, hold the patient's nostrils with the left hand (in an "OK" gesture), inhale normally, purse your lips around the patient's mouth, and blow gently, observing the changes in the patient's chest rise and fall. Release the left hand fingers for 2 seconds, and then provide another breath, with a compression-to-ventilation ratio of 30 ∶ 2.

(7) Effect Evaluation

The primary purpose of cardiopulmonary resuscitation is to restore the patient's autonomous breathing and heartbeat. So how to determine the effectiveness of cardiopulmonary resuscitation implementation and whether further respiratory support is needed can refer to the following indicators.

1) Pulse and Breathing

During the process of cardiopulmonary resuscitation, there involves carotid artery pulsation, and even after stopping compression, the pulse still beats. This indicates that the patient's spontaneous heartbeat has been restored.

2) Mindfulness and Autonomous Breathing

If spontaneous breathing is weak, respiratory support is still needed. If the patient returns to normal breathing, struggles

呼吸挣扎或有意识反应，说明复苏预后良好。

3. 头面口唇颜色

面色复苏有效时，面色和口唇会由发绀转为红润；如面色仍为灰白，说明复苏无效。

4. 瞳孔变化

瞳孔复苏有效时，可见瞳孔由大变小。如瞳孔由小变大、固定、角膜浑浊，说明复苏无效。如患者随后出现腱反射、流泪、吞咽动作、咳嗽反射、角膜反射、痛觉反应，说明复苏有效。

（八）安抚患者

若患者恢复自主循环，应即时安慰患者，"您刚才晕倒了，我对您实施了抢救，现在您没事了，您的财物都在您的身边，救护车和您的家人就在赶来的路上。现在我将您的头偏向一侧，以保证呼吸。"

三、心肺复苏技术注意事项

（一）胸外按压分数

胸外按压分数指的是按压时间占整个抢救时间（即确认心脏骤停到自主循环恢复的时间）的比值。目前，《中国心肺复苏指南》建议比值要大于 80%。此数值越高，说明在整个抢救过程中实行胸外按压的时间越长。胸外按压的目的是使机体产生血流，

with breathing, or has conscious reactions, it indicates a good recovery prognosis.

3) Color of Head, Face, Lips

When the complexion recovery is effective, the complexion and lips will change from cyanosis to redness; If the complexion is still grayish white, it indicates that the recovery is ineffective.

4) Pupillary Changes

When pupil resuscitation is effective, it can be seen that the pupil changes from large to small. If the pupil changes from small to large, becomes fixed, and the cornea becomes cloudy, it indicates that resuscitation is ineffective. If the patient subsequently experiences tendon reflex, tearing, swallowing movement, cough reflex, corneal reflex, and pain response, it indicates that the resuscitation is effective.

(8) Comfort the Patient

If the patient regains spontaneous circulation, comfort them immediately, "You fainted earlier; I have performed the rescue on you. Now you are fine. Your belongings are with you, and the ambulance and your family are on their way. Now, I will tilt your head to one side to ensure your breathing."

3. Precautions for Cardiopulmonary Resuscitation Techniques

(1) Compression-to-Flow Fraction (CCF)

The chest compression score refers to the ratio of compression time to the entire rescue time (the time from confirmed cardiac arrest to recovery of spontaneous circulation). Currently, Chinese Guidelines for Cardiopulmonary Resuscitation recommend a ratio greater than 80%. The higher this value, the longer the duration of chest compressions during the entire rescue process. The purpose of chest compressions is to generate blood flow in the body, thereby ensuring oxygen

从而保证组织的氧供。若按压中断的时间越长，那么组织得到的氧气就会减少，最终会降低自主循环的恢复概率以及生存率。

（二）按压速率

按压速率应保持 100 ～ 120 次 /min。当按压速率低于 100 次 /min 时，会明显降低自主循环恢复的概率。当高于 120 次 /min 时，表示按压太快，此时施救者并不能保证有效的按压深度。

（三）按压深度

按压深度应保持 5 ～ 6 cm。通俗而言，按压就是把心脏内的血液"挤"出去，给重要器官——心脏和大脑提供氧气。但是，如果按压的深度不够，就会导致"挤"出去的血太少，不能起到供氧的作用，进一步影响自主循环的恢复和最终的生存率。

（四）胸壁回弹情况

在胸壁完全恢复原位后再进行下一次按压。这主要是为了在按压时将血液从心脏挤出，随后通过胸廓的回弹，使静脉血回流进心脏。胸廓回弹得越好，回心血量越多，下 次有效按压时排出的血液也就越多。然而，许多施救者在紧张状态下只记得要快速按压，达到每分钟 100 次以上，因此会不自觉地将手掌一直压在胸骨上，未等胸廓充分回弹就开始下一次按压。这种做法会对冠状动脉灌注、大脑灌注、心脏指数

supply to tissues. If the interruption time of pressing is longer, the oxygen obtained by the tissue will decrease, ultimately reducing the chances of recovery and survival of autonomous circulation.

(2) Compression Rate

The compression rate should be maintained at 100−120 times per minute. A rate lower than 100 times per minute will significantly reduce the chances of spontaneous circulation recovery. Conversely, a rate higher than 120 times per minute indicates that compressions are too fast, and the rescuer may not be able to ensure effective compression depth.

(3) Compression Depth

Compression depth should be maintained at 5−6 centimeters. In simple terms, compression is about "squeezing" the blood out of the heart, providing oxygen to vital organs like the heart and brain. However, if the compression depth is insufficient, it will result in too little blood being "squeezed" out, failing to provide oxygenation and further affecting the recovery of spontaneous circulation and final survival rates.

(4) Chest Wall Recoil

Perform the next compression after the chest wall is fully restored to its original position. This is mainly to squeeze blood out of the heart during compression, and then allow venous blood to flow back into the heart through the chest rebound. The better the chest rebounds, the more heart blood is returned, and the more blood is discharged during the next effective compression. However, many rescuers only remember to press quickly in a tense state, reaching over 100 times per minute, so they unconsciously keep their palms pressed against the sternum and start the next press before their chest fully rebounds. This approach will have adverse effects on coronary artery perfusion, cerebral perfusion, cardiac index, and left ventricular myocardial blood flow.

以及左心室心肌血流等产生不利影响。

（五）通气要求

通气的目的是给予更多的氧气，以满足心脏和大脑对氧气的需求。目前推荐的是每分钟进行不超过10次的通气，或者按照推荐的胸外按压与通气比例进行（30：2），即30次胸外按压之后进行2次通气。当通气频率过高时，胸外按压与通气会产生冲突，不仅降低了通气效率，也降低了心肺复苏的效果。因此，目前并不建议太快的通气频率。

（六）其他注意事项

按压时，要让患者躺在较硬的地面或者背板上；按压时手臂要垂直于患者，手肘始终伸直。此外，考虑到胸外按压是一项高强度的体力活动，有条件的话，每2 min可以轮换一个人进行，从而保证按压始终处于高质量的状态。

思考二

1. 燃烧的基本条件和充分条件包括哪些？

2. 发生火灾时，我们应如何自救？

3. 灭火的措施包括哪些？

4. 发生洪涝自然灾害时，我们应注意什么？

5. 溺水时，我们应如何做才能自救并利于他人帮助自己？

(5) Ventilation Requirements

The purpose of ventilation is to provide more oxygen to meet the oxygen needs of the heart and brain. At present, it is recommended to ventilate no more than 10 times per minute, or follow the ratio of chest compressions to ventilation (30：2), that is, to ventilate twice after 30 chest compressions. When the ventilation frequency is too high, there is a conflict between chest compressions and ventilation, which not only reduces ventilation efficiency but also reduces the effectiveness of cardiopulmonary resuscitation. Therefore, it is currently not recommended to ventilate too quickly.

(6) Other Precautions

When pressing, the patient should be placed on a hard ground or backboard for pressing; when pressing, the arm should be perpendicular to the patient, and the elbow should always be straight. In addition, considering that chest compressions are a high-intensity physical activity, if conditions permit, one person can be rotated every 2 minutes to ensure that the compressions are always in a high-quality state.

Reflection 2

1. What are the basic and sufficient conditions for combustion?

2. What should we do to save ourselves in case of a fire?

3. What measures can be taken to extinguish a fire?

4. What should we pay attention to when natural disasters such as floods occur?

5. What should we do to save ourselves from drowning and facilitate others' help?

6. 发生运动软组织损伤后，处理时应遵循什么原则？

7. 为了防止运动损伤，在运动前我们应做的内容有哪些？

8. 心肺复苏的操作流程包括哪些步骤？

6. What principles should we follow when dealing with sports soft tissue injuries?

7. What should we do before exercising to prevent sports injuries?

8. What are the steps involved in cardiopulmonary resuscitation (CPR)?

第二章微课视频

第三章
常见刑事犯罪预防与控制

Chapter 3
Prevention and Control of Common Criminal Activities

第一节
犯罪相关理论

Section 1
Theories Related to Crime

犯罪学的理论发展脉络经历包括生物学、心理学及社会学等内容，如龙勃罗梭提出的犯罪人类学和犯罪生物学说，其立足于遗传学，认为人类遗传变异导致了原始善良的人性向恶性转变。社会学认为人类行为发展是一个社会化过程，犯罪行为乃是个体成长受到社会环境中的不良因素影响形成的。各层面的理论研究已有很多，而本教材并非完全是针对犯罪现象的研究，因此仅对比较主流的理论予以介绍，围绕"精神""学习""控制""紧张"，与心理与行为相关联的四个关键词展开。

The theoretical development of criminology has gone through various aspects such as biology, psychology, and sociology, such as the proposed theories of criminal anthropology and criminal biology by Lombroso, which is based on genetics, believing that genetic variations in humans lead to a transformation from primitive kindness to malignancy. Sociology believes that the development of human behavior is a socialization process, and criminal behavior is the result of influence of adverse factors in the social environment on individual growth. There have been many theoretical studies at various levels, but this course is not entirely focused on the study of criminal phenomena. Therefore, it only introduces mainstream theories, focusing on four key words related to psychology and behavior, including "mind", "learning", "control", and "tension".

一、精神分析理论

1. Psychoanalytic Theory

精神分析理论是由奥地利的心理学家弗洛伊德创立的。其理论可分为古典精神分析与新精神分析两个阶段。古典精神分析阶段提出个体无意识、性本能和防御机制等命题。新精神分析阶

The psychoanalytic theory was founded by Austrian psychologist Freud. Its theory can be divided into two stages: classical psychoanalysis and neo psychoanalysis. The classical psychoanalytic stage proposed propositions such as individual unconsciousness, sexual instincts, and defense mechanisms, while the neo psychoanalytic stage proposed the theory of

段提出了本能学说（生与死的本能）、人格结构和人格发展理论。

弗洛伊德本人并未研究犯罪，主要是研究精神疾病。后期学者根据其理论原理推断出对犯罪现象的解释，并发现了精神疾病与违法犯罪的一致性。在犯罪心理学领域中，精神分析以"无意识"和"性本能"为基本的研究对象，用精神疾病（消极能量的对内积累与扩展）、人格内部冲突、自我与环境文化的压力、罪恶感及心理防御等观点解释与探讨犯罪行为。总体而言，犯罪行为的产生是由于内在需要的压抑和扭曲致使人之本性改变而导致的。此处主要阐释精神分析理论的无意识、人格结构和性本能三个方面的内容。

（一）犯罪行为无意识与人格冲突

弗洛伊德提出的无意识、人格结构以及性本能三个概念是紧密相连的。弗洛伊德将人的思想分为不可感知的潜意识（无意识）和可感知的显意识，并将其比喻为海中冰山。其中的显意识为露出海平面能被感知到的部分，潜意识（无意识）是深藏水面以下的根基部分，虽无法被直接感知，但却影响和控制着整座冰山。

与无意识理论相对应，弗洛伊德将人格结构分为本我、自我和超我。显意识对应的是自我，自我遵循现实原则，是人类意识

instincts (the instincts of life and death), personality structure, and personality development theory.

Freud himself did not study crime, but mainly focused on mental illness. Later scholars inferred an explanation for criminal phenomena based on its theoretical principles and discovered the consistency between mental illness and illegal crime. In the field of criminal psychology, psychoanalysis takes "unconsciousness" and "sexual instinct" as the basic research objects, and interprets and explores criminal behavior from the perspectives of mental illness (internal accumulation and expansion of negative energy), internal conflicts of personality, pressure of self and environmental culture, guilt, and psychological defense. Overall, the emergence of criminal behavior is due to the suppression and distortion of internal needs, resulting in a change in human nature. This part mainly elaborates on the unconsciousness, personality structure, and sexual instinct aspects of psychoanalytic theory.

(1) Unconscious Criminal Behavior and Personality Conflict

The concepts of unconsciousness, personality structure, and sexual instinct proposed by Freud are closely related. Freud divided human mind into the imperceptible subconscious (unconscious) and the perceivable conscious, and likened it to an iceberg in the sea. The conscious is the part that is exposed above sea level that can be perceived, while the subconscious (unconscious) is the fundamental part hidden below the water surface. Although it cannot be directly perceived, it affects and controls the entire iceberg.

In contrast to the theory of unconsciousness, Freud divided personality structures into the id, ego, and superego. Consciousness corresponds to the ego, which follows the principles of reality and serves as the connection point

与现实世界的联结点。潜意识（无意识）与本我相对应。本我遵循快乐原则，表征着人类最基本的生理本能和心理本能，即弗洛伊德提出的性本能或生与死的本能。超我遵循理想原则，是社会道德规则内化于人类潜意识形成的内在心理约束机制，相当于良知。自我的主要作用是控制本我和超我的矛盾，即调节潜意识中的各类欲求和现实环境约束的关系。超我是个体社会经历在潜意识的反映，是自我控制能力的重要来源，主要对本我的原始欲望进行压制。

犯罪心理学家认为犯罪越轨行为的根源也在于人类潜意识中，由于童年时的创伤或需求剥夺，被压抑的内在需要和现实发生冲突，自我对于本我和超我的调和失败。当主体在现实中遭遇过多的挫折，例如排挤和欺压，自我囿于现实的社会规则，会压制和控制本我，但同时会促使本我的能量不断聚集。随着负面情绪的叠加，积累到特定程度时，自我就无法压制本我，进而导致过激行为的发生。例如日常生活中长期会发现认知中的老实的人，忽然爆发出强烈的情绪，并实施了过于暴力的行为，就是自我长期的压迫导致的本我极端展现。

between human consciousness and the real world. The subconscious(unconscious) corresponds to the id. The id follows the principle of happiness and represents the most basic physiological and psychological instincts of human beings, namely the sexual or life and death instincts proposed by Freud. The superego follows the principle of ideals, which is an internal psychological constraint mechanism internalized by social moral rules in the human subconscious, equivalent to conscience. The main function of the ego is to control the contradiction between the id and superego, that is, to regulate the relationships between various desires in the subconscious and the constraints of the real environment. The superego is a subconscious reflection of an individual's social experience and an important source of self-control, primarily suppressing the primitive desires of the id.

Criminal psychologists believe that the root of deviant behavior in crime also lies in the human subconscious. Due to childhood trauma or deprivation of needs, suppressed inner needs conflict with reality, and the ego fails to reconcile with the id and superego. When the individual encounters too many setbacks in reality, such as exclusion and oppression, and since the ego is confined to the social rules of reality, it will suppress and control the id, but it will encourage the energy of the id to continuously accumulate. With the accumulation of negative emotions, when the negative energy accumulates to a specific extent, the ego cannot suppress the id, leading to the occurrence of extreme behavior. For example, in daily life, it is often found that what we know as honest individuals suddenly experience strong emotions and engage in overly violent behavior, which is due to long-term ego oppression leading to the extreme manifestation of their id.

（二）犯罪权欲说

由于弗洛伊德理论对于人性本恶的观点过于绝对。为此，其学生阿德勒反对绝对意义的本能论与泛性论，提出个体心理学视角的犯罪权欲说。阿德勒认为犯罪既不是天生遗传的，也不是后天环境迫使的，而是一种社会心理：因为自卑，所以通过奋力追求补偿缺憾。该理论受到尼采的"权利意志"和"超人哲学"的影响，认为人人都有"向上意志"。若主体为实现特定目标，但与客体在互动过程中产生阻碍，就会产生自卑感。此阻碍既包括自然条件，也包括社会条件。

自卑与自尊相对应。阿德勒认为个体都有获得自尊的倾向，当个体产生自卑感后，就会通过特定行为重新获得自尊感或弥补其自卑感。其在著作《自卑与超越》中提出："在犯罪的各种活动与态度中，都显现出主体在挣扎着要成为优秀的人，要解决问题，要解决困难。"而违法犯罪就是在特定时间而进行的过度补偿的结果。阿德勒指出自卑感的产生有三种因素：a. 人的身体缺陷；b. 较差的经济条件；c. 极端的家庭教育方式（对孩子过于严厉或过于放纵或娇惯）[1]。正常人在碰到此类因素时，会基于符合社会规则进

(2) The Theory of Criminal Rights

Due to Freudian theory's overly absolute view on the inherent evil of human nature, his student Adler opposed the instinct theory and universality theory of absolute meaning, but proposed the theory of criminal desire from the perspective of individual psychology. Adler believed that crime is neither innate nor forced by environmental factors, but rather a social psychology that, due to inferiority, seeks to compensate for deficiencies through hard work. This theory was influenced by Nietzsche's "will to power" and "superhuman philosophy", believing that everyone has an "upward will". When the subject encounters obstacles in the process of interacting with the object in order to achieve specific goals, it will generate a sense of inferiority. This obstacle includes both natural and social conditions.

Inferiority corresponds to self-esteem. Adler believed that individuals have a tendency to gain self-esteem, and when they develop a sense of inferiority, they will regain self-esteem or compensate for inferiority through specific behaviors. The work *What life Should Mean to You* proposes that "in various criminal activities and attitudes, it is evident that the subject is struggling to become excellent, solve problems, and overcome difficulties." And illegal activities are the result of excessive compensation carried out at a specific time. Adler pointed out that there are three factors that lead to feelings of inferiority: a. physical defects in individuals; b. poor economic conditions; c. extreme family education methods (too strict or too indulgent or spoiled with children). Normal people, when encountering such factors, will provide appropriate compensation based on compliance with social rules to overcome their sense of inferiority. Criminals, due to their lack of understanding of

---

[1]　杨波，犯罪心理学 [M]. 北京：高等教育出版社，2015：57-58.

行适当补偿，以克服自卑感。犯罪者由于不了解社会，以及认知资源有限，补偿的方式受到限制，导致行为方式与社会的准则产生偏差。例如家庭的过于溺爱会使得个体在社会交往过程中发现，现实与理想存在很大偏差，进而在人际交往和竞争中受到阻碍，产生自卑感。自卑感就会导致反应性的嫉妒、敌意，最终产生冲突行为和攻击行为，并在规则的作用下产生罪恶感、自我惩罚和神经症性的恐惧。自我破坏的行为又会不断强化自卑、嫉妒与怨恨。为了平衡心理，又产生攻击行为，导致恶性循环。

society and limited cognitive resources, are limited in their compensation methods, leading to deviations in their behavior from social norms. For example, excessive indulgence in the family can lead individuals to discover a significant deviation between reality and ideals in social interactions, which can hinder interpersonal communication and competition, resulting in a sense of inferiority. Inferiority can lead to reactive jealousy and hostility, ultimately resulting in conflicting and aggressive behaviors, as well as feelings of guilt, self punishment, and neurotic fear under the influence of rules. Self destructive behavior will constantly reinforce inferiority, jealousy, and resentment. In order to balance psychology, it leads to aggressive behavior, resulting in a vicious cycle.

二、学习理论

学习理论是阐明人和动物学习的性质、过程和影响学习因素的各种学说。在犯罪学领域中，学习理论主要是分析和阐释犯罪行为的习得原因、过程和机制。

（一）学习理论发展概述

学习理论经历了经典行为主义、新行为主义和新新行为主义三个阶段。核心围绕"有条件下的学习机制"。经典行为主义是由约翰·华生基于巴甫洛夫的"条件反射理论"创立的。华生认为人和动物的所有行为都受外部环境的影响，特定的刺激就会引发特定的行为反应，刺激与反应

2. Learning Theory

Learning theory is an explanation of the nature, process, and factors influencing the acquisition of knowledge and behaviors in both humans and animals. In criminology, learning theory primarily analyzes and interprets the reasons, processes, and mechanisms behind the acquisition of criminal behavior.

(1) Overview of Learning Theories

Learning theory has gone through three stages: classical behaviorism, neo- behaviorism, and new neo-behaviorism. The core revolves around the "learning mechanism under certain conditions". Classical behaviorism was founded by John Watson based on Pavlov's theory of conditioned reflex. Watson believes that all behavior of humans and animals is influenced by the external environment, and specific stimuli can trigger specific behavioral responses, with a causal relationship between

呈因果关系。该理论缺陷是仅阐释了有机体如何被动地习得环境中具有关联性的刺激，缺失对主体行为主动地干预和影响其环境的行为习得机制的解释。

为此，以斯金纳为代表的新行为主义者在经典条件反射实验的基础上进行了修正与补充，在斯金纳箱实验的观察基础上提出了"操作性条件反射理论"。该理论认为有机体并不是被动地等待刺激的发生，而是通过行为主动引发环境刺激，并根据环境刺激的性质（奖励与惩罚），主动改变自己的行为，以期获得其最倾向获得的效果。同时，强化与惩罚对于行为的维持与改变具有重要作用。

综上，经典行为主义和新行为主义学派认为，所有习得行为的结果都是伴随一个外部刺激而发生的，是主体对这一次刺激做出的反射性回应。例如行为主义学派的挫折 – 攻击理论。该理论指出，挫折指任何阻碍享受快乐的外部条件。当遇到挫折时，攻击行为是宣泄的有效方式。每一个攻击行为背后都可寻觅到过往的某个挫折。

针对挫折 – 攻击理论，有学者提出反对的声音，认为不同主体面对相同的刺激，做出的行为反射并不是单一的，而是呈现多样性。即使无刺激条件，也会伴有新行为的发生。换言之，将经典与新行为主义应用于对人类意

stimuli and responses. The theoretical flaw is that it only explains how the passive acquisition of correlated stimuli in the environment by organisms, lacking the explanation of the behavioral acquisition mechanism that actively intervenes and influences the environment by the subject's behavior.

Therefore, the neo-behaviorists represented by Skinner has made revisions and supplements on the basis of the classical conditioned reflex experiment, and proposed the "operant conditioned reflex theory" based on the observation of the Skinner Shuttle Box Test. The theory suggests that organisms are not passively waiting for stimuli to occur, but are actively triggering environmental stimuli through behavior, and changing their behavior according to the nature of environmental stimuli (rewards and punishments) in order to achieve the desired effect. Meanwhile, reinforcement and punishment play an important role in maintaining and changing behavior.

In summary, both classical behaviorism and neo-behaviorism schools believe that the outcome of all learned behaviors is a reflexive response of the subject to an external stimulus. For example, the frustration-attack theory of the behaviorist school. This theory suggests that setbacks refer to any external conditions that hinder the enjoyment of happiness, and when faced with setbacks, aggressive behavior is an effective way to vent. Behind every attack, one can trace a past setback.

Regarding the frustration-attack theory, some scholars have raised objections, believing that different subjects facing the same stimulus do not exhibit singular behavioral reflexes, but rather exhibit diversity. Even under non-stimulus conditions, new behaviors may occur. In other words, when applying classical and neo-behaviorism to the global interpretation of human consciousness and behavioral systems,

识与行为系统的全局性解读时就会对其复杂性一筹莫展。

因此，第二次世界大战以后，随着认知心理学的发展，以托尔曼和班杜拉为代表的新的新行为主义吸收融合了认知主义和行为主义的理论，以解释人类复杂的社会化行为发展过程。理论认为个体受到的刺激与行为的单向维度中间，还存在中介变量——"认知"。

对学习理论的阐述将按照行为习得的最基本原理的普遍性表述、行为习得机制的系统性表述、行为习得具体内容的具体性表述的顺序，分别从宏观层、中观层、微观层予以阐明。

（二）社会学习理论

班杜拉的社会学习理论以三元交互理论为核心，以观察学习机制为补充，解释个体行为模式形成的普遍性原理，处于学习理论中的底层或宏观层。理论指出行为人的行为习得过程中，认知起枢纽的作用。行为的形成并非简单归因于外部的刺激，而是个体基于自身的需要对外界的解读。基于此，班杜拉提出了三元交互决定论、观察学习机制和自我效能决定论三个理论。在犯罪学领域中，三元交互决定论和观察学习机制能广泛地解释犯罪行为的习得机制。

one will be at a loss for their complexity.

Therefore, after World War II, with the development of cognitive psychology, neo-behaviorism represented by Tolman and Bandura absorbed and integrated theories of cognitivism and behaviorism to explain the complex process of human socialization behavior development. The theory suggests that there is a mediating variable—"cognition"—between the unidirectional dimensions of stimuli and behavior received by an individual.

The exposition of learning theory will be based on the universal expression of the most basic principles of behavioral acquisition, the systematic expression of behavioral acquisition mechanisms, and the specific expression of specific content of behavioral acquisition, respectively, from the macro level, meso level, and micro level.

(2) Social Learning Theory

Bandura's social learning theory is centered around the Triadic Reciprocal Determinism, supplemented by observational learning mechanisms, explaining the universal principles of individual behavior patterns, and is at the bottom of the learning theory. This theory suggests that cognition plays a pivotal role in the process of behavior acquisition, and the formation of behavior is not simply attributed to external stimuli, but rather an individual's interpretation of the outside world based on their own needs. Based on this, Bandura proposed three theories: observational learning mechanism, and self-efficacy determinism. In the field of criminology, the Triadic Reciprocal Determinism and observational learning mechanisms can widely explain the acquisition mechanisms of criminal behavior.

1. 三元交互理论

三元交互理论是对斯金纳刺激 – 反应模式的完善。班杜拉指出对行为者而言，理解行为结果如何改变行为的心理机制就必须分析认知等主体因素与行为和环境的交互影响。行为人会基于其固有认知结构解读环境刺激，并做出行为性的反应。环境、行为以及认知三者之间，每两者都具有双向的交互决定关系，按照交叉排列，交互影响机制有六种。

（1）环境影响认知和行为。

环境影响行为是对行为主义理论的直接继承；环境影响认知意指在尔虞我诈的环境会促使主体产生自我保护意识。

（2）认知影响行为与环境。

个体的不同认知结构将会决定那些刺激会被直接感知到，并以此为基础指导行为决策。例如经常上当受骗的人会怀疑自己的判断力，进而出现依赖他人和犹豫不决；一个经常与他人发生矛盾的人，往往会使得周围人对其充满敌意。

（3）行为影响认知与环境。

人的行为和行为后果会显著改变其思维模式，长期从事刑侦工作的人会疑心较重；认知结构的差异并不会从物理层面改变环境，但却会影响主体对环境刺激的解读。例如自信的人对于外界的信息解读倾向于鼓励，自卑的

1) Triadic Reciprocal Determinism

The Triadic Reciprocal Determinism is a refinement of Skinner's stimulus response model. Bandura pointed out that for actors, understanding how behavioral outcomes change the psychological mechanisms of behavior requires analyzing the interactive effects of cognitive and other subjective factors on behavior and environment. Behavioral individuals interpret environmental stimuli based on their inherent cognitive structure and make behavioral responses. There is a bidirectional interactive relationship between the environment, behavior, and cognition, and according to the cross arrangement, there are six types of interactive influence mechanisms.

① Environments impact cognition and behavior.

Environments impacting behavior is a direct inheritance of behaviorism theory; environmental impacting cognition refers to the tendency of individuals to develop self-protection awareness in a deceitful environment.

② Cognitive influence on behavior and environment.

The different cognitive structures of individuals will determine which stimuli will be directly perceived and guide behavioral decision-making based on this. For example, people who are often deceived may doubt their own judgment, leading to dependence on others and indecisiveness; a person who frequently conflicts with others often leads to hostility from those around them.

③ Behavior influences cognition and environment.

Human behavior and its consequences can significantly change their thinking patterns, and those who engage in criminal investigation work for a long time may be more suspicious; the differences in cognitive structures do not physically alter the environment, but they can affect the subject's interpretation of environmental stimuli. For example, confident people tend to interpret information as

个体则会倾向于批判。

2. 观察学习机制

观察学习机制将条件作用机制与信息加工机制结合。班杜拉通过对"波波玩偶攻击行为模仿实验"的观察发现，目睹成人对玩偶实施攻击行为的儿童，攻击性倾向会变高，即使在没有直接强化效应的条件下，儿童仍会倾向于模仿大人的行为。

为此，班杜拉认为在社会学习语境下，大部分的行为都是通过学习获得的，这一过程不需要主体有任何实际的行为操作，即可完成行为的习得。多数儿童更倾向于模仿与其关系亲密的成人及受欢迎的公众人物。观察学习分为四个阶段。

（1）注意过程。

观察者通过注意，选择性接受示范刺激，此过程是模仿的选择性。模仿者并不是对所有对象模仿，而是对其注意的对象启动观察学习。

（2）保持过程。

将示范行为编码，转化为符号化认知结构。示范者会将模仿对象的具体信息转化为抽象的认知符号，以便储存于记忆中。

（3）运动再现过程。

将符号化认知创造性地输出为具体行为。在适当的环境下，将存留的记忆与环境相联系的认知结构提取出来，能动地转化为具体的行为过程。

encouragement, while inferior people tend to take it as critics.

2) Observational Learning Mechanism

The observational learning mechanism combines conditional learning mechanisms with information processing mechanisms. Bandura's observation of the "Bobo Doll Experiment" revealed that children who witnessed adults engaging in aggressive behavior towards the dolls showed increased tendencies towards aggression, even without direct reinforcement.

Therefore, Bandura believes that in the context of social learning, most behaviors are acquired through learning, a process that does not require the subject to engage in any actual physical actions yet results in the acquisition of behavior. Most children are more likely to imitate adults they are close to and popular public figures. Observational learning occurs in four stages.

① Attentional process.

The observer selectively accepts model stimuli through attention. This process is selective imitation; the imitator does not mimic all objects but rather imitates the objects they pay attention to.

② Retention process.

The modeled behavior is encoded and transformed into symbolic cognitive structures. The modeler will convert specific information about the imitation object into abstract cognitive symbols for storage in memory.

③ Motor reproduction process.

Creatively output symbolic cognition into concrete behavior. In an appropriate environment, extract the cognitive structures of memories associated with the environment and actively transform into specific behavioral processes.

（4）行为的固化。

如果模仿了一个不良行为，加以制止就不会长久。动机过程是观察学习和条件强化作用机制的结合。个体仅通过观察、模仿习得的行为往往不具有可持续性，例如在公共场合大声喧哗。若家长及时批评、加以制止，则此不良行为不会持久；相反，若不良行为得到环境的积极反馈，如言语褒奖、物质奖励等，则行为固化与重复的可能性将大大增加。

（三）差异接触理论

差异接触理论是在社会学习理论提供的基本原理基础上，通过 9 个命题系统表述社会学习理论基本原理作用的过程与机制。

差异接触理论由美国犯罪学家萨瑟兰提出。背景是当时欧洲及美国的犯罪学家将犯罪现象归因于生物学和心理病态等方面，将犯罪帖上遗传学的标签，与社会下层紧密联系。但后期研究发现，实际的犯罪群体并非完全来自于官方统计的下层群体。因此，犯罪行为的遗传层面归因并不能完全解释犯罪现象。

常言道"近朱者赤，近墨者黑"，但与此相对立的是"出淤泥而不染"。即使在恶劣的环境也依然有人洁身自好；相反地，优异的环境也存在越轨者。对此，萨瑟兰认为"近朱者赤"并非指

④ Consolidation of behavior.

If an inappropriate behavior is imitated and then stopped or intercepted, it will not persist over a long period. Motivational processes are a combination of observational learning and conditioned reinforcement mechanisms. Behaviors that are learned through observation and imitation alone are often not sustainable, e.g., loud noises in public will not be sustained if parents criticize and stop the behavior. On the contrary, if the undesirable behavior receives positive feedback from the environment, such as verbal praise and material rewards, the likelihood that the behavior will be reinforced and repeated will be greatly increased.

(3) Differential Association Theory

Differential Association Theory, built upon the fundamental principles of social learning theory, articulates the processes and mechanisms underlying the role of these principles through a system of 9 propositions.

Proposed by American criminologist Sutherland, the theory emerged as a response to the tendency of European and American criminologists at the time to attribute criminal phenomena to biological and psychological pathologies, often associating crime with the lower strata of society. However, Sutherland's investigations revealed that the actual criminal groups did not exclusively originate from the officially documented lower classes. Consequently, genetic attributions to criminal behavior fell short in explaining the complexity of criminal phenomena.

Contrary to the saying "birds of a feather flock together", "rise from the mud unstained" refers to those that are noble still even in bad environments. Conversely, deviants also exist in good environments. Sutherland introduced the concept of "differential association" as opposed to mere cohabitation. Based on this concept, he formulated 9 propositions to

简单意义上的共处一室，提出了"有效接触"的概念。基于此概念，提出了9个命题去论证有效接触对人的行为模式产生实质影响的社会接触机理，并从其接触的人群中选择性学习之过程。

（1）犯罪行为和其他行为一致，都是习得的。此条否认了犯罪归因中的遗传和生理因素作用。同时表明了犯罪并非源于精神分析理论强调的个人内在因素，而是在环境的作用下产生。

（2）犯罪行为是在与他人的互动沟通中获得的。互动沟通不仅仅包括语言，也包括非话语的肢体语言和表情等。

（3）犯罪行为的习得主要发生于个人亲密群体内部。此条借鉴了模仿理论，说明其不仅是模仿的对象，也是反射机制中强化的刺激来源。

（4）犯罪行为习得的内容包括犯罪的技巧，犯罪的特定动机、目的、合理化解释及态度。犯罪动机的习得要严重于犯罪技巧的习得。犯罪行为实施的前提是犯罪动机的产生，而行为是内在思维与情绪的外显，如果缺少特定的内驱力和心理态度，犯罪行为就不会发生。

（5）对不同行为动机与态度的习得表现为将特定法律禁令定义为可接受的及不可接受的。犯罪人并非不知道那些行为是犯

demonstrate the differential mechanisms of effective associations, elucidating the intricate processes of social contacts that substantially impact human behavioral patterns through selective learning from their contact groups.

① Criminal behavior is consistent with other behaviors and is learned. This article denies the role of genetic and physiological factors in criminal attribution. At the same time, it indicates that crime is not an internal factor of individuals, but rather influenced by the environment.

② Criminal behavior is obtained through interaction and communication with others. Communication not only includes language, but also non-verbal body language and facial expressions.

③ The acquisition of criminal behavior mainly occurs within the personal intimate group. In this article, Sutherland drew inspiration from the theory of imitation, indicating that they are not only objects of imitation, but also sources of reinforcement stimuli in the reflex mechanism.

④ The content learned from criminal behavior includes techniques for committing crimes; The specific motive, purpose, rationalization explanation, and attitude of the crime. The acquisition of criminal motives is worse than the acquisition of criminal skills. The premise for the implementation of criminal behavior is the generation of criminal motives, and behavior is the manifestation of internal thinking and emotions. Without specific internal driving forces and psychological attitudes, criminal behavior will not occur.

⑤ The acquisition of different behavioral motivations and attitudes is characterized by specific legal prohibitions defined as acceptable and unacceptable. The perpetrator is not unaware of which actions are criminal and which are not

罪，而仅是因为他不认可。

（6）当对某法律禁令的不可接受压倒了对其可接受时，主体就会倾向于犯罪。每个个体都生活在各种环境影响源共存的复杂社会环境中，且一般会暴露在两个不同定义体系中，当不接受某法律禁令的定义体系的影响力强过可接受法律禁令的定义体系时，量变就会逐步促成质变，最终导致越轨行为的发生。

（7）接触的影响力差异受到四个因子的影响：频率，持续，优先，强度。四个因子变化的强弱决定哪个方向的接触影响会占据优势。其中频率和持续代表纯粹时间总量上的指标；优先指哪个对象有"近水楼台"的优势，即社会接触发生的时间先后，例如父母、从小的伙伴、老师；强度则是认知特征指标，与时间量无关，而是对影响力来源的重视程度。

（8）学习犯罪行为的过程和学习任何其他行为的过程所使用的学习机制是一样的，包括刺激、注意、认知、反射、模仿、强化，等等。

（9）尽管犯罪行为可以看作是对一些普遍性需求及价值观的极端表达，但是这些需求和价值观本身并不能解释犯罪行为，因为非犯罪行为一样是对这些普遍性需求和价值的表达。为此，犯罪行为是对社会的过度索求。例如性犯罪就是性欲过度，而很多

illegal, but simply because they do not approve.

⑥ When the unacceptable definition of a legal prohibition overwhelms the acceptable definition, there is a tendency towards crime. Every individual lives in a complex social environment where various environmental influences coexist, and is generally exposed to two different definition systems. When the impact of denial of legal prohibitions overpower that of acceptance, quantitative accumulation hit the qualitative point, the crime would occur.

⑦ The difference in the influence of contact is influenced by four factors: frequency, sustainability, priority, and strength. The strength of the four factor changes determines which direction of contact influence will dominate. Among them, frequency and sustainability represents a purely temporal indicator; priority means which object has the advantage of being closer; and intensity is a cognitive characteristic indicator, independent of the amount of time.

⑧ The process of learning criminal behavior involves the same learning mechanism as the process of learning any other behavior, including: stimulation; attention, cognition, reflection, imitation, reinforcement, etc.

⑨ Although criminal behavior can be seen as an expression of some universal needs and values, these needs and values themselves cannot explain criminal behavior, as non-criminal behavior is also an expression of these universal needs and values. For this reason, criminal behavior is an excessive demand. For example, sexual crimes are caused by excessive sexual desire, and the reason for financial crimes is that the explanation of money supremacy lacks persuasiveness,

合法求偶行为同样是受到性冲动驱使；谋财犯罪的原因是犯罪者认为金钱至上，而对金钱的向往是大多数合法商业牟利行为的最基本的驱动力。

虽然该理论极大扩展了犯罪学归因理论的视野，但也受到许多学者的批评。例如，核心概念缺乏操作性；关键概念的内涵与外延比较模糊，解读该理论时就会出现很大争议，也造成以这些概念为研究对象的实证结果不一致。

（四）中和技巧理论

中和技巧理论是差异接触理论的下位理论，是对其内容的细化和概念性填充。差异接触理论9个命题中的4、5命题指出，犯罪行为习得中，犯罪动机、目的、合理化解释及态度的习得比技巧的习得更可怕，因为它指代对特定法律禁令可接受与不可接受。而此类动机、目的及态度的具体内容是什么，就是中和技巧理论要阐明的问题。

中和技巧理论是大卫·马兹阿和格雷瑟姆·塞克斯提出的。他们发现在青少年犯罪中存在"道德漂移"现象。"道德漂移"指行为人并不完全把自己置于道德规范的对立面，但当道德规范的堤坝出现裂缝时，则利用各种借口实施越轨行为；一旦借口失效，则又重返道德规范的红线内，在红线内外不断游走，故称"道德

because many legitimate courtship behaviors are also driven by sexual impulses, and the desire for money is the most basic driving force for most legitimate commercial profit-making behaviors.

Although the theory broadens the scope of criminological attribution, criticisms arise, such as the lack of operational clarity in core concepts and an overemphasis on the passivity of learning, overlooking individual agency and creativity.

(4) Techniques of Neutralization

The theory of Techniques of Neutralization is a subordinate theory of Differential Association theory, which is a refinement and conceptual filling of its content. The fourth and fifth propositions of the theory of differential contact point out that in the acquisition of criminal behavior, the acquisition of criminal motivation, purpose, rational interpretation, and attitude is more terrifying than the acquisition of skills, because it refers to the acceptance or non-acceptance of specific legal prohibitions. The specific content of such motivations, purposes, and attitudes is the question that the Techniques of Neutralization aims to clarify.

The theory of Techniques of Neutralization was proposed by David Matza and Gresham Sykes. They found that there is a phenomenon of "moral drift" in juvenile delinquency. The so-called moral drift refers to the behavior of individuals who do not completely place themselves in opposition to moral norms, but when cracks appear in the dam of moral norms, they use various excuses to carry out deviant behavior. Once the excuses fail, they return to the red line of moral norms and constantly wander inside and outside the red line, hence the name "moral drift". They found through extensive practical

漂移"。他们通过大量的实际观测发现，行为人越轨行为提供道德上的合理化解读在效力上可分为文饰、表达、中和三个层次。

文饰指由于偶然过失或实施错误行为之后做出的辩解。例如，小孩子打破玻璃，就怪玻璃不太结实，一碰就碎。此层次无法在逻辑上自洽，因此，对抗道德追责的效果并不明显，难以支持重复的越轨行为。

表达指行为人的犯罪意图或动机已经成型，但缺少一个实施的理由和借口，若找到合理化的解释，则马上摆脱道德束缚，并付诸行动。例如，你与同事或同学存在矛盾，早就想教训对方，此时刚好同事与你发生了争吵，你马上对其实施了暴力行为。表达对抗道德追责的效果优于文饰，但只能运用于特定场景，无法支撑持续的越轨行为。

中和的本质是使越轨行为获得道德合理性的认知结构，是一种对普遍性规则的解读，可直接将法律禁令赋予的道德追责抹除，能无视环境，支持行为人长期稳定的越轨行为。以青少年的认知水平基本无法自主创造如此合理化的技巧，一般都是从其他成年人那里学习和模仿的。通过实证观察，常用的中和技巧有以下 5 种。

observations that the moral rationalization interpretation provided by the deviant behavior of the perpetrator can be divided into three levels in terms of effectiveness: decoration, expression, and neutralization.

Decoration refers to an excuse made due to accidental negligence or erroneous behavior. For example, when a child breaks glass, they blame it for not being too strong and easy to break. This level cannot be logically consistent, therefore, the effect of opposing morality is not significant, making it difficult to support repetitive deviant behavior.

Expression refers to the fact that the perpetrator's criminal intent or motive has already taken shape, but lacks a reason or excuse for implementation. If a reasonable explanation is found, they immediately break free from moral constraints and take action. For example, if there is friction between you and colleagues or classmates, and you have long wanted to teach them a lesson, then coincidentally, you have an argument, you can immediately engage in violent behavior towards them. The effect of expressing moral condemnation is better than decoration, but it can only be applied to specific scenarios and cannot support sustained deviant behavior.

The essence of neutralization refers to the cognitive structure that enables deviant behavior to achieve moral rationality. It is an interpretation of universal rules that directly erases the moral condemnation imposed by legal prohibitions, disregards the environment, and can support the long-term and stable deviant behavior of the perpetrator. Adolescents are generally unable to independently create such rationalization skills at their cognitive level. It is generally learned and imitated from other adults. Through empirical observation, there are five commonly used neutralization techniques.

1. 否定责任

行为人认为自己的行为并非出于自己的主观，而是由于环境造成的，导致自己身不由己。类似于"官逼民反"。

2. 否定伤害

通过避重就轻的方式否定伤害。例如认为受害人很有钱，"我偷的钱于他而言九牛一毛。"

3. 否定受害人

犯罪人通过将受害人描述为具有道德缺陷的方式否定自身实施的危害行为。

4. 指责谴责者

反客为主，对谴责其不当行为的社会主体的道德权威提出质疑，从而抵消行为的可谴责性。例如，违法占道摆摊的商贩谴责城管暴力执法或厚此薄彼，为自己不服管理的行为做出辩解。

5. 诉诸更高阶忠诚

犯罪者会将其行为诉诸于更高价值的追求，将自己的行为定义为"忠孝难两全"。例如街头斗殴的青年会将自己的行为定义为朋友两肋插刀，从而为自己的越轨行为辩解。

三、控制理论

控制理论为犯罪行为归因带来了革命性视角。传统的犯罪学理论总是阐释人为什么犯罪，而

1) Negate Responsibility

The perpetrator believes that their actions are not subjective, but are caused by the environment, resulting in involuntary actions, similar to "the government pressures the people rebel".

2) Negate Harm

Negate the harm by neglecting the heavy aspects. For example, if the victim has a lot of money, the criminal would say, "The money I took would be a drop in the bucket for him."

3) Negate the Victim

Criminals deny harmful acts committed by describing victims as morally deficient.

4) Blame Who Condemned

Call black white by questioning the moral authority of social entities condemning their improper behavior, offsetting the condemnability of behavior, such as illegal street vendors condemning violent law enforcement by urban management or playing the weak, in order to defend their behavior against management.

5) Appeal to Higher-level Loyalty

Criminals will resort to higher value pursuits for their actions, defining them as a "dilemma between loyalty and filial piety". For example, young people in street fights will define themselves as friends who are willing to sacrifice themselves for friends and defend their deviant behavior.

3. Control Theory

The control theory has brought a revolutionary perspective to the attribution of criminal behavior. Traditional criminological theories always explain why people commit

控制理论则是解释"人为什么不犯罪"。理论提出的前提是基于"人性之本恶"的立场，而人不犯罪则得益于控制的结果，即社会个体经历了正常的社会化成长过程，懂得遏制内心的邪恶天性，而越轨行为的发生则是不充分控制的结果。该理论将施加于个体的控制分为三种类型：直接控制、间接控制和内在控制。

直接控制指对错误行为的惩罚和服从行为的褒奖；间接控制指与守法人群的情感认同，即社会化的个体所重视的人际关系，从而引发对不良行为的抗拒心理；内在控制指道德规范的内化，或精神分析理论中弗洛伊德口中的良知或超我。

具有行为学意义的为间接控制和内在控制。直接控制的问题在于社会不具备足够资源监督所有个体，并对其行为施以相应的奖励和惩罚。即使具备充足的社会资源，如此做也会导致个体的自由受限，侵犯个人隐私权。但直接控制却是间接控制和内在控制确立的基础，即悬在头顶上方的达摩克利斯之剑。

具体而言，针对违反社会道德规范的行为进行惩罚，可使社会成员认识到大众对该类行为的谴责态度，并收敛其言行，如此就确立了间接控制的基础。而对特定的嘉言懿行进行褒奖，就可

crimes, while control theory explains "why people do not commit crimes". The premise of the theory is based on the standpoint of the "fundamental evil of human nature", and the non-crime of humans benefits from the result of control. Social individuals have gone through a normal process of socialized growth, and know how to restrain their evil nature, while the occurrence of deviant behavior is the result of insufficient control. This theory divides the control exerted on individuals into three types: direct control, indirect control, and intrinsic control.

Direct control refers to the punishment of erroneous behavior and the commendation of obedient behavior; indirect control refers to the emotional identification with law-abiding individuals, namely the interpersonal relationships valued by socialized individuals, which leads to resistance to bad behavior. Internal control refers to the internalization of moral norms, or Freud's concept of conscience and superego in psychoanalytic theory.

Indirect control and internal control have behavioral significance. The problem with direct control is that society does not have enough resources to supervise all individuals and reward and punish corresponding behaviors. Even with sufficient social resources, doing so can lead to restricted individual freedom and infringement of individual privacy rights. But direct control is the foundation of indirect control and internal control, which is the sword of Damocles hanging above the head.

Specifically, punishing behavior that violates social moral norms can make members of society aware of the public's condemnation of such behavior and restrain their words and actions, thus establishing the foundation of indirect control. Praising the excellent words and deeds of the special movement can cultivate everyone's moral inclination,

培养大家的良好道德倾向，自发向善，如此就强化了内在控制。

因此，在确立直接控制发挥其基本功能的前提下，控制理论的研究问题就在于怎么建立和优化间接控制和内在控制，即如何将对间接控制的深入研究发展成社会控制，以及如何对将内在控制的考察发展成自我控制。

（一）社会控制理论

特拉维斯·赫希通过对前人行为控制机制研究总结与整理提出了社会控制理论。社会控制理论建立的重要概念基础是杰克逊·托比提出的"服从的利害相关性"。如果人们做坏事都不一定会受到惩罚，为何还会控制自己不做坏事？概念指出，人们担忧违法犯罪会导致社会道德规范之设定的"服从的获利"被剥夺。例如，事业成功人士身处较好的生活环境，拥有良好的人际关系和身份地位，从而拥有良好的人生体验，而违法犯罪行为引起的社会负面反应则会导致积极的体验不复存在。所以，当社会个体通过社会联结获得积极的体验后，面对越轨行为或犯罪行为的诱惑时，就具备克制自我、遏制恶性的动力。相反，对社会化失败的个体而言，行无所失，几乎没有服从的利害相关性，因此就不具备抗拒越轨行为的动力。

基于杰克逊·托比的服从的

voluntary goodness, and thus strengthen internal control.

Therefore, on the premise of establishing direct control to play its basic function, the research problem of control theory is how to establish and optimize indirect control and internal control. That is, through in-depth research on indirect control, how it develops into social control, and through examination of internal control, how it develops into self-control.

(1) Social Control Theory

Travis Hirshi proposed the Social Control Theory by summarizing and organizing previous research on behavioral control mechanisms. The important concept established by Social Control Theory is based on Jackson Toby's proposal of "stake in conformity". If people do bad things, they may not necessarily be punished, them why do they still control ourselves from doing bad things? The concept points out that people are concerned that illegal activities may lead to the deprivation of the "profit of conformity" set by social moral norms. For example, successful individuals in their careers are in a good living environment, have good interpersonal relationships and social status, and thus have good life experiences. However, the negative social reactions caused by illegal and criminal behavior will lead to the disappearance of such positive experiences. Therefore, when individuals in society gain positive experiences through social connections and face the temptation of deviant or criminal behavior, they have the motivation to restrain themselves and curb malignancy. On the contrary, for individuals who fail socialization, they lack the motivation to resist deviant behavior because they not only fail but also have almost no interest in obedience.

Based on Jackson Toby's theory of the relevance of

利害相关性理论，赫希提出了社会控制理论的四要素：依恋，投入，参与和信念。

依恋指行为人对身边成员的感情和兴趣。换言之，即通过持续的社会化过程与他人建立的亲密人际关系；投入指对传统价值投入的时间、精力和努力，即行为人通过守法行为的承诺与践行所获得的社会化回报；参与指行为人参与社会化活动中所消耗的时间和精力，可强化依恋关系的形成，促进社会化投入的增加，是前两个要素的辅助条件；信念指对传统社会化秉持的道德规范合理性之认同，对社会控制起着基础性和全局性的影响。对反社会化的个体而言，其他要素的增加反而会促成相反的结果。四个因素处于叠加关系，作用机制是由于接受了法治价值观体系，依恋/依附于传统社会结构，并通过参与守法，积累与该信仰体系兼容的社会资本，为避免社会资本的减损而强化行为控制的意愿。

（二）自我控制理论

特拉维斯·赫希后续一系列验证性研究表明，社会控制理论无法解释当个体具有多个"服从的获利"时仍然犯罪的现象。按照社会控制理论，个体应当惧怕失去积极的人生体验（生活环境、人际关系、社会地位）而抑制犯罪的行为和想法。但多数欺诈、贪

obedience, Hirsch proposed four elements of social control theory: attachment, commitment, involvement, and belief.

Attachment refers to the emotions and interests of the actor towards the members around them, in other words, the intimate interpersonal relationships established with others through a continuous socialization process. Commitment refers to the time, energy, and effort invested in traditional values, that is, the social rewards obtained by the actor through the commitment and practice of law-abiding behavior; Involvement refers to the time and energy consumed by the actor in participating in social activities. Involvement can strengthen the formation of attachment relationships and promote an increase in social investment, which is the auxiliary condition for the first two elements. Belief refers to the recognition of the rationality of moral norms upheld in traditional socialization, which has a fundamental and global impact on social control. For antisocial individuals, the increase of other elements will actually achieve the opposite result. The four factors are in a superimposed relationship, and the mechanism of action is due to the acceptance of a law-abiding belief value system, attachment/attachment to traditional social structures, and the accumulation of social capital compatible with the belief system through participation in the combination of law-abiding socialization. In order to avoid the loss of social capital and strengthen the willingness to control behavior.

(2) Self Control Theory

Hirschi's subsequent series of confirmatory studies have shown that Social Control Theory cannot explain the phenomenon of individuals committing crimes even when they have multiple "profits of conformity". According to the theory, individuals should be afraid of losing positive life experiences (living environment, interpersonal relationships, social status) and suppress their criminal behaviors and ideas. However, most individuals who commit crimes such as fraud

污等犯罪行为人往往并不缺乏社会控制。因此提出自我控制理论。因为社会控制作为外部控制，只是通过外在环境正式与非正式社会控制机制的作用，促使行为人对特定积极的社会化体验产生向往和留念，并不产生行为的执行力。因此，行为人内在心理素质中涉及冲动型、理性思维能力及移情能力的指标才是在犯罪人与守法人之间划出界线的关键因素，即当行为人面对原始欲望驱动的犯罪诱惑时，仅有守法之意愿是不够的，还必须有压制欲念的守法之能力，而这种能力就来自自我控制。

那么内在心理素质的指标有哪些？低自我控制具有哪些特质？针对此类问题，后续学者将人格特质理论中重复犯罪人的性格特质描述与自我控制理论相对照发现，低自我控制是犯罪人普遍存在的人格特质。低自我控制作为一种性格特质集合，由三个主维度和主维度相互交叠而成的三个次生维度组成。

1. 认知能力维度——易冲动

低自我控制能力的人往往行事冲动，不善于考虑后果。从心理动机的角度看，冲动只是外在表现，内在本质是个体缺乏对行为之后果进行具象化想象的能力和认知能力。例如违章开快车或横冲直撞的行为人并非不知行为

and corruption often do not lack social control. Therefore, the theory of self-control is proposed. Because social control, as an external control, only through the formal and informal social control mechanisms of the external environment, promotes the desire and retention of specific positive social experiences by the perpetrator, and does not generate the execution power of the behavior. Therefore, Hirsch believes that the indicators related to impulsivity, rational thinking ability, and empathy in the intrinsic psychological qualities of the perpetrator are the key factors that draw the boundary between the criminal and the law-abided, when faced with the temptation of crime driven by primitive desires, the willingness to abide by the law alone is not enough. It is also necessary to have the ability to suppress desires and abide by the law, and this ability comes from self-control.

So what are the indicators of internal psychological quality? What are the characteristics of low self-control? In response to such issues, subsequent scholars have compared the description of personality traits of repeat criminals in personality trait theory with self-control theory and found that low self-control is a common personality trait among criminals. As a set of personality traits, it consists of three main dimensions and three secondary dimensions that overlap with each other.

1) Cognitive Dimension—Impulsivity

People with low self-control often act impulsively and are not good at considering the consequences. From the perspective of psychological motivation, impulsiveness is only an external manifestation, and the intrinsic essence is the individual's lack of ability to visualize the consequences of behavior and the cognitive ability. For example, when driving fast or recklessly in violation of regulations, the perpetrator is

的后果，而是不能将抽象的危险行为转化为车祸后身体的痛楚和事故惨状的具体场景。

2. 耐受能力维度——简单任务偏好

低自我控制能力的行为人都喜欢做较简单而结果易得的事，而不愿处理复杂的事务。因为复杂的事物并非一蹴而就，需要经历较长的重复性动作才能取得回报。因此简单任务偏好的本质在于行为人缺乏对挫折的耐受力。

3. 功利性满足来源维度——追求感官刺激

低自我控制能力的行为人偏好感官刺激而回避智力型或认知型活动。感官刺激指通过对大脑低端神经末梢的直接刺激，包括酒精、药物、生理欲求满足或其他简单情绪调动诱发神经递质分泌带来的直接刺激。以低端神经末梢为主的直接刺激存在钝化效应或者边际效应，随着刺激的增加，愉悦感会逐步降低，在循环往复的过程中人会逐渐进入欲壑难填的状态。因此，犯罪人往往追求物质刺激无法自拔，精神空虚。

4. 风险偏好（认知能力维度和功利性满足来源维度）

主要表现为行为人需要高度刺激的冒险行为才能获得快感，为此往往不考虑风险行为之后果。

not unaware of the consequences of the behavior, but cannot transform abstract dangerous behavior into specific scenes of physical pain and tragedy after the accident.

2) Tolerance Dimension—Preference for Simple Tasks

People with low self-control tend to prefer doing simple and easy-to-achieve tasks, rather than dealing with complex tasks, because complex things are not achieved overnight and require a long and repetitive period of time to achieve rewards. Therefore, the essence of simple task preference lies in the lack of tolerance for setbacks by the behaviorist.

3) The Source Dimension of Utilitarian Satisfaction—Pursuing Sensory Stimulation

Behavioral individuals with low self-control tend to prefer sensory stimuli and avoid intellectual or cognitive activities. Sensory stimulation refers to the direct stimulation of low-end nerve endings in the brain, including alcohol, drugs, physiological desire satisfaction, or other simple emotional stimuli that induce the secretion of neurotransmitters. The direct stimulation mainly based on low-end nerve endings has a passivation effect or marginal effect. As the stimulation increases, the sense of pleasure will gradually decrease, and in a cyclic process, it will gradually enter a state of insatiable desires. Therefore, criminals often pursue material stimulation and cannot extricate themselves, resulting in spiritual cmptincss.

4) Risk Preference (Cognitive Ability Dimension and Utilitarian Satisfaction Source Dimension)

The main manifestation is that the actor needs highly stimulating adventurous behavior to obtain pleasure, and often does not consider the consequences of risky behavior.

5. 简单化的自我中心性（耐受能力维度和功利性满足来源维度）

自我中心主义表现为做事从不替他人考虑，这种性格的核心是不懂得通过与他人的社会化互动来实现个人利益。

6. 坏脾气（认知能力维度和耐受能力维度）

主要指行为倾向于通过对抗甚至暴力的方式来处理人际冲突。一方面对暴力冲突的后果缺乏认知，另一方面是行为人不善于通过相对复杂的社会化策略达成目的，只能诉诸暴力手段解决问题。

四、紧张理论

紧张理论主要是借鉴涂尔干的失范理论。失范代表社会秩序的紊乱和道德规范的失衡。涂尔干通过考察社会整体与社会个体之间的关系，发现如果两者的关系平衡被打破或断裂，就会引发失范现象。美国社会学家默顿在涂尔干研究的基础上，从宏观层面提出了解释当时美国犯罪现象的紧张理论。后续学者又在紧张理论的基础上提出了相对剥夺感理论和一般紧张理论。

（一）结构紧张理论

默顿在其出版的《社会理论和社会结构》一书中指出，失范的根源在于社会所塑造的文化目

5) Simplified Egocentricity (Tolerance Dimension and Utilitarian Satisfaction Source Dimension)

Self centeredness manifests as never considering others when doing things, and the core of this personality is not understanding how to achieve personal interests through social interaction with others.

6) Bad Temper (Cognitive and Tolerance Dimensions)

This mainly refers to the tendency of behavior to handle interpersonal conflicts through confrontation or even violence. On the one hand, there is a lack of understanding of the consequences of violent conflicts, and on the other hand, the perpetrator is not good at achieving their goals through relatively complex socialization strategies and can only resort to violent means to solve problems.

4. Strain Theory

The Strain Theory mainly draws inspiration from Durkheim's Theory of Anomie. Anomie represents the disorder of social order and the imbalance of moral norms. Durkheim found through examining the relationship between the whole society and individual that if the balance between the two is disrupted or broken, it will lead to anomie. American sociologist Merton, based on Durkheim, proposed the Strain Theory from a macro perspective to explain the crime phenomenon in the United States at that time. Subsequent scholars have proposed the Theory of Relative Deprivation and the Theory of General Strain based on the Theory of Strain.

(1) Structural Strain Theory

Merton pointed out in his book *Social Theory and Social Structure* that the root of anomie lies in the tension between the cultural goals shaped by society and the institutional

标与实现特定目标的制度性手段之间存在张力与紧张。文化目标指社会文化在意识价值层面提倡和要求社会个体生存、生活和发展的目标，是社会个体整体性的参照框架，起着整合个体需要和行为动机的作用。社会制度性手段指界定和规范实现特定文化目标所被允许的、合法的、可接受的方式和方法。如果文化目标与社会制度性手段处于相对平衡的状态时，大多数社会成员能够利用合法的手段去实现文化目标，并从中获得满足感。如果产生失衡，社会个体无法利用制度性手段来实现文化目标时，就会产生紧张。例如当下社会的文化目标是有车有房有稳定工作，财富自由等，但部分社会成员不能够利用有限的合法渠道去实现这些目标时，便会倾向于转向其他不被允许但是有效的途径去实现这些目标，例如欺骗、暴力乃至犯罪等。

同时，默顿指出，社会制度性手段对于社会个体而言并非是公平的。社会和经济地位越高，所获得合法性手段就越多，因此就导致紧张状态在社会下层弥漫，使后者易通过犯罪手段追求文化目标。

（二）相对剥夺感理论

随着对紧张理论的深入研究，发现即使在合法性较高的中上层社会，也存在犯罪行为。基

means of achieving specific goals. Cultural goals refer to the goals advocated and required by social culture at the level of consciousness and value for the survival, life, and development of individual society. They serve as a reference framework for the overall social individual and play a role in integrating their needs and behavioral motivations. Social institutional means refer to the allowed, legal, and acceptable ways and methods that define and regulate the achievement of specific cultural goals. If cultural goals and social institutional means are in a relatively balanced state, most members of society can use legal means to achieve cultural goals and obtain a sense of satisfaction from them. If there is an imbalance and social individuals are unable to use institutional means to achieve cultural goals, strain will arise. For example, in today's society, the cultural goals are to have a car, a house, a stable job, financial freedom, etc. However, when certain members of society are unable to use limited legal channels to achieve these goals, they tend to turn to other prohibited but effective ways to achieve these goals, such as deception, violence, and even crime.

Meanwhile, Merton pointed out that social institutional measures are not fair and equal for individuals in society. The higher the social and economic status, the more legitimate means are obtained, which leads to strain spreading in the lower echelons of society and the pursuit of cultural goals through criminal means.

(2) Theory of Relative Deprivation

With in-depth research on the Theory of Strain, it has been found that even in the upper-and-middle class society with higher legitimacy, criminal behavior still exists. Based

于此，默顿在参照群体理论的基础上提出了相对剥夺感理论。理论指出，当社会个体在与参照群体（包括团体或个人）进行社会比较时，如果发现自身利益低于参照群体，就会产生不公平感和相对剥夺感。这种感受是一种主观体验或心理态度，只有在进行社会比较时才会产生。

美国社会学家布劳（Blau）夫妇将默顿的紧张理论与社会解组理论进行了整合，对相对剥夺论进行了系统而全面的阐述。《不平等的代价：都市结构与暴力犯罪》一文指出，相对剥夺感不仅包括与他人或群体的比较，还涉及与自己的过去和对未来的期望的比较。日益扩大的贫富差距会引发社会不公平感和相对剥夺感，这些内心感受会导致愤怒等紧张情绪，从而引发犯罪。下层阶级由于其种族和阶级地位的劣势，难以通过合法手段获得期望的物质财富，当他们在贫富交叉的城市区域目睹富人的富裕生活时，会感到被剥夺，产生不公平和不满感。这种由相对剥夺感引发的紧张情绪，导致了犯罪行为的发生。

过去，犯罪学家普遍认为，收入不平等是导致下层阶级紧张与犯罪的关键因素。下层阶级与中上层阶级之间的明显差距造成了下层阶级的紧张情绪。社会中的贫富悬殊会使相对处于劣势的

on this, Merton proposed the Theory of Relative Deprivation on the basis of the reference group theory. This theory suggests that when individuals in society compare themselves with reference groups (including groups or individuals), if they find that their own interests are lower than those of the reference group, they will experience a sense of unfairness and relative deprivation. This feeling is a subjective experience or psychological attitude that only arises when making social comparisons.

American sociologists Judith Blau and Peter Blau have integrated Merton's Strain Theory with Social Disorganization Theory, providing a systematic and comprehensive exposition of the theory of relative deprivation. "Metropolitan Structure and Violent Crime: Which Measures of Crime?" points out that relative deprivation not only involves comparison with others or groups, but also involves comparison with one's own past and expectations for the future. The widening wealth gap can trigger a sense of social inequality and relative deprivation, which can lead to tension such as anger and trigger crime. The Blau couple believe that the lower class, due to their disadvantaged race and class status, find it difficult to obtain the expected material wealth through legal means. When they witness the affluent life of the rich in urban areas where wealth intersects, they feel deprived, creating unfairness and dissatisfaction. This tension caused by relative deprivation leads to the occurrence of criminal behavior.

In the past, criminologists generally believed that income inequality was a key factor leading to strain and crime among the lower class. The obvious gap between the lower class and the upper-and-middle class has caused strain among the lower class. The wealth disparity in society can create a sense of relative deprivation among people who are relatively

人产生相对剥夺感，促使他们寻求获取财富和成功的途径。研究表明，由收入不平等引起的相对剥夺感可以预测下层阶级的财产和暴力犯罪行为。那么，这种相对剥夺感引发的紧张情绪是否仅存在于下层阶级呢？它能否预测中上阶级的犯罪情况呢？阿格纽（Agnew）认为，相对剥夺感同样能够解释中上阶级群体的犯罪行为。他指出，即使是美国最富有的人也会因为无法实现无限制的目标而感到紧张和失落。这意味着相对剥夺感与个人的富裕程度没有直接关系。中上阶级有他们自己的目标，当这些目标过高且难以实现时，也会产生紧张感。

（三）一般紧张理论

默顿紧张理论的视角主要在于对社会结构的解析，它用于解释宏观层面的紧张，但并没有解释不同个体的行为差异。为此，犯罪学家罗伯特·阿格纽在继承默顿紧张理论的基础上，综合借鉴了社会心理学、犯罪心理学、医学等学科的研究成果，对传统紧张理论进行了根本性的修改和扩展，提出了一般紧张理论。

罗伯特·阿格纽认为传统的紧张理论过于单一和局限，只强调了社会结构对个人追求文化目标的限制，而紧张不应局限于这种单一的形式。他将紧张的范围进一步扩大，包括认知、行为和

disadvantaged, prompting them to seek ways to obtain wealth and success. Research has shown that relative deprivation caused by income inequality can predict property and violent criminal behavior in the lower class. So, does the strain caused by this relative deprivation only exist in the lower class? Can it predict the crime situation of the upper-and-middle class? Agnew believes that a sense of relative deprivation can also explain the criminal behavior of upper-middle class groups. He pointed out that even the wealthiest people in the United States feel nervous and disappointed because they cannot achieve unlimited goals. This means that relative deprivation is not directly related to an individual's level of wealth. The upper-and-middle class has their own goals, and when these goals are too high and difficult to achieve, they can also generate tension.

(3) General Strain Theory

The perspective of Merton's tension theory mainly lies in the analysis of social structure, which is used to explain macro-level strain, but does not explain the behavioral differences of different individuals. Therefore, criminologist Robert Agnew inherited Merton's Strain Theory and comprehensively drew on the research achievements of social psychology, criminal psychology, medicine, and other disciplines to fundamentally modify and expand traditional Strain Theory, proposing the General Strain Theory.

Robert Agnew believes that the traditional Theory of Strain is too singular and limited, emphasizing only the limitations of social structure on individuals pursuing cultural goals, and strain should not be limited to this singular form. He further expands the scope of tension, including cognitive, behavioral, and emotional types. Specifically, the General

情绪等类型。具体而言，一般紧张理论认为个体的紧张主要包含以下三种类型。

第一种：个人无法或未能实现其想要实现的目标。此类型又包括三种情形。情形一，个体想要实现的目标与现实之间存在差距，这是默顿紧张理论的核心，即文化目标与合法手段之间的失衡。情形二，个人的主观期望与实际结果之间存在差距，例如想要考取好大学，但成绩不理想，或想要拥有一份稳定的工作，但一直无法如愿。情形三，应当获得的结果与实际获得的结果之间存在差距，例如付出比他人更多的时间和精力，但获得的报酬却不成比例。

第二种：个人被剥夺了积极且有价值的刺激或失去了积极向上且的欲望。例如经历亲人的去世、与伴侣分手、失去工作等。

第三种：遭遇消极刺激。例如童年时代受到虐待或校园欺凌，或经常被父母或老师严厉指责。

以上三种情形多源自负面的人际关系、同事关系、家庭关系等。这些情形会导致个体产生紧张感，进而产生失望、抑郁、恐惧、愤怒等负面情绪。尤其应注意愤怒，它是紧张与犯罪行为之间最重要的中介变量。愤怒增加了个体的受伤害感和报复欲望，降低了其对自身行为的约束，促

Strain Theory suggests that an individual's strain mainly includes the following three types.

The first type: Individuals are unable to achieve their desired goals. This type also includes three situations. Scenario 1: The gap between the individual's desired goals and reality is the core of Merton's Strain Theory, which is the imbalance between cultural goals and legal means. Scenario 2: The gap between personal subjective expectations and actual results, such as wanting to get into a good university but not achieving ideal results, or wanting to have a stable job but still unable to achieve it. Scenario 3: The gap between the expected and actual results, such as investing more time and effort than others but receiving disproportionate rewards.

The second type: Individuals are deprived of positive and valuable stimuli or lose their desire for positivity. For example, the death of a family member, breaking up with a partner, losing a job, etc.

The third type: Encounter negative stimuli. For example, being abused or bullied on campus during childhood, or often being harshly criticized by parents or teachers.

The above three situations mostly stem from negative interpersonal relationships, colleague relationships, family relationships, etc. These situations can lead to feelings of strain, leading to negative emotions such as disappointment, depression, fear, and anger, especially anger, which is the most important mediating variable between strain and criminal behavior. Anger increases an individual's sense of injury and desire for revenge, reduces constraints on their own behavior, and prompts them to take corresponding actions.

使其采取相应行动。

阿格纽认为，一旦出现负面刺激，个人必须采取一些必要的应对方式来调试和减轻紧张感，降低心理压力。否则，他们可能会采取一些社会不能接受的方式解决问题，违法犯罪行为就是其中之一。①

Agnew believes that once negative stimuli occur, individuals must adopt necessary coping strategies to adjust and reduce strain, and reduce psychological stress. Otherwise, they may adopt some socially unacceptable ways to solve these problems, and illegal and criminal behavior is one of them.

第二节
各类犯罪预防

Section 2
Prevention of Various Crimes

根据公安机关公布的关于2020—2021 年度刑事案件及构成数据，可分为杀人、伤害、抢劫及盗窃等案件类型（见表 3-1）。除

According to the data on criminal cases and their composition released by the public security organs of China from 2020 to 2021, they can be classified into types of cases such as murder, injury, robbery, and theft (Table 3-1). Except

表 3-1　2020—2021 全国各类刑事犯罪案件起数　Criminal Cases and Composition of Chinese Public Security Organs

案件类型 Case Type	立案 / 起 Number of Cases Filed		构成占比 /（％） Composition Proportion/(%)	
	2020	2021	2020	2021
杀人 Murder	7 157	6 522	0.15	0.13
伤害 Intentional Injury	79 662	82 476	1.67	1.64
抢劫 Robbery	11 303	9 700	0.24	0.19
强奸 Rape	33 579	39 577	0.70	0.79
盗窃 Pilferage	1 658 609	1 602 450	34.69	31.87
诈骗 Fraud	1 915 429	1 954 276	40.07	38.87

（数据来源：《国家统计局 2023 中国统计年鉴》）

(Data source: *National Bureau of Statistics 2023 China Statistical Yearbook*)

---

① 毛威 . 紧张理论视角下我国银行人员犯罪研究 [D]. 北京：中国人民公安大学，2020.

走私和伪造假币以外，其他案件类型都与我们的生活息息相关，每时每刻都在上演。

犯罪预防是对犯罪的事前防范活动，指国家、社会和个人采取的旨在消除犯罪原因、减少犯罪机会、威慑和矫正犯罪人，从而防止和减少犯罪发生的策略与措施的总和[①]。本节将在对各类犯罪案件的条件和原因分析的基础上，提出个人层面的防护措施。

一、暴力犯罪的预防

暴力犯罪是智力犯罪的对称，泛指以暴力作为犯罪手段严重危害社会的犯罪行为[②]。具体指行为人使用暴力手段或暴力相威胁，非法侵害公民的人身权利、财产权利、民主权利、和其他合法权益，以致这些合法权益受到危险的犯罪行为。根据国家统计局公布的标准，刑事立案类型属于以武力为手段、以肢体冲突为特征的犯罪包括凶杀、故意伤害、抢劫和强暴四种。

（一）防范凶杀

凶杀也称杀人犯罪，是指故意非法剥夺他人生命的行为。依据主体实施犯罪行为前是否预知会将受害人致死，可将凶杀分为

for smuggling and counterfeiting, other types of cases are closely related to our lives and are happening every moment.

Crime prevention is a pre-crime prevention activity that refers to the sum of strategies and measures adopted by the state, society, and individuals aimed at eliminating the causes of crime, reducing crime opportunities, deterring and correcting criminals, in order to prevent and reduce the occurrence of crime. Based on the analysis of the conditions and causes of various criminal cases, this section will propose personal protective measures.

1. Prevention of Violent Crimes

Violent crimes, the counterpart of intellectual crimes, encompass criminal acts that seriously endanger society through the use of violent means. This includes actions where individuals employ violent methods or threats of violence to unlawfully infringe upon the rights of citizens, such as personal, property, democratic, and other legal rights, placing these lawful interests in jeopardy. According to the types of criminal cases published by the National Bureau of Statistics, crimes categorized as using force and characterized by physical conflict include homicide, intentional injury, robbery, and rape.

(1) Preventing Homicide

Homicide, also known as murder, refers to the deliberate illegal deprivation of another person's life. Based on whether the perpetrator foresees causing the victim's death, homicide can be classified into intentional murder and manslaughter.

---

① 史振，曹文江 . 重新犯罪的原因分析及对策研究 [J]. 法制与社会 ,2016,(34):280-282.

② 林亚刚 . 暴力犯罪的内涵与外延 [J]. 现代法学 , 2001(6)：138-142.

故意杀人和过失杀人。生命是主体行使所有其他权力的物质基础和前提。为此，我国现行的刑法体系中量刑最重的就是侵犯生存权利的各类犯罪行为。

1. 凶杀犯罪分析

从认知角度而言，挫折－攻击理论认为犯罪动机的产生与个体的挫折经历有关。挫折是妨碍个人进行有目的行为的客观情境，和随之而产生的情绪有关。挫折往往会产生一种攻击驱力，攻击驱力进而引起攻击行为。驱力是生物具有的本能性行为动机，但人是具有理性的，并非仅仅依靠生物本能活动。为此，在挫折和攻击行为中间，还有犯罪动机作为中介变量，而犯罪动机的构成与否不仅关乎挫折的情境，同时也和个体对于环境的认知解读及抗挫折能力有关，其认知归因更偏向于敌意性。如听到同样一句话，有人归类于玩笑，有人则归类于嘲笑与讽刺。根据国内司法实证研究和回顾研究，故意杀人罪的犯罪人文化程度集中在小学和初中的达到74.9%，职业集中在无业、农民和工人三个职业群体的达到92.3%[1-2]。表现特征为犯罪者认知范围狭窄，缺乏灵活性和

Life serves as the material foundation and prerequisite for individuals to exercise all other rights in our legal system. Consequently, crimes infringing upon the right to life constitute the most severely punished offenses in the current criminal law system.

1) Analysis of Homicide Crimes

From a cognitive perspective, the setback-attack theory suggests that the generation of criminal motivation is related to an individual's experience of setbacks. Setbacks are objective situations that hinder individuals from engaging in purposeful behavior and the resulting emotions. Setbacks often generate an aggressive drive, which in turn leads to aggressive behavior. Drive is an instinctive behavioral motivation possessed by organisms, but humans are rational and not solely reliant on biological instinctual activities. Therefore, between setbacks and aggressive behavior, there is also criminal motivation as a mediating variable, and the composition of criminal motivation is not only related to the context of setbacks, but also to the individual's cognitive interpretation of the environment and their ability to resist setbacks. Its cognitive attribution tends to be more hostile. For example, hearing the same sentence, some people classify it as jokes, while others classify it as ridicule and satire. According to domestic judicial empirical research and retrospective research, the cultural level of the perpetrators of intentional homicide is concentrated between primary and secondary schools, accounting for 74.9%, and their occupations are concentrated in three occupational groups: unemployed, farmers, and workers, accounting for 92.3%. The characteristic manifestation is that criminals have a narrow cognitive range, lack flexibility and adaptability, and

---

① 汤家全，刘建锋.88例已破故意杀人案的回顾性分析[J].法医学杂志,2016,32(2):119-122.

② 尹明灿，李晓明.故意杀人罪实证研究：以493例故意杀人罪案例为视角[J].中国刑事法杂志,2009(6):105-115.

变通性，面对高压情境往往缺乏足够的认知资源来解决危机。

从情绪特征而言，无论是理智型杀人还是情绪性杀人，多伴有某种强烈的情绪和情感影响。尤其是情绪型，杀人多是因为情绪的发泄，而这种情绪的负面积累多来源于人际交往。犯罪人一般较为内向、不善于情感表达，而受害人则较为强势、缺乏理性。在人际交往中，犯罪人由于比较弱势，长期处于情绪压抑状态，当负面情绪积累到失衡时，原始的本我与社会的自我的平衡被打破，就会导致激情状态下的即时宣泄。例如案例一的马加爵案件，案件的原因看似是表明的打牌，但根源的问题是长期负面情绪的集中爆发，正如俗语言，"老实人的脾气，三伏天的炸雷。"

从动机特征而言，除加害者为精神异常或过失情形，很少无缘无故突然实施犯罪行为。动机一般可分为情绪性杀人和工具性杀人。犯罪更多地来源于熟人间人际交往层面的冲突，例如由婚姻不顺、奸情、分手等恋爱问题或仇恨、嫉妒、愤怒等报复性情绪引起的杀人；陌生人作案主要为图财型。另外，还存在无差别杀人，该类动机特征十分明确，即为了发泄自身的不满而报复社会。无差别杀人案件犯罪人具有共同点，即自身的生活往往不顺利，在工

often lack sufficient cognitive resources to solve crises in high-pressure situations.

From the perspective of emotional characteristics, whether it is rational homicide or emotional homicide, it is often accompanied by a strong emotional influence. Especially for emotional types, killing is often due to the release of emotions, and the negative accumulation of this emotion mostly comes from interpersonal communication. Criminals are generally introverted and not good at expressing emotions, while victims are more dominant and lack rationality. In interpersonal communication, due to being relatively weak and in a state of emotional suppression for a long time, when negative emotions accumulate and become imbalanced, the balance between the original id and the social ego is disrupted, leading to immediate release of passion of criminals. For example, in the case of Ma Jiajue in Case 1, the cause of the case may seem to be playing cards, but the root problem is the concentrated eruption of long-term negative emotions, as the saying goes, "The temper of an honest person is like thunder in the dog days."

From the perspective of motivational characteristics, unless the perpetrator is mentally abnormal or negligent, it is rare to see one suddenly commit criminal acts without reason. Motivation can generally be divided into emotional killing and instrumental killing. Crimes are more likely to originate from interpersonal conflicts among acquaintances, such as murder caused by relationship issues such as marriage fail, infidelity, break-ups, or retaliatory emotions such as hatred, jealousy, and anger; The main type of crime committed by strangers is for financial gain. In addition, there is indiscriminate killing, which has a very clear motivational characteristic of retaliating against society in order to vent one's dissatisfaction. The perpetrators of indiscriminate homicide cases have common ground, with their own lives being very difficult and

作、生活或感情方面遭遇重大挫折，长期对现实呈悲观态度。该类犯罪人消极情绪长期无法排解，并且将自身所遭遇的挫折归咎于社会，报复社会从而成为了犯罪人实施犯罪行为的驱动力。

【案例一 马加爵案件】

2004 年 2 月上旬，马加爵在昆明市云南大学宿舍内与同学唐某、邵某及杨某等人打牌。期间，邵某怀疑马加爵出牌作弊，两人当众发生争执。此次杀人的直接原因是他在打牌时被同学诬蔑作弊，并且他平时也常受到同学们的嘲笑和排斥。马加爵因遭到诬蔑和嘲笑便实施了杀人行为。

2. 凶杀犯罪预防

（1）待人平和，建立良好的人际关系。

遇事要保持冷静地思考，不可冲动。凡事三思，要考虑事情的后果；与他人建立良好的人际关系、互重互谅、互爱互助是原则。在与他人交往的过程中即使发生冲突，也要和平理性地处理，不能动辄诉诸武力，防止因矛盾进一步激化而酿成恶果。

（2）凡事换位思考，注意危险信号。

根据情绪的生成模式，愤怒属于人的第二次情绪，其背后还隐藏着很多其他的负面情绪，如不安、痛苦、寂寞、悲伤、难过等。这些隐藏起来的情绪为第一

experiencing significant setbacks in work, life, or relationships. They have a pessimistic attitude towards reality for a long time. The negative emotions of these criminals cannot be resolved for a long time, and they attribute their setbacks to society, thus retaliating against society has become the driving force for criminals to commit criminal acts.

[Case 1 Ma Jiajue case] In early February 2004, Ma Jiajue played cards with his classmates Tang, Shao, Yang, and others in the dormitory of Yunnan University in Kunming. During this period, Shao suspected Ma Jiajue of cheating while playing cards, and the two had a public dispute. The direct reason for the murder this time was that he was falsely accused of cheating by his classmates while playing cards, and he often received ridicule and rejection from his classmates. Ma Jiajue committed murder simply because he was accused and ridiculed.

2) Prevention of Homicide Crimes

① Approach others calmly, establish positive interpersonal relationships.

Maintain a calm demeanor and think rationally when faced with difficult situations, avoiding impulsive actions. Always consider the consequences of your actions. Building positive interpersonal relationships, with mutual respect, understanding, love, and assistance. Even in conflicts with others, prioritize peaceful and rational resolutions, avoiding resorting to violence to prevent the escalation of conflicts.

② Empathize and recognize danger signals.

Based on the generation pattern of emotions, anger is considered a second-order emotion, often masking underlying negative emotions like anxiety, pain, loneliness, sadness, etc. These hidden emotions are the first emotions. When emotions cannot be expressed smoothly for the first time, people will use

次情绪。当第一次情绪无法顺利表达，人们才会使用愤怒情绪来表达。为此，在与同事、邻居以及亲戚等人的社会交往过程中，如果发现有人经常处于焦躁、慌张状态，持续地抱怨某件事或者突然翻旧账向他人发火，则要警惕其可能出现的攻击性愤怒；发现有人粗暴地使用物品甚至破坏物品，意味着其愤怒情绪郁结，攻击指向可能由物品转向无辜的他人，应与其保持必要的距离。在矛盾激化、关系紧张的情况下尽量避免与其单独接触，切勿盲目冲动自我处理。

（3）转移注意，避免情绪激化。

如果个体察觉到自身存在愤怒情绪，可尝试把注意力放到其他需要集中精神做的事情上，暂时缓解愤怒情绪；或者强迫自己改变行为方向，而不是怒气冲冲地反对他人；也可以通过理性情绪想象的方法，回想愉快的经历和美好的感觉，尽量使这种感觉胜过对他人的敌意。在社会互动中，应当掌控自身情绪，保持健康的社会人格，与周围人群积极互动，追求正向的情感认同，避免做出搬弄是非、挑拨离间、见利忘义、背信弃义等不道德甚至是违法犯罪的行为。

【案例二 情绪失控伤害事件】

2021 年 7 月 5 日，杨浦区中山北二路某公司内发生持刀伤人事

anger to express themselves. Therefore, in the process of social interaction with colleagues, neighbors, and relatives, when individuals frequently exhibit irritability, anxiety, consistent complaints, or sudden outbursts of anger, be alert to potential aggressive tendencies. Violent use of objects or property destruction indicates suppressed anger, potentially redirecting aggression towards innocent individuals. Maintain necessary distance when encountering such individuals in situations of escalated conflict or tension, avoiding impulsive actions.

③ Shift focus, avoid escalation of emotions.

If an individual recognizes anger within themselves, try redirecting attention to other tasks that require concentration to temporarily alleviate anger. Alternatively, force yourself to change behavior patterns rather than vehemently oppose others. Rational emotional imagination, recalling pleasant experiences and positive feelings, can help overshadow hostile sentiments towards others. We should control emotions during social interactions, uphold a healthy social personality, engage positively with others, seek positive emotional connections, and avoid engaging in unethical or even criminal behaviors such as spreading rumors, sowing discord, opportunism, or betrayal.

[Case 2   Emotional loss of control injury event]

On July 5, 2021, a knife injury incident occurred in a company on Zhongshan North Second Road in Yangpu District. The

件。犯罪嫌疑人刘某因工作积怨已久，忍无可忍，伤害了同事徐某，导致其抢救无效死亡。

（4）夜间关好门窗

凶杀的起始原因可能并非故意杀人，而只是为了抢劫，是当被发现时犯罪人应激状态下的反应。通过对华东地区某市中级人民法院 2010—2014 年判决的杀人案件中随机抽取 200 个样本案例进行调查分析，结果表明发生在个人住宅的杀人犯罪比例最高，达到 59.4%[①]。一项针对中国裁判文书网收集到的四川省 471 例故意杀人案（2012 年～2016 年）进行的回顾性分析表明，发生于室内的案件有 250 例，占 53.08%[②]。这是因为被害者通常对自己的住宅有潜在的信赖习惯和无意识的安全感，在自己的住宅缺乏警惕，以致悲惨的结局。

【案例三 6·4 罗城入室抢劫杀人案】2020 年 6 月 4 日凌晨，何某携带作案工具进入受害人家中实施盗窃。犯罪人在作案过程中致一人重伤、一人死亡，并在抢走财物后逃离现场。

（二）防范故意伤害

故意伤害罪指故意非法损害他人身体健康的行为。本罪侵犯的客体是他人的身体权，所谓身

suspect Liu, who had accumulated resentment for a long time at work, could not bear it. He injured his colleague Xu with a knife, which led to his death.

④ Secure doors and windows at night.

The initiation of homicide might not be intentional, but could be for robbery. When discovered, criminals in a stressed state may react impulsively. A survey and analysis was conducted on 200 randomly selected murder cases from judgments made by a Intermediate People's Court in a city in East China from 2010 to 2014. The results showed that the highest proportion of murders occurred in private residences, accounting for 59.4%. A retrospective analysis of 471 intentional homicide cases in Sichuan Province (2012–2016), collected from the China Judgments Online database, revealed that 250 of the cases (53.08%) occurred indoors. This is because victims often have implicit trust and unconscious security in their homes, lacking vigilance and leading to tragic outcomes.

[**Case 3　6·4 Luocheng burglary and murder case**] In the early morning of June 4, 2020, He Shun entered the back door of the victim's house with tools, intending to commit theft. The perpetrator caused one person serious injury and another one dead, and left the crime scene with the robbed property.

(2) Prevent Intentional Harm

The crime of intentional harm refers to the deliberate and illegal act of causing harm to another person's physical health. The object violated by this crime is the bodily rights of others,

---

① 陈文昊. 杀人犯罪被害人研究 [J]. 河南司法警官职业学院学报 ,2016,14(01):49-55.

② 吴畏，陈晓刚，邓振华. 四川省 471 例故意杀人案特征回顾性分析 [J]. 证据科学 ,2019,27(01):105-125.

体权是指自然人以保持其肢体、器官和其他组织的完整性为内容的人格权。本罪在主观方面表现为故意，在客观方面表现为实施了非法损害他人身体的行为。

根据 2014 年最高人民法院、最高人民检察院、公安部、国家安全部和司法部颁布的《人体损伤程度鉴定标准》，可将伤害分为重伤、轻伤和轻微伤三种。其中重伤指使人肢体残废、毁容、丧失听觉、丧失视觉、丧失其他器官功能或者受到其他对于人身健康有重大伤害的损伤，包括重伤一级和重伤二级。轻伤指使人肢体或者容貌损害，听觉、视觉或者其他器官功能部分障碍或者其他对于人身健康有中度伤害的损伤，包括轻伤一级和轻伤二级。轻微伤指各种致伤因素所致的原发性损伤，造成组织器官结构轻微损害或者轻微功能障碍。致人伤残程度与判罚力度成正相关。

1. 故意伤害犯罪分析

凶杀犯罪与故意伤害犯罪在动机方面的区别在于，凶杀行为是在图谋财物、报复泄愤、宣泄情欲等各种心理动因推动下实施的。尽管犯罪动机各式各样，但杀人作案的唯一主观目的皆为剥夺他人生命。不同的杀人犯罪动机决定了杀人案件的具体性质类型，例如谋财害命杀人、私仇报复杀人、强奸杀人、奸情杀人、寻

defined as the personality rights encompassing the integrity of one's limbs, organs, and other tissues. The subjective aspect of this crime manifests as intent, while the objective aspect involves the commission of an illegal act causing harm to another person's body.

According to the Standards for the Assessment of Human Body Injury Degree issued in 2014 by the Supreme People's Court, Supreme People's Procuratorate, Ministry of Public Security, Ministry of State Security, and Ministry of Justice, injuries are categorized into severe, minor, and slight. Severe injuries result in significant harm, such as disability, disfigurement, loss of hearing or vision, or other organ functions. This includes first and second-degree severe injuries. Minor injuries lead to impairment of limbs or appearance, partial impairment of hearing or vision, or other organ functions, causing moderate harm to personal health. This category includes first and second-degree minor injuries. Slight injuries involve primary damage caused by various injurious factors, resulting in slight damage to the structure or minor functional impairment of tissues and organs. The degree of disability caused is positively correlated with the severity of the punishment.

1) Analysis of Intentional Harm Crimes

The distinction between homicide and intentional harm in terms of motivation lies in the fact that homicide is driven by various psychological motives, such as plotting for wealth, seeking revenge, expressing desires. Although the motives for crimes vary, the sole subjective purpose of homicide is to deprive others of life. Different motives in homicide determine the specific nature of the case, such as murder for wealth, revenge, rape, extramarital affairs, or quarrels leading to violence. Intentional harm, on the other hand, often stems from actions like getting revenge, smashing

衅斗殴杀人等。伤害行为常有报复泄愤、打砸抢、聚众斗殴等。一项针对西南地区多地 2014—2016 年轻伤二级及以上故意伤害案件 1 340 例的案例分析发现，作案动机因纠纷的 614 例，因财物问题的有 95 例，因情感纠纷的有 41 例，因仇怨的有 32 例[①]。据此，可根据场景的不同将故意伤害细分为校园欺凌型伤害、婚恋型故意伤害、邻里纠纷型伤害等类型。

校园欺凌型伤害中，初中和大学是学生之间产生冲突比例较高的阶段。初中阶段的学生正进入敏感的青春期，其显著特征是追求思想的独立性，意图摆脱他人的束缚。大学阶段的学生正处于价值观形成的重要时期，易受周围境变化的影响，出现固执、偏激、冲动等特征，最终导致暴力行为[②]，如案例四和案例五，由同学间的矛盾上升至身体伤害。一项针对 816 例未成年人故意伤害案件的分析显示，故意伤害未成年人案例的伤者多为男性，以 16～18 周岁最多见。其动机以过激行事为主，致伤物以锐器和钝器为主，颅脑、脊柱四肢损伤最为多见，损伤程度中轻微伤和轻伤二级位及首位，发生场所主

and grabbing, or engaging in group brawls. An analysis of 1,340 intentional harm cases involving minor injuries or above in several southwestern regions from 2014 to 2016 revealed that 614 cases were motivated by disputes, 95 by property issues, 41 by emotional conflicts, and 32 by grudges. Accordingly, intentional harm crimes can be divided into campus violence injuries, relationship-related intentional harm, and neighborhood-dispute intentional harm based on different scenerios.

In terms of campus violence injuries, middle school and university have a higher proportion of fights. The middle school stage is entering a sensitive adolescence, characterized by the pursuit of independent thinking and breaking free from the constraints of others. College students are in an important period of value formation and are easily influenced by changes in their surroundings. They exhibit characteristics such as stubbornness, extremism, impulsiveness, and others, ultimately leading to violent behavior, such as in Cases 4 and 5, which escalate from conflicts among classmates to physical harm. An analysis of 816 cases of intentional injury to minors showed that the majority of intentional injury cases were male, with the most common cases occurring between the ages of 16 and 18. The main motivation was passion, and the main causes of injury were sharp and blunt instruments. Craniocerebral, spinal, and limb injuries were the most common, with minor and minor injuries ranking second and first. The injuries mainly occurred in public places, with a high incidence in autumn

---

① 龙武，胡春梅，李思思，等 . 西南地区 1 340 例故意伤害案件的特征及相关因素分析 [J]. 法医学杂志，2019,35(4):433-436.

② 马洁，薛顶峰 . 天津市青少年故意伤害行为调查分析 [J]. 中国慢性病预防与控制 ,2014,22(6):679-682.

要为公共场所。秋季高发，且多在晚上[①]。

婚恋型故意伤害的动机原因包括婚恋纠纷激化、产生经济纠纷、婚姻与爱情产生强迫性、生活琐事引发争执、出轨报复等。该类犯罪的主要形成机制包括：犯罪人心理承受能力差，对日常生活琐事的容忍度低，遇伴侣间争吵易情绪失控；犯罪人有酗酒、吸毒等不良习性，酗酒后性格会变得更加冲动、行事更加大胆；还有一种被害人诱发的机制，即其背叛感情、逃避家庭责任和义务、收取犯罪人大量财物拒不返还、挑起争端等[②]。

邻里纠纷型伤害的犯罪动机比较明显，主要包括邻里之间民间利益关系纠纷、土地纠纷及生活纠纷。简言之，主要原因是相关方因为利益、土地使用权以及琐事等纠纷冲突后，犯罪人不知道如何或不能及时通过正当途径解决，致使矛盾激化，导致伤害犯罪。

通过对几类故意犯罪类型的综合分析，发现其存在如下共性：故意伤害犯罪中，犯罪行为大多都是外界因素的刺激导致的激情犯罪，极少具有预谋性，如案例五；与凶杀犯罪类型一样，故意

and mostly at night.

Motives for relationship-related intentional harm include escalated disputes, economic disputes, forced marriage and love, trivial domestic matters, and revenge for infidelity. Factors contributing to these motives include poor psychological resilience of the perpetrator, low tolerance for daily life trivialities; emotional instability due to alcohol or drug abuse; and betrayal by the victim, along with evasion of family responsibilities, refusal to return significant assets, or provocation leading to conflicts.

Neighborhood-dispute intentional harm exhibits clear motives, mainly arising from disputes related to local interests, land uses, and daily life conflicts. In summary, the main reasons are conflicts arising from disputes over interests, land use rights, and trivial matters that cannot be resolved through legal means in a timely manner, leading to escalated contradictions and resulting in harmful crimes.

Through a comprehensive analysis of various intentional crime types, common points include that most intentional harm crimes are passion crimes caused under external stimuli, with little premeditation, such as in Case 5. Similar to homicide crimes, perpetrators of intentional harm generally have a lower cognitive level, prone to impulsiveness and irascibility. Faced

---

① 王威，张世林，张宵，等.816例故意伤害未成年人案件的法医学分析 [J]. 法制博览,2023(12):13-17.
② 陈朝.婚恋型故意杀人及故意伤害犯罪研究 [D]. 南昌：江西财经大学，2023.

伤害犯罪人一般认知水平较低、易冲度和暴躁，面对刺激时，缺少足够的认知资源解决问题，如面对利益纠纷不懂得利用合法工具维护权益，只能诉诸武力。

【案例四　打架斗殴】 2016年11月24日，X市护士学校学生小阳与学生小杰于白天打雪仗嬉戏时产生摩擦，两人产生了肢体碰撞的打架行为。小杰于当天晚上9时，聚集一群手持刀具和钢管的社会不良人员，找到小阳的宿舍，在未找到小阳本人的情况下，将其宿舍下铺学生的被子、衣物扔到厕所。小阳得知情况后，从校外赶回，于当晚11时，纠集舍友小刘、小龙、小鑫、小然等人持铁管将小杰打成重伤，主要伤及眼角膜，医院判定小杰的伤情为一级伤残。

【案例五　陕西神木未成年人欺凌案】 李某玉在2024年1月18日下午召集了刘某等7人准备对李某燃和贾某杰实施欺凌行为。通过"快手"私聊，以共同玩耍为由，侵害人分别约李某燃、贾某杰见面，经过一系列引诱，将被侵害人带至无人处，对其进行了殴打并拍摄了现场视频。同日下午，他们又对贾某杰进行了殴打，并指使其他人参与，对被侵害人造成了严重的伤害。

with stimuli, they lack sufficient cognitive resources to resolve issues, such as using legal tools to protect their rights in the case of disputes over interests. Instead, they resort to violence.

[**Case 4　Fighting in groups**]　On November 24, 2016, a student named Xiaoyang and a student named Xiaojie from X Nurse School had friction while having a snowball fight during the day, resulting in a physical collision and fighting behavior between the two. At 9 p.m. that evening, Xiaojie gathered a group of socially undesirable individuals holding knives and steel pipes to find Xiaoyang's dormitory. Without finding Xiaoyang himself, he threw the student's bedding and clothes under the dormitory into the toilet. After learning about the situation, Xiao Yang rushed back from outside the school and gathered his roommates Xiao Liu, Xiao Long, Xiao Xin, Xiao Ran, and others to use iron pipes to severely injure Xiao Jie, mainly affecting his cornea. It is understood that the hospital determined that Xiao Jie's injury was level one disability.

[**Case 5　Shaanxi Shenmu juvenile bullying case**] On the afternoon of January 18, 2024, Li Mouyu convened seven individuals to prepare for bullying Li Moran and Jia Moujie. The perpetrators asked Li Mouran and Jia Moujie to meet respectively through "Kuaishou" private chat for the reason of playing together. After a series of enticement, they took the victim to a private place, then beat him and shot a live video. On the same afternoon, they assaulted Jia Moujie again and instructed others to participate, causing serious harm to the infringer.

【案例六 火锅服务员热汤烧伤顾客事件】 2015 年 8 月 24 日，浙江温州的林女士与先生携带孩子到"第一桥火锅店"吃饭。期间，林女士呼叫服务员过来添汤，但由于店里生意火爆，并未有服务员理会。此时，负责传菜的服务员小朱，正好给林女士的孩子送已点的饮料。被林女士催促尽快加汤，小朱道歉过后，表示马上就加。然而小朱回到后厨后，由于需要传的菜品较多，就忘却了加水的事，想起时，已是十几分钟后。当小朱拿着灌满热高汤的水壶到林女士一桌时，便受到林女士的指责，小朱赶忙道歉并一再安抚林女士。但对方持续训斥小朱，这点燃了小朱的怒火，他将热水倒向了林女士。该事件造成林女士全身 40% 的烧伤，定级为七级伤残。小朱因怀有报复心理做出过激举动，属于情节较为严重，被判处三年以上十年以下有期徒刑。

2. 故意伤害犯罪预防

根据故意伤害的几种类型的共性原因可知，故意犯罪的犯罪人的自控能力较差，容易在争吵与纠纷中爆发，缺乏认知资源解决矛盾，以及常伴有酗酒问题等。基于此，预防行为包括以下几种。

（1）和谐共处，与人为善。

在婚恋型故意伤害犯罪中，犯

［**Case 6 Hot pot waiter burns customer with hot soup incident**］ On August 24, 2015, Ms. Lin and her husband took their children to eat at the "First Bridge Hot Pot Restaurant" in Wenzhou, Zhejiang. During this time, Ms. Lin called for a waiter to come and add soup, but due to the hot business in the restaurant, no waiter paid attention. At this moment, the waiter in charge of delivering dishes, Xiao Zhu, happened to deliver the ordered beverage to Ms. Lin's child. After being urged by Ms. Lin to add soup as soon as possible, Xiao Zhu apologized and said he would add it immediately. However, when Xiao Zhu, who was responsible for passing the dishes, returned to the kitchen and forgot about adding water because there were many dishes to pass. When he remembered it, it was already more than ten minutes later. When Xiao Zhu came to Ms. Lin's table with a kettle filled with hot soup, he was criticized by Ms. Lin. Xiao Zhu quickly apologized and repeatedly comforted Ms. Lin, but she kept scolding him. Xiao Zhu, who had been criticized for a long time, could not suppress his emotions and poured all the hot water towards Ms. Lin, causing up to 40% of Ms. Lin's body burns, who was classified as level seven disability. Xiao Zhu was also sentenced to imprisonment for not less than three years and not more than ten years due to his retaliatory behavior, which is considered a more serious offense.

2) Prevention of Intentional Injury Crimes

From the common causes of different types of intentional injuries, we can see that offenders of intentional crimes generally have poor self-control, are prone to explosions during arguments and disputes, lack cognitive resources to solve conflicts, and may exhibit behaviors such as alcoholism and chaos. Based on these characteristics, preventive measures include the following ones.

① Harmonious coexistence and kindness to others.

In intentional injury crimes related to relationships, the

罪人多为男性。男性犯罪人多具有男权思想，认为妻子应当臣服于他，性格冲动，生活上稍有不顺心就会对配偶或伴侣动用暴力。

（2）遇到纠纷问题，诉诸合法手段。

当遇见校园同学间的冲突、邻里利益纠纷等情况无法处理时，应通过合法的手段解决，例如查询相关事件的处理方式、上报学校、咨询援助律师等。切勿通过暴力手段自己解决。

（3）遇见常酗酒人群，应尽量远离。

在生活中常会遇到喝酒的人无事生非，若与其产生争吵，其在酒精的麻痹下，无法充分认识行为所造成的严重后果，容易主动挑衅，发起进攻行为。

（4）不与性格火爆、易冲动的人过分争执。

易冲动的人在情绪激动时，可能难以控制自己的行为，容易导致争执升级为身体冲突甚至暴力行为。争执过程中可能出现失控的情况，带来身体伤害的风险。

（三）防范抢劫

抢劫是指以非法占有为目的，采用暴力、胁迫或者其他方法，强行劫取公私财物的行为[①]。通过定义可知，虽然嫌疑人的主要目标是金钱、首饰等贵重物品，

offender is often male. Male offenders tend to have patriarchal thoughts, believing that their wives should submit to them, and they are impulsive. If life is slightly unsatisfactory, they may resort to violence against their spouses or partners.

② Resolve disputes through legal means.

When encountering conflicts between classmates on campus, neighborhood interests disputes that cannot be resolved, legal means should be used, such as inquiring about the handling methods of relevant events, reporting to the school, consulting and assisting lawyers, and not resorting to violent means to resolve them on their own.

③ Avoid regular alcoholics.

In daily life, it is common to encounter people who drink alcohol and cause trouble. If there is an argument with them, under the paralysis of alcohol, they cannot fully understand the serious consequences of their behavior. They are easily provoked and initiate aggressive behavior

④ Avoid conflict with hot-tempered and impulsive individuals and excessive argumentation.

Impulsive people may have difficulty controlling their behavior when they are emotionally agitated, which can lead to disputes escalating into physical conflicts or even violent behavior. During the dispute, there may be a risk of losing control and causing physical injury.

(3) Preventing Robbery

Robbery refers to the act of forcibly taking the property of the victim with the purpose of illegal possession, using violence, coercion, or other methods. While the primary goal of the suspect is valuables such as money and jewelry, the use of violent actions serves as a means, threatening and violating

---

[①] 熊秋红.最高检首批刑事抗诉指导性案例评析 [J]. 中国检察官,2023(18):18-22.

暴力行为只是手段，但对当事人来说，其财产权和人身权均受到了威胁与侵犯。

1. 抢劫犯罪分析

盗窃、抢劫与诈骗虽同属于财产类犯罪，但抢劫相较于盗窃更公开，较于诈骗更简单粗暴。表明抢劫犯的聪慧性较低，敢为性等人格因素高。但并不表明此类犯罪是非理性的。相反，犯罪群体会将风险与收益等因素考虑在内。为此，环境很重要。

综合而言，抢劫违法行为具有多维度差异。从性别看，犯罪群体主要为男性，尤其是青壮年。从时间维度看，春秋两个季度较少，冬夏为犯罪高峰；白天较少，夜晚较多。从场所上看，城市中荒僻的街道，城乡结合部，部分公共场所如银行、商店等是抢劫的易发点。另外，犯罪多为群体犯罪，且携带凶器抢劫的比例高。

情绪方面。该类群体情绪不稳定、易激动，情绪反应速度快。尤其是与被害人直接接触时，情绪往往处于高度紧张状态，抑制犯罪的意志薄弱。为此，被害人的反抗往往会带来严重的后果，例如案例七。

动机方面。抢劫犯罪的动机很明确，即获取受害人的财物，暴力行为仅仅是手段。但亦有少数抢劫犯的犯罪动机并非出于财物掠夺，而是寻求刺激。此种类

both the property and personal rights of the individuals involved.

1) Analysis of Robbery Crimes

Theft, robbery, and fraud are all property related crimes. But robbery is more public than theft, and simpler and more brutal than fraud. This indicates that robbers have lower intelligence and higher personality factors such as daring to act. But it does not mean that such crimes are irrational. On the contrary, criminal groups will consider factors such as risk and benefits. For this reason, the environment is very important.

Overall, robbery violations have various differences. From a gender perspective, the criminal group is mainly male, especially young adults. From a temporal perspective, there are fewer crimes in spring and autumn, and the peak of crime is in winter and summer. There are fewer days crimes and more nights crimes. From a regional perspective, there are more cities crimes than rural areas crimes. Desolate streets, urban-rural fringe areas, and public places such as banks and shops are prone to robbery. In addition, most crimes are group crimes, and the proportion of armed robbery is high.

In terms of criminal emotions. This type of group has unstable emotions and is prone to quick emotional reactions. Especially when in direct contact with the victim, emotions are in a highly tense state. The will to suppress crime is weak, and as a result, the victim's resistance often leads to serious consequences, such as in Case 7.

In terms of motivation, the motive for robbery is very clear, which is to obtain the victim's property, and violent behavior is only a means. But there are also a few robbers who are not motivated by property, but seek stimulation, and this type is mostly juvenile delinquency.

型多为青少年犯罪。

【案例七　辽宁朝阳市 ATM 机抢劫案】　2013 年 8 月某一天夜里，一女子到银行自动取款机取钱。此时，一名男子走到女子身后，用枪指着其威胁交钱，女子非但没有服软反而挑衅，致使被激怒的歹徒扣下扳机，最终导致女子变成植物人。

2. 抢劫犯罪预防

（1）遇见抢劫，勿挑衅。

通过抢劫犯罪的分析可知，抢劫犯罪群体容易被激怒，且持械。若不幸遇见劫财的抢劫，切勿保财不要命，与犯罪人发生争执，导致犯罪人被激怒，可先选择服从，将财产全部交出，当脱离危险后，再选择报警。

（2）勿在夜间走偏僻小道。

抢劫存在环境与时间特征。在偏僻小道及夜间至凌晨的时间段，女性是犯罪者的首选目标，一是因为现金及其他贵重物品一般都放在其挎包里，给犯罪分子抢劫提供了便利条件，例如摩托车抢劫群体。二是因为夜间行路的单身女子自我保护能力差，且抢劫多为群体作案，遇见基本无力反抗。因此，夜间切勿独自出门至僻静街上行走，尤其是需要值夜班的群体。

（3）莫炫富张扬。

抢劫虽然具有随机性，但当

[**Case 7　An ATM robbery case in Chaoyang City, Liaoning Province**]　One night in August 2013, a woman went to a bank ATM to withdraw money. At this time, a man walked up behind her and pointed a gun at the woman, threatening her to give him the money The woman not only did not soften but provoked, irritating the criminal. The criminal pulled the trigger and directly shot the woman's head, causing her ultimately becoming a vegetative.

2) Prevention of Robbery Crimes

① When encountering a robbery, avoid provocation.

Analysis of robbery crimes reveals that perpetrators are easily provoked and often armed. If unfortunate enough to encounter a robbery motivated solely by material gain, it is crucial not to prioritize belongings over life. Avoid engaging in disputes with the criminals, as it may escalate the situation. Choosing compliance and surrendering all possessions first, prioritizing personal security, and then notifying the authorities is advisable.

② Avoid walking on isolated paths at night.

Robberies exhibit environmental and temporal characteristics. Women become prime targets during late-night to early-morning hours, especially on isolated paths. This is due to valuables, including cash, typically being stored in bags, providing convenience for criminals, such as those on motorcycles to commit robbery. Additionally, single women walking alone at night are vulnerable and often encounter group attacks, making resistance difficult. Therefore, it is crucial not to venture alone into quiet streets, especially for those working night shifts.

③ Avoid flaunting wealth.

Although robberies are somewhat random, entering

在危险场所(如僻静小道等)显露名贵物品时就已经为其成为被害人埋下了隐患。为此,不要露财(如在危险环境佩带贵重首饰)。另外,应减少大量取现行为,因为携带或是持有大量现金本身就意味着有遭遇抢劫或者被盗的风险。最后,还应强化犯罪被害防范意识。在日常生活中,通过细节有意识地培养预防犯罪意识,如减少与危险人群的接触、避免将自己置于易于被害的时空环境中,等等。总之,应该综合运用多种途径减少自我被害的风险,如案例八。

(4)莫粗心大意。

此点主要针对男性,一般男性认为自己身强力壮,没有人敢对自己怎么样,从而落入圈套中。如在案例九的色诱抢劫案中,面对女性男性几乎没有戒备之心,从而在谈话过程中将个人钱财信息透漏给犯罪人,随意跟犯罪人到出租屋或宾馆内,给犯罪分子提供了劫走其全部钱财的机会。

【案例八　周某系列持枪抢劫案】2004年4月22日中午12时左右,某酒店的出纳和会计两名职工到分理处取款后,遭遇歹徒周某。其在开枪打死1人、打伤1人后逃逸,抢走现金。2009年12月4日,周某持枪杀害从银行取款出来的郭某,抢走现金。2012年1月6日,周某在某银行

dangerous areas, like poorly monitored isolated paths, while displaying valuable items already creates a potential hazard. Avoid showcasing wealth in risky environments, such as wearing expensive jewelry, and be cautious not to reveal valuables. Furthermore, reduce the habit of carrying large amounts of cash, as it inherently increases the risk of robbery, assault, or theft. Lastly, strengthen awareness of crime prevention. In daily life, consciously cultivate an awareness of crime prevention through details, such as minimizing contact with potentially dangerous individuals and avoiding situations that increase vulnerability to crime. In summary, employ various measures to reduce the risk of self-victimization, as the Case 8.

④ Avoid carelessness and negligence.

This point mainly addresses males who may mistakenly believe in their physical strength, thinking they are invulnerable. In seduction robberies like Cases 9, where men are targeted by female perpetrators, the lack of vigilance can lead to falling into traps. In these instances, men may inadvertently disclose personal financial information during conversations with criminal actors, casually accompany them to rented rooms or hotels, providing criminals with an opportunity to rob them of all their money.

[**Case 8　Zhou series armed robbery cases**] On April 22, 2004, around noon, two employees, a cashier and an accountant from a hotel went to withdraw funds. Zhou shot and killed one person, injured the other, and fled, stealing cash. On December 4, 2009, Zhou held a gun and killed Guo, who had withdrawn funds from a bank, stealing cash. On January 6, 2012, Zhou was at the entrance of a bank. Zhou killed Li, who had just withdrawn money, and stole money and escaped the scene. There were 9 other

门口持枪杀害刚取款出来的李某，抢走现金后逃离现场。与此相似的案件共有9起，共11人遇难。

【案例九　色诱抢劫案】
2022年6月9日，犯罪人朱某、曾某以女性的身份通过交友软件添加了受害人小帅，并约好翌日见面。10日晚，犯罪人曾某开车将两名女性送去与小帅会面。见面后，二人找理由将小帅带至偏僻处，犯罪人朱某与曾某后对其进行抢劫。

（四）防范强暴

强暴也称强奸，是一种严重侵犯人身权利的犯罪。是性犯罪的一种，其不仅给被害人的身体带来伤害，同时也带来无比的精神痛苦。我国刑法对于强奸罪的规定为："强奸是违背妇女意志，使用暴力、胁迫或者其他手段，强行与女性发生性关系的行为。"

1. 强暴犯罪行为分析

精神分析理论认为该类行为是人的本能驱使而成（性本能和攻击本能），即生理兴奋性。换言之，当个体的性激素水平较高时，唤醒水平也较高；同时对性兴奋的抑制能力较弱，即自我控制较弱。道德水平低，外界监管不足加之男性本能与攻击本能成为强奸犯罪的生理动力。研究结果表明，75%的强奸犯罪人作案时小于30岁，青春期和性激素水平相关度较高。另外，犯罪人如实

similar cases, with 11 people killed.

[Case 9　Seduction robbery case] On June 9, 2022, criminals Zhu and Zeng added the victim Xiao Shuai through social media as women, and made an appointment to meet. On the evening of the 10th, the criminal Zeng drove two women to meet with the victim. Afterwards, they made up an excuse to take him to a quiet place, and the two perpetrators committed robbery.

(4) Prevention of Sexual Assault

Sexual assault, also known as rape, is a severe crime that violates personal rights. It is a form of sexual crime, causing physical harm and immense mental suffering to the victim. In China, the Criminal Law defines rape as "the act of forcibly engaging in sexual intercourse with a woman or committing lascivious acts with a minor, against the will of the female, through violence, coercion, or other means".

1) Analysis of Sexual Assault Criminal Behavior

According to psychoanalytic theory, such behavior is considered instinctual (sexual and aggressive instincts) and related to physiological arousal. In other words, when an individual has high levels of sex hormones, their arousal levels increase, and their ability to control sexual excitement weakens. Factors such as low moral standards, lack of external supervision, male instincts, and aggressive tendencies contribute to the physiological drive for sexual assault. Research indicates that 75% of sexual assault criminals are under the age of 30, correlating with adolescence and higher levels of sex hormones. Additionally, behaviors like alcohol and drug abuse significantly increase excitement, weaken

施酗酒和吸毒等行为也会提高其兴奋性，弱化自我抑制，促使自我放纵，降低行为人的自我控制能力。

强奸犯罪亦存在时间与空间上的特点。首先地点多为封闭空间。封闭空间相对来说更加隐秘、安全性高，不易被第三者发现。其次夜晚的发生概率更大。借助黑夜的掩护，即所谓的"去人性化"环境实施犯罪。一项针对河南省 100 份强奸犯罪审判决文书的实证研究发现，强奸犯的作案时间在夜晚到达最高水平，在晚间六点至凌晨六点的时间段内作案的比例高达总数的 78%。强奸犯罪行为同样高发于个人住宅（包括犯罪人与被害人）和环境较为封闭的酒店房间内，占比高达 84%。文化程度较低的犯罪被告人数量占比约为 87%。犯罪手段主要有使用暴力和威胁、引诱、欺骗、网络交友、使用监护或教育便利、使用酒精和迷药等[①]。

2. 强暴犯罪行为预防

（1）远离易发案环境。

KTV、酒吧等娱乐场所，人流量大，环境嘈杂，灯光昏暗，且本身为酒精提供场所，犯罪人的欲望越容易被激发，被害的易感性增大。尤其是对于女性大学生

self-control, and reduce the perpetrator's ability to restrain themselves.

Sexual assault crimes exhibit temporal and spatial characteristics. The locations are typically enclosed spaces, providing secrecy and high security, making it less likely to be noticed by third parties. The second highest occurrence probability is during the night, utilizing the cover of darkness known as the "dehumanization" phenomenon. A study analyzing 100 rape trial documents in Henan Province found that the majority of rape crimes occurred during the night, with 78% taking place between 6 p.m. and 6 a.m. The crimes predominantly occur in private residences (including those of the perpetrator and victim) and enclosed environments like hotel or motel rooms, accounting for 84% of cases. Perpetrators often have a lower level of education, with approximately 87% having lower educational backgrounds. Methods employed in sexual assault include violence, threats, enticement, deception, meeting victims through online social networks, exploiting guardianship or educational situations, and the use of alcohol and drugs.

2) Preventing Sexual Assault Criminal Behavior

① Avoid high-risk environments.

Entertainment venues like KTVs and bars, with large crowds, noisy environments, dim lighting, and alcohol consumption, easily stimulate criminal desires, increasing possibilities to crimes. For female college students, especially in campuses located in urban-rural transition areas, where

---

① 邵嘉. 论强奸犯罪的成因及防范对策：基于河南省 100 起样本分析 [J]. 商丘师范学院学报，2023，39(10):86-92.

而言，大多高校建立在城乡结合部，聚集着大量社会流动人口，夜间在校外游荡，极易被犯罪分子盯上陷入被害情境。为此，要按时就寝，避免在深夜独自出入相关场所。

（2）注意个人言行，减少被害的诱发性。

诱发性是指被害人的言行、状态容易使犯罪人实施犯罪行为的因素，对犯罪人起刺激作用。女性在着装上应尽量避免不必要的身体暴露，防止给潜在的犯罪人以刺激。在与异性交流和交往时，应把握尺度。同时，面对异性的试探，不要模棱两可，态度要坚决，避免给异性传递模糊信号。另外，女大学生要合理使用网络，谨慎交友，树立正确的交友观。

（3）不要轻信他人，提高安全意识。

大学生要树立正确的价值观，克服虚荣心。当下眼花缭乱的交友平台甚多，犯罪人会把自己包装人"高富帅"，通过花言巧语迎合女性的喜好。当建立信任后，则会实施进一步的犯罪行为，例如案例十。与在社交平台认识的异性会面，应尽量去熟悉的地方，不到陌生场所，尤其不要单独涉足野外无人的场合或空间死角，不喝不明饮料；不要将陌生人领

there's a concentration of transient populations, roaming outside during the night can make them easy targets for criminals. It is crucial to avoid wandering in secluded areas during late hours and adhere to regular sleeping schedules.

② Mind personal behavior to minimize provocation.

Provocation refers to the factors that make the words, actions, and state of the victim easily trigger the perpetrator to commit a criminal act, and have a stimulating effect on the perpetrator. In terms of clothing, they should try to avoid unnecessary physical exposure to avoid stimulating potential criminals. When communicating and interacting with others, one should grasp the scale and avoid excessive ambiguous behavior. At the same time, when facing the temptation of the opposite sex, do not be ambiguous, adopt a resolute attitude, and avoid sending blurry messages to the opposite sex. In addition, female college students should use the internet reasonably, be cautious in making friends, and establish a correct view of making friends.

③ Exercise caution, increase security awareness.

College students cultivating correct values and overcoming vanity is essential. With numerous friendship platforms, criminals may present themselves deceptively, catering to preferences to establish trust before committing crimes, as seen in Case 10. When meeting people from social platforms, choose familiar locations, avoid unfamiliar places, especially solitary ventures into remote areas or spaces with limited visibility. Avoid alcohol and unknown drinks. Refrain from bringing strangers to one's home or visiting unfamiliar homes late at night. Secure doors and windows during the night. Be cautious about nighttime visits from strangers and

至家中或深夜去不熟悉的异性家中拜访；夜间要关好门窗；深夜有陌生人来访时不要随意应门；不要随便搭乘陌生人的车；女性在夜间莫单独外出，尤其是经常上夜班回家的女性，应有伴同行，并随身携带自卫器具，不要图近而走偏僻陌巷或经过公园僻静的地方；不使用极少有人用的公厕。

（4）面临强暴行为，应呵声制止。

女性一旦被某些莫名其妙的招呼骚扰时，应该不予理睬或加以斥责；若对方还有进一步的身体动作，则应该大声加以斥责和呼救。在面临被害时，若消极抵抗、自我顺从、容忍，暴露出难以应对被害的心理弱势，往往会强化犯罪人犯罪动机，助长犯罪人的嚣张气焰。若喝斥无用，也应强烈反抗，使对方恢复理智。

【案例十　网络诱骗强奸案】2011 年 11 月，曹某利用微信结识了"90 后"女大学生小丽，在获取小丽信任后，两人约定见面。小丽见曹某条件不凡，便轻易信任。却遭到强奸。

二、非暴力犯罪预防

非暴力犯罪指未使用暴力手段的犯罪行为，如盗窃、诈骗、侵害知识产权、非法吸收公共财款等犯罪行为。非暴力犯罪的目标

refrain from opening the door casually. Avoid hitchhiking in unfamiliar vehicles. Women should avoid going out alone at night, especially those returning home late from night shifts, having companions and carrying self-defense tools, avoiding secluded alleys or quiet parks, and avoiding seldom-used public restrooms.

④ Confront assault.

When women are harassed by inexplicable greetings, they should ignore or reprimand them. If the other party makes further physical movements, they should loudly reprimand and protest. When facing victimization, if one passively resists, obeys, and tolerates, exposing a psychological weakness that is difficult to cope with, it often reinforces the criminal's motivation and promotes their arrogance. If drinking and scolding are useless, one should also strongly resist to restore the other person's rationality.

［**Case 10　Internet induced rape case**］ In November 2011, Cao met a female college student born in the 1990s named Xiaoli through WeChat. After gaining Xiaoli's trust, the two agreed to meet. Xiao Li easily trusted the perpetrator for he seemed rich and handsome, but then was raped.

2. Prevention of Non-violent Crimes

Non-violent crimes refer to criminal behaviors that do not involve the use of violence, such as theft, fraud, intellectual property theft, and illegal absorption of public funds. The non-violent crimes is the pursuit of property, but in the process of

是财物,但在获取财物的过程中则可能上升至暴力犯罪,如案例十一。为此,非暴力犯罪常与暴力犯罪交叉存在,如抢夺罪的目的是获取物质财产,而非对人身实施侵害,即犯罪行为上属于暴力犯罪,动机上属于非暴力犯罪。虽然非暴力犯罪对于公共安全的危害相对较轻,但防范意识仍要从财产安全上升至人身安全的高度。

【案例十一 阳光别墅杀人案】 2010 年 9 月 15 日,赵某潜入一别墅。在盗窃过程中被受害人胡某发现,双方发生了短暂打斗。赵某最终杀害了胡某在内共 4 人。

(一)防范盗窃

盗窃犯罪指以非法占有为目的,秘密窃取数额较大公私财物或多次窃取公私财物的行为。盗窃是传统类犯罪之一,是刑事案件中除诈骗外犯罪率最高的。根据是否与受害人有直接接触,可将盗窃犯罪可分为偷窃和扒窃。其中偷窃最常见的为入室盗窃。

根据不同的标准,盗窃的种类可作如下划分。根据盗窃物品种类,可分为一般财物盗窃、自行车盗窃、电动车盗窃、机动车盗窃、保险柜盗窃、珍贵文物盗窃、枪支弹药盗窃、信用卡盗窃,以及网游虚拟物品盗窃等。根据盗窃手法可分为"顺手牵羊"盗窃、调

obtaining the property, they may escalate to violent crimes, as Case 11. Therefore, non-violent crimes are not completely independent but interact with violent crimes, such as the crime of robbery aims at material property rather than personal injury, which is a violent crime in behavior but a non-violent crime in motivation. Although non-violent crimes pose a relatively lighter threat to public security, it is still necessary to elevate the importance of personal security alongside property security.

[Case 11　Sunshine villa murder case] On September 15, 2010, Zhao broke into a villa. During the theft, he was discovered by the victim, Hu, and a brief fight ensued. Zhao killed 4 people in the end.

(1) Prevention of Theft

Theft crimes refer to behaviors aimed at illegally possessing someone else's property through secretive removal of items of significant value from public or private premises, or through repeated stealing. Theft is one of the traditional types of crimes and, besides fraud, has the highest incidence rate in criminal cases. Depending on whether there is direct contact with the victim, theft crimes can be divided into larceny and pickpocketing, with larceny most commonly manifesting as burglary.

The types of theft can be categorized as follows: by the type of item stolen, such as general property theft, bicycle theft, electric vehicle theft, motor vehicle theft, safe theft, theft of valuable cultural relics, gunpowder and ammunition theft, credit card theft, and virtual item theft in online games; by the theft technique, such as grab-and-run theft, switch theft, bag snatching, slicing bags, pickpocketing, smashing vehicle theft, picking locks on safes, inside jobs, and cyber theft; by the

包盗窃、拎包盗窃、割包盗窃、扒窃、砸车盗窃、撬砸保险柜盗窃、网络盗窃，以及监守自盗等。根据盗窃的场所可分为公共场所盗窃、单位内部盗窃、家庭室内盗窃等。根据入室盗窃行为，可分为钻窗入室盗窃、撬门入室盗窃、技术开锁入室盗窃、挖墙翻墙入室盗窃、尾随入室盗窃、溜门入室盗窃、骗开房门入室盗窃等①。

1. 盗窃犯罪分析

不管是偷窃，还是扒窃，犯罪人的主要目的就是将他人财物占为己有。从众多盗窃案件的行为主体看，社会闲散、无业人员是盗窃案件的主要成员②。根据控制理论的阐释，该类群体缺少服从的利益相关性。从紧张理论角度论述，该类群体将自身经济拮据的原因归于社会的不公，自己付出了努力，但是无法获得理想的回报。从认知角度而言，盗窃类犯罪整体而言是理性犯罪，犯罪者意志力薄弱，无法摆脱大脑边缘系统的自然反应，即做贼心虚。从行为特征看。盗窃的典型特征除了侵占性外，还具有隐秘性。相较于其他刑事犯罪案件，盗窃的随机性和群体性更强，

location of the crime, such as public place theft, theft within an organization, and domestic interior theft; and by the method of entering the premises, such as window entry, door breaking, technical lock picking, wall climbing, following victims, door-slip entry, and deception to open doors.

1) Analysis of Theft Crimes

Whether it's larceny or pickpocketing, the thief's main goal is to take ownership of someone else's property. As for the perpetrators of many theft cases, socially unemployed or jobless individuals are the primary offenders. According to Control Theory, this group lacks the incentive to conform. From a Strain Theory perspective, they attribute their economic hardship to societal injustice, their efforts not being rewarded as they expect. Cognitively, theft crimes are generally rational, but the criminals have weak willpower and cannot overcome the natural response of the limbic system, which is to feel guilty when stealing. Behaviorally, in addition to possession, theft is characterized by its secrecy. Compared to other criminal cases, it has a higher randomness and group nature, mainly occurring in crowded and noisy areas where the target can be selected at any time.

---

① 刘宏斌. 当前我国盗窃犯罪的现状及治理 [J]. 中国人民公安大学学报 (社会科学版)，2011,27（4）: 118-112.

② 张应立，戴晶晶. 盗窃犯罪被害问题实证研究：以宁波市北仑区为例 [J]. 公安学刊 (浙江警察学院学报)，2021(2):86-95.

犯罪者主要是在人群杂乱、地段喧闹的场所蹲点，并根据时机选择作案对象。

为此，行为人在人多的情况下是不会行窃的，其作案必然选择隐秘的作案地点，并在无人的空隙时间实施盗窃。此外，目标具有准确性。犯罪行为人往往直接针对实施窃取的目标，如哪个有钱大学生或某贵重物品，了解其常放在什么地方、有没有锁在箱子中或柜子里、钥匙放在何处等。不动手便罢，一旦动手目标十分准确。

2. 盗窃犯罪预防

（1）识别危险场景。

扒窃是公共场所中较为常见的犯罪。盗窃多在隐秘场所进行，因此危险场景多集中在火车站、公交车上，以及节日时人员聚集场所。此类地点鱼龙混杂、目标易注意力分散，很容易遭窃。为此，在此类场景中应将物品包裹置于身前，而非身后。

（2）切勿心存侥幸，粗心大意。

侥幸心理促使人们认为盗窃违法行为发生在自己身上的概率很小，或容易处于性善论的角度，认为他人都是良好公民，不会发生此类事情。因此常常将财物随手放在暴露的公共区域，或在未锁车的情况下去寻拿其他物品。

（3）切勿懒惰，图方便。

人们出门时常常不反锁家门、

Therefore, the perpetrator will not steal in the presence of many people and will choose a location and time when unoccupied to commit the theft. Additionally, accuracy in targeting. The perpetrator often directly focuses on the specific target to steal, such as which college student has money or valuable items, where they are usually kept, whether they are locked in a box or a drawer, and where the keys are kept. If there is no immediate opportunity, they will wait, but once they act, the target is chosen with precision.

2) Prevention of Theft Crimes

① Identify high-risk scenarios.

Pickpocketing is a common crime in public places. Theft is usually carried out discreetly, so high-risk scenarios often occur at train stations, on buses, and in crowded places during festivals. These locations are characterized by a mix of people and diverted attention, making it easy to become a target. Therefore, it is advisable to keep valuables in front of you rather than behind you in these situations.

② Avoid overconfidence.

The psychology of overconfidence leads individuals to believe that the probability of being affected by theft is low, or from a perspective of moral innocence, they think that good citizens like themselves would not be involved in such incidents. Consequently, they often leave their belongings unattended in public areas or forget to lock their cars, making it convenient for thieves.

③ Avoid negligence for convenience.

Individuals often do not lock their doors when leaving

不关好门窗；门窗损毁或防盗设施损坏不及时修复；车门或电动车不锁。如果感觉非常麻烦而忽略细节，常常就会失窃。夜间休息与外出时，应关闭并锁住窗户，反锁房门，例如案例十二。

（4）加强安全措施，降低风险概率。

若自己的住所无警报、无监控、无街邻联防，或住在低层时，应加强窗户防盗，防止罪犯翻窗入室，"顺手牵羊"。

（5）降低好奇心。

盗窃还存在网上盗窃，即通过新奇的网页，吸引被害人；当受害人点击时，自己的私人信息被盗，从而导致网络游戏账号等有价值物品被盗。

（6）若被盗窃，不要激怒歹徒。

歹徒实施盗窃时往往已经处于紧张或激动的状态，激怒他们可能会导致他们采取更极端的行动，包括暴力伤害受害者。在此情况下，保持冷静和配合是最安全的选择。财物虽然重要，但远不及人身安全重要。激怒歹徒可能会让自己陷入危险的境地，甚至可能会危及生命。放弃财物而保全生命才是明智的选择。应保持冷静，尽可能多地记住歹徒的人体外貌特征细节，为后续警方破案提供线索。

the house, neglect to secure their windows and doors, or fail to repair damaged windows and doors or security measures. They may also consider it too troublesome to lock car doors or the electric bikes, which can lead to theft. It is important to lock and close windows and doors at night and when going out to reduce the risk of break-ins, as Case 12.

④ Strengthen security measures to reduce risk.

If your residence lacks alarms, surveillance, or neighborhood cooperation, or if you live on the ground floor, it is necessary to reinforce window guards to prevent window-entry burglaries and opportunistic theft.

⑤ Minimize curiosity.

Theft can also occur online through fishing websites that attract victims with intriguing content. When victims click on these links, their personal information is stolen, leading to the theft of valuable items such as online game accounts. Carelessness by residents, often forgetting to close doors and windows, can also lead to theft.

⑥ Do not provoke the thief.

If you become a victim of theft, avoid actions that may anger the perpetrator. When criminals commit theft, they are often already in a state of tension or excitement, which can anger them and lead them to take more extreme actions, including violent harm to the victim. In this situation, staying calm and cooperating is the safest option. Although property is important, it is far less important than personal security. Angering criminals may put oneself in a dangerous situation, and may even endanger one's life. Abandoning property and preserving life is a wise choice. Stay calm and remember more details about the criminal's physical appearance to provide clues for subsequent police investigations.

【案例十二　山西警察夫妇被害案】2010 年 11 月 10 日山西洪洞县警察夫妇被害案中，犯罪嫌疑人杀害两名被害人并实施抢劫。

（二）防范诈骗

诈骗是指以非法占有为目的，用虚构事实或者隐瞒真相的方法，骗取款额较大的公私财物的行为。不论是传统街头诈骗，还是集资、信用卡诈骗等现代犯罪形式，诈骗犯罪区别于抢劫、盗窃等犯罪行为的典型特征是犯罪人在犯罪过程中依靠自身的伪装能力，使被害人产生认知错误，主动将财物的某种处分权转移给自己。

1. 诈骗犯罪分析

从认知特征看，诈骗犯罪有以下特征。第一，犯罪人以中年群体为主。诈骗需要犯罪者具备使被害人产生信任感的能力，并能够虚构符合逻辑的故事，青年群体大多并不具备该能力。但由于电信网络诈骗信息化程度高，其犯罪者则以青年为主。第二，道德的自我谴责感弱。犯罪人会将非法所得归功于自己的"聪明才智"，或者如现在发达的电信诈骗，因不需要犯罪人与被害人面对面地交流，使其往往罪恶感低。第三，犯罪人深谙人性之道。犯罪人往往很了解人际交往中的社会心理，了解不同人具有的弱点，如对某些社会角色具有崇敬的心

[**Case 12　Police couple murdered in Shanxi Province**]

In the murder of a police couple in Hongdong County, Shanxi Province, on November 10, 2010, the suspect killed and robbed two victims.

(2) Prevention of Fraud

Fraud refers to the act of obtaining someone else's property by false pretenses or concealing the truth with the intention of illegal possession. Whether it's traditional street fraud or modern forms such as pyramid schemes, credit card fraud, the typical feature that distinguishes fraud from crimes like robbery and theft is that the criminal relies on their ability to disguise themselves, causing the victim to make a cognitive error and willingly transfer the right to dispose of the property to them.

1) Analysis of Fraud Crimes

Cognitively, fraud has the following Features. Firstly, fraudsters are primarily middle-aged individuals because fraud requires the ability to gain trust and fabricate logically consistent stories, which young individuals do not typically possess. However, telecommunications fraud, due to its high level of informatization, often targets the young. Secondly, fraudsters have a weak sense of moral self-condemnation, attributing their illegal gains to their own "intelligence" or the fact that telefraud often does not require face-to-face communication with the victim, leading to a lower sense of guilt. Thirdly, they have a deep understanding of human nature, knowing the social psychology of interpersonal relationships and the weaknesses of different individuals, such as the reverence for social roles and the desire for easy gains. Fourthly, they are personable in the presence of strangers, thus they are often extroverted, skilled in communication, enthusiastic, and good at hiding their emotions.

理、贪便宜等。第四，犯罪人在陌生人面前具有亲和力。犯罪人在性格方面往往较为外向，善于交际、为人热情，善于隐藏自己的情绪表现。

从行为特征看，诈骗犯罪有如下特征。第一，诈骗目标从随机到精准。传统电信诈骗往往通过"广撒网"的方式，随机性强。数据信息化的当下，各类新媒体平台都在不断收集用户的个人、社会信息及日常喜好，也为不法分子提供了可乘之机。诈骗集团会针对不同群体，根据非法获取的个人信息，量身定制诈骗剧本，实施精准诈骗。第二，集团性犯罪突出，作案人离散程度高。从当前我国侦破的多起电信网络诈骗案看，电信网络诈骗犯罪呈现职业化和集团化，内部有着严密的组织与分工。例如电影《孤注一掷》中提及的"千门八将"就是真实案例的缩影。诈骗集团紧跟社会热点，随时变化诈骗手法和"话术"，迷惑性强。此外，由于担心被"一锅端"，作案人员往往离散程度高，因此难以通过低层作案人员摸出其他作案人和集团内部的管理人员的线索。第三，作案手段多样，科技化程度愈来愈高。随着互联网及新媒体科技水平的更迭升级，电信网络诈骗的科技化程度也在不断提升，犯罪分子的科技素养显著提高，能

Behaviorally, fraud has the following features. Firstly, the targets of fraud range from random to precise. Traditional telefraud often involves "casting a wide net", with a high degree of randomness. In today's data-driven society, various new media platforms continuously collect users'personal, social information, and daily preferences, providing opportunities for criminals. Fraud groups tailor-make fraud scripts based on illegally obtained personal information to carry out precision fraud targeting different groups. Secondly, group crimes are prominent, with a high degree of dispersion among perpetrators. From the cases of telefraud solved in our country, telefraud crimes are becoming professionalized and grouped, with a strict organization and division of labor. For example, the "Notorious Eight" mentioned in the movie *No More Bets* is a reflection of real life. Fraud groups keep up with social hotspots and constantly change fraud methods and "scripts" , making them highly misleading. Additionally, due to the fear of being wiped out, perpetrators often have a high degree of dispersion, making it difficult to trace other perpetrators and the internal management of the group through low-level perpetrators. Thirdly, the means of committing the crime are diverse, with an increasing level of technification. With the upgrading of the Internet and new media technology, the level of high-tech fraud is also continuously improving, and the technical literacy of criminals has significantly increased, allowing them to skillfully use various hacking techniques, such as Trojan horse virus implantation, creation of phishing websites, theft of others'accounts, and establishment of illegal servers.

够熟练运用各种黑客技术，例如，木马病毒植入、钓鱼网站制作、盗取他人账号、搭建非法服务器等。

2. 常见诈骗类型与预防

2023 年公安部发布了刷单返利、虚假网络投资理财、虚假网络贷款、冒充电商物流客服、冒充公检法、虚假征信等 10 种高发电信网络诈骗犯罪类型，发案率占比 88.4%，其中刷单返利类诈骗发案率最高，约占发案率的 1/3；虚假网络投资理财诈骗造成的损失最大，占诈骗金额的 1/3 左右。本部分针对公安部发布的 10 种常见诈骗类型案件的作案手法及预防手段予以阐释，望提高警惕，切勿上当。

（1）刷单返利类诈骗。

作案手法：刷单返利诈骗通过各类网络平台和渠道发布招聘启事，任务通常包括刷单、点赞等。诈骗者先将受害人拉入群聊，发布任务并支付小额佣金。随后，安排"托"发布获得高额佣金的截图，利用"充值越多、抢单越多、返利越多"的诱惑条件，让受害人逐步陷入圈套。

预防措施：刷单本身就是违法行为，切勿被蝇头小利所诱惑。

（2）虚假网络投资理财类诈骗。

作案手法：虚假网络投资理

2) Common Types of Fraud and Prevention

In 2023, the Ministry of Public Security released 10 common types of fraud crimes, including tasks such as click farming, false online investment and financing, false online loans, impersonating e-commerce logistics customer service, posing as public security or procuratorial organs, and false credit reporting. These types of cases account for 88.4% of the incidence rate, with click farming frauds being the most common, accounting for 1/3 of the incidence rate, and false online investment and financing frauds causing the largest losses, accounting for about 1/3 of the fraud amount. This section explains the modus operandi and preventive measures for the 10 common types of fraud cases released by the Ministry of Public Security, in the hope of raising everyone's awareness and vigilance and preventing them from falling victim.

① Fraud of click farming.

Modus operandi: Fraud of click farming offers rebates. Recruitment tips are posted through various online platforms and channels, and tasks usually include click farming, liking, etc. The fraudster first pulls the victim into a group chat, posts a task, and pays a small commission. Subsequently, they arrange for the release of screenshots of high commissions, using the temptation of "more recharge, more grabbing orders, and more rebates" to gradually trap the victims.

Preventive measures: click farming is illegal, do not be tempted by petty gains.

② False online investment and financing fraud.

Modus operandi: False online investment and financial

财诈骗通过网络各媒体平台发布推送消息。受害人由于有投资需求，被诈骗者拉入所谓的投资群聊。诈骗者自称为"投资导师"，通过发送虚假成功投资信息或免费投资直播课等方式，骗取受害人的信任。此外，诈骗者还会通过婚恋交友平台与受害人建立暧昧关系，取得信任后，再以有特殊资源、少投入高回报等理由，诱骗受害人在虚假平台开设账户进行投资。受害人初期投入小额资金会获得回报，但在追加投资后，却发现无法提现。受害人群多为具有一定收入和资产的单身人士或热衷于投资、炒股的群体。

预防措施：凡是标榜稳定高额回报、内部消息的网络理财都是诈骗，切勿相信。

（3）虚假网络贷款类诈骗。

诈骗手法：诈骗人通过电话、短信，以及各类社交软件发布办理贷款、信用卡及提额套现等虚假广告，谎称贷款"无抵押、免征信、快速放贷"，引诱受害人下载虚假贷款 App 或登入虚假网站。然后，以贷款需先缴纳"手续费"或"保证金"，或者"刷流水"为理由，诱骗受害人支付各类费用。诈骗分子收到费用后，便会关闭虚假 App 并将受害人"拉黑"。

预防措施：任何贷款需求应通过正规渠道，切勿通过网络贷

fraud, which involves publishing notifications through various media platforms on the internet. The victim, due to their investment needs, was pulled into a so-called investment group chat by the fraudster. The fraudster claims to be an investment mentor and uses methods such as sending false successful investment information or free investment live classes to gain the trust of the victim. In addition, fraudsters may establish ambiguous relationships with victims through marriage and dating platforms, gain trust, and then use reasons such as having special resources, low investment and high returns to lure victims into opening accounts on fake platforms for investment. The victim initially receives returns by investing small amounts of funds, but after making additional investments, they find it impossible to withdraw. The victims are mostly single individuals with a certain income and assets, or groups who are enthusiastic about investing and trading stocks.

Preventive measures: Any online financial management that claims stable high returns and internal information is considered fraud, do not believe it.

③ False online loan scams.

Modus operandi: Perpetrators deceive individuals through phone calls, text messages, and various social media platforms by posting false advertisements for loan processing, credit cards, and cash advances, claiming loans are "unsecured, credit check-free, rapid". They lure victims to download fake loan apps or access bogus websites. Then, under the pretext of requiring fees like "processing fees" or "security deposits" or "transaction flow", they trick victims into paying various charges. After receiving the fees, scammers shut down the fake app and block the victim.

Preventive Measures: All loan requests should go through legitimate channels; avoid online loan methods. When

款手段。当得知需缴纳会员费、保证金或刷流水时，应立即终止行为。

（4）冒充电商物流客服类诈骗。

作案手法：冒充电商平台或物流快递公司，谎称受害人网购的商品出现质量问题，或售卖的商品因违规被下架，以"理赔退款"或"重新激活店铺"为由，要求受害人缴费，诱导其提供银行卡号和手机验证码等信息。他们还可能声称误将受害人升级为会员、授权为代理、开通商业分期业务等，威胁如果不取消上述业务将产生额外扣费；或者表示如果不订购"保证金""假一赔三"等服务将无法"理赔退款"或"重新激活店铺"，诱导受害人支付费用。此外，还会以受害人在电商平台的会员积分或信用积分不足为由，要求受害人申请贷款以提高积分，并诱骗其将贷款汇入指定账户。

预防措施：正当商家退货无需支付任何额外费用。切勿点击陌生链接，不要随意填写银行卡密码或短信验证码，更不要根据对方指示开启屏幕共享。

（5）冒充公检法类诈骗。

作案手法：通过非法渠道获取受害人的个人身份信息，冒充

asked to pay membership fees, deposits, or transaction flows, terminate the process immediately.

④ Impersonation of e-commerce logistics customer service scams.

Modus operandi: By impersonating an e-commerce platform or logistics courier company, falsely claiming that the victim's online shopping products have quality problems, or the products sold have been taken down due to violations, criminals demand the victim to pay fees and induce them to provide bank card and mobile verification code information under the pretext of "claims refund" or "reactivating the store". They may also claim that the victim was mistakenly upgraded to a VIP member, authorized as an agent, or engaged in commercial installment services, threatening to incur additional deductions if the aforementioned services are not cancelled; or it can be stated that if services such as "deposit" and "fake one compensation three" are not ordered, it will be impossible to "claim refunds" or "reactivate the store", inducing victims to pay fees. In addition, claiming that the victim's membership or credit points on the e-commerce platform are insufficient, the victim is required to apply for a loan to increase their points, and is deceived into transferring the loan to a designated account.

Preventive measures: Legitimate merchants do not need any fees for returns. Do not click on unfamiliar links, do not fill in bank card passwords or SMS verification codes casually, and do not turn on screen sharing according to the instructions of the other party.

⑤ Impersonation of public security and judicial authorities scams.

Modus operandi: Obtaining victims' personal information through illegal means, scammers impersonate

公检法机关工作人员,通过电话、微信、QQ 等与受害人取得联系,要求受害人配合工作。以受害人涉嫌洗钱、非法出入境、快递藏毒、护照有问题等罪名为由进行威逼、恐吓,要求配合调查并严格保密,同时向受害人展示虚假通缉令,财产冻结书等法律文书以增加可信度。

以帮助受害人洗脱罪名为由,诱导受害人到宾馆等独立封闭空间,阻断与外界联系,进而要求受害人配合调查或接受监控,将名下所有资金转至"安全账户";或要求其下载指定 App,引诱受害人从正规贷款平台借款转出,达到诈骗金额最大化的目的。

预防措施:公检法机关不会通过电话或网络办案,也不存在所谓的"安全账户"。要求转账的行为就是诈骗。如遇自称公检法人员主动联系,应及时与当地相关部门核实。

（6）虚假征信类诈骗。

作案手法:冒充银行、中国银行保险监督管理委员会工作人员或网络贷款平台工作人员,与受害人建立联系。犯罪人谎称受害人之前开通过校园贷、助学贷等账号未及时注销,需要注销相关账号;或谎称受害人信用卡、花呗、借呗等信用支付类工具存在不良记录,需要消除相关记录,

law enforcement personnel, contacting victims via phone, WeChat, QQ, etc., claiming the victim is involved in money laundering or illegal activities. Threatening and coercing victims to cooperate in investigations, they display fake arrest warrants and freeze orders to enhance credibility.

Pretending to help clear the victim's name, they isolate the victim in closed spaces, urging them to transfer funds or download specific apps, maximizing the scam amount.

Preventive measures: Public security, procuratorial and judicial organs will not handle cases through telephone or internet, and there are no "security accounts". The act of requesting a transfer is fraud. If a person claiming to be a public security, procuratorial, or judicial officer proactively contacts, they should promptly verify with the relevant local department.

⑥ False credit-related scams.

Modus operandi: Pretending to be bank or financial regulatory staff, scammers contact victims, alleging that accounts from previous loans need closure or that the victim has negative records affecting their credit. They induce victims to apply for loans on legitimate platforms, transferring funds to specified accounts under the guise of eliminating adverse credit records.

否则会影响个人征信；以消除不良征信记录、验证流水等为由，诱导受害人在正规网络贷款平台或互联网金融 App 进行贷款，并转到其指定的账户，从而诈骗钱财。

预防措施：凡是声称需要消除"校园贷"记录或升级学生账户，威胁会影响征信，并要求转账或"刷流水"的，都是诈骗。如对个人征信有疑问，应通过官方渠道咨询，切勿轻信陌生来电。

（7）虚假购物、服务类诈骗。

作案手法：在微信朋友圈、网购平台或其他网站发布低价打折、海外代购、"0 元"购物等诱人广告，或者提供论文代写、私家侦探、跟踪定位等特殊服务的广告。一旦与受害人取得联系，犯罪人将诱导其通过微信、QQ 或其他社交软件添加好友进行商议，并以私下交易可节省手续费或更便捷为理由，要求受害人进行私下转账。受害人一旦付款，犯罪分子会以缴纳关税、定金、交易税、手续费等为由，继续诱骗受害人转账汇款，完成后将受害人拉黑。

预防措施：购物或购买服务时，一定要选择正规的渠道，避免使用代购等私下交易方式，因为此交易方式存在较大风险。在社交平台上进行交易时，务必详细了解商家的真实信息，并在交易时选择官方认可的正规平台。

Preventive measures: Any claim that it is necessary to eliminate "campus loan" records or upgrade student accounts, otherwise it will affect credit reporting and require transfer or transaction flow, is considered fraud. If you have any questions about personal credit reporting, you should consult through official channels and do not trust unfamiliar calls.

⑦ False shopping and service scams.

Modus operandi: Posting tempting advertisements such as low-price discounts, overseas purchasing, and "zero-yuan" shopping on WeChat Moments, online shopping platforms, or other websites, or providing special services such as essay writing, private detective, and tracking and positioning. Once in contact with the victim, criminals induce them to add friends through WeChat, QQ, or other social media platforms for discussion, and request the victim to make a private transfer on the grounds that private transactions can save transaction fees or be more convenient. Once the victim makes the payment, the criminals will continue to lure the victim into transferring money under the pretext of paying tariffs, deposits, transaction taxes, handling fees, etc. After completion, they will blackmail the victim.

Preventive measures: When shopping or purchasing services, it is important to choose legitimate channels and avoid using private transaction methods such as purchasing agents, as this type of transaction carries significant risks. When conducting transactions on social media platforms, it is important to have a detailed understanding of the true information of the merchant and choose an officially

（8）冒充领导、熟人类诈骗。

作案手法：诈骗分子采用多种手段，包括使用受害人领导、熟人、子女或老师的照片和姓名来伪装社交账号，向受害人发送添加好友请求，或将其拉入特定群聊，甚至潜入受害人所在的群聊。他们会以领导、熟人的身份对受害人进行虚情假意的问候，模仿领导或老师的语气，以此获取受害人的信任。当冒充领导时，诈骗分子常以有事不便出面或不方便接电话为理由要求受害人代为转账，并发送虚假转账截图以假装已完成转账。接着，他们会催促受害人尽快向指定账户转账。在冒充企业领导或老师时，犯罪人也会模仿相应身份的语气，向受害人发出转账或缴纳费用的指令，并以时间紧迫或机会难得等为理由，督促受害人尽快行动。

预防措施：当遇到自称为领导或熟人要求转账时，务必保持警惕。在确认对方身份之前，绝对不要轻易转账。

（9）网络游戏产品虚假交易类诈骗。

作案手法：在社交、游戏平台发布买卖网络游戏账号、道具、点卡的广告，免费或低价获取游戏道具、参加抽奖活动资格等相关信息。以在其他平台交易或私下

recognized and legitimate platform during the transaction.

⑧ Impersonation of leaders and acquaintances scams.

Modus operandi: Scammers use various means, including using photos and names of the victim's leader, acquaintances, or children's teachers to disguise their social accounts, sending requests to add friends to the victim, or pulling them into specific group chats, and even sneaking into the victim's group chat. They will offer sincere greetings to the victim as leaders or acquaintances, imitating the tone of the leader or teacher, in order to gain the victim's trust. When impersonating a leader, fraudsters often request the victim to transfer money on their behalf, citing reasons such as inconvenience in answering phone calls, and send false transfer screenshots to pretend that the transfer has been completed. Next, they will urge the victim to transfer funds to the designated account as soon as possible. When impersonating corporate leaders or teachers, they will also imitate the tone of their corresponding identity, issue instructions to the victim to transfer funds or pay fees, and use reasons such as time constraints or rare opportunities to urge the victim to take action as soon as possible.

Preventive measures: When encountering self-proclaimed leaders or acquaintances who request a transfer, be vigilant. Never transfer money easily before confirming the other party's identity.

⑨ False trading of online game products scams.

Modus operandi: Posting advertisements on social and gaming platforms for buying and selling online game accounts, props, and point cards, obtaining game props at low prices or for free, and participating in lottery activities. Inducing victims to bypass legitimate third-party platforms or requiring

交易更便宜、更方便为由，诱导受害人绕过正规的第三方平台，或者要求受害人添加所谓的客服账号参加抽奖活动。以受害人操作失误、等级不够为由，要求受害人支付"注册费""解冻费""会员费"等费用，随后将受害人拉黑。

预防措施：在购买游戏账号和装备时，务必选择正规的官方渠道，而不轻信陌生网友。要提高警惕，对于"低价充值、高价回收账号"等宣传要格外警惕，其很可能是诈骗。

（10）婚恋、交友类诈骗。

作案手法：诈骗分子首先通过网络收集大量"白富美"和"高富帅"的自拍及生活照，其次根据预先设计的剧本打造不同的虚假身份。这些身份被发布在婚恋和交友网站上，以吸引潜在受害者。建立联系后，诈骗分子通过照片和预先设计的个人经历，丰富其虚假身份以获取受害人的信任，并与其建立恋爱关系。在取得信任后，诈骗分子会以遭遇变故急需用钱或维持恋爱关系为由，向受害人索要钱财。他们会根据受害人的财力情况不断变化借口，要求转账，直到受害人发觉被骗或无力继续转账为止。

预防措施：网络交友存在风险。打着"恋爱"和"交友"的旗号要求你转账的多数情况都是诈骗。要时刻保持警惕，不轻易相信。

them to add so-called customer service accounts to participate in lottery activities, citing that trading on other platforms or privately is cheaper and more convenient. Fraudsters commit the crimes by requesting victims to pay so-called "registration fees", "unfreezing fees", "membership fees", and other fees on the grounds of manipulating food and not having enough grade, and then blacklisting the victims.

Preventive measures: When purchasing game accounts and equipment, be sure to choose legitimate official channels instead of trusting unfamiliar netizens. Be vigilant, especially when it comes to advertising such as "low-price recharge and high-price account recycling", as it may be fraudulent.

⑩ Romance and dating scams.

Modus operandi: Scammers first collect a large number of selfies and life photos of "bai fumei" and "gao fushuai" (the beautiful rich women and the handsome rich men) through the internet, and create different false identities based on pre designed scripts. These identities are posted on marriage and dating websites to attract potential victims. After establishing contact, fraudsters enrich their false identities through photos and pre-designed personal experiences to gain the trust of victims and establish romantic relationships with them. After gaining trust, fraudsters will demand money from victims on the grounds of urgently needing money or maintaining a romantic relationship due to unforeseen circumstances. They will constantly use excuses based on the victim's financial situation to request a transfer until the victim realizes they have been deceived or unable to continue the transfer.

Preventive measures: There are risks in online dating. In most cases, asking you to transfer money under the banner of "relationship" and "making friends" is a scam. Always remain vigilant and not easily believe.

思考三

1. 犯罪的归因都包括哪些?

2. 越轨行为的主要源头是什么,受哪些因素影响?

3. 人们受到挫折就一定会攻击吗?

4. 凶杀和故意伤害的预防措施有何不同?

5. 抢劫包括哪些情况,应如何应对?

6. 针对个人而言,我们应注意哪些行为,以防止强暴?

7. 生活中,容易受到诈骗的行为有哪些?

Reflection 3

1.What are the attributions of crimes?

2.What are the main sources of deviant behaviors and what are the factors influencing them?

3.Do people always attack when they encounter setbacks?

4.What are the differences in preventive measures between murder and intentional injury?

5.What are the scenarios of robbery? How do we deal with them?

6.What behaviors should we pay attention to to prevent rape?

7.What are the behaviors that are prone to fraud in daily life?

第三章微课视频

第四章
智　斗

Chapter 4
Smart Battle

智斗是指在紧急情况下，能够足智多谋地与敌人斡旋，凭借各类策略机智脱身，而非格斗的方式。本章主要介绍一般的智斗过程中脱身的原则和较为可行的模式。

Smart battle refers to the ability to cleverly mediate with the enemy in emergency situations, relying on various strategies and wit to escape, rather than engaging in combat. This chapter mainly introduces the principles and feasible models of detachment in general intellectual battles.

第一节
急智脱身

Section 1
Quick Release

一、应付歹徒和攻击的急智原则

1. The Principle of Quick Release in Dealing with Criminals and Attacks

遭到歹徒攻击时，临场思考出万全之策并非易事。一是对歹徒的底细、动机、目的都不甚了解。二是缺少思考时间，有时需在几秒钟内就做出重大决策，是对个人反应能力的极高考验。换个角度思考，许多公司在信息齐全、"智囊团"傍身的前提下，做出重大决策时也需长时间的头脑风暴，且无法保证决策的正确性。而既无信息又无时间的个人在生命遭遇危机的情况下，如何能想

It is not easy to think of a foolproof solution on the spot when attacked by criminals. One is a lack of understanding of the criminal's background, motivation, and purpose, and the other is a lack of thinking time, sometimes requiring significant decisions to be made within a few seconds, which is an extreme personal test to reaction. Looking at it from a different perspective, a company, with complete information and a think tank nearby, also requires long-term brainstorming when making major decisions, and cannot guarantee the correctness of the decisions. How can self-defenders come up with a foolproof solution when facing a personal life crisis with neither information nor time? Therefore, the probability

出万全之策呢？因而在遭到攻击时，自卫者安全脱身的概率很难预测，通常只能依靠运气和即时的反应尽量保护自己。

美国专家沃尔德1994年提出了一套在遭受攻击时的决策模式：

（1）避开强于现场退让；

（2）现场退让强于受伤；

（3）受伤强于变成残废；

（4）变成残废强于杀人；

（5）杀人强于被人杀害。

沃尔德的模式列出了决策的轻重缓急，建议选伤害轻者而为之。这一模式对帮助人们在遭受攻击时，作决策很有启迪。

沃尔德还提出了应付歹徒攻击的七步模式：

（1）能谈则谈；

（2）道歉撤出；

（3）引旁人注意以求帮助；

（4）尖声喊叫或逃走；

（5）如被困住，只有在歹徒真正攻击时才可以反抗；

（6）在面对抢劫时，不要反抗；

（7）如你感到不管怎么做都会被严重伤害时，立即攻击歹徒。

此七步虽不系统，但尚可作为现场应付歹徒的指导原则，但对第五步则需再次考量。如若让歹徒先动手，则自卫者必败无疑。伯汝沃此点的提出是基于法律方面的考量，而非实战方面。

of self-defender escaping safely when attacked is difficult to predict.

In 1994, American expert Wald proposed a decision-making model when under attack:

① Avoidance is better than on-site concession;

② Giving way on site is better than getting injured;

③ It is better to be injured than to become disabled;

④ Becoming disabled is better than killing someone;

⑤ Killing is better than being killed by someone else.

Wald's model lists the importance and urgency of decision-making, and suggests that people choose the one with less harm, which is very enlightening for helping people make decisions when under attack.

Wald proposed a seven-step model for dealing with criminal attacks:

① If you can talk, talk;

② Apologize and withdraw;

③ Attract the attention of others for help;

④ Scream or run away;

⑤ If trapped, one can only resist when the criminals truly attack;

⑥ When facing robbery, do not resist;

⑦ If you feel that no matter what you do, you will be seriously injured, immediately attack the criminal.

Although these seven steps are not systematic, they can still serve as guiding principles for dealing with criminals on site, but the fifth step needs further discussion. If the criminals were to take action first, the self-defense would undoubtedly be defeated. Wald considers the issue from a legal perspective rather than from a practical perspective at this point.

二、临场对付歹徒的常见模式

下面讨论的智能型措施（与格斗相对应），旨在帮助学生在遭到歹徒攻击时避免直接对抗，而保护自己的生命安全。这些措施来自于一些真实案例，被一些自卫者成功地使用过，并被自卫防身学所推荐。但没有一项急智措施能百分之百地保证自卫者能安全脱身，因为每个自卫者所遇到的情况都不尽相同。自卫者应根据自己的情况和环境灵活运用。

急智脱身措施的最大好处是不需要实质性的格斗，因此格斗受伤的可能性较低。另外，由于自卫者不用武力抵抗，歹徒亦有可能降低其攻击的暴力程度。然而，这些措施亦有其共同的最大缺点，即不管自卫者采取何种智能型措施，如妥协、舌战（言语交流）等等，最终决定权仍掌握在歹徒手中，自卫者对现场及结果没有丝毫控制权。因此在采用这些措施的同时，自卫者必须做好随时格斗的准备。在下文的讨论中，不同的急智措施将以不同的模式呈现，以帮助学生理解和应用这些措施。

（一）走为上策——兔子模式

兔子模式，即"三十六计，走为上策"，这一军事原则同样适用于安全自卫。在遭遇歹徒攻击时，选择转身逃走有诸多好处。

2. Common Patterns of Dealing with Criminals on the Spot

The intelligent measures discussed below (opposite to combat) aim to help students avoid direct confrontation when attacked by criminals and protect their own lives. These measures come from some real-life cases, have been successfully used by some self-defenders, and have been recommended by self-defense studies. But there is no one urgent measure that can guarantee 100% security for self-defense, because the situations encountered by each self-defender are not the same. Self-defenders should use it flexibly according to their own situation and environment.

The biggest benefit of quick release measures is that there is no need for substantial combat, so the likelihood of injury during combat is lower. In addition, as self-defenders do not use force to resist, criminals may also reduce the level of violence in their attacks. However, these measures also have their common biggest drawback, which is that regardless of the intelligent measures taken by the self-defense, such as compromise, verbal communication, etc., the final decision is still in the hands of the criminals, whether to let you go or attack you, and the self-defender has no control over the scene and the outcome. Therefore, while adopting these measures, self-defenders must be prepared to engage in combat at any time. In the following discussion, different urgent measures will be presented in different modes to help students understand and apply these measures.

(1) The Best Strategy is to Go—Rabbit Mode

"Thirty six strategies, walking away is the best strategy." This military principle also applies to security and self-defense. Turning around and running away when attacked by criminals has many benefits. One is that it is easy to do and

一是较为简单可行，不需要任何专门技术。二是避免了如采用格斗而可能造成的伤害，同时也避免了留在现场而受歹徒摆布的危险局面。三是可以立即将危险甩掉，因为歹徒一般不愿在容易被人看到的情况下追杀自卫者。此模式的安全性、实用性较高，所以被广泛推荐。但兔子模式亦有其局限性，一是在很多情况下自卫者被堵在屋内或被抓住、捆住而无路可逃。二是因穿戴不当、跑得不快或缺乏耐力而不易脱逃。三是有的受害者被吓得双腿发软，失去逃跑能力。

自卫者在遇到以下情况时，可考虑采用兔子模式。第一是当歹徒身材与力量占明显优势、持刀枪或团伙攻击时，自卫者应毫不犹豫地跑掉。第二是当歹徒威逼自卫者去僻静之处时，自卫者应以"走为上"。第三是在歹徒还未下手之际。第四是自卫者对其他急智措施或格斗没有信心和把握，而奔跑能力较强时。

兔子模式在实际应用上可以有很多变化。自卫者可以一见歹徒转身就立即逃跑，什么都不要了，歹徒往往会因为没料到这一招而愣神，进而失去攻击机会；自卫者还可以先大声呼喊一个假名字，如"李强，我在这儿"，同

does not require any technology. The second is that escaping avoids the potential harm caused by fighting, and also avoids the dangerous situation of staying at the scene and being manipulated by criminals. The third is to immediately shake off the danger when escaping. Criminals generally do not want to pursue self-defenders in situations where they are easily visible. This mode has high security and practicality, so it is widely recommended. But the rabbit mode also has its limitations. Firstly, in many cases, the self-defender is blocked inside the house or caught and tied up without a way to escape. Secondly, improper wearing, slow running, or lack of endurance make it difficult to escape. Thirdly, sometimes the victim is frightened and their legs become weak, losing their ability to escape.

Self-defenders may consider using rabbit mode when encountering the following situations. Firstly, when the criminals have a significant advantage in physical strength, wielding knives and guns, or engaging in gang attacks, the self-defender should run away without hesitation. Secondly, when criminals threaten the self-defender to go to secluded places, the self-defender should prioritize escaping. Thirdly, when the criminals have not yet taken action, or when they are in combat or using quick witted measures to create opportunities for escape. Fourthly, when the self-defender lacks confidence and confidence in other urgent measures or combat, but has strong running ability.

The rabbit mode can have many changes in practical applications, such as running away at the sight of the criminal, turning around and not wanting anything. The criminal often becomes stunned by this move and loses the opportunity to attack. The defender can also shout a fake name for help like "Li Qiang, I am here" first and run away quickly, so that the criminals will feel that the defender has companions and dare

时疾速逃跑，这样歹徒会感到自卫者有同伴而不敢尾随。专家们还推荐在遭遇抢劫时，不要把钱交到歹徒手里而是"掉"在地上或一边，同时向反方向逃走，并高声呼救，歹徒一般都会抢钱跑掉。这一招亦称"蜥蜴模式"，由蜥蜴在受到攻击时使用的断尾蒙骗之计而来。另一种更富有攻击性的逃跑方式是先朝歹徒背后大喊一声"警察快来"，趁歹徒心虚转身、分神之际踢打其裆部等弱处，然后逃走。此招受到章鱼遇险时释放烟雾以逃脱启发，亦称"章鱼模式"。

（二）妥协服从——病人模式

病人模式指自卫者完全听命于歹徒而不作任何反抗，以求歹徒不会用更严重的暴力，进而在其达到目的后放过自卫者，或希望歹徒因此而松懈下来，从而为自卫者创造使用其他策略的良机。该名称之由来是病人在医生面前从来都是服从状态，因此命名"病人模式"。

妥协服从的好处有如下几点。第一，不会激怒歹徒，使歹徒感到受害者不会反抗，因而无需增加其使用暴力的程度。第二，歹徒会感到自己掌控了局势，让自卫者只能被动接受摆布，因而放松警惕，使自卫者有机可乘。第三，自卫者可利用妥协服从推迟歹徒下手的时间，以寻找其他

not follow. Experts also recommend that when facing robbery, do not hand over money to criminals but instead "drop" it to the ground or one side, while running in the opposite direction and shouting for help. Generally, criminals will grab the money and run away. This move, also known as the "lizard mode", is derived from the trick of a lizard cutting off its tail to deceive when attacked. Another more aggressive way of escaping is to shout "Police, come quickly" from behind the criminal, turn around to see what's going on, and then kick and hit the weak areas such as the crotch while the criminal is feeling guilty, and then run away. This move imitates the octopus's method of escaping by emitting smoke, also known as the "octopus mode".

(2) Compromise and Obedience—Patient Mode

The patient mode refers to the situation where the self-defender completely obeys the orders of the criminals without any resistance, in order to prevent them from using more severe violence and to spare the self-defender after achieving their goals, or to hope that the self-defender will relax as a result, thereby creating a good opportunity for the self-defender to use other strategies. The name comes from the fact that patients are always in a submissive state in front of doctors, hence the name "patient mode".

The benefits of compromise and obedience are as follow. Firstly, they will not provoke the criminals and make them feel that the victims will not resist, so there is no need to increase their level of violence. Secondly, criminals will feel that they have taken control of the situation and relax their vigilance, allowing self-defender to take advantage of it. Thirdly, self-defenders can use compromise and obedience to delay the time when criminals take action, in order to seek other opportunities. But this method also has its limitations. The first

机会。但此方法也有其局限性。第一，自卫者使用此计时，对局势没有任何主动权，只能受歹徒摆布。一旦歹徒无论如何也不放过自卫者，还需另做脱身打算，但时间可能也来不及了。第二，歹徒可能会利用大多数受害者"听话就能保命"的心理，而把自卫者逐步引入圈套。当自卫者发现自己被捆绑，失去了最后的反抗机会，而歹徒又欲行凶时，则只能任人宰割。

　　应用此办法对付歹徒有两种时机。第一，当自卫者没有机会反抗或逃脱，并且拒绝服从歹徒会立即使生命处于危险时，自卫者不得不使用此策略。如自卫者被抓住捆牢、或刀枪顶腹、或歹徒已经杀害不服从的其他自卫者。第二，自卫者主动应用此计以平稳歹徒情绪和解除即刻的生命危险，然后伺机逃走或格斗。有很多自卫者使用过此措施，但没有研究表明此办法的应用效果如何。案例研究发现，有的受害者安全无事，而有的则仍被杀害。由于歹徒的动机及案件的具体情况不同，受害者使用此计安全脱身的概率是无法预料的。

　　使用此计的最重要原则是建立妥协服从的底线，即在什么程度上可以妥协服从，而在什么情况下不能继续再妥协服从，必须逃走或反抗。如果自卫者认为继

is that the self-defender uses this timing to defend themselves. The defender has no initiative in the situation and can only be manipulated by the criminals. And once the criminals do not spare the victims in any way, they need to make other plans, but time may not be enough. The second possibility is that criminals may take advantage of the mentality that most self-defenders can save their lives by being obedient, leading them step by step into a trap. When the self-defender finds themselves tied up and loses the last chance to resist, and the perpetrator intends to commit the crime, the self-defender can only be slaughtered.

　　There are two opportunities to apply this method to deal with criminals. The first is when the victim does not have the opportunity to resist or escape, and disobeying the perpetrator immediately puts their life in danger, the self-defender has to use this method. For example, if the self-defender is caught and tied tightly, or if the perpetrator has already killed other disobedient victims, this is a passive application. The second type is for self-defender to actively apply this strategy to calm the emotions of the criminals and relieve immediate life-threatening situations, and then wait for an opportunity to escape or engage in combat. Many self-defenders have used this measure, but there is no research indicating the effectiveness of its application. Case studies have found that some self-defenders are safe and unharmed, while others are still killed. Due to the different motivations of the criminals and the specific circumstances of the case, the probability of the self-defender using this method to safely escape is unpredictable.

　　The most important principle of using this strategy is to establish a bottom line of compromise and obedience. To what extent can one compromise and obey, and under what circumstances can one no longer compromise and obey, and must flee or resist. If the self-defender believes that continuing

续妥协听命会使他们丧失最后的反抗机会,如被捆绑起来或带到僻静无人之处时,则应当机立断、改变策略,即便是有生命危险也必须奋力反抗或逃走。

（三）舌战——推销员模式

一名优秀的推销员一般都会用出色的口才让顾客心动、下单。人们在面对强壮歹徒、面对枪口刀尖而不能逃跑时,或身体赢弱且无技术、无信心格斗反抗时,往往会试图采用推销员模式。其目的是使歹徒改变初衷、或让歹徒心软而不加害于自己、或拖延时间寻找其他机会。

此模式的好处有如下几点。第一,不像格斗或逃跑那样容易激怒歹徒,从而可减少歹徒采取更严厉手段的可能性。第二,在某些情况下,如歹徒良心未泯,该模式能使歹徒产生同情心理而不使用暴力。第三,在与歹徒交谈时发现可利用的信息,以制定对策寻找脱身的机会。然而,此模式也有局限性。一是自卫者可能根本没有开口机会。二是由于惊吓,受害者脑子一片空白,已想好的措辞无法表达出来。第三,无论自卫者如何努力说服,仍无法改变歹徒的加害之意,因为多数歹徒都没有同情心,他们常常对自卫者的乞求不屑一顾。因此,此计效果难料。

此模式的具体运用方式有多

to compromise and obey will cause them to lose their last chance of resistance, such as being bound or taken to a secluded place, they should make a decisive decision, change their strategy, and even if their life is in danger, they must fight back or escape with all their might.

(3)Tongue Battle—Salesman Mode

Salespeople usually use sweet words to attract customers. People often try to use the mode when facing strong criminals, or when they cannot escape when facing the tip of a gun or knife, or when they are physically weak and have no skills or confidence to fight and resist. Its purpose is to change the original intention of the criminals, or to soften their hearts without harming the victims, or to delay time in seeking other opportunities.

The advantages of this mode include the following ones. Firstly, it is not as easy to provoke criminals as fighting or running away, thus reducing the possibility of criminals taking more severe measures. Secondly, in certain situations, such as when the perpetrator is not extremely vicious, insane, or has a strong conscience, it can cause the perpetrator to develop sympathy and not use violence. Thirdly, when conversing with criminals, discover available information to formulate countermeasures or seek opportunities for escape. However, this mode also has limitations. Firstly, the self-defender may not have had the opportunity to speak up at all, and secondly, due to shock, the self-defender's mind is blank and the measures they have already planned cannot be expressed. Thirdly, no matter how hard the victim tries to persuade, they still cannot change the perpetrator's intention of harm, because most criminals lack empathy and often disregard the self-defender's requests. Therefore, the effect of this plan is unpredictable.

There are various specific ways to apply this method.

种。第一种是谈判式，如自卫者同意交出更多藏起的钱财以换取生命安全，或保证不透露歹徒长相、不报警，以免歹徒杀人灭口。第二种是规劝式，自卫者试图以规劝来唤起歹徒的良知，让其停止因一时冲动而引起犯罪行动。第三种是欺骗式，自卫者利用各种借口，欺骗歹徒以求新的脱身机会。如骗劫财歹徒去取钱而半路逃跑，或以感染性病为由吓退欲行强奸的歹徒。此模式的运用时机包括当自卫者没机会逃走或格斗时，或当歹徒不过于凶恶蛮横时，或当自卫者需要拖延时间、改变环境时。

（四）吓唬——吠犬模式

此模式旨在警告和威胁歹徒，让他们明白自卫者并非如想象般的软弱可欺；相反，如果歹徒硬要攻击，不仅难以得逞，甚至可能自食其果。歹徒一般喜欢选择软弱、毫无防备及容易得手的目标，因为成功率高且风险低。而当自卫者摆出正规格斗的姿势及拼命的神情时，歹徒很有可能望而生畏、知难而退，转而寻找更容易得手的目标。此模式的名称源于准备攻击时呲牙咧嘴的狗，其虽不一定会咬人，但十分吓人。

应用此策略时需要选择合适的时机。一般而言，若歹徒在身体素质或武器等方面不具备优势，感觉并非志在必得时，自卫

Negotiative style is a way in which the self-defender agrees to hand over more hidden money in exchange for life security, or does not report the look of the perpetrator, or does not report to the police to prevent the perpetrator from killing and putting an end to the situation. Persuasion style is another form of change, in which self-defenders attempt to awaken the conscience of criminals or stop criminal actions caused by momentary impulses through persuasion. Deception is another change, where self-defenders use various pretexts to deceive criminals in order to seek new opportunities for escape. If scamming criminals to get money and running away on the way, or using getting sexual diseases as an excuse to scare off criminals who want to commit rape. The timing of using this method includes when the self-defender does not have a chance to escape or engage in combat, or when the perpetrator is not as aggressive, or when the defender needs to delay or change the environment.

(4) Scare—Barking Dog Mode

This mode aims to warn and threaten criminals, making them understand that the self-defender is not as weak and deceptive as imagined. On the contrary, if criminals insist on attacking, not only will it be difficult to succeed, but they may even reap the consequences themselves. Criminals generally prefer to choose targets that are weak, unprepared, and easy to achieve because of their high success rate and low risk. When the self-defender takes on a formal combat posture and looks desperate, the criminals are likely to be intimidated and retreat, seeking easier targets. The name of this mode comes from a dog that grins its teeth and cracks its mouth. Although it may not necessarily bite people, it makes people feel very scared.

When applying this strategy, it is necessary to choose the appropriate timing. Generally speaking, if criminals do not have an advantage in physical fitness or weapons, feel that they are not determined or lack confidence, show timidity,

者若有信心对付歹徒且没有即刻的生命危险，可考虑应用此模式。具体操作上，自卫者可摆出架式并喝斥"住手，免得伤了你"或"想和黑带过几招吗"等等。当歹徒不了解底细时，此招通常很有效，让歹徒以为碰上高手了，从而逃之夭夭。

此策略有如下作用。一是在吓唬歹徒时，自卫者也能增强自身的抗敌勇气。二是吓唬会出乎歹徒意料之外，使歹徒在心理上缺乏制服自卫者的信心。三是歹徒不清楚自卫者有多么厉害，吓唬可能使歹徒先退缩。四是歹徒会担心短时间内无法得手而被人发现。此策略也有其局限性。当歹徒了解自卫者底细、或歹徒明显占据优势、或歹徒志在必得时，可能很难奏效。另外，吓唬可能会激怒歹徒，促使他们使用更危险的暴力手段制服受害者。

（五）弄脏自己——黄鼠狼模式

此模式旨在使自卫者变得污秽不堪，从而让歹徒失去兴趣甚至感到厌恶而罢手。主要用来对付强奸和性骚扰。当受到熟人攻击时效果更佳，因为熟人一般不会被激怒而采取更严重的暴力行为。在受到陌生人攻击时，也能拖延歹徒的进攻，从而寻找脱身机会。此模式的灵感来源于黄鼠狼的御敌模式。

and self-defense is confident in dealing with criminals without immediate life-threatening situations, this mode can be considered. In terms of specific operations, the self-defense person can put on a stance and scold, "Stop, so as not to hurt you", or "You don't want to play a few moves with the black belt" and so on. When criminals do not understand the details, this move is usually very effective, making them think they have encountered a master and thus escape.

This strategy has the following effects. Firstly, when intimidating criminals, self-defenders can also enhance their courage to resist the enemy. Secondly, intimidation may surprise the criminals, causing them to lack the confidence to subdue the self-defense psychologically. Thirdly, criminals are not clear about how powerful the self-defenders are, and scaring them may cause them to retreat first. Fourthly, criminals may worry that they may not be able to succeed in a short period of time and may be discovered by others. This strategy also has its limitations. It may be difficult for criminals to succeed when they understand the details of their self-defense, or when they have a clear advantage, or when they are determined to win. In addition, intimidation may anger criminals and encourage them to use more dangerous forms of violence to subdue victims.

(5) Dirty Yourself—Weasel Mode

This mode aims to make the self-defender dirty and unbearable, causing the criminals to lose interest or even feel disgusted and stop. It is mainly used to deal with rape and sexual harassment. The effect is better when attacked by acquaintances, as acquaintances are generally not provoked to engage in more serious violent behavior. When attacked by strangers, it is also possible to delay the attacker's attack and seek a chance to escape. The inspiration for this mode comes from the weasel's defense mode.

有多种方法可以使自己变脏，如呕吐、故意尿裤子、把各种酱类洒得满身皆是、在泥里打个滚等。把自己搞脏的作用是改变受害者的形象，由光鲜亮丽变成肮脏不堪，从而引发歹徒产生厌恶感并降低攻击欲望。歹徒通常缺乏心理准备和经验应对这样的自卫方式，因此可能会犹豫或放弃。

然而，策略也有一些局限性。首先，不管自卫者把自己搞得多么肮脏不堪，最终还是取决于歹徒的反应，自卫者无法完全控制局势。其次，自卫者未必总有机会或条件实施此策略。最后，歹徒可能会为了达成目的而采取更严重的暴力行为。此外，此策略对强奸效果更好，对其他类型的犯罪作用有限。

（六）装疯卖傻——小丑模式

此策略通过让自卫者表现出歹徒未预料到的怪异行为，使歹徒感到困惑，并因缺乏应对经验和信心而选择退让。这种方法有多种形式，以下是几个实例说明。

例子一：一位老妇人在等待汽车时遭遇歹徒抢劫，她突然转身打招呼说："喂，我认识你妈，她最近好吗？"歹徒愣住了，没想到对方居然认识自己的母亲，自然不敢攻击，以免被告发。

例子二：一位女教授在夜间遭遇一伙流氓时，装作精神病患

There are various ways to make yourself dirty, such as vomiting, intentionally wetting your pants, spilling various sauces all over your body, and rolling in the mud. The purpose of dirtying oneself is to change the image of the victim, from clean to dirty, thereby triggering a sense of disgust among the criminals and reducing their desires to attack. Criminals often lack psychological preparation and experience to deal with such self-defense methods, so they may hesitate or give up.

However, the strategy also has some limitations. Firstly, no matter how dirty the defender makes themselves, it ultimately depends on the reaction of the criminals, and the defender cannot fully control the situation. Secondly, self-defenders may not always have the opportunity or conditions to implement this strategy. Thirdly, criminals may resort to more serious acts of violence in order to achieve their goals. In addition, this strategy is only effective for rape and has limited impact on other types of crimes.

(6) Playing Mad and Foolish—Joker Mode

This strategy confuses the criminals by causing them to exhibit unexpected and bizarre behavior, and they choose to back down due to a lack of coping experience and confidence. There are various forms of this method, and the following are a few examples to illustrate.

Example 1: An old woman was robbed by an assailant while waiting for a car. She suddenly turned around and said, "Hey, I know your mother. How is she recently?" The assailant was stunned. Unexpectedly, the other party knew his mother. Naturally, she did not dare to attack to avoid being reported.

Example 2: A female professor escaped by pretending to be a mentally ill patient when encountering a group of

者逃过一劫。歹徒们全都愣住，眼睁睁看着她离去，不知道该怎么办。

例子三：一位去参加聚餐的人遇到攻击时，扬起手中的酒瓶装成醉汉，歹徒觉得醉汉神志不清、可控制程度低，结果让他脱身。

例子四：一位女士在遭遇性攻击时，主动装作脱衣服，同时抱怨自己感染了艾滋病，结果吓退了歹徒。

例子五：一位外国学生遭遇攻击时装作不懂歹徒的语言，从而成功逃脱。

此策略通过让歹徒感到困惑，使他们在心理上产生犹豫，只得重新调整心态和目标，结果丧失进攻机会；或者使歹徒因为缺乏应对这类情况的经验和信心而放弃。但这种策略有其局限性。自卫者在遭受攻击时可能没有机会实施此计，使用此计也需要具备一定的胆量和机智，且最终主动权仍掌握在歹徒手中。

综观以上各种急智脱身措施可发现并非都很有效且作用有限。专家推荐最多的是兔子、病人和吠犬模式，效果因人而异。

criminals at night. The criminals were all stunned, watching her leave without knowing what to do.

Example 3: When a person attending a gathering encounters an attack, they raise their wine bottle and pretend to be drunk. The perpetrator feels that the drunkards are not sane and are hard to control, as a result, they let him escape.

Example 4: When a woman was sexually assaulted, she pretended to take off her clothes and complained that she was infected with AIDS, which scared off the criminal.

Example 5: A foreign student successfully escaped an attack by pretending not to understand the criminal's language.

This strategy confuses criminals, causing them to hesitate psychologically, requiring them to readjust their mindset and goals, resulting in losing the opportunity to attack or giving up due to a lack of experience and confidence in dealing with such defenders. But this strategy has its limitations. Self-defenders may not have the opportunity to implement this plan when attacked, and using this plan also requires a certain level of courage and wit under the threat of criminals, with the ultimate initiative still in the hands of the criminals.

Overall, not all of the above emergency measures are very effective and have limited effects. The most recommended modes by experts are rabbit, patient, and barking dog, and the effects vary from person to person.

第二节
临阵对付各种犯罪的措施与方法

Section 2
Measures and Methods for Dealing with Various Crimes on the Spot

临场对付歹徒攻击的最大困难是不知道歹徒想干什么。因而人们常常使用妥协、逃跑、格斗等方法本能地保护自己。但如果知道歹徒想干什么，即了解歹徒的犯罪目的，可更有针对性地选择应对措施。

The biggest difficulty in dealing with criminal attacks on the spot is not knowing what the criminal wants to do. Therefore, people often use methods such as compromise, escape, and fighting to instinctively protect themselves. Because these measures are effective against any type of attack. But if you know what the criminal wants to do, that is, understand the criminal purpose of the criminal, you can choose more targeted response measures.

一、对付抢劫

1. Dealing with Robbery

对付抢劫虽然危险，但作决定却并不难。歹徒一般要钱不伤及人身安全，但有时也会在抢劫后杀人灭口或强奸，因此专家们提出以下几个对付抢劫的办法：

（1）马上交钱，决不为保钱财而冒险。

（2）扔了钱就跑，以免歹徒得了钱后继续施暴。

（3）不要试图去记住歹徒的面貌，以免招致杀身之祸。

（4）如果歹徒得手后还想带走或伤害受害者，则受害者应立即逃跑或拼命格斗。

Although dealing with robbery is dangerous, making decisions is not difficult. Criminals usually ask for money and don't want to hurt anyone, but sometimes they may kill or rape people after robbery. Experts propose the following ways to deal with robbery:

① Pay the money immediately and never take risks to protect your wealth.

② Throw away the money and run away to prevent the criminals from continuing to commit violence after receiving the money.

③ Don't try to remember the appearance of the criminal, as it may lead to murder.

④ If the perpetrator still wants to take away or harm the victim after winning, the victim should immediately escape or fight desperately.

二、对付劫车

（1）如果歹徒尚在车外，应立即加大油门，迅速逃离现场。

（2）如果歹徒扒住车身，可通过突然加速和急停来甩掉他，或者靠近树旁以剐蹭方式摆脱他。

（3）如果歹徒已进入车内并持有刀枪，不要在车内进行搏斗，因为狭小的空间会限制你的动作。应等待时机，再采取行动。

（4）当歹徒劫车杀人意图十分明显，或猜不透歹徒的意图但感到危险时，可开车撞向其他车辆或有人的地方，例如电线杆或邮筒，等等。此类事故常常会引人他人的注意，从而吓退歹徒，亦有可能使歹徒受伤。注意撞击后应立即下车逃走并呼救。

三、对付入室行窃

（1）如发现家门被撬，不要急于检查损失状况，应立即去邻居家报警。

（2）如人在家时遭遇歹徒撬门或破窗，可调高电视音量、或高喊男性名字、或大喊"拿刀来"等以吓退歹徒。

（3）持刀或持棍时，应先发制人攻击歹徒，趁其立足未稳将其打退。

（4）如与入室行窃歹徒打上

2. Dealing with Car Robbery

① If the criminal is still outside the car, immediately speed up and quickly escape the scene.

② If the criminal grabs the car body, you can get rid of him by suddenly accelerating and stopping, or by getting close to the tree and rubbing against him.

③ If the criminal has entered the car and is holding a knife or gun, do not engage in combat inside the car, as the narrow space will limit your movements. You should wait for the opportunity before taking action.

④ When the intention of the robber to rob a car or kill someone is very obvious, or when they cannot guess the culprit's intention but feel dangerous, they can drive into other vehicles or places with people, such as power poles or mailboxes. Such accidents often attract the attention of others, thereby scaring off criminals and potentially injuring them. Pay attention to getting off the car immediately and calling for help after the impact.

3. Dealing with Burglary

① If you find your home door being pried, don't rush to check for damage. You should immediately go to your neighbor's house to report the incident.

② If a person encounters a burglar prying a door or breaking a window at home, they can adjust the TV volume, shout male names, or shout "bring me a knife" to scare off the burglar.

③ When wielding a knife or stick, one should take the initiative to attack the criminal and take advantage of their unstable footing to drive them back.

④ If you have a face-to-face conversation with a burglar,

照面，可假意打声招呼，请对方坐下喝茶，并表示要去邻居家叫歹徒要找的人回来，趁机溜走。

（5）如面对持刀持枪的歹徒，则交出钱物，但如果歹徒意图杀人灭口，必须尽全力反抗。

四、对付强奸

（一）对付熟人强暴

（1）态度坚决、严辞拒绝。

（2）警告对方将负法律责任。

（3）威胁对方自己会以牙还牙、拼死反抗，强调如果对方坚持攻击则后果自负，至少两败俱伤。

（4）给对方一个台阶下，让其不失面子地退场。

（5）找个借口，如处于生理期等。

（二）对付陌生人强暴

（1）如无生命危险，喊叫求援以吓退歹徒。

（2）跑向有人的地方。

（3）警告并威胁对方，表示自己不好惹。

（4）拉开格斗架式，准备一拼。

（5）使用各种正规与非正规格斗技术反击。

（6）在不服从便有生命危险时，暂时妥协，保全性命。

（7）假意表示愿意合作，并让对方找个舒适地方。同时，寻

you can pretend to say hello, ask the other person to sit down and have tea, and indicate that you want to call the person the burglar is looking for from your neighbor's house, then take the opportunity to sneak away.

⑤ If facing criminals with knives and guns, hand over money and belongings, but if the criminals intend to kill and silence, you must do your best to resist.

4. Dealing with Rape

(1) Dealing with Rape by Acquaintances

① Keep a resolute attitude, and stern refusal.

② Warn the other party that he will bear legal responsibility.

③ Threaten the other party that he will lead to retaliation and desperate resistance, emphasizing that if the other party insists on attacking, the consequences will be at their own risk, at least causing both parties to suffer.

④ Give the other party a step down and end the game without losing face.

⑤ Find an excuse, such as menstrual cycle, etc.

(2) Dealing with Stranger Rape

① If there is no life-threatening situation, shout for help to scare off the criminals.

② Run towards where there are people.

③ Warn and threaten the other party, indicating that you are not easy to provoke.

④ Take the fighting stance and prepare for a fight.

⑤ Use various formal and informal fighting techniques to counterattack.

⑥ If you don't obey, your life is in danger, you have to compromise temporarily to save your life.

⑦ When necessary, you can also pretend to cooperate and ask the other party to find a comfortable place. Meanwhile,

找机会脱身。

seek opportunities to escape.

五、对付攻击伤人

（1）一旦形成冲突并发现歹徒有暴力倾向，应立即撤退以避免武斗，迅速离开。

（2）如歹徒持续攻击，可跑向有人的地方求助。

（3）如没有生命危险，可威胁歹徒再敢挑衅后果自负，至少两败俱伤，谁也占不到便宜。

（4）如对方不肯罢手，且自己又无退路，应全力反击，以击退歹徒。

六、对付凶杀

（1）如果对方执意要杀害受害者，唯一的选择是逃命，逃走就是胜利。

（2）当发现歹徒不会放过自己时，应抓住时机格斗反抗。尽管危险性比较大，但总比任人宰割强。

七、对付绑架

（1）如有生命危险，切不可妄动，应妥协服从，同时寻找脱身机会。

（2）留心环境，丢下点证物以利于警察寻找。

（3）不要把全部底细都透露给

5. Dealing with Attacks and Injuries

① Once a conflict arises and there is a tendency towards violence, one should immediately withdraw to avoid fighting and leave.

② If the criminals continue to attack, you can run to places with people for help.

③ If there is no danger to life, warn and threaten criminals. If they dare to provoke again, they will bear the consequences. At least both parties will be harmed, and no one can take advantage of it.

④ If the other party refuses to stop and there is no way out for oneself, the defender can only fight back with all their might to repel and injure the criminals.

6. Dealing with Murder

① If the other party insists on killing the victim, the only option is to escape, and escape is victory.

② When it is discovered that the criminals will not let themselves go, the defender should seize the opportunity to fight and resist. Although the danger is relatively high, it is always better than being slaughtered by others.

7. Dealing with Kidnapping

① If there is a danger to your life, you must not act recklessly, compromise and obey, and at the same time seek opportunities to escape.

② Pay attention to the environment and discard evidence to facilitate the police's search.

③ Do not reveal all the details to the criminals, in case

歹徒，以防被认为无用而被杀害。

（4）若发现歹徒有松懈或打算杀害自己时，应努力逃走或拼命突围。

（5）观察歹徒的神情变化，勿多嘴多舌引起歹徒厌恶，以避免受到直接伤害。

（6）如遇警察围捕，远离门窗等地，并隐藏好自己。

they are deemed useless and killed.

④ If it is found that the criminals have slackened or intend to kill the victims, efforts should be made to escape or break through desperately.

⑤ Observe the changes in the expression of the criminals, avoid talking too much to cause disgust and avoid direct harm.

⑥ If surrounded by police, stay away from doors, windows, and other places, and hide yourself.

思考四

1. 应付歹徒攻击的急智原则包括哪些？

2. 临床对付歹徒的常见模式包括哪些？

3. 临场对付各类犯罪的措施包括哪些？

Reflection 4

1.What are the principles of impatience in dealing with criminal attacks?

2. What are the common patterns of dealing with criminals in clinical practice?

3.What are the measures to deal with various crimes on the spot?

第五章
正当防卫与案例评析

Chapter 5
Legitimate Defense and Case Analysis

第一节
正当防卫基本理论

Section 1
Basic Theory of Legitimate Defense

2020 年"两高一部"为依法准确适用正当防卫制度，维护公民的正当防卫权利，鼓励见义勇为，弘扬社会正气，把社会主义核心价值观融入刑事司法工作，根据《中华人民共和国刑法》和《中华人民共和国刑事诉讼法》的有关规定，联合印发了《关于依法适用正当防卫制度的指导意见》（以下简称《意见》）。《意见》对于正当防卫、防卫过当以及特殊防卫的具体适用都进行了细化与说明。

In 2020, in accordance with the relevant provisions of the *Criminal Law of the People's Republic of China* and the *Criminal Procedure Law of the People's Republic of China*, the Supreme People's court, the Supreme People's Procuratorate, and the Ministry of Public Security jointly issued the Guiding Opinions on the Application of the Legitimate Defense System (The Opinions in short) in accordance with the law, in order to accurately apply the legitimate defense system in accordance with the law, safeguard the legitimate defense rights of citizens, encourage courageous actions in righteousness, promote social righteousness, and integrate socialist core values into criminal justice work. The Opinions have elaborated and explained the specific application of justifiable defense, excessive defense, and special defense.

一、正当防卫概念

1. The Concept of Legitimate Defense

正当防卫与暴力犯罪是一对孪生体。后者指行使暴力手段危害公民的人身或财产安全的犯罪主体，前者指对犯罪主体的对抗。正当防卫源于人类的自我防卫本能，其制度化本质是对人类自我防卫保护行为的法律认可。《中华

Legitimate defense and violent crime are twins. The latter refers to the criminal subject who exercises violent means to endanger the personal or property security of citizens, while the former refers to the confrontation against the criminal subject. Legitimate defense originates from human self-defense instinct, and its institutionalized essence is the legal recognition of human self-defense protection

人民共和国刑法》中第二十条指出："为了使国家、公共利益、本人或者他人的人身、财产和其他权利免受正在进行的不法侵害，而采取的制止不法侵害的行为，对不法侵害人造成损害的，属于正当防卫。"另外，"对正在进行行凶、杀人、抢劫、强奸、绑架以及其他严重危及人身安全的暴力犯罪，采取防卫行为，造成不法侵害人伤亡的，不属于防卫过当，不负刑事责任。"

二、正当防卫的成立条件

（一）起因条件

正当防卫的前提是他人对生命权，健康权，人身自由以及公私财产等权利的侵犯。不法侵犯是客观存在的，并不是主观臆测的。例如长春女大学生搭乘网约车，因犯困误以为司机下药将其划伤就属于主观臆断，不属于正当防卫。另外，《意见》指出不法侵害既包括针对本人的不法侵害，也包括危害国家、公共利益或者针对他人的不法侵害。例如乘坐公交车时，面对拉拽方向盘、殴打司机等妨害安全驾驶、危害公共安全的违法犯罪行为，可以实行防卫。成年人对于未成年人正在实施的针对其他未成年人的不法侵害，应当劝阻、制止；劝

behavior. The provision on justifiable defense in Article 20, Paragraph 1 of the *Criminal Law of the People's Republic of China* states, "Actions taken to stop unlawful infringement in order to protect the interests of the state, the public, the personal, property, and other rights of oneself or others from ongoing unlawful infringement, which cause harm to the unlawful infringer, belong to justifiable defense." In addition, "taking defensive actions against ongoing violent crimes such as murder, robbery, rape, kidnapping, and other serious threats to personal security that cause injury or death to the unlawful infringer does not constitute excessive defense and does not bear criminal responsibility."

2. The Conditions for the Establishment of Legitimate Defense

(1) Causal Conditions

The premise of legitimate defense is the infringement of rights such as the right to life, health, personal freedom, and public and private property. Meanwhile, illegal infringement is an objective existence, not subjective speculation. For example, when a female college student from Changchun takes a ride hailing service, she mistakenly thinks that the driver has drugged her and scratched her due to drowsiness, which is subjective speculation and not legitimate defense. In addition, The Opinions points out that illegal and unlawful infringement includes both unlawful infringement against oneself and unlawful infringement against the state, public interests, or others. For example, when taking a bus, illegal activities such as pulling the steering wheel, assaulting the driver, etc. that hinder safe driving and endanger public security can be defended. Adults should dissuade and stop the illegal infringement against other minors being carried out by minors; if persuasion or cessation is ineffective, defense may

阻、制止无效的，可以实行防卫。

（二）时间条件

《意见》指出正当防卫必须是针对正在进行的不法侵害。换言之，对于发生在不法侵害行为之前的防卫行为则不成立。对于不法侵害已经形成现实、紧迫危险的，应当认定为不法侵害已经开始。

另外，以往认为不法侵害行为停止之后的防卫行为不能被称为正当防卫，包括是事前防卫和事后防卫。但《意见》做出了细化与整改，指出不法侵害虽然暂时中断或者被暂时制止，但不法侵害人仍有继续实施侵害的现实可能性的，应当认定为不法侵害仍在进行；在财产犯罪中，不法侵害人虽已取得财物，但通过追赶、阻击等措施能够追回财物的，可以视为不法侵害仍在进行；对于不法侵害人确已失去侵害能力或者确已放弃侵害的，应当认定为不法侵害已经结束。对于不法侵害是否已经开始或者结束，应当立足防卫人在防卫时所处情境，按照社会公众的一般认知，依法做出合乎情理的判断，不能苛求防卫人。对于防卫人因为恐慌、紧张等心理，对不法侵害是否已经开始或者结束产生错误认识的，应当根据主客观相统一原则，依法做出妥当处理。

be implemented.

(2) Time Conditions

The Opinions points out that legitimate defense must be aimed at ongoing illegal infringement. In other words, defense actions that occurred before the occurrence of illegal infringement are not valid. For those who have already formed a real and urgent danger of illegal infringement, it should be recognized that the illegal infringement has begun;

In addition, it was previously believed that defensive actions after the cessation of unlawful infringement could not be referred to as legitimate defense. They are pre-defense and post-defense, respectively. But The Opinions have been refined and rectified, pointing out that even if the illegal infringement is temporarily interrupted or stopped, the illegal infringer still has a realistic possibility of continuing to carry out the infringement, it should be recognized as the illegal infringement is still ongoing; in property crimes, if the illegal infringer has already obtained property but can recover it through measures such as chasing and blocking, it can be considered that the illegal infringement is still ongoing; if the unlawful infringer has indeed lost the ability to infringe or has indeed abandoned the infringement, it shall be deemed that the unlawful infringement has ended. For whether the illegal infringement has already begun or ended, it should be based on the situation in which the defender is in defense, according to the general understanding of the public, make reasonable judgments in accordance with the law, and cannot demand the defender excessively. For defenders who have a mistaken understanding of whether the illegal infringement has already begun or ended due to panic, tension, and other psychological factors, appropriate measures should be taken in accordance with the principle of subjective and objective unity and in accordance with the law.

（三）对象条件

正当防卫必须针对不法侵害人进行，对于多人共同实施不法侵害的，既可以针对直接实施不法侵害的人进行防卫，也可以针对在现场共同实施不法侵害的人进行防卫。但不能针对其他不相关的人。如张三对李四正在实施不法侵害，但张三的同伴正在规劝和阻拦，张三的同伴并未参与侵害行为，不能进行连坐式伤害。明知侵害人是无刑事责任能力人或者限制刑事责任能力人的，应当尽量使用其他方式避免或者制止侵害；没有其他方式可以避免、制止不法侵害，或者不法侵害严重危及人身安全的，可以进行反击。

（四）主观条件

正当防卫必须是为了使国家、公共利益、本人或者他人的人身、财产和其他权利免受不法侵害。对于故意以语言、行为等挑动对方侵害自己再予以反击的防卫挑拨，不应认定为防卫行为。

（五）限度条件

为了防止防卫权的滥用。《意见》指出对于显著轻微的不法侵害，行为人在可以辨识的情况下，直接使用足以致人重伤或者死亡的方式进行制止的，不应认定为防卫行为。例如犯罪人只是实施了盗窃，可预见地不会造成人身安全威胁时，行为人就不能使用

(3) Object Conditions

Legitimate defense must be aimed at the perpetrator of the unlawful infringement. If multiple people jointly commit the unlawful infringement, defense can be taken against both the person who directly committed the unlawful infringement and the person who jointly committed the unlawful infringement on site. But it cannot target other unrelated individuals. If Zhang San is committing illegal infringement against Li Si, but his companions are persuading and obstructing him, and Zhang San's companions have not participated in the infringement behavior, they cannot engage in seated injuries. If it is known that the infringer is a person without criminal liability or with limited criminal liability, other means should be used as much as possible to avoid or stop the infringement; if there is no other way to avoid or stop illegal infringement, or if the illegal infringement seriously endangers personal security, a counterattack can be carried out.

(4) Subjective Conditions

Legitimate defense must be aimed at protecting the state, public interests, personal, property, and other rights of oneself or others from unlawful infringement. Defense provocation that intentionally provokes the other party to harm oneself through language, behavior, etc. and then retaliates should not be considered as a defensive act.

(5) Limit Conditions

To prevent the abuse of defense rights. The Opinions points out that for significant and minor illegal infringement, if the perpetrator directly uses a method that can cause serious injury or death to stop it in identifiable circumstances, it should not be recognized as a defensive act. For example, if a criminal only commits theft and it is foreseeable that it will not threaten personal security, they cannot use violent means to deprive others' right to life. In addition, if the illegal infringement is

暴力手段剥夺他人生命权。另外，不法侵害系因行为人的重大过错引发，行为人在可以使用其他手段避免侵害的情况下，仍故意使用足以致人重伤或者死亡的方式还击的，不应认定为防卫行为。

（六）其他情况

因琐事发生争执，双方均不能保持克制而引发打斗，有过错的一方先动手且手段明显过激，或者一方先动手，在对方努力避免冲突的情况下仍继续侵害的，还击一方的行为一般应当认定为防卫行为。双方因琐事发生冲突，冲突结束后，一方又实施不法侵害，对方还击，包括使用工具还击的，一般应当认定为防卫行为。不能仅因行为人事先进行防卫准备，就影响对其防卫意图的认定。

三、特殊防卫

特殊防卫，也称为无限防卫权或预防性正当防卫，与一般防卫有所不同。特殊防卫指的是在某些特定情况下，行为人实施正当防卫时不受强度限制，对防卫行为的后果不负刑事责任。根据刑法第二十条第三款的规定，特殊防卫适用于特定情况，包括"行凶"、"杀人、抢劫、强奸、绑架"，以及"其他严重危及人身安

caused by the perpetrator's gross fault, and the perpetrator intentionally uses a method that is sufficient to cause serious injury or death to retaliate, even when other means can be used to avoid the infringement, it should not be considered as a defensive act.

(6) Other Situations

If a dispute arises due to trivial matters and neither party is able to exercise restraint, leading to a fight, and if the party at fault takes action first and the means are clearly excessive, or if one party takes action first and continues to infringe despite the other party's efforts to avoid conflict, the act of retaliating against the other party should generally be recognized as defensive behavior. If there is a conflict between the two parties due to trivial matters, and after the conflict ends, one party commits illegal infringement, and the other party retaliates, including using tools, it should generally be recognized as a defensive act. Just because the perpetrator has made defense preparations beforehand cannot affect the determination of their defense intention.

3. Special Defense

Special defense, also known as unlimited defense rights or preventive justifiable defense, is different from general defense. Special defense refers to the situation where, in certain specific circumstances, the perpetrator is not subject to intensity restrictions when exercising legitimate defense and is not criminally responsible for the consequences of the defense act. According to the provisions of Article 20, Paragraph 3 of the Criminal Law, special defense applies to specific situations, including "assault", "murder, robbery, rape, kidnapping", and "other violent

全的暴力犯罪"。

《意见》指出,对于不符合特殊防卫条件的防卫行为,如果没有明显超过必要限度,导致不法侵害人伤亡的,也应当认定为正当防卫,不负刑事责任。行为没有严重危及人身安全的,应适用一般防卫的法律规定。

"行凶"是指使用致命性凶器,严重危及他人人身安全;或者虽然未使用凶器,但根据不法侵害的人数、打击部位和力度等情况,确实严重危及他人人身安全;即使尚未造成实际损害,但已对人身安全构成严重、紧迫危险的,也可认定为"行凶"。

"杀人、抢劫、强奸、绑架"指具体的犯罪行为,而非具体罪名。在实施不法侵害过程中,存在杀人、抢劫、强奸、绑架等严重危及人身安全的暴力犯罪行为,如以暴力手段抢劫枪支、弹药、爆炸物,或者以绑架手段拐卖妇女、儿童的,可以实行特殊防卫。

"其他严重危及人身安全的暴力犯罪"指与杀人、抢劫、强奸、绑架行为相当,并具有致人重伤或死亡的紧迫危险和现实可能的暴力犯罪。

四、防卫过当

《中华人民共和国刑法》第二十条第二款的规定,防卫过当

crimes that seriously endanger personal security".

The Opinions points out that for defense actions that do not meet the special defense conditions, if they do not clearly exceed the necessary limit and cause injury or death to the unlawful infringer, they should also be recognized as legitimate defense and not bear criminal responsibility. If the behavior does not seriously endanger personal security, general defense laws and regulations should be applied.

"Assault" refers to the use of lethal weapons that seriously endanger the personal security of others; or even if the weapon is not used, it does seriously endanger the personal security of others based on the number of illegal infringements, the location and intensity of the strike, and other factors; even if no actual damage has been caused, but it has posed a serious and urgent danger to personal security, it can still be considered as "assault".

"Murder, robbery, rape, and kidnapping" refer to specific criminal acts rather than specific charges. In the process of carrying out illegal infringement, there are violent criminal acts that seriously endanger personal security, such as murder, robbery, rape, kidnapping, etc., including robbing firearms, ammunition, explosives by violent means, or trafficking women and children by kidnapping, special defense can be implemented.

"Other violent crimes that seriously endanger personal security" refer to violent crimes that are equivalent to murder, robbery, rape, and kidnapping, and have an urgent risk of causing serious injury or death, as well as a realistic possibility of violence.

4. Excessive Defense

According to the second paragraph of Article 20 of the *Criminal Law of the People's Republic of China*, excessive

应当同时具备"明显超过必要限度"和"造成重大损害"两个条件，缺一不可。《意见》指出，防卫过当应负刑事责任，但是应当减轻或者免除处罚。

（一）明显超过必要限度

判断防卫行为是否"明显超过必要限度"时，需要综合考虑以下因素：不法侵害的性质、手段、强度、危害程度，以及防卫的时机、手段、强度和损害后果。同时，还要对比双方的力量，立足于防卫人在当时情境下的情况，结合社会公众的一般认知进行判断。

在评估不法侵害的危害程度时，既要考虑已经造成的损害，还要考虑其进一步损害的紧迫性和现实可能性。不应苛求防卫人必须采取与不法侵害基本相当的反击方式和强度。通过综合考量，对于防卫行为与不法侵害相差悬殊、明显过激的，应认定为防卫明显超过必要限度。

（二）造成重大损害

"造成重大损害"是指造成不法侵害人重伤、死亡。造成轻伤及以下损害的，不属于重大损害。防卫行为虽然明显超过必要限度但没有造成重大损害的，不应认定为防卫过当。

defense should meet both the conditions of "obviously exceeding the necessary limit" and "causing significant damage". The Opinions points out that excessive defense should bear criminal responsibility, but the punishment should be reduced or exempted.

(1) Clearly Exceeding Necessary Limits

When determining whether a defensive action clearly "exceeds the necessary limit", the following factors need to be comprehensively considered: nature, means, intensity, degree of harm of unlawful infringement, as well as the timing, means, intensity, and consequences of defense. At the same time, it is necessary to compare the strength of both sides, based on the situation of the defender in the current situation, and make judgments based on the general understanding of the public.

When evaluating the degree of harm caused by illegal infringement, it is necessary to consider not only the damage already caused, but also the urgency and realistic possibility of further damage. Defenders should not be required to adopt a counterattack method and intensity that is basically equivalent to illegal infringement. After comprehensive consideration, if there is a significant difference between defensive behavior and unlawful infringement, and it is clearly excessive, it should be deemed that defense clearly exceeds the necessary limit.

(2) Causing Significant Damage

"Causing significant damage" refers to causing serious injury or death to the unlawful infringer. Causing minor injuries or below does not constitute significant damage. Defense behavior that clearly exceeds the necessary limit but does not cause significant damage should not be considered as excessive defense.

第二节
正当防卫案例评析

Section 2
Analysis of Justifiable Defense Cases

为了帮助大家更为深刻地了解《关于依法适用正当防卫制度的指导意见》指出的关于正当防卫、特殊防卫以及防卫过当的条例，与此相配套地发布了七条案例。本节就正当防卫、特殊防卫、滥用防卫权，以及正当防卫与打架斗殴的分界四个方面，各摘取一个案例进行探讨，供大家参考。

In order to help everyone have a deeper understanding of the regulations on justifiable defense, special defense, and excessive defense pointed out in the Guiding Opinions on the Application of the Legitimate Defense System in accordance with the law, seven cases have been issued in conjunction with this. This section divides justifiable defense, special defense, excessive defense, and the boundary between justifiable defense and fighting into four aspects, with one case selected for your reference.

一、汪天佑正当防卫案——正当防卫条件的把握

1. Wang Tianyou's Case of Justifiable Defense—Grasping the Conditions for the Cause of Justifiable Defense

（一）案例描述

被告人汪天佑与邻居汪某某曾因建房问题发生冲突，后经调解解决。但在 2017 年 8 月，汪某某的女婿和其朋友赵某与杨某驾车来到汪天佑家准备质问此事。燕某某和赵某敲汪天佑家的北门，汪天佑因不认识他们，遂询问二人有什么事，但燕某某等始终未表明身份，汪天佑拒绝开门。

燕某某和赵某踹开纱门，闯入汪天佑家的过道屋。汪天佑被突然开启的纱门打伤右脸，从过道屋西侧的橱柜上拿起一根铁质摩托车减震器，与燕某某和赵某厮打。汪天佑用摩托车减震器先

(1) Case Description

The defendant Wang Tianyou and his neighbor Wang had a conflict over building a house, which was later resolved through mediation. But in August 2017, Wang's son-in-law and his friends Zhao and Yang drove to Wang Tianyou's house to inquire about the matter. Yan and Zhao knocked on the north door of Wang Tianyou's house. Wang Tianyou didn't know them, so he asked them what they had to do. However, Yan and others never revealed their identities, so Wang Tianyou refused to open the door.

Yan and Zhao kicked open the screen door and broke into the hallway of Wang Tianyou's house. Wang Tianyou was injured in the right face by the sudden opening of the screen door. He picked up an iron motorcycle shock absorber from the cabinet on the west side of the hallway and fought with Yan and Zhao. Wang Tianyou used motorcycle shock

后将燕某某和赵某头部打伤，致赵某轻伤一级、燕某某轻微伤。在此期间，汪天佑的妻子电话报警。最终判定汪天佑属于正当防卫，不负刑事责任。

（二）判定依据

（1）对受害人实施不法侵害。燕某某和赵某与汪天佑并不相识，在不表明身份的情况下，于天黑时强行端开纱门闯入汪天佑家。其非法侵入住宅行为不仅侵害了他人的居住安宁，还对他人的人身和财产造成了严重威胁，应当认定为"不法侵害"，可以进行防卫。因此，汪天佑为制止不法侵害，随手拿起摩托车减震器，在双方厮打过程中将燕某某和赵某打伤，致一人轻伤一级、一人轻微伤的行为属于正当防卫。

（2）受害人制止不法侵害。本案中，汪天佑与邻居汪某某曾因汪某某家建房产生矛盾，但该矛盾已经调解解决。之后，汪某某的女婿燕某某驾车与赵某、杨某来到汪天佑家准备质问此事，进而实施了非法侵入住宅的行为。综合全案可以发现，汪天佑随手拿起摩托车减震器进行还击，系为制止不法侵害，并无斗殴意图，故最终认定其还击行为属于正当防卫。

absorber to successively injure Yan and Zhao in the head, resulting in Zhao being lightly injured at level one and Yan being slightly injured. During this period, Wang Tianyou's wife called the police. It was ultimately determined that Wang Tianyou was engaged in justifiable defense and did not bear criminal responsibility.

(2) Judgment Basis

① Engage in unlawful infringement against the victim. Yan and Zhao, who were not acquainted with Wang Tianyou, forcefully kicked open the screen door and broke into Wang Tianyou's house in the dark without revealing their identities. Their illegal intrusion into residential areas not only infringes on the residential tranquility of others, but also poses a serious threat to their personal and property. It should be recognized as "illegal infringement" and can be used for defense. Therefore, in order to stop illegal infringement, Wang Tianyou casually picked up the motorcycle shock absorber and injured Yan and Zhao during a fight, causing one person to be lightly injured and one person to be slightly injured, which is considered justifiable defense.

② The victim stops the illegal infringement. In this case, Wang Tianyou and his neighbor Wang had a conflict over Wang's house construction, but the conflict has been resolved through mediation. Afterwards, Wang's son-in-law Yan drove with Zhao and Yang to Wang Tianyou's house to inquire about the matter, and subsequently carried out illegal intrusion into the residence. Taking into account the entire case, it can be found that Wang Tianyou casually picked up the motorcycle shock absorber to retaliate, in order to stop illegal infringement and without any intention of fighting. Therefore, it was ultimately determined that his retaliatory behavior was justifiable defense.

二、陈月浮正当防卫案——特殊防卫的具体适用

（一）案例描述

2009年1月，被害人陈某某酒后来到被告人陈月浮家，用随身携带的一把菜刀敲击陈月浮家的铁门，叫嚣让陈月浮出来打架。陈月浮的妻子下楼，谎称陈月浮不在家。然而，陈某某继续敲击铁门。陈月浮便下楼打开铁门，陈某某用菜刀砍中陈月浮的脸部，致其轻伤。陈某某再次砍向陈月浮时，被陈月浮挡开，菜刀掉在地上。陈月浮上前拳击陈某某的胸部等部位，二人在地上扭打。最终，陈某某因钝性物体作用胸部致心包、心脏破裂，导致失血性休克死亡。法院判定认为，陈月浮为了使自己免受正在进行的不法侵害，对正在进行的危害人身安全的暴力犯罪采取防卫行为，造成不法侵害人陈某某死亡的，不属于防卫过当，不负刑事责任。

（二）判定依据

（1）侵害人行凶行为判定。陈某某无故持菜刀凌晨上门砍伤陈月浮，属于使用致命性凶器实施的严重危及他人人身安全的不法侵害，应当认定为"行凶"，对此陈月浮可以实行特殊防卫。

（2）被害人高度惊恐的情绪下，无法判断侵害人的进一步动

2. Chen Yuefu's Justifiable Defense Case—Specific Application of Special Defense

(1) Case Description

In January 2009, the victim Chen came to the defendant Chen Yuefu's house under the influence of alcohol and used a kitchen knife he carried with him to knock on the iron door of Chen Yuefu's house, shouting that Chen Yuefu should come out and fight. Chen Yuefu's wife went downstairs and falsely claimed that Chen Yuefu was not at home. However, Chen continued to knock on the iron door. Chen Yuefu went downstairs and opened the iron door. Chen used a kitchen knife to strike Chen Yuefu in the face, causing him minor injuries. When Chen was chopping towards Chen Yuefu again, he was blocked by Chen Yuefu and his kitchen knife fell to the ground. Chen Yuefu stepped forward to punch Chen's chest and other parts, and the two of them wrestled on the ground. In the end, Chen died of hemorrhagic shock due to the rupture of the pericardium and heart caused by blunt objects acting on the chest. The court ruled that Chen Yuefu's defensive actions against the ongoing violent crime that endangers personal security in order to protect himself from the ongoing illegal infringement, resulting in the death of the perpetrator Chen, do not constitute excessive defense and do not bear criminal responsibility.

(2) Judgment Basis

① Judgment of the perpetrator's violent behavior. Chen came to the door with a kitchen knife without reason and attacked Chen Yuefu in the early hours of the morning. This is a serious illegal infringement that endangers the personal security of others using a deadly weapon, and should be recognized as the "perpetrator". Chen Yuefu can exercise special defense against this.

② In the highly frightened state of the victim, it is impossible to determine the further motivation of the

机。陈某某持菜刀砍中陈月浮脸部致其轻伤，陈某某再次砍向陈月浮时被其挡开，菜刀掉到地上。在这种情况下，要求陈月浮在被菜刀砍伤后保持高度冷静，在将行凶者打倒之后，还要仔细判断行凶者有没有继续行凶的能力，这对于在黑夜之中高度惊恐的防卫人，是强人所难。因此，应当认为在陈某某菜刀掉到地上之后，陈月浮仍然可以实行防卫。

三、刘金胜故意伤害案——滥用防卫权行为的认定

（一）案例描述

2016 年 10 月某天，刘金胜因家庭和情感问题与黄某甲发生争吵，期间刘金胜打了黄某甲两耳光。黄某甲随后到她哥哥黄某乙的水果店，告诉黄某乙自己被刘金胜打了耳光，并请求他调解她与刘金胜的分手和孩子抚养问题。黄某乙于是叫上在店内聊天的李某某、毛某某和陈某某，由黄某甲带领，一行人于当晚 10 时许来到刘金胜的住处。

黄某乙质问刘金胜，双方发生争吵。黄某乙和李某某各打了坐在床上的刘金胜一耳光，刘金胜随即从被子下拿出一把菜刀砍伤黄某乙的头部，黄某乙随即逃离现场。李某某见状想跑，却被刘金胜拽住并持菜刀向李某某头

perpetrator. Chen hit Chen Yuefu in the face with a kitchen knife, causing minor injuries. When Chen tried to cut at Chen Yuefu again, he was blocked and the knife fell to the ground. In this situation, Chen Yuefu is required to maintain a high level of composure after being cut by a kitchen knife. After knocking down the perpetrator, it is also necessary to carefully assess whether the perpetrator has the ability to continue the attack. This is difficult for highly frightened defenders in the dark. Therefore, it should be considered that even after Chen's kitchen knife fell to the ground, Chen Yuefu could still take defense.

3. Liu Jinsheng's Intentional Injury Case—Determination of Abuse of Defense Rights

(1) Case Description

In October 2016, Liu Jinsheng had an argument with Huang Moujia over family and emotional issues, during which he slapped Huang Moujia twice. Huang Moujia then went to her brother Huang Mouyi's fruit shop and told him that she had been slapped by Liu Jinsheng, and requested him to mediate her breakup with Liu Jinsheng and the issue of child rearing. Huang Yi then called on Li, Mao, and Chen, who were chatting in the store, and Huang Moujia led them to Liu Jinsheng's residence at around 10 p.m. that evening.

Huang Mouyi questioned Liu Jinsheng and both sides had an argument. Huang Mouyi and Li each slapped Liu Jinsheng, who was sitting in bed. Liu Jinsheng then took out a kitchen knife from under the blanket and injured Huang's head. Huang Mouyi fled the scene immediately. Li wanted to run when he saw this, but was grabbed by Liu Jinsheng and wielded a kitchen knife to cut Li's head three times in a row.

部连砍三刀。毛某某、陈某某和黄某甲立即上前劝阻，毛某某和陈某某抱住刘金胜并夺下菜刀后，随即跟随李某某跑下楼报警。

经鉴定，黄某乙的伤情属于轻伤一级，李某某的伤情属于轻伤二级。最终，刘金胜因故意伤害罪被判处有期徒刑一年。该判决已生效。

（二）判定依据

（1）侵害人属于泄愤行为。黄某乙和李某某打刘金胜耳光的行为是一般争吵中的轻微暴力行为，不同于以伤害他人为目的的攻击性不法侵害行为。因此，刘金胜因家庭婚姻情感问题矛盾激化被打了两耳光后，持菜刀连砍他人头部，致人轻伤的行为，没有防卫意图，而是泄愤行为，不应认定为防卫行为。

（2）侵害人在事件的起因，存在重大过错。刘金胜与黄某甲因家庭和情感问题发生争吵，并打了黄某甲两耳光，这是引发黄某乙、李某某等人上门质问争吵的直接原因。换言之，事件因家庭琐事引发，且刘金胜在此过程中负有重大过错。

四、陈天杰正当防卫案——正当防卫与打架斗殴的分界

（一）案例描述

2014 年 3 月，陈天杰和其妻

Mao, Chen, and Huang Moujia immediately stepped forward to dissuade Liu Jinsheng. After grabbing the kitchen knife, Mao and Chen immediately followed Li downstairs to report the incident.

After appraisal, Huang Mouyi's injury belongs to level one minor injury, while Li's injury belongs to level two minor injury. In the end, Liu Jinsheng was sentenced to one year in prison for the crime of intentional injury. The judgment has taken effect.

(2) Judgment Basis

① The infringer was venting their anger. The act of Huang Mouyi and Li slapping Liu Jinsheng in the face is a minor violent behavior in general arguments, different from aggressive and unlawful infringement aimed at harming others. Therefore, Liu Jinsheng's behavior of repeatedly chopping someone's head with a kitchen knife after being slapped twice due to the intensification of family and marital emotional conflicts, causing minor injuries, has no intention of defense, but rather a venting of anger, and should not be recognized as a defensive act.

② The infringer was at fault in the cause of the incident. Liu Jinsheng and Huang Moujia had an argument over family and emotional issues, and slapped Huang Moujia twice. This was the direct reason for Huang Mouyi, Li Mouyi, and others to come and question the argument. In other words, the incident was caused by trivial family matters, and Liu Jinsheng was at major fault in this process.

4. Chen Tianjie's Legitimate Defense Case—The Boundary Between Legitimate Defense and Mutual Fighting

(1) Case Description

One day in March 2014, Chen Tianjie and his wife Sun

子孙某某等水泥工在海南省三亚市某工地加班运送混凝土。某晚22时许，周某某、容某甲、容某乙和纪某某饮酒后，看到孙某某在一人卸混凝土，便言语调戏她。孙某某将此事告诉了正在装混凝土的陈天杰，陈天杰生气地叫容某乙等人离开，但他们不予理会。

接着，周某某摸了一下孙某某的大腿，陈天杰与周某某等人发生争吵。周某某冲上去要打陈天杰，陈天杰也准备反击。孙某某和从不远处跑来的刘某甲站在中间，将双方架开。周某某从工地上拿起一把约2 m长的铁铲冲向陈天杰，但被孙某某拦住。周某某扔下铁铲，空手冲向陈天杰。孙某某在劝架时被周某某推倒在地，哭了起来。陈天杰准备上前扶孙某某时，周某某、容某乙和纪某某先后冲过来对陈天杰拳打脚踢，陈天杰边退边还击。

随后，容某乙、纪某某从地上捡起1 m长的钢管，冲上去打陈天杰。孙某某、刘某甲、容某甲都曾试图阻拦。容某甲阻拦周某某时被挣脱，纪某某被刘某甲抱住但一直挣扎。当纪某某和刘某甲靠近陈天杰时，纪某某将刘某甲甩倒在地，并持钢管朝陈天杰的头部打去。因陈天杰头戴安全帽，钢管滑到陈天杰的左上臂。陈天杰在保护孙某某时，用随身携带的折叠式单刃小刀乱挥

and other cement workers worked overtime at a construction site in Sanya, Hainan Province to transport concrete. At around 10 p.m., after drinking alcohol, Zhou, Rong A, Rong B, and Ji saw Sun unloading concrete alone, so they verbally teased her. Sun told Chen Tianjie, who was loading concrete, about this matter. Chen Tianjie angrily asked Rong and others to leave, but they ignored it.

Then, Zhou touched Sun's thigh, and Chen Tianjie had an argument with Zhou and others. Zhou rushed forward to attack Chen Tianjie, who was also preparing to counterattack. Sun and Liu Moujia, who were running from afar, stood in the middle and separated the two sides. Zhou picked up a shovel about 2 meters long from the construction site and rushed towards Chen Tianjie, but was stopped by Sun. Zhou threw down his shovel and charged towards Chen Tianjie empty handed. Sun was pushed to the ground by Zhou while trying to persuade him to fight, and he started crying. When Chen Tianjie was about to step forward to help Sun, Zhou, Rong B, and Ji rushed over and punched Chen Tianjie, who fought back as he retreated.

Subsequently, Rong B and Ji picked up a one meter long steel pipe from the ground and rushed up to hit Chen Tianjie. Sun, Liu Moujia, and Rong have all attempted to obstruct. When Rong A tried to stop Zhou, he broke free, while Ji was held by Liu but struggled. When Ji and Liu Jia approached Chen Tianjie, Ji threw Liu Moujia to the ground and hit Chen Tianjie's head with a steel pipe. Due to Chen Tianjie wearing a security helmet, the steel pipe slipped onto his left upper arm. While protecting Sun, Chen Tianjie used a foldable single edged knife that he carried with him to randomly swing and stab, causing injuries to Rong B, Zhou, Ji, and Liu Moujia.

乱捅，导致容某乙、周某某、纪某某、刘某甲受伤。

水泥工刘某乙闻讯赶到现场，周某某、容某乙和纪某某见状逃离，逃跑时还拿石头和酒瓶砸向陈天杰。容某乙被捅伤后跑到工地的地下室里倒地，后因失血过多死亡。经鉴定，周某某的伤情为轻伤二级；纪某某、刘某甲、陈天杰的伤情均为轻微伤。最终，法院判定陈天杰属于正当防卫，依法不负刑事责任。

（二）判定依据

（1）维护妻子的尊严与人身安全。妻子孙某某被调戏、自己被辱骂的情况下，陈天杰面对冲上来欲殴打他的周某某，也准备还击，但被孙某某和刘某甲拦住。当陈天杰去扶被推倒在地的孙某某时，周某某、容某乙和纪某某先后冲过来对他拳打脚踢，并持械殴打他。陈天杰持刀捅伤被害人时，正是被容某乙等人持械殴打的紧迫期间。因此，陈天杰在其妻子被羞辱、自己被打后，为维护自己与妻子的尊严和人身安全，被动进行还击，其行为属于防卫而非斗殴。

（2）行为符合特殊防卫条件。容某乙等人持械击打陈天杰的头部，这是人体的重要部位。在陈天杰戴安全帽的情况下，仍导致头部轻微伤，钢管打到安全帽后滑到手臂，造成手臂皮内、皮下

Cement worker Liu Mouyi rushed to the scene upon hearing the news, and Zhou, Rong B, and Ji fled upon seeing the situation. While fleeing, they even smashed stones and wine bottles at Chen Tianjie. After being stabbed, Rong B ran to the basement of the construction site and fell to the ground, but died due to excessive bleeding. After appraisal, Zhou's injury was classified as minor injury level 2; Ji, Liu Moujia, and Chen Tianjie all suffered minor injuries. In the end, the court ruled that Chen Tianjie was engaged in legitimate defense and did not bear criminal responsibility in accordance with the law.

(2) Judgment Basis

① Chen's behavior was to maintain the dignity and personal security of the wife. In the situation where his wife Sun was teased and he was insulted, Chen Tianjie was also prepared to fight back against Zhou who rushed to beat him, but was stopped by Sun and Liu Moujia. When Chen Tianjie went to help Sun, who had been pushed to the ground, Zhou, Rong B, and Ji rushed over and punched and kicked him, as well as physically assaulted him. When Chen Tianjie stabbed the victim with a knife, it was during an urgent period of being physically assaulted by Rong B and others. Therefore, after his wife was humiliated and he was beaten, Chen Tianjie passively retaliated to maintain the dignity and personal security of himself and his wife, and his behavior was considered self-defense rather than fighting.

② The behavior meets the special defense conditions. Rong B and others used weapons to hit Chen Tianjie's head, which is an important part of the human body. Despite wearing a security helmet, Chen Tianjie still suffered a minor head injury. The steel pipe hit the helmet and slid onto the arm, causing intradermal and subcutaneous bleeding in

出血，可见打击力度之大。在当时的情形下，陈天杰只能根据对方的人数和所持工具判断自身的处境。容某乙、纪某某、周某某三人都喝了酒，气势汹汹，持有足以严重危及他人人身安全的凶器。在场的孙某某和刘某甲曾试图阻拦，但孙某某被推倒，刘某甲也被甩开。而且，陈天杰半蹲着左手护住妻子孙某某，右手持小刀防卫，这种姿势是一种被动防御的姿势，且他手持的刀刃只有 6 cm 的小刀，只要对方不主动靠近攻击就不会被捅刺到。因此，本案符合特殊防卫的条件，陈天杰的防卫行为造成不法侵害人伤亡的，不属于防卫过当，不负刑事责任。

（3）行为符合正当防卫条件。虽然击打陈天杰头部的是纪某某，但容某乙当时也围在陈天杰身边，手持钢管殴打他，亦属于不法侵害人，陈天杰可以对其实行防卫。当时，陈天杰被围打，疲于应对，场面混乱。容某乙等人持有足以严重危及他人人身安全的凶器主动攻击陈天杰，严重侵犯了陈天杰和孙某某的人身权利。在这种情况下，陈天杰用小刀刺、划正在围殴他的容某乙等人，符合正当防卫的条件，属于正当防卫。

the arm, indicating the strength of the impact. At that time, Chen Tianjie could only judge his own situation based on the number of people and tools held by the other party. Rong B, Ji, and Zhou all drank alcohol with a strong aura, holding weapons that could seriously endanger the personal security of others. Sun and Liu Moujia who were present attempted to stop, but Sun was pushed down and Liu Moujia was also thrown away. Moreover, Chen Tianjie squatted with his left hand to protect his wife Sun, and held a small knife in his right hand for defense. This position was a passive defense, and the blade he held was only a 6-centimeter small knife. As long as the opponent did not actively approach and attack, he would not be stabbed. Therefore, this case meets the conditions for special defense. If Chen Tianjie's defense behavior causes injury or death to the unlawful infringer, it does not constitute excessive defense and does not bear criminal responsibility.

③ The behavior meets the conditions for legitimate defense. Although Ji was the one who hit Chen Tianjie on the head, Rong B was also surrounded by him at the time, holding a steel pipe and assaulting him, which was also considered a criminal offender. Chen Tianjie could defend himself against it. At that time, Chen Tianjie was surrounded and beaten, exhausted from responding, and the scene was chaotic. Rong B and others held weapons that could seriously endanger the personal security of others and actively attacked Chen Tianjie, seriously infringing on the personal rights of Chen Tianjie and Sun. In this situation, Chen Tianjie stabbed and scratched Rong B and others who were surrounding him with a small knife, which met the conditions for legitimate defense and belonged to legitimate defense.

思考五

1. 正当防卫的概念是什么？

2. 正当防卫的成立条件包括哪些要素？

3. 一般正当防卫与特殊正当防卫的区别有哪些？

4. 如何区分正当防卫和打架斗殴？

5. 在日常生活中，如何借助法律的武器——正当防卫，保护自身安全？

Reflection 5

1. What is the concept of justifiable defense?

2. What are the elements required for the establishment of justifiable defense?

3. What is the difference between general justifiable defense and special justifiable defense?

4. How to distinguish between justifiable defense and fighting?

5. In daily life, how to use the weapon of the law—justifiable defense to protect one's own security?

第二部分　格斗技术篇

PART II　Combat Techniques

第六章
格斗基础

Chapter 6
Basics of Combat Techniques

第一节
基本格斗姿势与移动

Section 1
Basic Fighting Posture and Movement

一、基本格斗势

基本格斗势也称实战预备姿势或格斗势，是后续格斗技术运用的起始。格斗势应符合"便于进攻、便于防守、便于移动"的原则。便于进攻指实战姿势中两手及两脚的位置便于灵活转换和迅速发动。便于防守指身体的投影面（暴露面）要小，防守面要大。便于移动指能够根据攻防的要求和特点，在不同时机和距离能快速地转换步法和姿势。按照该要求，基本格斗姿势各部位要求如下（见图6-1）：

（1）下肢：两脚平行站立，脚内侧与肩同宽。随后，右脚向后撤一步，右脚尖与左脚后跟对齐，两脚脚尖朝右斜前方45°平行移动。重心在两腿之间，两腿微屈，后脚跟轻微抬起，前脚微内扣，使身体处于"弹性"状态。

1. Basic Fighting Posture

Basic fighting posture, also known as combat readiness posture or fighting posture, is the starting point for the subsequent application of fighting techniques. The fighting style should adhere to the principles of "easy to attack, easy to defend, and easy to move". Easy to attack refers to the position of both hands and feet in actual combat, which is easy to flexibly switch and quickly launch. Easy to defend refers to having a smaller projection surface (exposed surface) of the body and a larger defensive surface. Easy to move refers to the ability to continuously and quickly change footwork and posture at different times and distances according to the requirements and characteristics of offense and defense. According to this requirement, the basic combat posture and various parts are required as follows (see Figure 6-1):

① Lower limbs: Stand with both feet parallel, with the inner side of the feet shoulder width apart. Subsequently, take a step back with your right foot, aligning the tip of your right foot with the heel of your left foot, and then move the tips of your two feet parallel at a 45 degree angle diagonally forward to the right. The center of gravity is between the legs, with the legs slightly bent, the heels slightly raised, and the front feet slightly inward buckled to keep the body in an "elastic" state.

（2）躯干：含胸收腹，侧向站立。目的是减少暴露面积。

（3）上肢：竖项梗脖，下颌微收，合齿闭唇，缩小咽喉的暴露面。双手四指卷曲并拢，大拇指置于食指和中指的第二指关节成握拳。双臂弯曲，肘关节朝下，右拳置于右颌，右肘紧贴右肋。左手置于体前，与眼同高，目平视，护住头部、躯干等要害部位。

② Trunk (torso): Hold the chest and abdomen, stand sideways. The purpose is to reduce the exposure area.

③ Upper limbs: Straighten the neck, slightly retract the lower jaw, close the teeth and lips, and reduce the exposed surface of the throat; fold the four fingers of both hands together, and place the thumb on the second joint of the index and middle fingers to form a fist. Bend both arms, with the elbow joint facing downwards, place the right fist in the right jaw, and press the right elbow tightly against the right rib. Place your left hand in front of your body, at the same height as your eyes, and look straight at them. Protect critical areas such as the head and torso.

图 6-1 基本格斗姿势 Basic fighting stance

二、步伐移动

2. Footwork

"打拳容易，走步难"。在与歹徒搏斗的现实场景中，双方的位置和攻防距离常常处于不断的移动变化中，是根据"远踢、近打、贴身摔"原则不断调整的。攻防距离的变化主要依靠脚下的步法，灵活机动的步法意味着拥有进攻与防守的选择权与主动权。

"Boxing is easy, but footwork is difficult." In the real-life scene of fighting criminals, distance between two parties is often constantly moving and changing, not standing still, but constantly adjusting according to the principles of "far kick, close hit, and close fall". The change in distance mainly depends on the footwork under one's feet, which means the choice of attack and defense, as well as the grasp of initiative.

此外，俗语讲"步不快则拳慢，步不稳则拳乱""手到步不到，打人不为妙，拳到步也到，打人如拔草"。可见，步法的移动和变换是习得各类格斗技术的基础，是提高拳腿组合技术的核心要义。步法如缺乏灵活性和机动性，将导致上下肢失调、动作僵硬、下盘不稳、力量传递不充分、组合动作衔接不连贯等问题，严重影响整体的格斗技术水平。本章视频课程主要介绍进退步和滑步（见本章二维码）。

In addition, as the saying goes, "If the footwork is not fast, the punch will be slow, and if the footwork is not stable, the punch will be chaotic." "If the hand cannot follow the footwork, hitting is not good, and if the punch can follow the footwork, hitting is like pulling grass." It can be seen that the movement and transformation of footwork are the foundation for learning various combat techniques and the core essence of improving the combination of fist and leg techniques. The lack of flexibility and mobility in footwork can lead to upper and lower limb disorders, stiff movements, unstable lower parts, insufficient power transmission, and inconsistent combination movements, seriously affecting the overall level of combat skills. This section mainly introduces forward and backward footwork and sliding footwork (see QR code of this chapter).

第二节
格斗应用原则

Section 2
Principles of Fighting Application

一、全面的技术准备

1. Comprehensive Technical Preparation

抢劫、暴力伤害等案件形式具有多变性，案发地点具有多样性，如拥堵的公交车、狭窄的小巷、逼仄的角落、公共卫生间等地点都有可能。案件形式及案发地点的不确定性使得攻击方式也难以预料。此类因素都属于不可控因素，且应对策略应根据不可控因素的不同而调整。为了提高自卫格斗胜算的概率，自卫者应在可控因素——技术与策略做好全方位的准备，充分掌握近战、

Scenarios of robbery, violent injury, and other cases can take various forms, including congested buses, narrow alleys, cramped corners, and public restrooms. In addition, the attack methods are also unpredictable, and the methods are cruel and crude. These factors are all uncontrollable, and the coping strategies will change due to different uncontrollable factors. In order to increase the probability of winning in self-defense combat, self-defenders need to be well prepared in all aspects of training, fully master various techniques such as close combat, long-range combat, throwing, ground combat, and grappling, cope with various uncontrollable situations, and not put themselves in a passive position.

远战、摔法、地面战、擒拿格斗等各类技术，以及应对各类不可控情景的智斗策略，不将自己置于被动的局面。

二、连续格斗

面对各类暴力刑事案件，一招制敌往往是理论层面的美好期许。对于大部分普通群体而言，囿于直接经验、技能熟练度及身体素质等的不足，三拳两脚并不能解决战斗，反而会陷入持续时间较长的缠斗中。因此，一方面要具备连续作战的能力，应付歹徒不同形式的进攻；另一方面要具备连续组合的能力，即掌握拳法、腿法、摔法，以及擒拿等格斗技术的不同组合使用。

三、综合技术与应用

综合技术与应用强调的是真实格斗场景的瞬息万变。从远战到近战、从摔法到地面战、从腿法到摔法、从擒拿到解脱，随着时空的变化，技术也需不断调整。在技术层面要求将各部分有机地整合到一起，避免机械地将各个技术分解独立，导致见树不见林。

四、标准技术实用化

格斗技术的学习过程中总是

2. Continuous Fighting

Faced with various violent criminal cases, defeating the enemy with one move is often a beautiful expectation at the theoretical level. For most ordinary people, due to insufficiency in direct experience, skill proficiency, and physical fitness, small moves cannot win the battle and often lead to prolonged entanglement. In this way, on the one hand, it is required to have the ability to deal with different forms of attacks by criminals and have the ability to engage in continuous combat. On the other hand, it requires the ability to combine continuously, such as boxing, leg techniques, throwing techniques, and the continuous use of grappling techniques.

3. Integrated Techniques and Applications

The integration of techniques and application emphasizes the ever-changing nature of real combat scenes. From long-range combat to close combat, from throwing techniques to ground combat, from leg techniques to throwing techniques, from capture to release, as time and space change, techniques should also be constantly adjusted. Technically, it is required to organically integrate various parts together, avoiding mechanical decomposition and independence of each technology.

4. Practical Application of Standard Techniques

In the process of learning combat techniques, practice

按照特定的标准、特定的路线练习与强化。在现实场景中，歹徒是动态变化的，而训练中学习的标准格斗技术则是静态的，若按照刻舟求剑的思路应对突发的暴力冲突则无异于缘木求鱼。为此，在日常的学习和练习过程中勿陷入固性思维中，应以实用为先，以效果为先。例如近战格斗技术中的反身横肘，应根据歹徒与自己的身高差调整横击的高度。

and reinforcement are always carried out according to specific standards and routes. In real-life scenarios, criminals are dynamically changing, while the standard fighting techniques learned during training are static. If one follows the strategy of marking the boat find the lost sword to deal with sudden violent conflicts, it is no different from seeking fish from climbing a tree. Therefore, in daily learning and practice, do not fall into fixed thinking, and prioritize practicality and effectiveness. For example, in close combat operations techniques, the reverse transverse elbow should be adjusted according to the height difference between the perpetrator and oneself.

五、技术应用无限制

5. Unlimited Application of Techniques

暴力刑事犯罪危害的是当事人的生命权，面对生命安全受到威胁的情况，虽然部分技术会对犯罪人造成较为严重的损害，如击打要害部位，包括踢裆、戳眼等，但自卫者不应手下留情，心存善念，为自己设限。对敌人仁慈就是对自己残忍。

Violent criminal offenses endanger the right to life of the parties involved. In the face of a threat to life security, although some techniques may cause serious damage to the attacker, such as kicking the crotch and poking the eye. But those who defend themselves should not show mercy, have good intentions, and set limits for themselves. At this time, being kind to the enemy is cruel to oneself.

六、先下手为强

6. It's Better to Start First

进攻是最好的防守。面对抢劫和盗窃等犯罪，不要一味地等待敌人先动手，机会稍纵即逝，若时机恰当，应抢占先机，先下手为强，控制住敌人，掐断潜在危险的引线。

Attack is the best defense. When facing crimes such as robbery and theft, do not simply wait for the enemy to take action first. Opportunities are fleeting. If the timing is appropriate, seize the opportunity, take the initiative first, control the enemy, and cut off potential dangerous leads.

七、攻守平衡

7. Attack and Defense Balance

进攻是最有效的防守，防守

Attack is the most effective defense, and defense is to better

是为了更好地组织进攻，两者互为前提，相互依存。在与歹徒的搏斗中，应先建立防守线，在避免受伤害的前提下，组织有效的进攻。例如格斗准备姿势中，对于各部位的要求应贯穿始终，不能在施展格斗技术的过程中就荡然无存。此外，在平常的练习过程中应建立防守反击的意识，如敌人摆拳进攻时，应运用格挡技术的基础上立即实施勾拳或直拳，并寻觅时机快速拉开距离。

八、格斗技术与思维

格斗并不是技术与体力的较量，硬碰硬的想法不可有。应学会避实就虚、随机应势、随机应变、以巧取胜。遇见身材魁梧、持械的歹徒，在以少对多或可立即逃脱的情境下，应掌握各类逃脱策略，利用环境等各方面的条件，迅速逃离。

九、速度优于力量

天下武功，无坚不摧，唯快不破。肌纤维再粗、绝对力量再强，缺少速度与爆发力，每轮进攻总是慢一拍或总是被闪躲，都是无效进攻。因此，各类格斗技术练习过程中，单个技术要快速迅捷，组合技术动作要连贯紧密、一气呵成。

organize the attack. The two are prerequisites and interdependent. In the fight against criminals, a defensive line should be established first, and effective attacks should be organized on the premise of avoiding harm. For example, in the preparation posture for combat, the requirements for each part should be consistent throughout, and cannot be completely eliminated in the performance of combat techniques. In addition, in the normal practice process, one should establish a sense of defense and counterattack. For example, when the enemy swings their fists to attack, they should use blocking techniques and immediately implement hook or straight punches, and look for opportunities to quickly distance themselves.

8. Fighting Techniques and Thinking

Fighting is not a competition between skills and physical strength, and there must not be a strong idea of confrontation. We should learn to avoid the real and resort to the virtual, adapt consistently to the situation, and win with cleverness. When encountering a burly, armed criminal who can escape in a few-to-many or immediate runaway situation, one should master various escape strategies and utilize the advantages of the environment and other aspects to quickly escape.

9. Speed is Better than Strength

The world's martial arts are not invincible, only strength and speed are excluded. No matter how thick the muscle fibers are, no matter how strong the absolute strength is, it is ineffective attack when there is a lack of speed and explosive power. Therefore, in the process of practicing various combat techniques, individual techniques should be fast and agile, and combined technical movements should be coherent and tight, completed in one go.

思考六

1. 格斗准备姿势的原则是什么？

2. 格斗准备各部位姿势的要求是什么，有什么目的？

3. 步法移动在格斗技术中占据多大重要性？

4. 格斗技术中应遵循哪些原则？

5. 格斗应用原则中的"技术应用无限制"是否有场景限制？

Reflection 6

1.What are the principles of combat readiness posture?

2. What are the requirements for each part of the combat readiness posture and what is the purpose?

3. How important is footwork in combat techniques?

4.What principles should be followed in fighting techniques?

5. Is there any scenario limitation in the principle of "unlimited technical application" in combat application?

第六章微课视频

第七章
远战格斗技术

Chapter 7
Long–Range Fighting Techniques

　　远战格斗指自卫者与歹徒之间保持两臂以上的距离时所采用的格斗技术。远战的主要目的是使自卫者能在格斗中与歹徒保持一定的安全距离，以使歹徒无法抓住或击打自卫者。自卫者在保持安全距离的基础上，亦有一定的时间对歹徒的攻击意图及时反应，做出相应的对策。因此，于自卫者而言，远战格斗方式相对安全，具备近可攻，退可守的优势。

　　当遇见歹徒时，自卫者应优先选择远战技术，尤其是在歹徒靠近或抓住自卫者之前，或在解脱搂抱之后，或当歹徒有刀时。自卫者远战格斗的主要武器是拳脚。攻击的目标是歹徒的软弱和致命部位。最主要的打击目标是头和裆部。攻击这些部位可严重击伤歹徒以削弱其进攻能力。次要打击目标是膝、肘、肋及下腹，也可给歹徒造成一定程度的伤害。同时，自卫者在远战格斗时，对自己的要害部位也应严加防护。

　　Long-range fighting techniques refer to the fighting techniques self-defenders use to maintain a distance of more than two arms between self-defender and criminals. The main purpose of long-range fighting is to enable the self-defender to keep a certain safe distance from the criminals in combat, so that the criminals cannot catch or hit the self-defender. The self-defender also have a certain amount of time and distance to respond promptly to the attack intentions of the criminals and make corresponding countermeasures. Therefore, for self-defense, long-range combat is relatively safe and has the advantage of being close to attack and able to retreat and defend.

　　When encountering a criminal, self-defender should prioritize long-range combat techniques, especially before the criminal approaches or captures the self-defender, or after being released from embrace, or when the criminal has a knife. The main weapons used in long-distance combat by the Self-defender Force are fists and feet. The target of the attack is the weak and deadly parts of the criminal. The main targets are the head and crotch. Attacking these areas can seriously injure the criminal and weaken their attacking ability. The secondary targets are the knees, elbows, ribs, and lower abdomen, and can also cause a certain degree of damage to the perpetrator. At the same time, self-defender should also take strict precautions against their vital parts during long-distance combat.

第一节
远战进攻技术

Section 1
Long-Range Offensive Techniques

远战进攻技术主要指腿法技术。俗语讲"欲上搏击场，腿脚必称王"。可见腿法在格斗技术体系中的重要作用。另外，武术谚语中比喻长兵器为"一寸长，一寸强"，腿法亦是如此。腿的长度约占身高的 1/2，使用腿法可在安全线范围内进攻和防守。腿法的路线可分为由下至上的弹腿、水平弧形的鞭腿，以及由后向前的蹬腿和踹腿。除腿法外，直拳和摆拳也是远战进攻技术体系的重要组成部分，可与腿法配合，形成拳腿组合。

Long-Range offensive techniques mainly refer to leg techniques. As the saying goes, "If you want to enter the fighting arena, your legs and feet will be king". It can be seen that leg techniques play an important role in the combat technical system. In addition, in martial arts proverbs, the metaphor for a long weapon is "one inch long, one inch strong", and the same goes for leg techniques. The length of the legs accounts for about half of the height and can be used for attack and defense within a safe range. The leg techniques can be divided into bottom-up bouncing, horizontally curved whip leg, and backward forward kicking and kicking. In addition to leg techniques, straight punches and swinging punches are also important components of the long-range offensive technical system, which can be combined with leg techniques to form a combination of punches and legs.

一、远战拳击技术

1. Long-Range Boxing Techniques

（一）直拳技术

直拳技术是运动路线为直线的拳击技术。直拳的特点是直打直收。两点之间直线最短，为此，直拳在快速进攻的同时，也能快速回防。直拳往往是一连串攻击组合的开端，是其他技术的开路者，是格斗过程中最直接有效的拳法之一。

动作说明：前手直拳以捎节的拳面为引领，直线向人体中线

(1) Straight Fist Technique

Straight fist technique is a technique in boxing where the movement route is a straight line. The characteristic of straight fist is to strike straight and receive straight. The straight line between two points is the shortest, so the straight fist can quickly attack and also quickly defend. Straight punches are often the beginning of a series of attack combinations, the pioneer of other techniques, and one of the most direct and effective punches in combat.

Action instruction: The front hand straight fist should be guided by the full range of the joint, and strike straight

打出；前脚蹬地向右转腰发力，力达拳面（见图7-1）；后手直拳从右下颌出手，直接向中线打出，后脚蹬地，向左转腰发力（见图7-2）。出拳时，肘与肩关节不能先动，导致架肘，架肩；不能向后拉拳后再出拳，身体不可过于向前倾斜，导致动作幅度和预兆过大。发力时应蹬地，合髋，转腰，再出手。

towards the midline of the human body. The front foot should step on the ground and turn to the right waist to exert force, reaching the face of the fist (see Figure 7-1); Take a straight punch from the right lower jaw and strike directly towards the midline, then kick the ground with the back foot and turn the waist to the left to exert force (see Figure 7-2).When punching, the elbow and shoulder joints cannot move first, causing the elbow to stand and the shoulder to stand; Do not pull the fist backwards before punching again, and do not tilt the body too far forward, which may cause excessive movement amplitude and premonition. When exerting force, one should push the ground, close the hips, and turn the waist before making a move.

动作应用：直拳技术路线最短，速度最快，尤其是前手直拳，身体转动角度小，具有极强的突击性，使敌人缺少反应时间，难以防备。使用直拳进攻技术可直接击打歹徒的面部三角区。

Action application: The straight fist technique has the shortest route and fastest speed, especially the front hand straight fist, which has a small body rotation angle and extremely strong assault ability, making the enemy extremely short of reaction time and difficult to defend against. The use of straight fist attack technique can directly hit the facial triangle of the criminal.

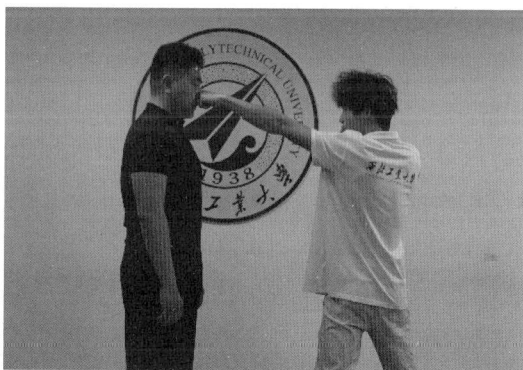

图 7-1　前手直拳　Front hand straight fist

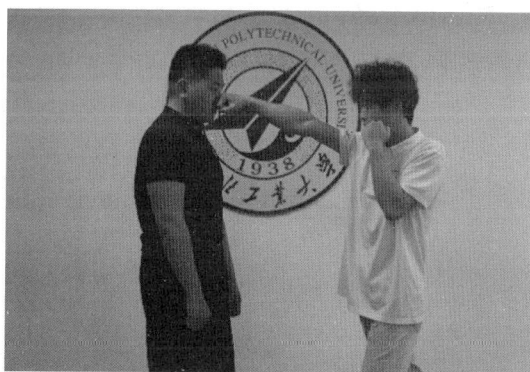

图 7-2　后手直拳　Back hand straight fist

（二）摆拳技术

摆拳技术又称为侧勾拳，是冲击运动路线为水平弧线的技术。摆拳的缺点为攻击路线长，幅度大，离心力大。优点为通过

(2) Swinging Fist Technique

Swinging fist technique, also known as side hook fist, is a technique in boxing techniques where the movement route is a horizontal arc. The disadvantages of swing boxing are long attack routes, large amplitudes, and high centrifugal forces.

腰部的旋转，可增加摆动幅度，增强动作惯性，使力量最大化。

动作说明：以左摆拳为例。实战姿势准备，重心微下降，身体向左回旋（旋转约45°），肩关节抬起（内旋），从左向右侧弧形击打至对手中线位置，力达拳面／拳峰。同时，左脚蹬地，拧腰转胯（见图7-3）。右摆拳除了不需要再右回旋蓄力外，其余环节与左摆拳相同，方向相反（见图7-4）。

摆拳动作预兆要小，勿出现拉臂或身体前倾，导致做功距离和漏洞增大；腰部转动幅度不要过大，导致上下肢脱节。

动作应用：摆拳技术主要是以侧面击打敌人的面部或其他要害部位的形式进行。使用时配合直拳技术，效果更佳。

The advantage is that it can increase the swing amplitude through the rotation of the waist, enhance movement inertia, and maximize strength.

Action instruction: Taking the left swing fist as an example. Prepare for actual combat posture, slightly lower the center of gravity, rotate the body to the left by 45 degrees, lift the elbow joint (internal rotation)., and strike in an arc from left to right to the midline position, reaching the fist face/peak with force. At the same time, step on the ground with your left foot, twist your waist and turn your hips (see Figure 7-3). The right swing fist does not require a right turn to accumulate power, and the other steps are the same as the left swing fist, with the opposite direction (see Figure 7-4).

Require that the premonition of the action is small, and do not pull the arm or lean forward, which may increase the distance and loopholes during work; Do not rotate the waist too much to prevent upper and lower limb dislocations.

Action application: The swinging technique can use large and small swinging punches based on the distance between the criminal and the self-defense person. The main difference between the big swing fist and the small swing fist is the magnitude of the arc. If the distance with the criminal is close, there is a small swing fist, otherwise the opposite is true. The main striking area is the temple on the face or vital parts.. When used in conjunction with straight fist techniques, the effect is better.

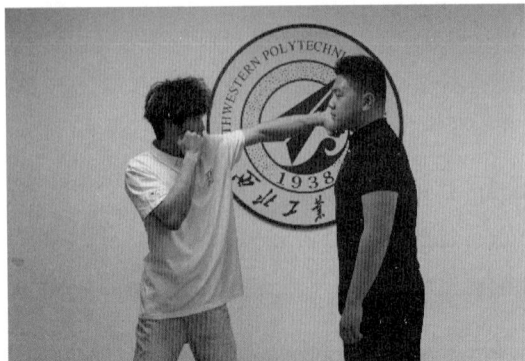

图 7-3　前手摆拳　Front hand punching

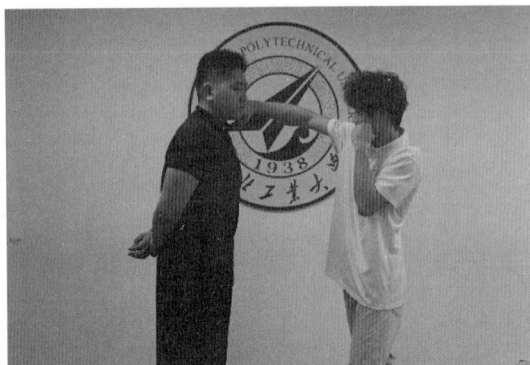

图 7-4　后手摆拳　Back hand punching

二、腿法技术

（一）弹腿技术

弹腿是远距离格斗中使用频率较高的一种腿法。以快速屈伸出以激力，如弹射之势而故名。

动作说明：以左弹腿为例。格斗姿势准备，屈膝屈髋，提膝至水平以上。脚背伸（绷直）。同时，膝关节快速由屈至伸，向前弹击，力达脚尖（见图 7-5）。

动作应用：弹腿速度在远战格斗技术中速度较快，具有出其不意的效果。当与歹徒处于合适的距离时，可使用弹腿技术快速弹击歹徒的裆部（见图 7-5）、腹部，以及下颌位置（见图 7-6）。

2. Leg Techniques

(1) Bouncing Leg Technique

Bouncing leg is a technique commonly used in long-distance combat. It is named after its rapid bending and extension to stimulate force, as in the form of a catapult.

Action instruction: Taking the left leg as an example. Prepare for combat posture, bend knees and hips, and lift knees to level. Extend (straighten). the back of the foot. At the same time, the knee quickly moves from flexion to extension, bouncing forward with force reaching the toes (see Figure 7-5).

Action application: Bouncing speed is faster in long-distance combat techniques and has unexpected effects. When at an appropriate distance from the perpetrator, leg bouncing techniques can be used to quickly hit the perpetrator's crotch (see Figure 7-5), abdomen, and jaw position (see Figure 7-6).

图 7-5　弹腿踢击裆部　Kicking the crotch with a bouncing leg

图 7-6　弹腿踢击下颌　Kicking the jaw with a spring leg

（二）蹬腿技术

不管是在格斗比赛中，还是在遭遇特殊情境时，正蹬腿的使用频率是最高的。其与人正常行走迈步的结构类似，符合人体行为习惯。行走或奔跑时，都会有提膝和落膝的动作过程，正蹬腿

(2) Leg Extension Technique

Whether in competitive combat or when we encounter special situations, the frequency of using leg extension is the highest. It has a structure similar to that of normal walking and walking, which is in line with human behavioral habits. When walking or running, there is a process of lifting the knee and falling, while leg extension increases the extension of the knee

则是在提膝后增加了伸膝的动作。正蹬腿具有放长击远和命中率高等特点。

动作说明： 右正蹬腿时，前脚（左脚）外撇45°且作为支撑腿。后脚（右脚）迅速提膝至高于水平，脚背屈，脚面朝向前方。随后，伸髋伸膝，向前用力蹬出，力达脚面（见图7-7）。

动作应用： 可通过蹬击对方腹部、膝盖及胯部进行堵击（见图7-7）或截击，阻碍歹徒的进攻（见图7-8）。随即选择逃跑或进攻。

after lifting it. The forward leg has the characteristics of long reach and high hit rate.

Action instruction: When kicking the right leg, the front foot (left foot) should be turned outward at a 45 degree angle and used as a supporting leg. Quickly raise the hind foot (right foot) above the knee level, bend the instep, and keep the top of the foot facing forward. Then, stretch your hips and knees, push forward with force, reaching the top of your feet (see Figure 7-7).

Action application: It can block or intercept the opponent's abdomen, knees, and hips by kicking them (see Figure 7-7). Obstructing the criminal's attack (see Figure 7-8), then choosing to flee or attack.

图7-7 蹬腿堵击 Kick and block

图7-8 蹬腿截击 Leg extension and intercept

（三）踹腿技术

踹腿是远战格斗中不可或缺的腿法。其具有放长击远、坐髋击短、大而凶猛等特点。踹腿灵活多变，进攻方向可从正、侧、后多个方向踹击，攻击的位置亦可从大腿上至面部，控制对方下、中、上三盘。此外，可通过身体的扭转，增加踹腿的弹性势能，增强踹击的力度。该技术的缺

(3) Kicking Technique

Kicking is an indispensable leg technique in long-distance combat. It has the characteristics of being able to strike long, hitting short while sitting on the hip, being small yet flexible, and being large yet fierce. Kicking is flexible and versatile, with multiple attacking directions from front, side, and back. The attacking position can also be from the thigh to the face, controlling the opponent's bottom, middle, and top three sets. In addition, by twisting the body, the elastic potential energy of the kicking leg can be increased,

点是动作幅度较大。

动作说明：以左端腿为例。格斗姿势准备，身体重心移向右腿，并微屈支撑；左腿屈膝屈髋，提膝至高于水平，大腿外翻（外旋），脚尖勾起（脚背屈）。随后，伸髋伸膝，力达脚面；上体微侧倾（见图7-9）。

动作应用：当歹徒欲朝自卫者逼近时，可使用该技术蹬击歹徒的胸腹部、头部或大腿根部，以阻击进攻技术，拉远距离。另外，当面对前后左右夹击时，可在面朝前方的同时，向后端腿堵击敌人。

enhancing the strength of the kicking, but the disadvantage is that the movement amplitude is relatively large.

Action instruction: Taking the left kick as an example. Prepare for combat posture, shift the weight of the body towards the right leg, and slightly bend and support the right leg; Bend the left knee and hip, lift the knee to the same height as the waist, turn the thigh outward (outward rotation), and raise the toe. Subsequently, extend the hips and knees, reaching the soles of the feet with force; Slight tilting of the upper body (see Figure 7-9).

Action application: When the perpetrator intends to approach the defender, this technique can be used to kick the perpetrator's chest, abdomen, head, or thighs to block the use of offensive techniques and bring them closer. In addition, when facing a pincer attack from front, back, left, and right, you can also kick your legs backwards to block the enemy while facing forward.

图7-9　端腿技术　Kicking technique

（四）鞭腿技术

鞭腿也称边腿，以形喻势。将大腿根部比喻为鞭把，膝关节为鞭体，脚面为鞭梢，通过整个身体的扭转，如同摔鞭子一样，将腿鞭摔出去。鞭腿属于弧线性路线腿法，可从侧面的上、中、下

(4) Whip Leg Technique

Whip legs, also known as edge legs, are used to metaphorically describe the shape of the thigh as a whip handle, the knee joint as a whip kick, and the foot as a whip tip. Through the twisting of the entire body, the leg whip is thrown out like a whip. Whip leg belongs to the curved leg technique, which can strike enemies from the upper, middle,

三路击打敌人，具有出腿快、杀伤力强和灵活性好等特点。

动作说明： 以右鞭腿为例。格斗姿势准备，左腿支撑，左脚外撇45°；右腿屈膝内扣（内旋），展髋，脚背绷直。随即，转腰伸膝，鞭甩小腿，力达脚背。

动作应用： 鞭腿主要运用于迂回阻击对方攻击或直接进攻对方。主要进攻对方大小腿内外侧（见图7-10）、躯干及头侧等部位（见图7-11）。防守反击时，防上击下或结合步法后撤躲闪，再以鞭腿还击对方。

and lower sides. It has the characteristics of fast leg release, strong killing power, and good flexibility.

Action instruction: Taking the left whip leg as an example. Prepare for combat posture, slightly bend and support your right leg, and tilt your upper body slightly to the right; Bend the left leg and swing it to the left, buckle the knee, keep your feet straight, then lift the knee whip forward and swing the calf, reaching the back of the foot to the front lower end of the calf.

Action application: Whip legs are mainly used to detour and block the opponent's attack or directly engage the opponent. Mainly attack the inner and outer sides of the opponent's legs (see Figure 7–10), torso, and head (see Figure 7–11). When defending and counterattacking, defend by hitting up and down or combining footwork to retreat and dodge, and then use whip legs to counterattack the opponent.

图7-10　鞭腿击打腿部　Whip leg hitting leg

图7-11　鞭腿击打躯干　Whip leg hitting torso

第二节
远战防守技术

Section 2
Long-Range Defense Techniques

一、接触性防守

1. Contact Defense

远战接触性防守包括应对拳击技术直拳和摆拳的拍击和格肘

Long-range contact defense includes slapping and checking elbows against boxing techniques of straight

等进攻时，防守敌的进攻拳，或应对蹬腿、鞭腿等腿法进攻时，防卫者预判进攻路线，使用抄抱等技术截击敌人进攻腿，使敌人单腿支撑；并配合近战进攻技术或配合摔法技术实施打击。

and swing punches, or refers to when the attacker uses leg techniques such as kicking and whipping to attack, the defender anticipates the attack route, uses techniques such as grabbing, hanging in, and cutting out to intercept the enemy's attacking leg, so that the enemy can support one leg, and cooperates with close combat attack techniques or throwing techniques to carry out the attack.

（一）拍击

动作说明： 以左手拍击为例。格斗姿势准备，肘关节弯曲略大于 90°，并向外旋臂约 45°。随后，前脚（左脚）蹬地，转腰转髋，前手（左手）内旋，拍打敌人腕关节，力达掌心，改变其运动方向（见图 7-12 和图 7-13）。

动作应用： 当歹徒使用直拳技术向自卫者面部或胸部击打时，使用拍击格挡。

(1) Clapping

Action instruction: Prepare for combat posture, bend the elbow slightly more than 90 degrees, and rotate the arm outward by about 45 degrees. Subsequently, the front foot (left foot). kicks the ground and rotates inward, turning the waist and hips, the front hand (left hand). rotates inward, pats the enemy's wrist joint, reaches the palm of the hand, and changes its direction of movement (see Figure 7-12 and Figure 7-13).

Action application: When the opponent uses straight fist technique to hit my face or chest, use a slap block (see Figure 7-12 and Figure 7-13).

图 7-12　左手拍击　Left hand clamping

图 7-13　右手拍击　Right hand clamping

（二）格肘

动作说明： 以左手格肘为例，格斗姿势准备，当对方进攻时，手臂微内旋，随后，由内向外格挡，力达小臂（见图 7-14 和

(2) Grid Elbow

Action instruction: Taking the left elbow as an example, prepare for combat posture. When the opponent attacks, rotate the arm slightly inward, then block from the inside out, reaching the forearm with force (see Figure 7-14 and Figure 7-15).

图 7-15)。

动作应用: 当歹徒使用诸如下短拳等弧线路线拳法击打自卫者面部时,使用格肘技术。

Action application: When the opponent uses arc lines such as swinging punches to hit my side, use blocking techniques.

图 7-14　左手格肘　Left hand grid elbow

图 7-15　右手格肘　Right hand grid elbow

(三)抄抱技术

根据敌人所使用腿法技术的不同,对抄抱技术的要求也略有不同。

动作说明: 鞭腿抄抱。格斗姿势准备,当敌人使用鞭腿技术时,左臂屈肘外旋,使用手腕钩住敌人腿上部,右臂屈肘,由下向上抄抱,钩住敌人腿下部,形成环抱之势(见图 7-16)。正蹬腿抄抱。含胸收腹,左臂屈肘由下向上抄抱敌人踝关节,右臂屈肘,掌指朝左置于敌人脚背处(见图 7-17)。侧端腿抄抱。含胸收腹,左臂屈肘由下向上抄抱敌人踝关节,右臂屈肘,掌指朝下置于敌人脚背处(见图 7-18)。

动作应用: 抄抱技术主要是用手、臂抄抱对手的小腿和踝关

(3) Picking Technique

According to the different leg techniques used by the enemy, the requirements for the grab technique also vary slightly, as shown below.

Action instruction: Whip the leg to grab. Prepare for combat posture. When the enemy uses whip leg technique, bend the left arm and rotate outward, hook the upper part of the enemy's leg with the wrist, bend the right arm and grab from bottom to top, hook the lower part of the enemy's leg, and form an embrace (see Figure 7-16); kicking and embracing. Hold the chest and abdomen, bend the elbow with the left arm and hug the enemy's ankle joint from bottom to top, bend the elbow with the right arm, and place the palms and fingers facing left on the enemy's foot (see Figure 7-17), side kick and grab. Hold the chest and abdomen, bend the elbow with the left arm from bottom to top and grab the enemy's ankle joint, bend the elbow with the right arm, and place the palms and fingers facing down on the enemy's foot (see Figure 7-18).

Action application: The grab technique mainly involves using hands and arms to grab the opponent's

图 7-16 鞭腿抄抱技术 Whip leg grab technique

图 7-17 正蹬腿抄抱技术 Straight leg grab technique

图 7-18 侧踹腿抄抱技术 Side kick grab technique

节，使敌人落入单腿支撑，平衡不稳的状态，并进一步施展摔法和拳法技术。

（四）挡踢技术

动作说明：格斗姿势准备。重心移至左腿支撑，同时右脚屈膝提起，格挡敌人的腿法进攻（见图 7-19）。

动作应用：当歹徒使用鞭腿进攻时，可使用挡踢技术防守，同时用膝盖部位迎合歹徒迎面骨部位。当歹徒使用正蹬腿或侧踹腿时，提膝可保护腹部或裆部，避免要害部位受到打击。

calves and ankles, causing them to fall into a single leg supported, unbalanced state, and further utilizing throwing and boxing techniques.

(4) Blocking Kick Technique

Action instruction: Move the center of gravity to the right leg for support, while bending the left knee to lift and block the enemy's attacking leg technique (see Figure 7-19).

Action application: When criminals use whip leg attacks, blocking kick technique can be used to defend, while using the knee area to cater to the attacker's frontal bone area. When criminals use leg kicks or side kicks, lifting the knee can protect the abdomen or crotch from being hit by vital parts.

图 7-19　提膝格挡　Knee lift block

二、非接触性防守技术

非接触防守是利用身体姿势的变化或双脚的移动，如潜身、后闪、腾身、闪步和退步等方法来闪避歹徒的进攻。非接触防守应准确掌握、娴熟应用，使其各尽其效，以凸显防守在实战中的价值。其中后撤躲闪最安全，即当敌人进攻时，立即后跳步躲闪，可拉开与敌人的距离（参考格斗基础部分的后滑步）。

（一）下潜

动作说明： 格斗姿势准备，当敌人进攻时，含胸收腹，收下颌，两手护于头部两侧。同时，身体保持直立位，屈髋屈膝，迅速下蹲至接近水平。要求下蹲时勿抬臀俯身，致使重心前移，否则即不利于向后步法移动，陷入被动局面，也将导致头部暴露在敌人面前（见图 7-20）。

动作应用： 当敌人使用直拳、

2. Non-contact Defensive Techniques

Non-contact defense is the use of changes in body posture or foot movements, such as diving, backstabbing, leaping, and stepping back, to dodge the opponent's attack. Non contact defense should be accurately mastered and skillfully applied to achieve its full effectiveness, in order to highlight the value of defense in practical combat. The safest maneuver is the retreating dodge, meaning that when the enemy attacks, you immediately perform a backward jump to dodge, which can create distance between you and the enemy (refer to the backward slide step in the basic combat section).

(1) Dive

Action instruction: Prepare for combat posture. When the enemy attacks, hold your chest and abdomen, lower your jaw, and protect both sides of your head with your hands. At the same time, maintain an upright position, bend the hips and knees, and quickly squat down to near horizontal. When squatting, it is required not to lift your hips and bend down, causing the center of gravity to move forward. Otherwise, it will not be conducive to backward movement, leading to passive situations and causing your head to leak in front of the enemy (see Figure 7-20).

Action application: When the enemy uses techniques

图 7-20 下潜躲闪 Diving and dodging

摆拳或鞭拳等技术攻打自卫者面部时，使用下潜技术，并快速使用勾拳击打敌人腹部或使用直拳击打对手裆部。

（二）左右侧闪

动作说明： 以左侧闪为例。格斗姿势准备，当敌人进攻时，重心微下降，左脚向体左侧斜前方微上一步，右脚以前脚掌为轴，蹬地内扣。同时，身体微向左侧旋转（见图 7-21）。右侧闪动作路线相同，方向相反（见图 7-22）

动作应用： 当敌人使用直拳等技术时，两手护住头部，身体向同侧微旋转躲闪、移动。

such as straight punches, swing punches, or whip punches to attack my face, use diving techniques and quickly use hook punches to hit the enemy's abdomen or use straight punches to hit the opponent's crotch.

(2) Shake Left and Right to Flash

Action instruction: Left and right swaying and flashing is a continuation of diving techniques, combined with footwork techniques. For example, prepare for a combat posture with a left shake flash. When the opponent is attacking, after diving, take a step to the left with your left foot (see Figure 7-21), followed by a step to the left with your right foot, and move to the side of the enemy's body (see Figure 7-22)

Action application: The left and right shake flash technique is mainly used by enemies to dodge while moving to the enemy's side, and quickly use techniques such as swing to counterattack.

图 7-21 左侧闪 Left flashing

图 7-22 右侧闪 Right flashing

（三）后闪

动作说明：当敌人进攻时，前脚不动，后脚向后撤一步。同时上肢后仰接近 45°，进行闪躲。下颌微收，目视前方（见图 7-23）。

动作应用：当敌人使用直拳或摆拳等拳法进攻时，使用后闪技术进行闪躲。

(3) Backflash

Action instruction: When the enemy attacks, keep your front foot still, take a step back with your back foot, tilt your upper limbs back nearly 45 degrees, dodge, lower your jaw slightly, and look ahead (see Figure 7-23).

Action application: Backward dodge technique is used to dodge when the enemy uses straight or swinging punches to attack.

图 7-23　后闪技术　Flashback

（四）左右摇闪

动作说明：左右摇闪是下潜动作技术的延续，并配合左右横移步的技术。以左摇闪为例。格斗姿势准备，当敌人进攻时，先下潜［见图 7-24（a）］。随后，左脚向体左侧横迈一步［见图 7-24（b）］。旋即，右脚向左侧紧跟一步，闪移至敌人身体旁侧［见图 7-24（c）］。

动作应用：左右侧闪技术主要应用于当敌人使用摆拳等技术时，下潜躲避的同时移动到敌人的一侧，并快速使用摆拳等技术进行反击。

(4) Left and Right Side Flashing

Action instruction: The left and right swish is a continuation of the diving technique, combined with the technique of left and right lateral steps. Taking left shake flash as an example.Prepare for combat posture and dive first [see Figure 7-24(a)] when the opponent attacks. Then, take a horizontal step with your left foot towards the left side of your body [Figure 7-24(b)]. Immediately, tighten your right foot one step further to the left and dodge to the side of the enemy's body [Figure 7-24(c)].

Action application: The left and right side swipe technique is mainly used when the enemy uses techniques such as swinging fists, diving to avoid while moving to the enemy's side, and quickly using techniques such as swinging fists to counterattack.

（a）

（b）

（c）

图 7-24 左右摇闪 Left and right side flashing

第三节
远战策略

Section 3
Long-Range Strategy

远战策略包括进攻型策略和防守型策略。远战格斗成功与否不仅取决于技术优劣，也取决于策略运用的合理性。自卫者要根据敌我双方情况灵活运用。

Long-range strategy includes offensive strategy and defensive strategy. The success or failure of long-distance combat depends not only on the quality of technology, but also on the rationality of strategic application. Self defenders need to use it flexibly based on the situation of both the enemy and ourselves.

一、进攻型策略

自卫者并非消极等待歹徒进攻、被动挨打，而是主动出击，以攻为守击伤、击退、或吓退歹徒。当自卫者只有击伤歹徒才能保护自己或出于其他各类原因（如歹徒有后援或自己耐力不足），想尽快打退歹徒时，或歹徒身高力量都不占优势时，可考虑应用此策略。策略运用方法有以下几种。

（1）用巧计诱骗歹徒，待其松懈时猛攻。

（2）用假动作及组合拳连续攻击歹徒。

（3）摆出一副拼命的打斗架式，即使挨上一两拳也不在乎。两军相逢勇者胜，在气势上要能压住对方。

二、防守型策略

此策略主要是躲避歹徒锋芒，以逸待劳。当歹徒十分强壮凶猛或持刀，或急于抓住自卫者以求速战速决，或自卫者对主动攻击缺乏能力与信心时，应考虑采用此策略。其主要的实施方法包括下面几种。

（1）不断移动，保持安全距离。

（2）节省体力，不要轻易出腿出拳。

（3）如歹徒进逼至无处后退时，应以重踹逼退对方。

1. Attack Strategy

Self defenders are not passively waiting for criminals to attack and be beaten, but actively taking the initiative to attack or repel criminals or scare them away. Whenever a defender has to injure a criminal in order to protect themselves, or for various reasons (such as the criminal having backup or having poor endurance), they want to quickly repel the criminal, or when the criminal's height and strength are not superior, this strategy can be considered. The application methods of this strategy include the following points.

① Use clever tricks to lure criminals and attack them fiercely when they slack off.

② Use fake movements and combination punches to continuously attack criminals.

③ Put on a desperate fighting posture, even if you get punched or punched, you don't care. When two armies meet, the brave will win, and they must be able to suppress each other in terms of momentum.

2. Defensive Strategy

This strategy is mainly to avoid the sharpness of criminals and wait for trouble. When the criminals are very strong and fierce, or hold knives, or are eager to catch the self-defender for quick action, or when the self-defender lacks the ability and confidence to launch an attack, the self-defender should consider adopting this strategy. The main implementation methods include the following.

① Keep moving and maintain a safe distance.

② Save energy and do not easily throw legs or punches.

③ If there is no place for the criminals to retreat, they should use a heavy kick to force the other party to retreat.

（4）留心环境以利用地形并寻找武器。

（5）采用积极的战术，准备与歹徒长时间对峙，有机会则打，无机会则打了就跑。

两种策略各有优缺点。进攻型策略有声有势、积极主动，但易消耗体力。另外，进攻时太靠近歹徒也增加了危险性。防守型格斗则灵活机动、节省体力，但在活动范围受限制时作用不大。两种策略的成功运用依赖于双方的水平能力及具体的格斗情况。一般来讲，防守型较适合于初学者。

思考七

1. 什么是远战格斗？

2. 远战进攻技术包括哪些？

3. 远战接触性防守技术包括哪些？

4. 远战进攻技术中蹬腿与踹腿的区别是什么？

5. 远战非接触性防守技术与接触性防守的优缺点有哪些？

④ Pay attention to the environment to utilize terrain and search for weapons.

⑤ Adopt proactive tactics, prepare for a prolonged confrontation with the criminals, fight whenever there is a chance, and run away if you do.

Both strategies have their own advantages and disadvantages. The offensive strategy is both verbal and aggressive, proactive, but can easily consume energy and increase danger due to being too close to the criminals during the attack. Defensive fighting is flexible and saves energy, but it has little effect when the range of movement is limited. The successful application of the two strategies depends on the level and ability of both parties, as well as the specific combat situation. Generally speaking, defensive strategies are more suitable for beginners.

Reflection 7

1. What is long-range combat?

2. What are the techniques for close combat attack?

3. What are the techniques for long-range contact defense?

4.What is the difference between a stomp and a kick in long-distance attack techniques?

5. What are the advantages and disadvantages of non-contact defense techniques and contact defense in long-distance combat?

第七、八章微课视频

第八章
近战格斗技术

Chapter 8
Close Combat Fighting Techniques

近战指自卫者与歹徒距离在一臂之内时所采用的格斗技术。近战格斗技术主要包括短拳、肘撞、膝法等进攻技术。对自卫者而言，近战格斗容易被抓被打，危险性和受伤的概率也大大增加。由于双方距离较近，自卫者没有时间和空间思考招数，攻守亦不十分明晰，双方常常是混战成一团。

Close combat refers to the situation where the defender is within arm's length of the perpetrator. The main techniques of Close combat operations include attacking techniques such as fist, elbow, and knee techniques, as well as corresponding defensive techniques. For self-defense fighters, Close combat operations is prone to being caught and beaten, and the danger and likelihood of injury greatly increase. Due to the close distance between the two sides, the self-defender does not have time and space to think about tactics, and the attack and defense are not very clear, often resulting in a melee between the two sides.

第一节
近战进攻技术

Section 1
Close Combat Offensive Techniques

一、近战短拳技术

1. Short Boxing Techniques

根据运动路线的不同可将短拳技术分为上、下短拳，以及冲天炮。两种拳法分别对应水平弧线和从下至上的运动。另外，为了更好地区分和描述左右手的动作说明，以基本格斗势正架为例（左手前，右手后），将左手称为前手，右手称为后手；反架则相反（右手前，左手后）。因此，正架左手短拳可称为前手短拳，右

According to different sports routes, boxing techniques can be divided into three types: upper short punch, lower short punch, and rocket. The two boxing techniques correspond to straight line, horizontal bending, and bottom-up curved movements. In addition, in order to better distinguish and describe the left and right hand movements of various boxing techniques, taking the basic fighting posture of the front frame as an example (left hand is front, right hand is behind), the left hand is called the front hand, the right hand is called the back hand, and the reverse frame is the opposite (right hand is front,

手短拳则可称为后手短拳。

　　勾拳技术是近距离贴身近战拳法的代表之一，运动路线为由下向上。勾拳力量大，距离可根据肘关节弯曲的角度调整，一般多在防守反击或近战纠缠时使用。

　　动作说明：以前手下短拳为例，站立格斗姿势准备。身体向左微旋转，左手小臂高度微下落。随后，左脚蹬腿发力，左拳向前，向上迅速勾击；手腕微内扣，力达拳面。击打后，按照原有路线，恢复至初始状态（见图8-1），右勾拳与左勾拳动作路线相同，方向相反（见图8-2）。发力时，身体不可挺腹后仰，重心上提，不可拉臂。

　　动作应用：勾拳技术的路线是从下往上的。为此，使用该技术时，主要击打的部位为腹部及要害部位颌骨位置。由下向上击

left hand is behind). The upright left hand straight punch can also be called the front hand short punch, while the right hand short punch can be called the back hand straight punch.

Uppercut boxing technique is one of the representatives of close range and close combat boxing, with the movement route from bottom to top. Uppercut punches have great strength and the distance can be adjusted according to the angle of elbow joint bending. They are generally used for defensive counterattacks or close combat entanglement.

Action instruction: Taking the left uppercut punch as an example, prepare for standing combat posture, rotate the body slightly to the left, slightly lower the arm height, exert force on the left foot, and quickly hook the left fist forward and upward, with the wrist slightly inward clasped, reaching the face of the fist. After hitting, follow the original route and return to the initial state (see Figure 8-1). The right uppercut punch follows the same movement route as the left uppercut punch, but in the opposite direction (see Figure 8-2). When exerting force, the body should not lean back, the center of gravity should be lifted, and arms should not be pulled.

Action application: The route of uppercut punch technique is from bottom to top. Therefore, when using this technique, the main areas of impact are the lower abdomen and jawbone, and the lower jaw, also known as a rocket, is hit from bottom to top.

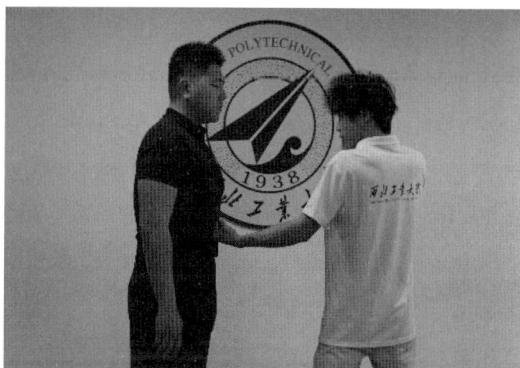

图8-1　前手勾拳　Front hand hook fist

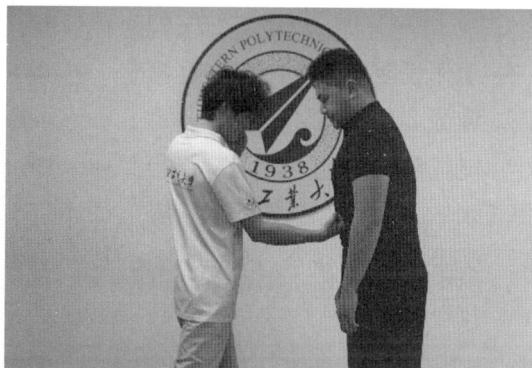

图8-2　后手勾拳　Back hand hook fist

打下颌也称冲天炮。

二、肘法技术

俗语讲"宁挨十拳，不挨一肘"。原因有如下几点。第一是力量的传递更好。力从足起，通过蹬地，扣膝，转髋，转腰，然后传递到上肢的肩、肘、手部位。相较于拳法，肘法的发力环节减少了一环，如此，力量的流失更少。第二是压强更大。肘法的力点为肘尖，相较于拳面而言面积更小。因此在力量相等情况下，压强更大。第三是肘关节的骨密度要比拳大。根据肘法运动方向的不同，可将肘法分为水平屈伸的横肘、上至下的砸肘、前后路线的刺肘、下至上的挑肘。

（一）刺肘技术

根据方向的不同，刺肘可以分为前刺肘和后刺肘。

动作说明： 前刺肘以左侧为例。实战姿势准备，左手大小臂尽可能折叠，保持屈肘状态，并上提至水平，与胸齐；拳心朝下。随后，身体向异侧（右侧）旋转，手臂回带蓄力，左脚（前脚）微内扣。旋即，转腰转髋，带动肘关节向前顶击，力达肘尖（见图8-3）。

2. Elbow Techniques

As the saying goes, "It's better to get ten punches than one elbow". There are several reasons for this: firstly, the transmission of power. Power starts from the feet, passes through kicking the ground, buttoning the knees, turning the hips, turning the waist, and then transmits to the shoulders, elbows, and hands of the upper limbs. Compared to fist techniques, the elbow technique reduces the power output by one link, resulting in less loss of strength. The second is pressure. The force point of the elbow method is the tip of the elbow, which has a much smaller area compared to the overall area. When the force is equal, the area of the elbow method is smaller and the pressure is greater. The third is bone density. The bone density of the elbow joint is higher than that of the fist. According to the different directions of elbow movement, elbow movements can be divided into horizontal flexion and extension of the horizontal elbow, top-down smashing of the elbow, and top elbow in the front and back lines; Lift the elbow from bottom to top.

(1) Elbow Piercing Technique

According to the different directions, the top elbow can be divided into the Anterior thrust elbow and the backhand top elbow.

Action instruction: Take the left side as an example for the anterior elbow. Prepare for practical combat posture, fold your left and small arms as much as possible, maintain a bent elbow position, lift up to the level, level with your chest, and have your fist facing down; Arm retraction, rotate the body towards the opposite side (right side). to accumulate force, and slightly inward buckle the left foot (front foot). Subsequently, rotate the waist and hip, driving the elbow joint to push forward

后刺肘以左侧为例，左臂肘关节弯曲90°，向体前带臂，右手掌置于左拳面上（助力）。随后，右脚蹬地，转腰转髋，带动左臂向身体后侧顶击，力达肘尖（图8-4）。

动作应用：前刺肘主要击打部位为歹徒的心窝、面部三角区等部位。后刺肘预设的情景为歹徒从背后搂抱自卫者，且双臂被固定时，可通过腰部转动的惯性，向后击打敌人腹部，进行摆脱。

with force reaching the tip of the elbow (see Figure 8-3).

Taking the backhand top elbow as an example, bend the elbow joint of the left arm 90 degrees, bring the arm forward, and place the palm of the right hand on the left fist surface (assist). Subsequently, press the right foot onto the ground, turn the waist and hip, and drive the left arm to push towards the back of the body, reaching the tip of the elbow (see Figure 8-4).

Action application: The main striking area of the Anterior thrust elbow is the criminal's heart, facial triangle, and other areas. The scenario of backhand elbow thrust is for the criminal to embrace the defender from behind, and when both arms are fixed, they can use the inertia of waist rotation to strike the enemy's abdomen backwards to escape.

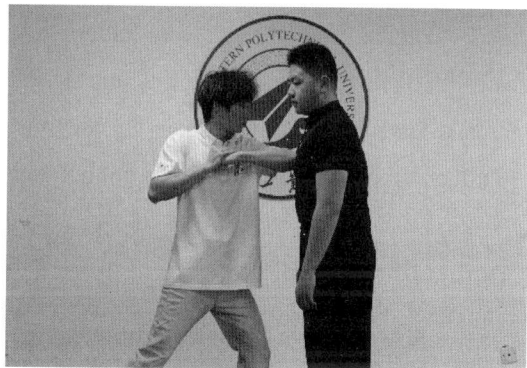

图 8-3　前刺肘　Pushing elbow forward

图 8-4　后刺肘　Pushing elbow backhand

（二）挑肘技术

动作说明：以前手挑肘为例。格斗姿势准备，左手大小臂尽量折叠。同时，左腿蹬地向左侧转腰转髋，左肘紧贴躯干由下向上挑击，力达肘尖（见图8-5），后手挑肘动作路线相同，方向相反（见图8-6）。

动作应用：当自卫者和歹徒缠斗时，歹徒使用摆拳等拳法进攻时，可在防守的基础上，寻找

(2) Elbow Lifting Technique

Action instruction: Taking the left elbow as an example. Prepare for combat posture, fold your left and large arms as much as possible. At the same time, push the left leg to the right and turn the waist to the hip (see Figure 8-5), lift the left elbow from bottom to top, and press the left arm tightly against the torso, reaching the tip of the elbow (see Figure 8-6).

Action application: When the self-defense fighter and the criminal are engaged in a fight, the criminal can use boxing techniques such as swinging to attack. Based on defense,

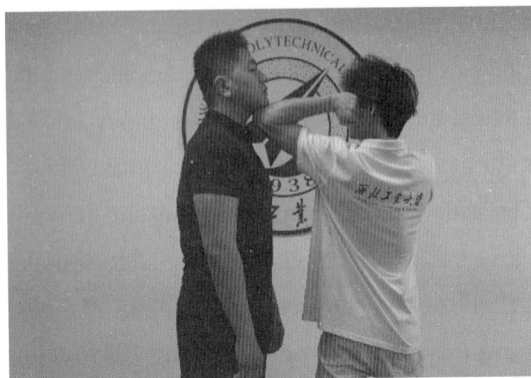

图 8-5 前手挑肘 Forehand elbow lift

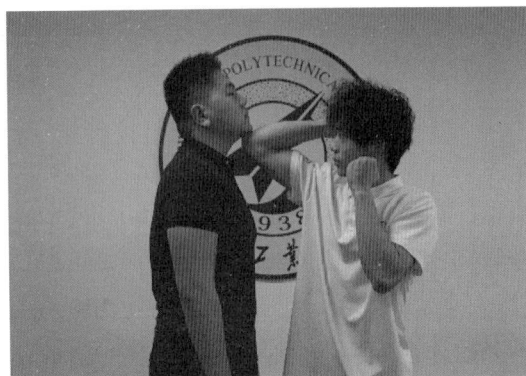

图 8-6 后手挑肘 Backhand elbow lift

时机，迅速上步，击打对方的下颌位置。

（三）砸肘技术

动作说明：以前手砸肘为例。格斗姿势准备，左臂向右旋转上抬，拳面朝上。随后，左腿蹬地转腰收腹，由上向下肘击（见图8-7），后手砸肘动作路线相同，方向相反（见图8-8）。

动作应用：当歹徒下潜抱住自卫者双腿或腰部，准备实施摔法技术时，自卫者一方面压低重心，进行防守。另一方面，使用肘尖击打歹徒背部或后颈部位置，实施进攻。

they can search for opportunities, quickly step up, and hit the opponent's jaw position.

(3) Elbow Smashing Technique

Action instruction: Taking the left elbow smash as an example. Prepare for combat posture, rotate your left arm and lift it up with your fist facing up. Subsequently, turn the left leg to the ground and lower the waist to tighten the abdomen (see Figure 8-7), then elbow strike from top to bottom (see Figure 8-8).

Action application: When the attacker dives and embraces the defender's legs or waist, preparing to perform the throwing technique, the defender lowers their center of gravity to defend. On the other hand, use the elbow tip to hit the enemy's back or back neck position to carry out an attack.

图 8-7 前手砸肘 Forward elbow smashing

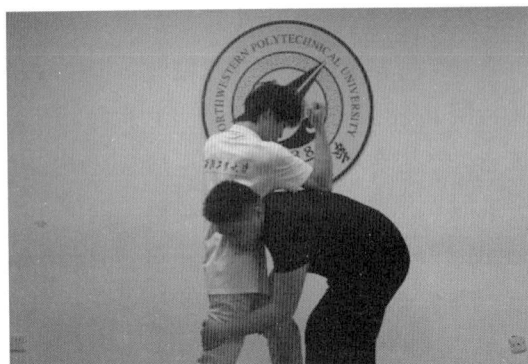

图 8-8 后手砸肘 Backhand elbow smashing

（四）横肘技术

根据方向的不同，横肘可以分为前横肘和后横肘。

动作说明： 前横肘以左侧为例。格斗姿势准备，左手大小臂尽量折叠，向后掀肘至水平，拳面朝前。随后，右脚蹬地转腰转髋，由后向前水平摆击，力达肘尖（见图8-9）。

后横肘以左侧为例，左手大小臂尽量折叠，掀肘至水平回带至体前，肘尖朝前，右手掌置于左手拳面上，左脚脚尖踮地并内扣。随后，右脚蹬地内扣，转腰转髋，带动手臂向后上方/水平摆击（根据身高差），力达肘尖（见图8-10）。

(4) Lateral Elbow Technique

According to the different directions, the transverse elbow can be divided into the anterior (front) transverse elbow and the posterior transverse elbow.

Action instruction: Take the left side as an example for the front elbow. Prepare for combat posture, fold your left arm as much as possible, lift your elbow back to level, and face your fist forward. Subsequently, turn the waist and hip with the right foot, and swing horizontally from the back to the front, reaching the tip of the elbow with force (see Figure 8–9).

Taking the left side as an example, fold the upper and lower arms of the left hand as much as possible, lift the elbow horizontally and bring it back to the front of the body, with the elbow tip facing forward. Place the right palm on the left fist surface, and the left foot tiptoe on the ground and buckle inside. Subsequently, press the right foot inward and turn the waist and hip, driving the arm to swing backwards/horizontally (depending on height difference), reaching the elbow tip (see Figure 8–10).

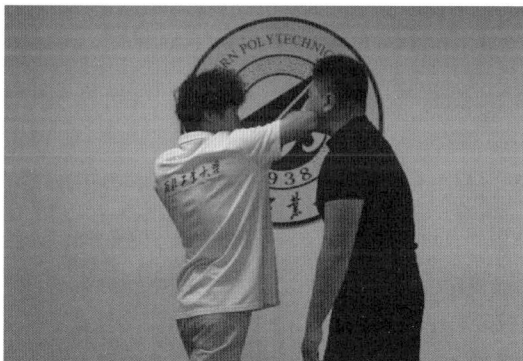

图8-9 前横肘 Forward transverse elbow

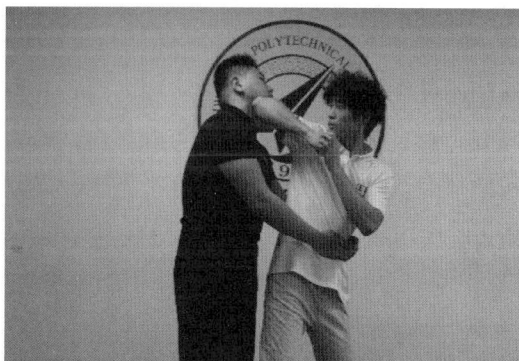

图8-10 反身横肘 Backhand transverse elbow

动作应用： 当与敌人处于缠斗状态时，可使用前横肘击打敌人头部位置。反身横肘的使用场景为当歹徒从后方抱住自卫者腰部，但双手未被控制，准备使用摔法时。先压低重心，同时向后

Action application: When in a state of entanglement with the enemy, you can use the anterior transverse elbow to hit the enemy's head position. The usage scenario of the reverse transverse elbow is when the attacker embraces the defender's waist from behind, but their hands are not controlled and they are ready to use the throwing technique. Lower the center

横肘至敌人头部。使用该技术时，需转腰转髋，增加旋转幅度，否则会导致无法击打到后方的敌人。

of gravity while bending your elbow backwards to reach the enemy's head. When using this technique, it is necessary to rotate the waist and hip to increase the rotation amplitude, otherwise it will result in the inability to hit the enemy in the rear.

三、膝法技术

膝法主要指以膝关节为力点，实施进攻的技术方法。膝击要求屈膝叠腿，使膝部突起击打敌人。膝法与肘法的特点类似，力量传递的环节少、动作幅度小、速度快、力量大、距离近、隐蔽性更强，主要用来打击歹徒裆部、大腿及下腹。若击中要害部位则可使歹徒立即失去反抗能力，即使击中腿部这样的强壮部位也会大大削弱歹徒的攻击能力，是出奇制胜的关键武器。除此以外，膝法还可作为远距离格斗的防守基础。换言之，膝法具有攻防兼备的特点，运用恰当可起到事半功倍的作用。

（一）撞膝技术

动作说明： 以左顶膝为例。格斗姿势准备，左腿屈髋屈膝，大小腿折叠。随后，双手夹固敌人脖颈，将敌人向下回拉。随后，提膝伸髋，向前顶击，力达膝关节（见图8-11）。

动作应用： 常见技术为箍颈撞膝。当与歹徒近身缠斗时，可

3. Knee Techniques

Knee technique refers to the technique of using the knee joint as the force point to carry out an attack. Knee strike requires bending the knees and folding the legs, causing the knees to protrude and hit the enemy. The characteristics of knee and elbow techniques are similar, with fewer stages of power transmission, smaller movement amplitude, faster speed, greater strength,closer distance, and stronger concealment. They are mainly used to strike the crotch, thighs and lower abdomen of criminals. If hitting the crucial area, it can immediately make the criminal lose their resistance ability. Even if hitting a strong part like the leg, it will greatly weaken the criminal's attack ability, making it a key dangerous weapon for surprise victories. In addition, knee technique can also serve as the defensive foundation for long-distance combat. In other words, the knee technique has the characteristic of both offense and defense, and proper use can achieve twice the result with half the effort.

(1) Top Knee Technique

Action instruction: Taking the left top knee as an example. Prepare for combat posture, bend the left leg to the hip and knees, and fold the big and small legs. Subsequently, clamp the enemy's neck with both hands and pull them forward and down,. Then, lift the knee and extend the hip, and push forward to reach the knee joint (see Figure 8-11).

Action application: The common technique is to clamp the neck against the knee. When engaging in close combat

快速抓住对手的衣领或搂紧脖颈，快速向己侧方向回拉用力，同时提膝向敌人的裆部或腹部等要害部位实施打击。

with criminals, you can quickly grab the opponent's collar or hug their neck, pull back and exert force towards your side, and at the same time, lift your knees to strike the enemy's vital parts such as the crotch or abdomen,

图 8-11　撞膝技术　Knee top technique

四、其他技术

4. Other Techniques

（一）短踢技术

动作说明： 以左腿短踢为例。格斗姿势准备，前腿（左腿）屈膝屈髋向胸前提起，脚尖勾起，左腿外翻，脚面朝向斜下方。随后，伸膝伸髋，向斜下方踢击力达脚外延（见图 8-12 和图 8-13 ）。

(1) Short Kick Technique

Action instruction: Taking the left leg short kick as an example. Prepare for combat posture, bend the knee and hip of the front leg (left leg). to lift towards the chest, raise the toes, turn the left leg outward, and face the foot diagonally downwards. Subsequently, extend the knee and hip, and kick diagonally downwards to reach the outside of the foot (see Figure 8-12 and Figure 8-13).

图 8-12　左腿短踢　Short left leg kick

图 8-13　右腿短踢　Short right leg kick

动作应用：短踢技术是利用歹徒保护上体时，前后腿隐蔽地攻击其膝盖或胫骨的一种踢法。击中歹徒后，可使其失去或削弱进攻能力。

（二）头撞技术

根据动作路线的不同，头撞可分为向前头撞和向后头撞。

动作说明：向前头撞时，脖颈肌肉收缩固定，身体微后倾。随后，收腹带动上体前移，力达脑门位置（见图 8-14）；向后头撞时，身体微前倾，脖颈肌肉收缩固定。随后，挺腹展髋，带动上体后倾，力达后脑勺（见图 8-15）。

Action application: Short kick technique is a kicking technique that uses the front and back legs of a criminal to covertly attack their knee or tibia while protecting their upper body. After hitting the criminal, it can cause them to lose or weaken their attacking ability.

(2) Head Impact Technology

According to the different action routes, head collisions can be divided into forward head collisions and backward head collisions.

Action instruction: When hitting the head forward, the neck muscles contract and fix, and the body leans slightly backwards. Subsequently, abdominal contraction drives the upper body to move forward, reaching the brainstem with force (see Figure 8-14). When hitting the head backwards, the body leans slightly forward and the neck muscles contract and fix. Subsequently, straighten the abdomen and hips, driving the upper body to tilt backwards, reaching the back of the head (see Figure 8-15).

图 8-14　向前头撞　Forward head collision

图 8-15　向后头撞　Backward head collision

动作应用：头撞技术可运用于当歹徒从前或从后搂抱防卫者时，撞击歹徒鼻梁或下巴。如双手不能动弹时，自卫者身体微前倾，然后迅速用后脑勺猛烈撞击歹徒的面部。歹徒面部鼻梁、

Action application: Head butting technology can be applied when a criminal embraces a defender from front or back, hitting the criminal's nose bridge or chin. When both hands cannot move. The defender leaned forward slightly and quickly slammed the back of his head into the face of the criminal. The criminal's face, nose bridge, and jaw were hit

下颌受到撞击疼痛撒手时，迅速解脱。

（三）肩顶技术

动作说明：格斗姿势准备，两手臂收于体内侧，含胸收腹。随后，后腿蹬地向前顶击，力达肩关节（见图 8-16）。

动作应用：肩顶技术主要撞击歹徒胸部迫其后退，将歹徒撞出其有效攻击距离之外，以便保持安全距离并准备下一步的攻击或迅速逃离。

and painful, and he quickly let go.

(3) Shoulder Top Technique

Action instruction: Prepare for combat posture, with both arms tucked in on the inside of the body, including the chest and abdomen. Subsequently, push forward with the hind legs, reaching the shoulder joint with force (see Figure 8-16).

Action application: Shoulder top technique mainly impacts the perpetrator's chest to force them to retreat, pushing them beyond their effective attack distance, in order to maintain a safe distance and prepare for the next attack or quick escape.

图 8-16 肩顶技术 Shoulder top technology

第二节
近战防守技术

Section 2
Close Combat Defense Techniques

拳谚讲："攻中有守不丢丑，守中有攻拳家走。"只有保护好要害部位，避免受到严重的打击，才能进一步组织有效的进攻。防守和进攻同等重要，切不可忽视。另外，近战接触性防守中也可与远战接触性防守中的提膝格挡技

As the saying goes, "When attacking, there is no shame in defending, and when defending, there is an attack." Only by protecting critical areas and avoiding serious attacks can effective attacks be further organized. Defense and offense are equally important and cannot be ignored. In addition, close combat contact defense can also be combined with knee lifting and blocking techniques in long-range contact defense, making

术配合，如此防守更加严密，使躯干和下肢皆在保护范围内。

defense more rigorous. Both the trunk and lower limbs are within the protection range.

接触性防守

Contact Defense

近战接触性防守是防卫者利用肢体通过格挡、掩肘等方法防止面部、躯干等要害部位受到打击的技术。

Close combat contact defense is the use of the defender's body to prevent critical areas such as the face and torso from being hit by tapping, blocking, and shelving.

（一）掩肘

动作说明：格斗姿势准备，当对手进攻时，重心微下降，两臂弯曲并拢，置于躯干位置，含胸收腹（见图 8-17）。

动作应用：当敌人使用从下向上的上短拳、冲天炮等短拳技术击打腹部时，使用掩肘技术保护胸腹部等要害部位。

(1) Elbow Covering

Action instruction: Prepare for combat posture. When the opponent attacks, the center of gravity slightly decreases, arms are bent and closed, placed in the trunk position, with chest and abdomen (see Figure 8-17).

Action application: When the enemy uses a bottom-up hook technique to hit the abdomen, use elbow covering technique to protect critical areas such as the chest and abdomen.

图 8-17 掩肘技术 Elbow covering technique

（二）推裆

动作说明：格斗姿势准备，当敌人用膝法进攻时含胸收腹，两手臂弯曲略大于90°，双手掌心朝下，下压推挡敌人的大腿中部位置，阻挡其后续动作的实现（见

(2) Pushing Gears

Action instruction: Prepare for combat posture. When the enemy uses knee techniques to attack, hold your chest and abdomen in, bend your arms slightly more than 90 degrees, palms facing down, and press down on the middle of the opponent's thighs to block their subsequent movements

图 8-18)。并寻找时机, 使用勾拳技术进行反击 (见图 8-19)。

动作要求: 推挡技术主要是针对近战格斗技术中的膝撞 (顶膝)。

(see Figure 8-18). And look for opportunities to use hook techniques to counterattack (see Figure 8-19).

Action requirements: The thrust technique is mainly aimed at knee collisions (top knee). in Close combat operations techniques.

图 8-18　推挡　Pusher

图 8-19　推挡勾拳　Pushing hook fist

第三节
近战格斗技术策略

Section 3
Technical Strategies for Close Combat Fighting

在格斗过程中要秉持综合运用、连续格斗以及攻守兼备的原则。作为防守的一方, 保护好自己是前提。应在建立防御线的基础上, 再施展进攻技术。弧线进攻技术时被阻挡后, 应快速转换其他线路技术, 使敌人处于疲于应付的防御状态, 不断寻找敌人的破绽。切勿重复使用单一技术。

In the process of fighting, we should adhere to the principles of comprehensive utilization, continuous fighting, and both offense and defense. As the defensive side, protecting oneself is a prerequisite, and offensive techniques should be applied on the basis of establishing a defensive line. After being blocked in a straight line attack technique, one should quickly switch to other line boxing techniques to keep the enemy in a state of exhausted defense and constantly search for their weaknesses. Do not reuse a single technology.

思考八

1. 近战格斗技术包含哪几类？

2. 近战各类技术的特点有哪些？

3. 近战格斗技术中的肘法技术包括哪些？

Reflection 8

1.How many types of close combat techniques are there?

2.What are the characteristics of various techniques in close combat?

3.What are the elbow techniques in close combat techniques?

第七、八章微课视频

第九章
摔法格斗技术

Chapter 9
Wrestling and Fighting Techniques

第一节
保护性倒地

Section 1
Protective Falling to the Ground

保护性倒地也称跌法，指被敌人使用摔法摔倒或失足跌倒，为了保护要害部位而采用的各类倒地动作。"有摔就有跌"，两者互为前提。武术拳谚讲"未学打人，先学挨打"，摔法亦是如此，"未学摔人，先学挨摔"。只有先保护好自己，才能组织和实施有效的进攻。为此，学习保护性倒地是学习摔法的前置条件。

保护性倒地包括跌扑与滚翻两类。在此基础上，根据跌倒方向和身体接触面的不同，将跌扑类技术分为前倒、后倒、左右侧倒。滚翻类技术可分为前滚翻和后滚翻。缓冲、勾头、团身、闭气、臂内旋是保护性倒地各技术的共有特征和要求。在学习和练习保护性倒地时，应以总纲为领，不断练习。

Protective fall, also known as fall method, refers to various fall actions taken by enemies to protect critical areas when they fall or slip. "If there is a fall, there is a fall", both are prerequisites for each other. The saying in martial arts boxing goes, "If you haven't learned how to hit someone, learn how to get hit first." The same goes for throwing techniques. If " you haven't learned how to hit someone, learn how to get hit first." Only by protecting yourself can you organize and implement effective attacks. Therefore, learning protective falling is a prerequisite for learning throwing techniques.

According to the different directions of falls and body contact surfaces, protective falls can be classified into static forward, backward, left and right side falls, as well as dynamic forward and backward rolls. The common characteristics and requirements of protective falling to the ground are buffering, hooking, bulging, breathing, arm rotation. When learning and practicing protective falls, one should take the overall outline as the guide and continuously practice.

一、前倒技术

动作说明： 站立姿势准备，向前倒地时，两手臂逐步弯曲，保持缓冲，掌心朝下，呈正三角形状接触地面；两腿间距略宽于肩，两腿脚尖触地，脚后跟抬起；躯干、大腿和小腿肌肉保持紧张状态，避免接触地面。接触地面时应闭气，增加肌肉张力（见图9-1）。

动作应用： 当不慎滑倒并向前倒地时，或被敌人从后面实施抱腿摔倒地时，应按照前倒的要求接触地面，避免要害部位的损伤。

1. Forward Fall Technique

Action instruction: Prepare for standing posture. As you fall forward, gradually bend your arms, maintain cushioning, palms facing down, and make contact with the ground in a triangular shape; The distance between the legs is slightly wider than the shoulders, the toes of the legs touch the ground, and the heels are lifted; Keep the trunk, thighs, and calf muscles tense and avoid contact with the ground. When in contact with the ground, one should hold their breath and increase muscle tension (see Figure 9-1).

Action application: When accidentally slipping and falling forward to the ground, or when being lifted by an enemy from behind and falling to the ground, contact the ground according to the requirements of falling forward to avoid damage to critical parts.

图9-1 前倒技术 Forward inversion technique

二、后倒技术

动作说明： 站立姿势准备。向后倒地时，两腿抬离地面，髋关节与膝关节呈90°，两脚间距与肩同宽，脚面朝前；两手掌心朝

2. Backward Fall Technique

Action instruction: Prepare for standing posture. When falling backwards, lift both legs off the ground, bend the hip and knee joints at a 90° angle, with the feet shoulder width apart and facing forward; Place your palms facing down and

下，向身体两侧前斜 45° 方向拍地、勾头、腹部收紧，使身体处于团身状态，下背部接触地面（见图 9-2）。

动作应用： 当不慎滑倒或歹徒使用正面下潜抱摔向后倒地时，应按照后倒的技术要求接触地面。

pat the ground at a 45° angle forward on both sides of your body. Hook your head and tighten your abdomen to keep your body in a ball state, with your lower back touching the ground (see Figure 9-2).

Action application: When accidentally slipping or the perpetrator uses a frontal diving hug to fall backwards to the ground, they should follow the technical requirements for backwards falling and make contact with the ground.

图 9-2　后倒技术　Backward inversion technique

三、侧倒技术

3. Lateral Fall Technique

动作说明： 以右侧为例。右侧脚向前抬腿，脚面外翻，横向向身体斜前侧蹬出，左侧膝关节弯曲支撑；右手掌心朝下，向身体右侧前斜 45° 方向拍地，左手臂架于额头斜上方；身体侧屈，抬头目视前方（见图 9-3）。

动作应用： 当单侧脚不慎打滑或歹徒实施单腿抱摔时，应使用侧倒技术接触地面，保护要害部位。

Action instruction: Taking the right side as an example. Lift your right foot forward, flip your foot outward, and push it sideways towards the front of your body. Bend and support your left knee joint; With the palm of the right hand facing downwards, pat the ground in a 45 ° forward tilt towards the right side of the body, and the left arm rest diagonally above the forehead; Bend your body sideways, look up and ahead (see Figure 9-3).

Action application: When one side of the foot accidentally slides, or when the perpetrator performs a single leg grab, the side down technique should be used to contact the ground and protect the vital parts.

图 9-3　侧倒技术　Inverted technique

四、前滚翻技术

动作说明：两腿微屈，团身勾头，向前翻滚。由蹲撑开始，两腿微屈，同时弯曲双臂、低头、提臀［见图 9-4(a)］、团身向前滚翻。在前滚的过程中，肩部、背部和臀部要依次着地［见图 9-4(b)］，背部着地的时候要迅速弯曲小腿，上体与膝盖紧紧靠在一起，两手抱住小腿［见图 9-4(c)］，向前滚动后迅速站起［见图 9-4(d)］。

动作应用：当有人从后面推击或向前滑倒，且动量过大时，应使用前滚翻技术，缓冲泄力。

4. Front Roll over Technique

Action instruction: Bend your legs slightly, curl your body and hook your head, and roll forward. Squat up, straighten your legs, bend your arms, lower your head, lift your hips [see Figure 9-4(a)], and roll your body forward. During the forward rolling process, the back of the head, as well as the shoulders, back, and hips, should land on the ground in sequence [see Figure 9-4(b)]. When landing on the back, the calves should be quickly bent, and the upper body should be tightly pressed against the knees [see Figure 9-4(c)]. Hold the calves with both hands and roll forward into a squat position [see Figure 9-4(d)].

Action application: When someone pushes or slides forward from behind and falls to the ground with excessive momentum, forward rolling technique should be used to cushion the release force.

(a)

(b)

(c)

(d)

图 9-4 前滚翻技术 Front roll over technology

五、后滚翻技术

5.Rear Roll over Technique

动作说明：后倒时［见图 9-5(a)］，两手向身体两侧拍地，颈部向左侧屈。随后，抬髋收腹，两脚向身体后方发力，经颈部右侧，向后翻滚［见图 9-5(b)］。翻滚时，臀部、背部、颈部、头依次着地。双脚着地瞬间，迅速抬头，双手支撑推地［见图 9-5(c)］，迅速站起［见图 9-5(d)］。

动作应用：当有人从前面推击或向后滑倒，且动量过大时，应使用后滚翻技术，缓冲泄力。

Action instruction: When falling backwards [see Figure 9-5(a)], pat the ground with both hands on both sides of the body and bend the neck to the left. Subsequently, lift the hips and tighten the abdomen, exert force with both feet towards the back of the body, and roll the body backwards through the right side of the neck [see Figure 9-5(b)]. When rolling, land on the hips, back, neck, and head in sequence. When both feet are on the ground, quickly raise your head, support and push the ground with both hands [see Figure 9-5(c)], and stand up quickly [see Figure 9-5(d)].

Action application: When someone pushes from the front or slides backwards and falls to the ground, and the momentum is too large, the back roll technique should be used to cushion the release force.

(a)

(b)

(c)   (d)

图 9-5 后滚翻技术   Rear roll over technology

第二节
摔法进攻技术

Section 2
Throwing Attack Techniques

拳加跤，艺更高。根据歹徒与自卫者的距离，以及是否主动进攻，将摔法分为贴身摔和接腿摔两类。贴身摔指自卫者与歹徒处于贴身缠斗中使用的技法，包含夹脖、抱腿及抱腰等不同部位的贴身摔法。接招摔主要指歹徒实施远距离腿法后，通过接触性防守后反摔的技法，即防守反击。但在实际情境搏斗中，歹徒不会静立不动，等待自卫者实施摔法。为此，即使是主动进攻的贴身摔也常伴有纠缠或其他技术。

本节针对使用率较高的贴身摔介绍三种，使用难度较高的接腿摔介绍两种。贴身摔对应抱腿和夹颈，并预设攻击者实施直拳和摆拳进攻后的应对措施。接腿摔是针对攻击者实施远战腿法时，如正蹬腿、侧踹腿等直线

Boxing and wrestling make one more skilled. According to the distance between the attacker and the defender, as well as whether to actively attack, the throwing method is divided into two categories, close to body throwing and leg catching throwing. Close to body throwing refers to the technique used by defenders and attackers in close combat, including neck pinching, leg hugging, and waist hugging. The technique of catching and throwing mainly refers to the attacker's defensive counterattack, which involves using contact defense after implementing long-range leg techniques. But in actual combat situations, the attacker will not stand still and wait for the self-defense to execute the throwing technique. For this reason, even active attacks with close falls are often accompanied by entanglement or other techniques.

This section introduces three types of close fitting falls with high usage rates and two types of leg extension falls with high difficulty in use. Close to body falls correspond to leg hugging and neck pinching respectively, and the attacker's response measures after implementing straight and swing attacks are pre-set. The leg catching and throwing technique is mainly used when the attacker is using long-range leg techniques such as straight leg

腿法和弧线腿法的鞭腿的防守摔法。

techniques like forward kicking and side kicking, as well as whip leg defensive throwing techniques such as curved leg techniques.

一、贴身摔

（一）下潜抱腿摔

动作说明：实战姿势准备。躯干保持直立位，屈膝下蹲至接近水平后［见图 9-6(a)］，左脚快速上步，前插至歹徒两腿中间位置；两手快速搂抱敌人双腿膝窝下部［见图 9-6(b)］。随后，两手臂向上抗举敌人的同时，用左肩向前顶击敌人左腰部或腹部，同时两手向回拉，前后协同用力，破坏敌人重心点，将敌人摔倒［见图 9-6(c)］。

动作应用：在进攻者毫无防备的情况下，出其不意地迅速下潜抱摔，或当攻击者使用直拳或摆拳进攻头部时，在采用下潜闪躲的基础上，快速跟进，实施抱摔。

1. Close Throw

(1) Diving with Leg Hugging and Throwing

Action instruction: Prepare for actual combat posture. Keep the torso in an upright position, bend the knees and squat down to near horizontal [see Figure 9-6(a)], then quickly step up with the left foot and insert it forward to the middle of the criminal's legs; Quickly embrace the lower part of the enemy's legs and knee sockets with both hands [see Figure9-6(b)]. Subsequently, while lifting the enemy with both arms upwards, use your left shoulder to push forward to the enemy's left waist or abdomen, push your body forward, pull your hands back, and work together to destroy the enemy's center of gravity, causing them to fall [see Figure 9-6(c)].

Action application: Quickly dive and grab the attacker off guard. Or when the attacker uses a straight or swinging fist to attack the head, they can quickly follow up and implement a throw while diving and dodging.

(a)　　　　　　　　(b)　　　　　　　　(c)

图 9-6　下潜抱腿摔　Diving with leg hugging and falling

（二）夹颈过背摔

动作说明：实战姿势准备。在敌人进攻格挡后［见图 9-7(a) ］，右腿快速向敌人对侧腿迈步，身体向左旋转，在右臂快速搂夹对方颈部的同时，左手快速置于右手腕部进行加固。旋即，左脚回撤一步，使两脚平行站立，背部贴近敌人胸腹部，右腰部紧顶对方身体，作为破坏重心点［见图 9-7(b) ］。旋即，蹬地伸膝，低头收腹挺髋，向左回旋发力，将敌人摔倒［见图 9-7(c) ］。

动作应用：当敌人用摆拳时，在可使用格肘防守的同时，快速夹紧对方脖颈实施此技术。此外，若感觉敌我双方体重较为悬殊，则可在过背摔的基础上，实施绊腿技术。即在过背摔的基础上，使用右小腿向后横打敌人小腿外侧。

(2) Neck Pinch over Back Throw

Action instruction: Prepare for actual combat posture. When the enemy attacks and blocks [see Figure 9-7(a)], take a quick step towards the opponent's right leg with your right leg, rotate your body to the left, and quickly wrap your right arm around the opponent's neck. Place your left hand on your right wrist for reinforcement. Then, take a step back with your left foot, standing parallel with your back close to the enemy's chest and abdomen, and pressing your right waist against their body as the center of gravity for destruction [see Figure 9-7(b)]. Immediately, push the ground and extend the knees, lower your head, tighten your abdomen and hips, turn left and exert force, and fall the enemy [see Figure 9-7(c)].

Action application: When the attacker uses a swing fist, they can use a grid elbow defense while quickly clamping the opponent's neck to implement this technique. In addition, if you feel that there is a significant weight difference between the enemy and us, you can implement leg tripping techniques on the basis of a backfall. On the basis of the over back fall, use the right calf to strike the enemy's outer calf backwards horizontally.

(a)　　　　　　　　(b)　　　　　　　　(c)

图 9-7　夹颈过背摔　Neck clip over back fall

（三）绊腿摔

动作说明：和敌人缠斗时，搂抱或夹固敌方颈部，并向回拽拉，敌人会下意识向前上步，并本能地对抗后仰[见图9-8(a)]。此时，抓住机会迅速向前迈步到敌人腿后[见图9-8(b)]，在向后绊击的同时，两手向前推击，将敌人摔倒[见图9-8(c)]。

动作应用：当和敌人进入近身缠斗时，可使用该技术改变局势。

(3) Tripped Leg Throw

Action instruction: When engaging in a fight with an enemy, hold or clamp the enemy's neck and pull forward. The enemy will instinctively step forward and instinctively resist tilting backwards [Figure 9-8(a)]. At this point, seize the opportunity and quickly step forward to the enemy's leg [Figure 9-8(b)], tripping backwards. At the same time, push forward with both hands, causing the enemy to fall [Figure 9-8(c)].

Action application: When engaging in close combat with enemies, this technique can be used to change the situation.

(a)　　(b)　　(c)

图 9-8　绊腿摔　Trip leg fall

二、接腿摔

2. Leg Extension and Throw

（一）抱腿挑摔

动作说明：以接敌人右腿为例。实战姿势准备。当敌人以鞭腿击打自卫者胸腹部时，自卫者找准敌人腿法路线，使用两手抄抱技术，扣住其右小腿[见图9-9(a)]；向前上一步，拉进与敌人距离。随后，左手臂由屈至伸，

(1) Leg Hugging and Throwing

Action instruction: Taking the right leg of the enemy as an example. Prepare for practical combat posture. When the attacker strikes the defender's chest and abdomen with a whip leg [see Figure 9-9(a)], identify the enemy's leg route, use the technique of two handed grab (see throwing defense), and buckle his right calf; Press forward slightly and pull in the distance from the enemy. Subsequently, the left arm is

在向斜上方抬高其悬空腿高度的同时,右脚回勾敌人支撑腿[见图 9-9(b)],使敌人失去支撑并摔倒[见图 9-9(c)]。

动作要求:抬高敌人悬空腿,回勾支撑腿,两个动作要协调同步完成。

bent to extended, and the height of its suspended leg is raised diagonally upwards [see Figure 9-9(b)]. At the same time, the right leg hooks and kicks the enemy's supporting leg, causing the enemy to lose and fall [see Figure 9-9(c)].

Action requirements: Raise the enemy's suspended leg, and coordinate the two movements of the back hook support leg to complete synchronously.

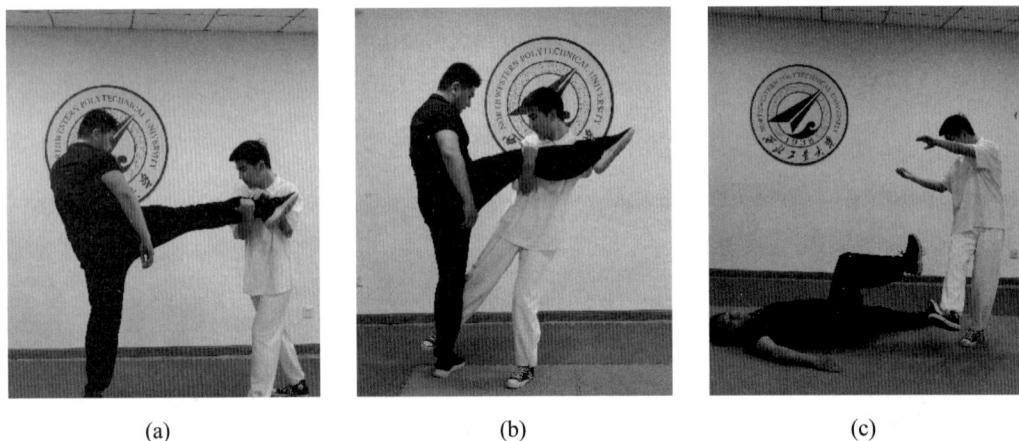

(a)　　　　　　　(b)　　　　　　　(c)

图 9-9　抱腿挑摔　Leg hugging and throwing

（二）抱腿压摔

动作说明:以接右鞭腿为例。当敌方用鞭腿进攻时,两手抄抱其鞭腿[见图 9-10(a)]。随后,向前上一步,拉近距离;左手抄抱敌人小腿部位,右手抱住其大腿上部,前(右)肩紧顶敌人同侧腰部。旋即,左脚向后回旋 90°,将抱住的腿往两腿中间回拉[见图 9-10(b)]。同时,身体微前压,双手贴近对方大腿根部和腹部,用胸臂下压敌人腰胯部,形成一上一下之力,破坏敌人重心,将其摔倒[见图 9-10(c)]。

(2) Leg Hugging Pressure Drop

Action instruction: Taking the right whip leg as an example. When the enemy attacks with whip legs, take a step towards the diagonal direction of the attacking leg, dissolve the strength, and hold the whip legs with both hands, while using the body to press against the shins of the calf [see Figure 9-10(a)]. Then, take a step forward with your right foot towards the enemy and bring them closer; Report the enemy's calf area with the left hand, hold the upper thigh with the right hand, and press the front (right). shoulder tightly against the enemy's waist on the same side. Immediately, turn the left foot back 90 degrees and pull the leg you are holding back towards the middle of both legs [see Figure 9-10(b)]. At the same time, press your body forward slightly, put your hands close to the base of the opponent's thighs and abdomen, and use your chest and arms to press down on the enemy's waist and hips, creating an upward and downward force, disrupting the enemy's center of gravity and causing them to fall [see Figure 9-10(c)].

动作要求： 实施抱腿摔时，回旋、下压及抬高腿部三个动作应协同配合，同时完成。

Action requirements: When performing a leg hugging throw, the three movements of spinning, pressing down, and lifting the leg should be coordinated and completed simultaneously.

(a)

(b)

(c)

图 9-10 抱腿压摔 Leg hugging and pressure drop

第三节
摔法防守技术

Section 3
Throwing Defense Techniques

摔法防守技术也称破摔技。使用时，应秉持以下原则。第一，贴身摔应拉开与敌人距离。推开歹徒的肩部和跨跟等根节部位，并屈腿俯身，降低中心，摆脱贴合状态。第二，接腿摔应摆脱被接腿的控制。本节针对使用比较广泛的摔法技术分别提出相应的防守方法，可根据一般的原则将其和具体技术的特征结合使用。

Defensive throwing technique, also known as breaking throwing technique. When using, the following principles should be adhered to: first, throwing close to oneself to distance oneself from the enemy. Push away the culprit's shoulders and heel joints, and bend down to lower the center, breaking free from the fit. second, The control of the leg should be overcome when attempting to catch a leg. This section proposes corresponding defensive methods for the widely used throwing techniques, which can be combined based on general principles and specific technical characteristics.

一、贴身摔防守

（一）下潜抱腿摔防守

动作说明： 当歹徒下潜搂抱自卫者双腿，准备实施摔法时，在两腿快速屈腿下蹲的同时，后腿后撤，身体前压，降低重心点，避免身体悬空。旋即，两手推击对方的肩部、头部或体侧，拉开敌我之间的距离，阻止敌人成功施展下潜摔法（见图 9-11）。阻挡后，可使用顶膝技术快速击打敌人腹部或头部，或砸肘击打敌人背部或后颈部位，或使用断头台技术夹固敌方脖颈部位。

（二）夹颈过背摔防守

动作说明： 过背摔的核心点是利用腰部的杠杆作用摔倒敌人。为此，当敌人准备施展过背摔时，应首先屈膝下蹲，降低重心点，同时用两手推击敌人肩部和髋部位置，拉开与敌方的距离，防止被摔（见图 9-12）。另外，敌人的腹部位置处于空档位置，可配合使用勾拳。

1. Close Throw Defense

(1) Diving with Leg Hugging and Throwing Defense

Action instruction: When the criminal dives and embraces the defender's legs in preparation for the fall, the legs should be quickly bent and squatted, while the hind legs should be pulled back and the body should be pressed forward to lower the center of gravity and avoid being suspended. At the same time, push the opponent's shoulders or head with both hands to widen the distance between us and the enemy, and prevent them from successfully using the diving technique. After blocking, you can use the top knee technique to quickly hit the enemy's abdomen or head, or smash the enemy's back or neck with an elbow, or use the guillotine technique to clamp the enemy's neck (see Figure 9-11).

(2) Neck Pinch over Back Fall Defense

Action instruction: The core point of backfall is to use the leverage of the waist to fall the enemy. Therefore, when the enemy is preparing to perform a backfall, they should first bend their knees and squat down, lower their center of gravity, and at the same time use both hands to push the enemy's shoulders and hips to widen the distance from the enemy and prevent falling (see Figure 9-12). In addition, the enemy's abdomen is in neutral position and can be used in conjunction with hook punches.

图 9-11　下潜抱腿摔防守　Diving with leg hugging and falling defense

图 9-12　过背摔防守　Overfall defense

（三）绊腿摔防守

动作说明： 绊腿摔的核心点是将敌人上肢向后推击，下肢则通过向前摆动腿，并快速向后回踢敌人支撑腿，破坏重心。为此，当敌人准备实施绊腿摔时［见图9-13(a)］，首先对抗敌人向后推挤的力量，同时，后脚向后撤一步，在减少敌方用力空间的同时，化被动为主动，将敌人摔倒［见图9-13(b)］。

(3) Tripping and Throwing Defense

Action instruction: The core point of leg tripping is to push the enemy's upper limb backwards, while the lower limb swings the leg forward and quickly kicks the enemy's supporting leg backwards, disrupting the center of gravity. For this reason, when the local authorities are preparing to implement leg tripping [see Figure 9-13(a)], they should first counter the enemy's backward pushing force, and at the same time, take a step back with their hind feet, making the enemy lack space to exert force and passively take the initiative [see Figure 9-13(b)].

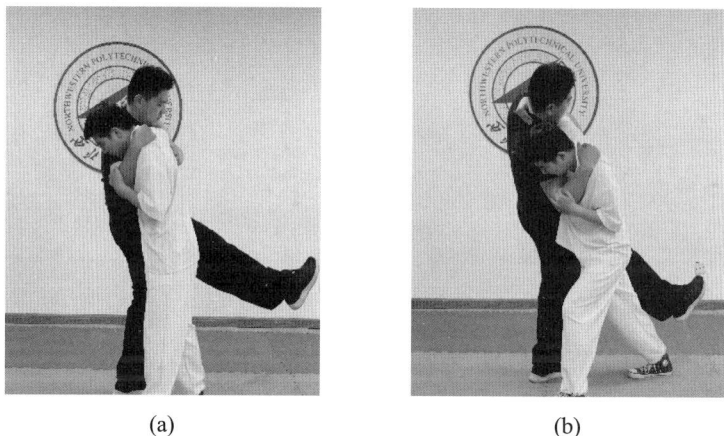

(a)　　　　　　　　　　(b)

图 9-13　绊腿摔防守　Leg tripping defense

二、接腿摔防守

2. Leg Catching and Throwing Defense

（一）抱腿挑摔防守

动作说明： 当使用腿法被敌人控制时，悬空腿应立即屈膝前顶，并使用双手按压或抱住其头部。当敌人勾踢时，支撑腿适时跳起或后撤，使踢击动作落空。随后，旋转大腿至膝关节朝下，并屈膝下压，抽出控制腿（见图9-14）。

(1) Leg Hugging and Throwing Defense

Action instruction: When using leg techniques and being controlled by the enemy, the suspended leg should immediately bend its knees and press or hug the opponent's head with both hands. When the opponent hooks and kicks, the supporting leg should jump or retreat in a timely manner to make the kicking action fall through. Subsequently, rotate the thigh until the knee joint is facing downwards and bend the knee to press down, pulling out the control leg. Quickly retreat backwards and widen the distance from the enemy (see Figure 9−14).

（二）抱腿压摔防守

动作说明： 当使用腿法被接住，歹徒准备施展抱腿压摔时，应迅速屈膝下压，降低重心，抽出控制腿，并用双手夹固对方的颈部，向下按压，控制对方（见图9−15）。

(2) Leg Hugging Pressure Drop Defense

Action instruction: When the leg technique was intercepted and the criminal was about to use the leg hugging pressure drop, he quickly bent his knees and pressed down, lowered his center of gravity, pulled out the control leg, and clamped the enemy's neck with both hands, pressing down to control the enemy (see Figure 9−15).

图 9−14　抱腿挑摔防守　Leg hugging and throwing defense

图 9−15　抱腿压摔防守　Leg hugging pressure drop defense

第四节
摔法使用策略

Section 4
Strategies for Using Throwing Techniques

摔法技术具有"借势、掀底、别根、靠身"的技法要求。掌握此四点，能帮助大家高屋建瓴地掌握摔法技术。借势指借助攻击者重心不稳或即将失去平衡的姿势，顺其失衡的同侧方位或发力方向施加外力，摔倒对方；掀底指破坏对方的支撑，采用掀、拉、摇、托等方式摔倒对方，例如上

The throwing technique has the technical requirements of "taking advantage of the situation, lifting the bottom, sticking to the root, and leaning against the body". Mastering these four points can help everyone master throwing techniques from a high perspective. Taking advantage of an attacker's unstable center of gravity or imminent loss of balance. Apply external force in the same direction or direction of force that is unbalanced, and fall the opponent; Lifting the bottom refers to breaking the support of the opponent, using methods such as lifting, pulling, shaking,

文的接腿上托；别根指通过身体的某一部位别绊对方支撑重心的根部，破坏支撑点，例如上文的拌腿摔，靠身指通过身体向前靠压的方法将对方绊倒。

实施摔法时，动作要衔接紧密，一气呵成。若中间留有空隙，则敌人就有充分的准备时间和反击空间；把位要紧，即在缠斗过程中，抓握和固定的部位要牢固。否则将导致歹徒迅速逃脱。

and supporting. For example, the leg extension support in the following text; Do not trip the base of the opponent's support center of gravity through a certain part of the body, damaging the support point. For example, the leg tripping throw mentioned earlier. To lean forward refers to the method of using the body to press forward and trip the other person.

When implementing the throwing technique, the movements should be closely connected and completed in one go. If there is a gap in the middle, the enemy will have sufficient preparation time and give them space to counterattack. The position is crucial, that is, the part that can be grasped and fixed during the entanglement process. Otherwise, it will lead to the criminals escaping quickly.

思考九

1. 保护性倒地在摔法中有多重要？

2. 保护性倒地的接触包括哪些？

3. 保护性倒地主要目的是什么？

4. 摔法的进攻技术包括几类，区别是什么？

5. 摔法的防守技术的原则是什么？

Reflection 9

1.How important is protective fall in throwing techniques?

2. What are the protective measures for falling to the ground?

3.What is the main purpose of protective falls?

4.How many types of attack techniques are included in the throwing technique, and what are the differences?

5.What are the principles of defensive techniques in throwing techniques?

第九章微课视频

第十章
擒拿解脱格斗技术

Chapter 10
Capture and Release Fighting Techniques

第一节
擒拿解脱技术

Section 1
Capture and Release Techniques

　　擒拿是根据人的骨关节结构及其活动功能的局限，运用锁、缠、扣、抓等多种手法迫使对手做反关节或超限运动，将对方制服的格斗技术。擒拿属于贴身格斗，技术体系围绕着人体结构自然缺陷和功能要害而展开，人体结构的复杂性决定了该技术的复杂性。一方面，要在对手运动过程中准确抓拿其要害绝非易事；另一方面，把位角度的轻微变化就会出现"拿不稳，抓不死"的情况。因此，不利于新手的掌握和学习。

　　因此，本章主要介绍被他人抓拿身体关节或部位时的被动解脱技术。解脱术是以挣脱对手的抓拿和控制为主要目的，在了解人体解剖结构、生理机能、关节的结构和反关节的原理的基础上，利用其弱点实施相应的反击自卫格斗术。解脱术是擒拿术的重要内容之一，对于没有接受任何武术等训练的人群而言是防身

　　Capturing is a combat technique that uses various techniques such as locking, wrapping, clasping, and grabbing to force the opponent to engage in anti joint or over limit movements based on the limitations of human bone and joint structure and mobility, in order to subdue the opponent. Capturing belongs to close combat, and the technical system revolves around the natural defects and key functions of the human body structure. The complexity of the human body structure determines its technical complexity. On the one hand, accurately grasping the key points of an opponent's movement is not an easy task, and on the other hand, slight changes in the grip angle can lead to "unstable grip and inability to grasp firmly". Therefore, it is not conducive to the mastery and learning of beginners.

　　Therefore, this chapter mainly introduces the release techniques when someone grabs a joint or part of the body. Liberation techniques are primarily aimed at breaking free from the grasp and control of opponents. Based on understanding the anatomical structure and physiological functions of the human body, the structure of joints, and the principles of anti joint movements, they utilize their weaknesses to implement corresponding counterattack self-defense combat techniques. Liberation technique is one of the important contents of grappling, and it is the best choice

自卫的最佳选择。零基础、易上手、即学即用是其显著特点。本节围绕容易被抓拿的头、颈、胸、手臂，以及腰等五个部位的解脱技术展开。

for self-defense for those who do not have any training in martial arts. "Zero foundation, easy to learn, and easy to use" are its prominent characteristics. This section focuses on the release techniques for the easily grabbed head, neck, chest, arms, and waist.

一、抓发解脱

1. Release from Hair Grabbing

动作说明：当歹徒用手抓握自卫者头发时，双手横向扣抓歹徒的手背，进行固定，防止逃脱［见图 10−1(a)］。旋即，身体前倾，将整个身体的重量移至歹徒的腕关节的同时，下蹲并后退，使歹徒身体前倾跪地［见图 10−1(b)］。

Action instruction: When the criminal grasps the hair of the self-defense person with their hands, they horizontally clasp the back of the criminal's hand with both hands to secure it and prevent escape [see Figure 10−1(a)]. Immediately, the body leaned forward, transferring the weight of the entire body to the perpetrator's wrist joint while squatting and retreating, causing the perpetrator's body to lean forward and kneel to the ground without moving [see Figure 10−1(b)].

动作要求：此技术针对的是腕关节。腕关节在额状轴上做屈伸运动，活动范围通常不超过 180°。为此，此技术最重要的核心点是通过整个身体的重量，致使敌人腕部手背屈超过 180°。

Action requirements: This technology is targeted at the wrist joint. The wrist joint performs flexion and extension movements on the frontal axis, with a range of motion typically not exceeding 180°. The most important core point of this technology is to use the weight of the entire body to cause the enemy's wrist and hand to bend over 180°.

(a)　　　　　　　　　　　　　　(b)

图 10−1　抓发解脱　　Release from hair grabbing

二、抓颈解脱

被掐脖时，首先应耸肩梗脖，限制对方用力。在此前提下，根据抓颈位置的不同予以应对。抓颈一般分为体前单手掐脖、双手掐脖和背后掐脖三种情况。

（一）单手掐脖解脱

动作说明： 当被敌人体前单手掐脖时，自卫者使用异侧手固定敌方的手腕。随后，提起同侧手臂，向下砸肘攻击敌人肘关节位置［见图 10-2(a)］，逼迫其松手的同时，使用顶肘技术攻击敌人面部［见图 10-2(b)］。右手可根据敌方反应，灵活变动，保护要害部位。

动作要求： 为了使砸肘更加有利，要转腰转髋，动用全身力量；砸肘和顶肘的衔接要快。

2. Neck Grasping Release

When being pinched, the first thing to do is to shrug and gag the neck, limiting the opponent's strength. Under this premise, make corresponding responses according to the different positions of neck grabbing. Neck grabbing is generally divided into four situations: front one hand neck grabbing, both hands neck grabbing, back neck grabbing, and neck clamping.

(1) Neck Pinched with One Hand

Action instruction: Taking being pinched by the enemy's left hand on the neck as an example. The defender uses the opposite hand to fix the enemy's wrist, while lifting the same arm and using the elbow smashing technique [see Figure 10-2(a)] . to attack the enemy's elbow joint position, forcing them to release their hand while using the elbow pushing technique to attack the enemy's face [see Figure 10-2(b)]. The right hand can flexibly adjust according to enemy reactions to protect critical areas.

Action requirements: In order to smash the elbow more effectively, turn the waist and hips, and use full body strength; The connection between smashing the elbow and pushing the elbow should be fast.

(a)   (b)

图 10-2　单手掐脖解脱　One handed neck pinch release

（二）双手掐脖解脱

动作说明： 当敌人用双手掐脖时，敌人胸腹部和裆部处于未防守的空隙。自卫者从身体两侧举臂，并快速从上向下拍击敌人的腕部［见图 10-3(a)］。摆脱被掐状态后，使用掌根部快速推击敌人下颌部位［见图 10-3(b)］。

动作要求： 用手臂拍击敌人腕部时，若仅动用腕部的力量将会导致力度不够，无法挣脱，为此应收腹坐髋，将全身的力量传递到腕部。此外，若技术不熟练导致无法摆脱时，应利用敌人的防守漏洞，用双拳峰击打其肋骨或用腿踢其裆部。

(2) Hands Pinched at the Neck

Action instruction: When the enemy pinches their neck with both hands, their chest, abdomen, and crotch are in an undefended gap. The defender raises his arms from both sides of his body and quickly slaps the enemy's wrist downwards [see Figure 10-3(a)]. After getting rid of the back pinch state, use the base of the palm to quickly push the enemy's jaw area [see Figure 10-3(b)].

Action requirements: When tapping the enemy's wrist with the arm, if only the strength of the wrist is used, it will result in insufficient force and inability to break free. Therefore, the abdomen should be closed and the hip should be sitting to transfer the full body strength to the wrist. In addition, if the lack of technical proficiency makes it impossible to get rid of it, one should take advantage of the enemy's defensive loopholes, hit their ribs with double fists or kick their crotch with their legs.

(a)　　　　　　　　　　　(b)

图 10-3　双手掐脖解脱　Pinching the neck with both hands to release

（三）背后掐脖解脱

动作说明： 歹徒从背后使用裸绞控制自卫者颈部时，用左手/右手向下拉拽歹徒的手腕［见图 10-4(a)］，将咽喉侧向一边；挺腹后仰，右/左臂向前摆起［见图

(3) Pinch Your Neck from Behind

Action instruction: When the criminal twisted the neck of the defender with their right arm from behind. Use your left/right hand to pull down the perpetrator's wrist and turn your throat to one side [see Figure 10-4(a)]; Lean your body back and straighten your abdomen, and swing your right arm forward [see

10-4(b)〕。随后，收腹转腰，迅速向臀后摆动右臂，用左拳或掌猛烈撞击歹徒的裆部〔见图10-4(c)〕。歹徒的裆部受到撞击，疼痛难忍撒手蹲地，自卫者迅速解脱。

动作要求：向前摆臂和向后撩击要迅速；挺腹和收腹要明显，如此摆动臂才更有利，打击效果更佳。

Figure 10−4(b)]. Then, quickly swing your right arm behind your buttocks and forcefully hit the perpetrator's crotch with your left fist or palm [see Figure 10−4(c)]. The perpetrator's crotch was hit and painful, and he couldn't bear to let go and squat on the ground. The defender quickly released himself.

Action requirements: Swinging arms forward and flicking backwards should be done quickly; Protruding and contracting the abdomen should be obvious, so that swinging the arm is more advantageous and the impact effect is better.

(a)   (b)   (c)

图 10-4 背后掐脖解脱 Back neck pinch release

三、抓臂解脱

（一）同侧抓握手臂解脱

动作说明：当歹徒左手抓自卫者同侧右手腕时〔见图10-5(a)〕，自卫者用左手扣按抓歹徒左手背，进行固定〔见图10-5(b)〕。随后，右手前臂翻转切压歹徒左手腕〔见图10-5(c)〕。

动作要求：首先，扣抓一定要牢。其次，要转腰转髋，利用整体的力量致使歹徒手腕过度外翻，疼痛解脱。

3. Grab Arm Release

(1) Same Side Grip

Action instruction: When the criminal's left hand grabs the right wrist of the self-defense victim in reverse [see Figure 10−5(a)], the self-defense victim uses their left hand to grab the back of the victim's left hand [see Figure 10−5(b)], and then flips and presses the victim's left wrist with their right forearm. Kneel down in pain [see Figure 10−5(c)].

Action requirements: Firstly, the grip must be firm, and secondly, the waist and hip should be rotated to use the overall strength to cause the enemy's wrist to excessively evert and relieve the pain.

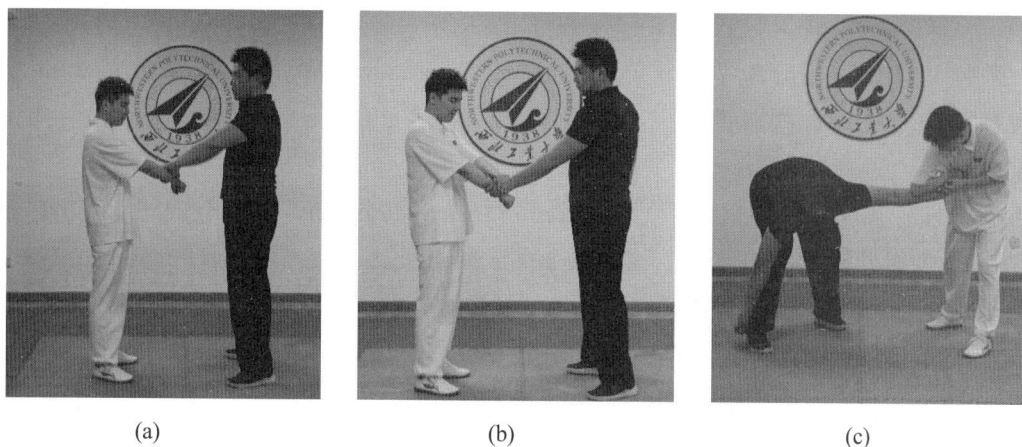

(a)　　　　　　　　　　(b)　　　　　　　　　　(c)

图 10-5　同侧抓握手臂解脱　Same side grip

（二）异侧抓握手臂解脱

动作说明：当歹徒用右手抓握自卫者异侧右手腕时，左手扣按歹徒右手背，进行固定［见图 10-6(a)］，左手呈 C 字形路线，顺时针上绕至歹徒手腕外侧［见图 10-6(b)］。随后，用右手掌切压歹徒右手腕［见图 10-6(c)］。

动作要求：按压固定与切腕动作要迅速，否则歹徒就有反应之机，从而降低成功率。

(2) Opposite Grip

Action instruction: When the perpetrator grabs the right wrist of the self-defense victim with the opposite side of their right hand [see Figure 10-6(a)], their left hand is pressed against the back of the perpetrator's right hand, and their left hand is clockwise wrapped around the perpetrator's wrist [see Figure 10-6(b)]. Simultaneously use the root of the right palm and fingers to cut and press the hook onto the criminal's right wrist [see Figure 10-6(c)].

Action requirements: The pressing and wrist cutting movements should be quick, otherwise the culprit will have a chance to react and reduce the success rate.

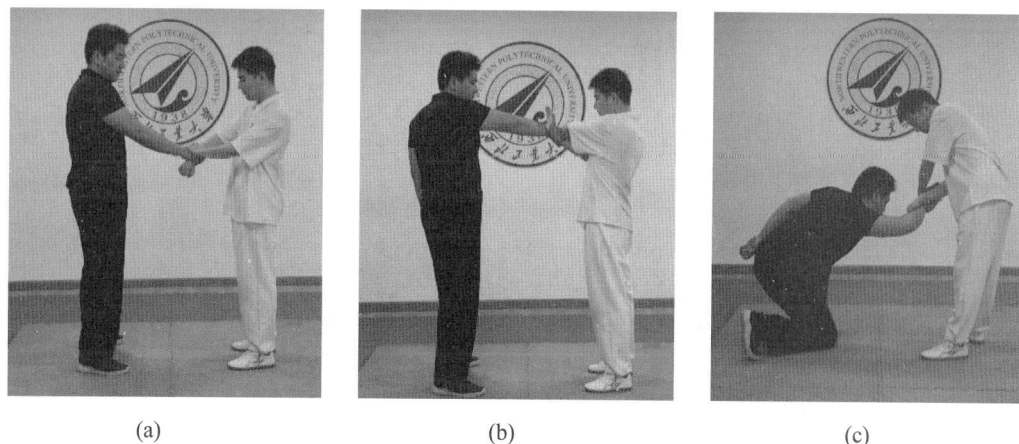

(a)　　　　　　　　　　(b)　　　　　　　　　　(c)

图 10-6　异侧抓握手臂解脱　Opposite grip

（三）抓握手臂挣脱

抓握手臂挣脱可分为单手抓握挣脱和双手抓握挣脱两种情况。

动作说明： 当歹徒单手抓握右手臂时，向左微转腰，并向上抬臂［见图 10-7(a)］。随后，快速向右转腰，手臂向后回带，挣脱敌人控制［见图 10-7(b)］；当歹徒双手抓握右手臂时，左手抓握被固定手臂的腕关节［见图 10-7(c)］。随后，向抓握手臂的相反方向转腰带动手臂，挣脱敌人的抓握［见图 10-7(d)］。

(3) Grip Release

Grasping the arm to break free can be divided into two situations: one hand grasping to break free and two hands grasping to break free.

Action instruction: When the criminal grabs the right arm with one hand, turn slightly to the left and lift the arm upwards [see Figure 10-7(a)]. Then, quickly turn your waist to the right, wrap your arms back, and break free from enemy control [see Figure 10-7(b)]; When the perpetrator grasps his right arm with both hands, his left hand grasps the wrist joint of the fixed arm [see Figure 10-7(c)]. Then, turn your waist in the opposite direction of gripping your arm to drive it and break free from the enemy's grip [see Figure 10-7(d)].

(a)

(b)

(c)

(d)

图 10-7　抓握手臂挣脱　Grasping the arm to break free

动作要求： 挣脱时，若仅动用手臂的力量无法有效摆脱控制；需转腰转髋，利用全身的力量。

Action requirements: When breaking free, if only the strength of the arm is used, it is not possible to effectively break free from control. Need to rotate the waist and hips, utilizing the strength of the whole body.

四、抓胸解脱

4. Chest Capture and Release

动作说明： 歹徒用左手同侧顺抓自卫者右肩时，左手固定抓握手臂［见图10-8(a)］。随后，用腰带动右肩做顺时针或逆时针绕环［见图10-8(b)］。肱骨顺时针旋转切压甲方手腕或逆时针旋转顶掀歹徒手腕内侧时，歹徒由于抓握不足，将不得不放手，从而逃脱。

Action instruction: When the perpetrator grabs the right shoulder of the self-defense victim with the same side of their left hand, the left hand firmly grasps the arm [see Figure 10-8(a)]. Subsequently, use the waist belt to move the right shoulder in a clockwise or counterclockwise loop [see Figure 10-8(b)]. When the humerus rotates clockwise to cut and press the wrist of Party A or counterclockwise to lift the inside of the criminal's wrist, the criminal will have to let go and escape due to insufficient grip.

动作要求： 摆动手臂时要转腰转髋，动用全身力量。否则仅用单一手臂的力量很难挣脱。

Action requirements: When swinging the arm, turn the waist and hips, and use full body strength. Otherwise, it is difficult to break free with the force of a single arm.

(a)　　　　　　　　　　　　(b)

图 10-8　抓胸解脱　Chest and shoulder release

五、抱腰解脱

5. Waist Hugging Release

被歹徒抱腰可分为从前搂抱和从后搂抱。其中从前搂抱可参

Being hugged by criminals can be divided into hugging from the past and hugging from the back. Previously, hugging can

考下潜抱腿摔防守的内容。向后搂抱可参考近战技术部分的头撞和肘法技术。另外，歹徒搂抱的主要意图是限制自卫者行动并实施摔法。为此，应做好防摔的同时实施解脱。此部分再介绍一种从后搂抱解脱的技术，供大家参考。

动作说明： 当敌人从背后用两臂搂抱自卫者腰包时[见图10-9(a)]。两手抓握敌人的腕部向下拽拉，身体向左旋转，左脚向敌人后方迈出一步。随后，左手向后屈肘摆绕，从敌人左耳侧插入至敌人面部[见图10-9(b)]。旋即，右手抓握敌人右手不放，左手推掀敌人的下颌，迫使其后仰倒地[见图10-9(c)]。

动作要求： 两手配合紧密，动作流畅。左步后撤身体左转的同时，左臂的绕环要迅速到位。右手拉伸与左手的推掀形成挣力。

refer to the content of diving and leg throwing defense. Backward embrace can refer to the head bump and elbow technique in the melee technique section. In addition, the main intention of the criminal's embrace is to restrict the movement of the self-defense and implement the throwing method, so it is necessary to do a good job of preventing falls and implementing release. This section will introduce another technique for releasing from the back embrace for your reference.

Action instruction: When the enemy embraces the defender from behind with both arms or strangles the defender's neck with their right arm [see Figure 10-9(a)]. Grasp the enemy's right wrist and pull downwards with your right hand, rotate your body to the left, and take a step towards the enemy's rear with your left foot, then, bend your left hand backwards and swing it around, inserting it from the enemy's left ear to the enemy's face [see Figure 10-9(b)]. Immediately, grab the enemy's right hand with your right hand and hold it, push the enemy's jaw with your left hand, and the enemy will tilt their head back to the left [Figure 10-9(c)].

Action requirements: Close coordination of both hands and smooth movements. While taking a left step back and turning left, the left arm loop should be quickly in place. The stretching of the right hand and the pushing and lifting of the left hand form a pulling force.

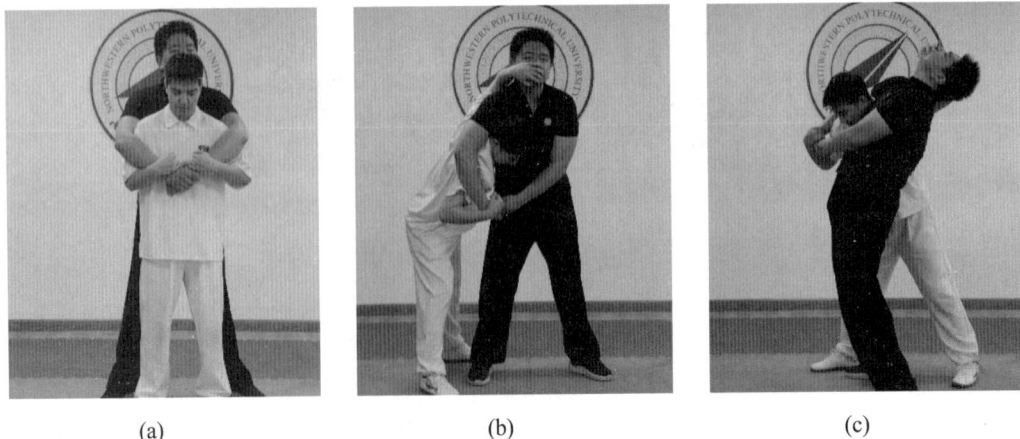

(a)　　　　(b)　　　　(c)

图 10-9　抱腰解脱　Waist hugging releas

第二节
击打要害部位解脱技术

Section 2
Release Techniques for Hitting Critical Areas

　　要害部位指人体遭受到打击或挤压时，最易使人昏迷、伤残和致死的部位。要害部位多集中于神经血管丰富、软骨组织较多的部位。符合该要求的有太阳穴、眼睛、鼻子、耳朵、裆部、肋骨、剑突等部位。此处仅介绍最为常用和有效的部位击打技术。

　　需要注意的是，由于要害部位造成的技伤害性大，且造成的部分伤害是不可逆或致死的。为此，使用该类技术时，应处于迫不得已的情况下，例如威胁到个人生命安危之时，若只是朋友间或同学间的口角之争或不和导致的打架斗殴，勿使用此类技术。

　　The crucial parts refer to the parts of the human body that are most likely to cause coma, disability, and death when subjected to impact or compression. The key areas are mostly concentrated in areas with abundant nerves, blood vessels, and cartilage tissue. Those who meet this requirement include the temples, eyes, noses, ears, ribs, crotch, xiphoid, and other parts of the head. This article only introduces the most commonly used and effective techniques for hitting parts. Waiting for functional abilities, as well as sword protrusions and crotch.

　　It should be noted that due to the significant technical damage caused by critical areas, and the resulting partial damage is irreversible or fatal. Therefore, when using this type of technology, one should be in a situation of necessity, such as when it threatens personal security. If it is only a quarrel between friends or classmates that leads to a fight, do not use this technology.

一、眼睛

1. Eyes

　　眼睛是人体最重要的视觉器官，同时也是最敏感和最脆弱的部位。眼睛富含大量毛细血管和视神经。受到外力打击时，可造成毛细血管破裂，引起出血。打击力度过大还会导致瞳孔移位，对视力造成严重损伤，影响人的行动和方位辨别能力。

　　The eyes are the most important visual organ in the human body, as well as the most sensitive and vulnerable part. The eyes are rich in numerous capillaries and optic nerves. When subjected to external force, it can cause capillary rupture and cause bleeding. Excessive impact can also lead to pupil displacement, causing serious damage to vision, and affecting a person's ability to move and identify directions.

自卫手段：拍打［见图 10-10(a)］。手掌放松，由上向下拍打对方眼睛。拍打的面积更大，容错率高。"二龙戏珠"［见图 10-10(b)］。食指和中指并拢伸直，其余三指并拢弯曲，大拇指按在小拇指和无名指上，使用食指和中指戳击敌人眼睛。

Self-defender measures: slapping [see Figure 10-10(a)]. Relax your palm and pat the other person's eyes from top to bottom. The tapping area is larger and the fault tolerance is higher. Two dragons playing with pearls [Figure 10-10(b)]. The index and middle fingers should be stretched together, while the other three fingers should be bent together. Place the thumb on the little and ring fingers, and use the index and middle fingers to poke the enemy's eyes.

(a) (b)

图 10-10　击要害部位——眼睛　Critical area — eyes

二、耳朵

2. Ears

耳廓神经离大脑较近，受到打击或挤压后，轻则导致耳穿孔或耳出血，损害人体平衡机能；重则脑震荡。

自卫手段：双峰贯耳技术（见图 10-11）。五指并拢，掌心内凹。随后两手弧形向对方耳朵拍打。当掌心内凹产生的空气被迫进入耳道，强汽波袭入耳薄膜，会导致薄膜破裂，使对手耳鸣目眩和剧烈疼痛。

The auricular nerve is closer to the brain and can cause ear perforation or bleeding when subjected to impact or compression, which can damage the body's balance function. In severe cases, it can cause cerebral concussion.

Self-defense measures: bimodal penetrating ear technique. Five fingers together, palm inward concave. Then he arched his hands and slapped each other's ears (see Figure 10-11). When the air generated by the concave palm is forced into the ear canal, and strong vapor waves strike the ear membrane, it can cause the membrane to rupture, causing tinnitus, dizziness, and severe pain in the hands.

图 10-11 击打要害部位——耳朵 Hitting the key part—ears

三、喉部

喉部的要害主要为咽喉和喉结。在颈部前面、两锁骨内侧、胸骨柄上缘有一个凹陷，该部位通常被称为咽喉。凹陷内有下行的无名静脉，气管食管，以及膈神经和迷走神经分支。在中医经络学上，凹陷又被称为"天突穴"。少林拳法中有"二捅天突穴，锁喉致昏哑"之说。手指用力直戳天突穴，可以猛烈地压迫气管，刺激迷走神经和膈神经，引起反射性的呼吸困难和剧烈咳嗽，甚至引起窒息。

喉结在颈部正中，由软骨构成支架，其中甲状软骨为最大的一块。甲状软骨在颈的突出部分即为喉结。喉结上通咽、口和鼻腔，下连气管，是肺脏与外界进行气体交换的通气要道。打击喉结、扼喉、勒颈、以及锐器切颈是致命的杀伤手段。

3. Throat

The key points of the throat are mainly the throat and Adam's apple. In front of the neck, there is a depression on the inner side of the two collarbones and the upper edge of the sternum handle, which is commonly referred to as the throat. There are descending unnamed veins, tracheoesophageal, and branches of the phrenic and vagus nerves within the depression. In traditional Chinese medicine, the depression is also known as the "Tiantu acupoint". In Shaolin boxing, there is a saying that "two punctures of the Tiantu acupoint can lock the throat and cause dizziness and hoarseness". Fingers forcefully poking the Tiantu acupoint can forcefully compress the trachea, stimulate the vagus and diaphragmatic nerves, cause reflexive breathing difficulties and severe coughing, and even cause ventricular rest.

The Adam's apple is located in the center of the neck and is supported by cartilage. The thyroid cartilage is the largest piece, and the protruding part of the thyroid cartilage in the neck is called the Adam's apple. The upper part of the larynx is connected to the pharynx, mouth, and nasal cavity, while the lower part is connected to the trachea, which is the main ventilation passage for the lungs to exchange gas with the outside world. Striking the Adam's apple, choking the throat, strangling the neck, and cutting the neck with sharp tools are deadly methods of killing.

自卫手段：可使用插掌［见图10-12(a)］、标指［见图10-12(b)］等技术击打咽喉部位。咽喉处有颈部动脉。该两条位于气管的两侧，是负责给大脑供氧的唯一主路径，打击或压迫其会导致缺氧休克。

Self-defense measures: techniques such as palm insertion and finger pointing [see Figure 10-12(a)] can be used to strike, or naked strangulation techniques [see Figure 10-12(b)] can be used to compress the throat or throat area. There is a cervical artery in the throat. These two are located on both sides of the trachea and are the only main pathways responsible for supplying oxygen to the brain. Shock or compression can cause hypoxia.

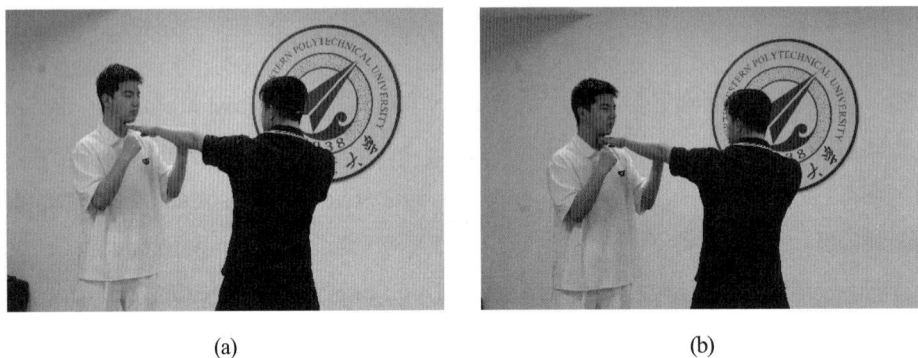

(a)　　　　　　　　　　　　　(b)

图 10-12　击打要害部位——喉部　Critical area—throat

四、裆部

4. Crotch

裆部又称会阴，是人体最薄弱的部位之一，也是自卫防身攻击的重点要害部位。裆部主要是指肛门与外生殖器之间的部位。裆部不仅有人的生殖器官，而且又是神经、血管最为密集的地方。以膝顶、脚踢男子裆部或以手揪、掐阴囊等方式，可造成阴囊挫伤或睾丸破裂，轻则疼痛难忍，跪膝倒地，重则会发生神经性休克，甚至引起死亡。因此，攻击裆部可以轻易使人失去抵抗能力，束

The crotch, also known as the perineum, is the weakest part of the human body and a key area for self-defense and self-defense attacks. The crotch mainly refers to the area between the anus and the external genitalia. The crotch not only contains human reproductive organs, but also serves as the most densely populated area of nerves and blood vessels. Kicking a man's crotch with his knees or feet, or pulling or pinching the scrotum with his hands, can cause scrotal contusion or testicular rupture. Mild pain can be unbearable, kneeling on the ground can lead to neurological shock, and even death. Therefore, attacking the crotch can easily cause a person to lose their resistance, be at the mercy of others, or

手任人摆布，也可轻易致人于死地。因此，当妇女、儿童被歹徒近身侵犯时乘其不备猛击裆部是最为有效的解脱方法。

自卫手段： 近战格斗技术中的下潜下冲拳和撩阴掌，远战格斗技术中的弹腿技术。

easily lead to death. Therefore, when women and children are physically assaulted by criminals, taking advantage of the situation and forcefully hitting the crotch is the most effective way to relieve them.

Self-defense measures: diving punch and yin palm in Close combat operations techniques, and bullet leg technique in long-range combat techniques.

第三节
擒拿与解脱格斗技术运用策略

Section 3
Strategies for the Application of Capture and Release Fighting Techniques

擒拿既不同于站立格斗中简洁明快的踢打技术，也不同于通过破坏对方重心使其倒地的贴身摔法技术。该技术相对复杂，把位稍纵即逝，攻防刹那转换。因此，擒拿解脱一定要"快、准、狠、稳"。

武术谚语中"巧拿不如拙打"指擒拿技术若不熟练，则失败概率高，而后易遭受对方的反抗和袭击，远远不如正面的击打防守更为保险。为此，勿将取胜的关键砝码放在"一招制敌"上，应留有后手，随时应对失败后突如其来的攻击和各种应激性反抗。

另外，人体关节结构具有极好的关联性，可"拿一点而控全身"。只要一节被控死，其他关节的运动能力就大大削弱，甚至丧失运动功能。因此，擒拿技术是

Capturing is not only different from the simple and straightforward kicking techniques in standing combat, but also from the intimate throwing techniques that disrupt the opponent's center of gravity and cause them to fall to the ground. The technology is relatively complex, the position is fleeting, and the attack and defense switch instantly. Therefore, the capture and release must be fast, accurate, ruthless, and stable.

The martial arts proverb goes, "It is better to strike skillfully than to strike clumsily". The technique of grasping is not proficient, with a high probability of failure, and is prone to resistance and attacks from the opponent, making it far less secure than frontal hitting defense. For this reason, do not place the key weight of victory on "one move to defeat the enemy". Keep a back hand and be ready to deal with sudden attacks and various emergency resistance after failure.

In addition, the joint structure of the human body has excellent correlation, controlling the whole body with just a little bit. As long as one joint is controlled to die, the movement ability of other joints is greatly weakened, and

巧的技术，要能够"以小博大，以弱胜强"。为此要多加练习，正所谓"久练为熟，熟能生巧，巧能生精"。除此之外，要对人体解剖知识有所了解，对重要关节结构烂熟于心，最大限度地利用好杠杆作用，以达到以小制大、以巧胜力的训练效果。但巧不可能是绝对的，毕竟"一力降十会"，学好擒拿必须以具备一定的力量基础。

even the movement function is lost. Therefore, the technique of catching is a clever technique that can "use the small to be broad, and use the weak to win the strong". To achieve this, it is necessary to practice more. As the saying goes, "Practice for a long time produces skill, which can produce skill, and skill can produce essence". In addition, it is necessary to have an understanding of human anatomy, be familiar with important joint structures, and make the most of leverage to achieve a training effect of using small to large and skillful to win strength. But coincidence cannot be absolute, after all, "one force reduces ten skills". Learning to capture well requires a certain level of strength as the foundation.

思考十

1. 擒拿是什么？

2. 擒拿解脱是什么？

3. 擒拿解脱技术主要包括哪些内容？

4. 要害部位包括？

5. 为什么击打要害部位能快速解脱？

Reflection 10

1.What is capture?

2.What is capture and release?

3. What are the main contents of capture and release techniques?

4. What are the key parts?

5.Why can hitting the critical area quickly release? and long-range contact defense?

第十章微课视频

第十一章
地面格斗技术

Chapter 11
Ground Fighting Techniques

地面格斗也是安全防卫学不可缺少的格斗技术，是在摔法的基础上产生的一方倒地，敌我双方基于腿法、拳法、地面锁技和绞技不断斡旋的格斗形式，其实质是站立格斗技术的地面延伸。由摔法导致的站立姿势改变，就产生了上位与下位。上位处于压制位，更有利于实施打击技术；下位是被压制的一方，所以相对而言，下位选手较为劣势。简言之，地面站就是位置之战。很多案例的统计表明，在遭到突然袭击时，自卫者尤其是女性往往在五六秒之内就被歹徒摔倒在地，并处于下位劣势。为此，在面对突然敌人的偷袭或敌我双方身体素质悬殊的情境下，不幸落入不利的下位，如何转换站位并格斗逃离就显得尤为重要。

Ground combat is also an indispensable combat technique in security and defense studies. It is a form of combat where one side falls to the ground based on the throwing technique, and the enemy and us constantly mediate based on leg techniques, fist techniques, ground locking techniques, and twisting techniques. The change in standing posture caused by the throwing technique results in upper and lower positions. The upper level is more conducive to implementing strike techniques, so the lower level players are relatively disadvantaged and are the suppressed side. In short, ground stations are a battle of location. Statistics from many cases indicate that in the event of a sudden attack, self-defense activists, especially women, often fall to the ground by criminals within five or six seconds and are in a lower position. Therefore, in the face of sudden enemy attacks or a significant physical disparity between the enemy and ourselves, unfortunately falling into a disadvantageous position, it is particularly important to change positions and develop.

第一节
地面远战

Section 1
Ground Long Range Fight

地面远战即自卫者处于未站立状态，且与进攻者并未产生肢

Ground combat refers to the defender being in an unsteaded state and not making physical contact

体接触的战斗。一般而言，自卫者处于未站立状态的下位较为劣势，应快速转变为站立状态。但站立状态的转变的过程需要不断防守歹徒的进攻或骑乘于自卫者身体上，变成更加不利的地面近战。为此自卫者应在倒地后，在防守的基础上不断调整至站立状态。本节根据从仰卧姿态到站立姿态的过程分为三种防守姿态。

一、仰卧防守

动作说明：倒地后，仰卧于地面。屈颈、屈肘、含胸收腹、膝盖与髋部各弯曲呈90°；双臂护头，脚面朝向敌人，保持团身状态。该状态防守严密，两腿防止敌人快速切入，双手防止敌人的拳击（见图11-1）。但缺点是不利于移动。为此，在仰卧防守的基础上，应寻觅时机快速切入坐式防守。

动作应用：仰卧防守时，当歹徒不断调整方向，寻找切入点时，左脚（右脚）落地支撑，以身体为支点，逆/顺时针调整方向，始终面朝敌人。同时，当歹徒欲试图接近自卫者时，可使用远战技术中的弹腿和蹬腿等技术，阻击歹徒，保持安全距离。

with the attacker. Generally speaking, when a defender is in a lower position without standing, they should quickly transition to a standing position. But the process of changing the standing state requires continuous defense against the attacks of criminals or riding on the self-defense body, becoming more disadvantageous ground close combat. For this reason, defenders should continuously adjust their defense after falling to the ground. This section is divided into three defensive postures based on the process from supine to standing posture.

1. Supine Defense

Action instruction: After falling to the ground, lie on your back. Bend the neck, elbow, chest and abdomen, bend the knees and hips at a 90°angle, protect the head with both arms, face the enemy with feet, and maintain a full body position. This state of defense is tight, with both legs to prevent the enemy from quickly cutting in and both hands to prevent the enemy from boxing. But the disadvantage is that it is not conducive to movement. Therefore, on the basis of supine defense, it is important to seek opportunities to quickly engage in seated defense (see Figure 11-1).

Action application: When lying on the back for defense, as the thug constantly adjusts direction and seeks a point of entry, the left foot (right foot). lands to support, using the body as a fulcrum, and adjusts direction counterclockwise/clockwise, always facing the enemy. At the same time, when criminals attempt to approach self-defense, they can use long-range techniques such as bouncing and kicking to intercept the enemy and maintain a safe distance.

二、坐式防守

动作说明：以右侧为例。在仰卧防守的基础上，身体迅速向右侧转，左腿屈膝支撑，右腿屈膝前伸，同侧手臂内旋屈肘撑地，形成两点支撑，便于移动和前伸腿进攻和防守。另外一侧手架于头顶上方，防止站立的敌人实施腿法和拳法进攻（见图 11-2）。

动作应用：当歹徒欲接近自卫者时，自卫者以左脚支撑其身体，右腿以踹腿、正蹬腿等技术阻击敌人。并为转换成半跪式防守创造机会。

2. Sitting Defense

Action instruction: Taking the right side as an example. On the basis of supine defense, quickly turn the body to the right, bend the left leg to support, bend the right leg to extend forward, and rotate the same arm inward to bend the elbow and support the ground, forming two points of support for easy movement and forward leg attack and defense. The other hand is placed above the head to prevent standing enemies from carrying out whip leg and boxing attacks (see Figure 11-2).

Action application: When the enemy wants to approach the defender, the defender can support their body with their left foot, and use techniques such as kicking or kicking to block the enemy with their right leg. And create opportunities for transitioning to semi kneeling defense.

图 11-1　仰卧防守　Supine defense

图 11-2　坐式防守　Sitting defense

三、半跪式防守

动作说明：以右侧为例。坐式防守的基础上，首先左腿支撑。其次右腿迅速收髋后撤，膝关节内侧接触地面，呈 90° 弯曲，前脚支撑地面，两手成格斗式抱架（见图 11-3）。最后，两脚由屈至

3. Half Kneeling Defense

Action instruction: Taking the right side as an example. On the basis of sitting defense, support with the left leg. Subsequently, the right leg quickly retracted its hip and pulled back, with the inner side of the knee joint touching the ground in a 90 degree bend, and the front foot supporting the ground. Two hands in a fighting style embrace (see Figure 11-3).

伸,重返站姿状态。

Finally, return to a standing position with both feet bent to extended.

动作应用：当歹徒逼近自卫者并使用腿法进攻时,可通过近战中的拍击、格肘等技术进行防守。在此基础上,快速转换为站姿状态,并快速拉开距离。

Action application: When the enemy approaches the defender and uses leg techniques to attack, it can quickly switch to a standing position and quickly widen the distance based on defensive techniques such as slapping and elbow blocking in close combat.

图 11-3　半跪式防守　　Half kneeling defense

第二节
地面近战

Section 2
Ground Close Combat

地面近战即一方未处于站立,且防守者与进攻者处于肢体接触状态下所使用的格斗技术。

Ground close combat refers to a situation where one side is not standing and the defender and attacker are in physical contact.

一、防守与挣脱技术

1. Defensive and Breakaway Techniques

(一)阻挡

(1) Obstruction

动作说明：两手屈臂握拳置于面部,上端护住面部,下端护于肋部,两肘间留有缝隙,以便于观察歹徒状态(见图 11-4)。

Action instruction: Bend your arms and place your fist on your face, with the upper end protecting your face and the lower end protecting your ribs. Leave a gap between your elbows for easy observation of the criminal's condition. At the same time, push both feet on the ground, straighten the hips, and destroy the enemy's center of gravity (see Figure 11-4).

动作应用: 当歹徒处于完全骑乘或封闭式骑乘,并用捶击等技术进攻时,可使用阻挡技术,先做好防守,再寻找机会逃脱。

Action application: When the enemy is on a fully mounted or enclosed mount and using offensive techniques such as pounding, blocking techniques can be used to defend first and then seek opportunities to escape.

图 11-4　阻挡　　Obstruction

(二)手肘逃脱法

动作说明: 手肘逃脱法又称虾行。以左侧虾行技术为例。当对手骑乘位置于自卫者上方时。右腿伸直,脚尖朝上,左腿膝盖弯曲约90°,且前脚掌支撑地面,尽可能贴紧臀部[见图 11-5(a)]。随后,身体猛然转向左侧呈侧躺,重心移至左肩,一手按住对手髋关节根部位置,一手按住其大腿部位[见图 11-5(b)]。旋即,左腿向后蹬腿发力,两手向前推,使得身体向后移动,臀部得以抽出[见图 11-5(c)]。身体旋转至另一侧,重复前面动作,直至完全脱离其骑乘状态[见图 11-5(d)]。

动作应用: 可与起桥技术搭配使用。

(2) Elbow Escape

Action instruction: Taking the left shrimp row technique as an example. When the opponent's riding position is above the defender. Extend the left leg straight, with the toes facing upwards, bend the right knee about 90 degrees, support the ground with the forefoot, and press it as close to the hips as possible [see Figure 11-5(a)]. Subsequently, the body suddenly turned to the left and lay on its side, shifting its center of gravity to the left shoulder. With one hand, it pressed down on the base of the opponent's hip joint, and with the other hand, it pressed down on the thigh near the knee [see Figure 11-5(b)]. Immediately, push the right leg backwards to exert force, and push both hands forward to move the body backwards, allowing the buttocks to be pulled out [see Figure 11-5(c)]. Rotate the body to the other side and repeat the previous movement [see Figure 11-5(d)].

Action application: can be used in conjunction with bridge lifting technology.

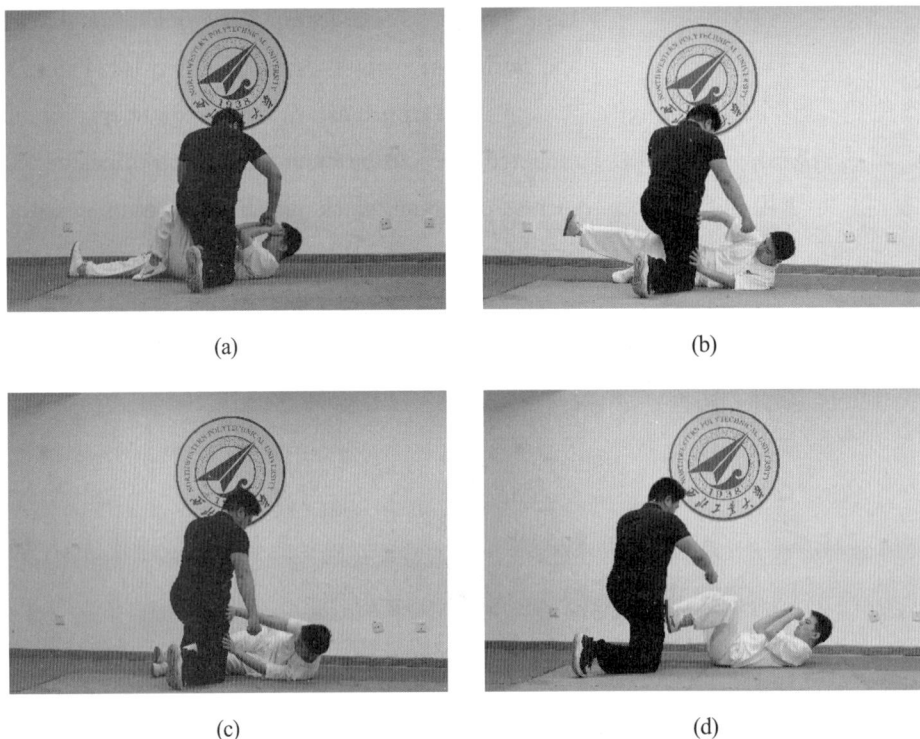

(a)

(b)

(c)

(d)

图 11-5　手肘逃脱法　Elbow escape method

（三）起桥

动作说明： 敌人进攻时，首先使用阻挡技术防守［见图 11-6(a)］。同时，大腿与小腿尽可能贴紧，两腿前脚掌着地。旋即，向上蹬地发力，伸膝挺髋，迫使敌人上肢前倾［见图 11-6(b)］，并环抱敌方肩臂躯干位置，进行控制。

动作应用： 当敌人完全骑乘在自卫者的髋部位置时，可利用格斗技术防守的同时，趁敌人不备，以腰部为杠杆改变敌人重心，减小敌人的进攻空间，并控制其躯干。

(3) Bridging

Action instruction: When the enemy attacks, first use blocking techniques to defend [see Figure 11-6(a)]. At the same time, the thighs and calves should be as close as possible, and the front soles of both legs should be on the ground. Immediately, push upwards and exert force, extend your knees and hips, forcing the enemy's upper limbs to lean forward [see Figure 11-6(b)], and embrace the enemy's shoulder, arm, and torso position for control.

Action application: When the enemy is completely riding on the defender's hip position, combat techniques can be used to defend while using the waist as a lever to change the enemy's center of gravity, weaken their attacking space, and control their torso when the enemy is unprepared.

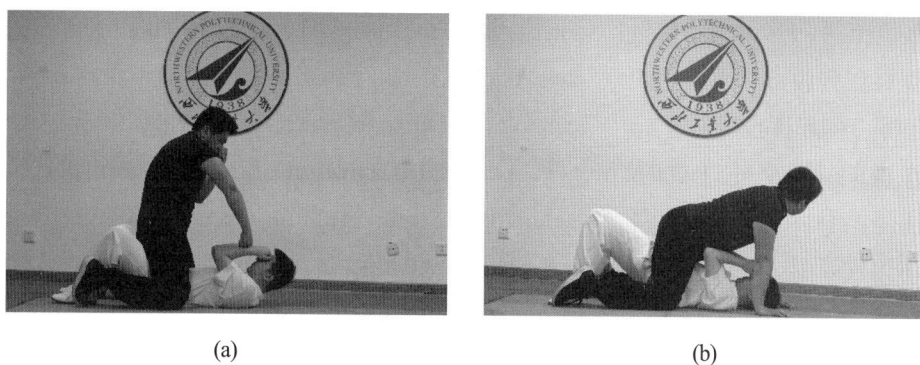

(a)　　　　　　　　　　　　(b)

图 11-6　起桥技术　Bridging

二、位置转换技术

"降服必先抢位"，地面缠斗的实质为位置之战。根据双方位置的不同可将地面近战分为骑乘位、侧骑乘位、封闭式防守、半封闭式防守及背后防守五种。此处主要介绍实际搏斗常见的骑乘位、侧骑乘位、封闭式防守及背后防守四类。下位即防守位，当被歹徒摔倒后，常处于被压制和不利的局面，应立即通过各类技术摆脱下位的不利局面。现就四种位置分别介绍下位逃脱之法。

（一）完全骑乘位置转换

骑乘位指自卫者摔倒在地后，被歹徒完全骑在躯干上并控制住身体。在完全骑乘姿势中，歹徒骑在自卫者的躯干上，四肢没有受到任何约束，而且身体重量都倾压在自卫者身上，居高临下，可以肆无忌惮地挥拳摆臂击自卫者的脑部。下位选手往往非常被动，毫无还击之力。遇见该

2. Position Conversion Technique

"To surrender, one must first seize a position, and the essence of ground fighting is a battle of positions." According to the different positions of both sides, ground close combat can be divided into five types: riding position, side riding position, closed defense, semi closed defense, and behind the back. This article mainly introduces the four common types of actual combat: riding, side riding, closed defense, and back riding. Lower position refers to defensive position. When a criminal falls down, they are often in a suppressed and disadvantageous situation, and should be immediately overcome through various techniques. Here are four different ways to escape from lower positions.

(1) Complete Riding Position Conversion

Riding position refers to the situation where the defender falls to the ground and is completely ridden on the torso and controlled by the perpetrator. In the fully riding position, the assailant rides on the self-defender's torso, without any restraint on his limbs, and his entire weight is leaning on defender opponent, standing high and down. Attacker can freely swing his fists and arms to hit his opponent's head, and the lower contestant is often very passive, without any fighting force. When encountering this situation, to avoid further

情形，为避免进一步恶化，应防止敌人骑乘在胸腹部位置。此处介绍上起桥＋侧起桥技术。

动作说明：当歹徒进攻时，首先使用阻挡技术防守，使用上起桥动作迫使歹徒上肢前倾［见图 11-7(a)］，并环抱歹徒肩臂躯干位置，进行控制。随后，使用侧起桥技术。左脚掌支撑地面，且用脚钩住对方脚踝，防止歹徒伸腿支撑［见图 11-7(b)］。随后，左腿蹬地发力，将重心移至左肩，右手经歹徒腋下，向左斜上方 45° 发力，迫使歹徒翻滚［见图 11-7(c)］，转换为上位的进攻方［见图 11-7(d)］。

动作应用：当歹徒完全骑乘于自卫者上方并单手撑按自卫者胸部，不断挥拳时，自卫者应在使用两手进行阻挡的基础上，配合侧起桥技术。

deterioration, the enemy should be avoided from riding in the chest and abdomen positions. This introduces introduce the technology of upper bridge and side bridge lifting.

Action instruction: Firstly, combining blocking technology with bridge lifting technology. When the enemy attacks, first use blocking techniques to defend. At the same time, the thighs and calves should be as close as possible, and the front soles of both feet should be on the ground [see Figure 11-7(a)]. Immediately, push up and exert force, extend your knees and hips, force the enemy's upper limbs to lean forward, and embrace the enemy's shoulder, arm, and torso position for control. Subsequently, the lateral bridging technique was used. Support the ground with your left foot and hook your foot onto the opponent's ankle to prevent them from extending their legs for support [see Figure 11-7(b)].Subsequently, the left leg kicked the ground and exerted force, shifting the center of gravity to the left shoulder. The right hand passed under the assailant's armpit and exerted force at a 45 degree angle to the left [see Figure 11-7(c)], forcing the enemy to roll and transform into an upper attacking force [see Figure 11-7(d)].

Action application: When the enemy shakes their hands and hits me, bend their arms and block their face, and cooperate with their head to dodge. When the opponent is completely riding above me and pressing my chest with one hand, continuously punching, using both hands to block, combined with the bridge lifting technique.

(a)

(b)

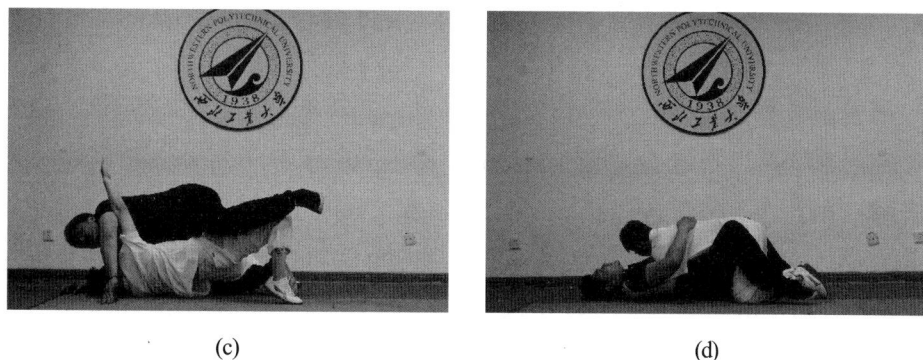

(c)　　　　　　　　　　　　　　(d)

图11-7　完全骑乘位置转换——侧起桥　Bridge lifting technology

（二）封闭式防守位置转换

封闭式防守指歹徒骑在自卫者躯干，但自卫者使用双腿缠绕在敌人腰间并且双脚交叉锁在对方身后，将敌方的臀部靠近下位己方的臀部，达到髋关节控制敌人重心的目的。另外，封闭式防守应注意双腿缠绕在敌方腰部的同时，两腿及膝盖部位一定要夹紧对方的身体两侧腰肋位置，并以双腿膝盖顶靠在对手双侧腋窝下，将其身体牢牢固定住。此处主要介绍剪刀扫技术。

动作说明：当歹徒使用摆拳等拳法进攻时，先使用格挡技术［见图11-8(a)］。随后，左手臂揽紧对手进攻手臂，控制于腋下，右手臂绕过敌方的颈后，双手共同控制其上肢，避免进一步打击。随后，左脚蹬踩敌方的同侧胯根位置，向左虾行，右腿迅速屈膝收腿，使右膝盖呈斜45°方向，顶住对方的小腹重心处，脚踝钩住对方的

(2) Closed Defensive Position Transition

Closed defensive position transition refers to the act of a criminal riding on the defender's torso, but the defender uses his legs to wrap around the enemy's waist and cross his feet to lock behind the opponent, bringing the enemy's buttocks closer to his own buttocks, achieving the goal of hip joint control of the enemy's center of gravity. In addition, closed defense should pay attention to wrapping both legs around the opponent's waist, while also gripping the opponent's waist ribs on both sides of the body with both legs and knees, and pressing the knees against the opponent's armpits on both sides to firmly secure their body. This mainly introduces the scissor scanning technology.

Action instruction: When the enemy uses fist techniques such as swinging to attack, use blocking techniques first [see Figure 11-8(a)]. Subsequently, the left arm tightly embraces the opponent's attacking arm, controlling it under the armpit. The right arm wraps around the enemy's neck, and both hands work together to control their upper limbs to avoid further attacks. Subsequently, step on the same side of the enemy's crotch with your left foot, shrimp to the left, and quickly bend your right leg to retract it, making your right knee inclined at a 45°angle, pressing against the center of gravity of the opponent's

身体一侧，避免对手过腿［见图 11-8(b)］。旋即，右腿向上向左用力，左腿向右用力横扫对方腿部，两腿呈左右剪式用力，并配合身体旋转迫使对方翻转［见图 11-8(c)］，之后迅速骑乘控制歹徒［见图 11-8(d)］。

动作要求：使用剪刀扫时，应挺起身体将歹徒上肢往身前拉，将其重心移至前方；膝盖顶住敌方身体时应保持斜方向，过低易导致被歹徒按压控制，过高易导致被掀开；伸直腿扫剪时，应先快速蓄力向外摆动。

lower abdomen, and hooking your ankle onto one side of the opponent's body to avoid crossing the leg [see Figure 11-8(b)]. Immediately, push your right leg up and left, and sweep your left leg across the opponent's leg with force. Cut your legs in a left and right motion and rotate your body to force the opponent to flip over [see Figure 11-8(c)]. Then, quickly ride and control your opponent [see Figure 11-8(d)].

Action requirements: When using scissors to sweep, the perpetrator should straighten their body and pull their upper limbs forward, moving their center of gravity to the front; when the knee is pressed against the enemy's body, it should be kept in an oblique direction. If it is too low, it is easy to be controlled by the enemy's pressure, and if it is too high, it is easy to be lifted; when sweeping and shearing with straight legs, one should first quickly swing outward to accumulate force

(a)

(b)

(c)

(d)

图 11-8　封闭式位置转换——剪刀扫　Scissor sweep

（三）侧面位置转换

侧骑乘有"千斤顶"之称。侧面位置是指自卫者摔倒后，歹徒从自卫者身体一侧进行压制，两者的身体位置呈大约90°。

动作说明： 当歹徒从自卫者身体一侧进行压制时［见图11－9(a)］。自卫者左手屈臂抵住歹徒的颈部，右手撑推其右侧髋部，以保持空隙距离［见图11－9(b)］。随后，右手臂环绕敌方同侧手臂的肘关节处［见图11－9(c)］，两脚前脚掌用力，左肩作为支撑，向左侧起桥［见图11－9(d)］。由于敌方的肘关节处于反关节状态，不得不按照劲力的方向翻滚。

(3) Side Position Conversion

Side riding, also known as a jack, refers to the position on the side where the perpetrator presses down from one side of the defender's body after a fall, with both bodies positioned at a 90°angle.

Action instruction: When the enemy suppresses the defender from one side of my body [see Figure 11-9(a)]. The defender bends his left arm against the enemy's neck and supports his right hip with his right hand to maintain a gap distance [see Figure 11-9(b)]. Subsequently, wrap your right arm around the elbow joint of the enemy's arm on the same side [see Figure 11-9(c)], exert force on the forefoot of both feet, and use your left shoulder as support to lift the bridge towards the upper left side of your body [see Figure 11-9(d)]. Due to the enemy's elbow joint being in a reverse joint state, they had to roll in the direction of force.

(a)

(b)

(c)

(d)

图 11-9 侧面位置转换 Side escape technique

动作要求： 为了留有反抗空间，左手要放在歹徒的颈部，并向前推击，右手要放在歹徒的髋部。

（四）背后位置转换

背后位置又称后骑乘，指歹徒处于自卫者身后。在柔术和综合格斗中一般将后骑乘位称为终极优势位置。自卫者无法看见歹徒做什么，不仅面临挨打的危险，同时也面临被绞脖的风险。所以下位是最不利的位置。为此，处于下位时首先要缩脖，防止绞脖；若处于俯卧位置，应立即翻身至仰卧位置。

动作说明： 首先双手拉扯对方手臂，以缓解其勒扼力度。迅速低头，收紧下颌，弯腰弓背屈腿，身体呈跪地团缩状。随后，勾头收腹，两脚蹬地，向前做抢背动作［见图 11−10(a)］，翻滚后循迅速控制敌人躯干，转换拿背的不利局面［见图 11−10(b)］。

动作要求： 翻滚时要控牢敌方的手臂，并迅速收腹，向前翻滚。

Action requirements: To avoid gaps, place your left hand on the enemy's neck and push forward, and your right hand on the enemy's crotch.

(4) Back Position Transition

The back is also known as a back riding, which refers to the enemy being behind the defender and using their feet to hook and control their body. In jujitsu and comprehensive combat, the rear riding position is generally referred to as the ultimate advantage position. Self-defenders are unable to see what the enemy is doing, facing not only the risk of being beaten, but also the risk of neck wrenching. So the lower position is the most unfavorable position. Therefore, the lower position should first shrink their neck to prevent twisting their neck; If in a prone position, immediately turn over to a supine position.

Action instruction: First, we use both hands to pull on the other person's arm to relieve their grip. Quickly lower your head, tighten your jaw, bend your waist, bow your back, and bend your legs, with your body in a kneeling and huddled shape. Subsequently, hook your head and tuck in your abdomen, kick your feet on the ground, perform a back grab move forward [see Figure 11−10(a)], roll and follow quickly to control the enemy's torso, and switch to a disadvantageous situation of holding your back [see Figure 11−10(b)].

Action requirements: When rolling, control the enemy's arms firmly, quickly tuck in your abdomen, and roll forward.

(a)　　　　　　　　　　(b)

图 11−10　背后位置转换——翻滚　Back rollover

三、控制降伏技术

降伏技也称关节技或绞技。通过绞技对敌方的脖颈实施压迫、阻断其大脑供血使其窒息。关节技是通过对人体关节造成非正常扭曲及变形，让对手剧痛难忍，迫使其投降认输的技术。处于上位的敌人由于手脚不受束缚，可用的降伏技较多。而下位的降伏技术多用于封闭式防守中。封闭式防守中，自卫者可使用十字搭扣技术控制敌方（见图11-11）。当处于下位防守时，若无法逃脱，或降伏技使用较为熟练时，可尽量转换为封闭式防守位置，实施相应控制技。此部分介绍两种常见的关节技和绞技。

3. Control and Subduing Technique

Subduing technique, also known as joint technique or twisting technique. The technique of exerting pressure on the opponent's neck through twisting techniques, cutting off their brain blood supply to suffocate them, or causing abnormal distortion and deformation of the human joints through joint techniques, causing intense pain and forcing the athlete to surrender and give up. Enemies in higher positions have more surrender techniques available due to their unrestrained hands and feet. The lower level subduing technique is often used in closed defense. In closed defense, the defender uses a cross buckle to control the opponent and can advance or retreat (see Figure 11-11). Therefore, when in a lower position defense, if it is impossible to escape or if the use of surrender techniques is more proficient, it is advisable to switch to a closed defense as much as possible. Here are several common techniques for subduction.

图 11-11　十字搭扣　Cross buckle

（一）关节技

1. 十字固

动作说明： 自卫者在封闭式防守中的下位时，使用十字搭扣控制对手。当敌人使用摆拳进攻时，使用格挡技术的同时［见图11-12(a)］，抓握住敌人的手臂，

(1) Arthrology

1) Cross Fixation

Action instruction: In a closed defense, the defender takes a lower position and uses cross buckles to control the opponent. When the enemy uses boxing techniques to attack, while using blocking techniques [see Figure 11-12(a)], they grasp the enemy's arm and tighten it towards their chest, firmly securing it

并向胸前揽紧,牢牢固定在己胸部。随后,左手推压敌方的脖颈,并迅速打开搭扣的双脚,左脚蹬敌方的髋部,推动身体向右侧移动[见图 11-12(b)],右腿顺势置于其肩部腋窝处并下压。旋即,左腿抬腿至敌方脖颈后部并下压[见图 11-12(c)]。之后,向上挺髋,伸展腰部,迫使其肩关节过度伸展[见图 11-12(d)]。

动作要求: 左腿跨越到对手头部的过程中,要始终保持对敌人的控制;十字固初步形成时与对手的身体呈十字形,挺髋伸展,身体协同用力对其肘关节形成十字臂锁;被固定的敌方手臂应使

to their chest. Subsequently, the right hand controls the enemy's arm, the left hand pushes and presses the enemy's neck, and quickly opens the buckle feet. The left foot kicks the opponent's hip, pushing the body towards the left side [see Figure 11-12(b)]. The right leg is placed in the opponent's shoulder armpit, and works together with the body to press and tightly control the opponent's upper body. Immediately,. Slip your left leg tightly against the outside of your opponent's body and slide over their head [see Figure 11-12(c)]. Afterwards, straighten your hips upwards, extend your waist, and block your opponent's right arm with both arms, forming a cross arm lock on their right elbow joint [see Figure 11-12(d)].

Action requirements: During the process of crossing the left leg over the opponent's head, always maintain control over the enemy; When the initial formation of the cross arm is formed, it forms a cross shape with the opponent's body, with the hips extended and the body working together to form a

(a)

(b)

(c)

(d)

图 11-12 封闭式位置转换——剪刀扫 Scissor Sweep

其大拇指朝上。

2. 木村锁（肩锁）

动作说明：自卫者处于封闭式防守的下位时，用双脚紧紧缠绕对方的腰部，以控制其重心。在控制敌人的基础上，伺机从内向外打开对手的双臂，迫使其双手触地［见图 11-13(a)］，迅速用右手的虎口位置抓牢敌人同侧小臂，并向后推，使敌人手臂后伸。随即，打开锁扣的双脚，左脚蹬地推动身体向右侧虾行，臀部后移之后，身体向右侧拧转半坐起，左臂经敌人左肩腋下，快速从敌人左肩上方绕至己方小臂处，握紧右手腕，双手协同锁扣敌人左手臂［见图 11-13(b)］。随后，左腿蹬地推动身体向左方虾行，右腿顺势跨越对手腰部控制其身体，避免对方逃脱。在此基础上，左臂下压敌人肩关节的同时，双手与身体协同用力，向斜上方抬拉敌人的左手臂，迫使敌方肩关节过度外旋［见图 11-13(c)］。

动作要求：将身体从敌人身体下方辗转出来时要借助双腿的摆动；双手协同锁扣对手手腕要牢固；右腿推撑对手身体，瞬间转出。转出后，右腿顺势跨越敌人腰部，控制腰身并向下压制，避免逃脱。动作形成时身体的位置与敌人不在一条直线上，向上向外推拉对手手臂，动作要连贯协同，一气呵成。

cross arm lock on the elbow joint; The fixed enemy arm should have its thumb facing upwards.

2) Kimura Lock (Shoulder Lock)

Action instruction: When the defender is in a closed defense position, tightly wrap their feet around the opponent's waist to control their center of gravity. On the basis of controlling the enemy, wait for an opportunity to open the opponent's arms from the inside out, force them to touch the ground with both hands [see Figure 11-13(a)], and quickly grasp the enemy's forearm on the same side with the tiger's mouth position of the right arm with the right hand, and push back to extend the enemy's arms. Immediately. Open the locking feet, push the body to the left with the right foot, move the buttocks back, twist the body to the left and sit up halfway. Pass the left arm under the enemy's left shoulder and quickly wrap it from above the enemy's left shoulder to your forearm, grip the right wrist, and work together to lock the enemy's left arm [see Figure 11-13(b)]. Afterwards, push the body to the right with the left leg, and cross the opponent's waist with the right leg to control their body and prevent them from escaping. On this basis, work together with your hands and body to push and pull the enemy's left arm diagonally upwards. At the same time, press down on your left shoulder, pull up with both hands, and lift up your right arm [see Figure 11-13(c)].

Action requirements: When rolling the body out from under the enemy's body, use the swinging of both legs. Collaborate with both hands to lock the opponent's wrist firmly, push and support the opponent's body with the right leg, and instantly turn it out. After turning out, cross the enemy's waist with your right leg, control your waist and press down to avoid escaping. When forming an action, the position of the body is not in a straight line with the enemy. Push and pull the opponent's arm upwards and outward, and the action should be coherent and coordinated in one go.

(a)

(b)

(c)

图 11-13 木村锁 Kimura lock

（二）绞技

1. 三角绞

动作说明：自卫者位于封闭式防守的下位，用双脚紧紧缠绕敌人。当敌人使用拳法进攻时［见图 11-14(a)］，自卫者伺机抓握敌人的左手腕并推向其腹部［见图 11-14(b)］。随后，迅速打开锁扣的双脚，挺髋挺腹，右脚勾压敌人脖颈后部［见图 11-14(c)］，左腿膝关节膝窝搭在右腿脚踝处。随后，收腹下压，并用两手扣压敌人头部，形成臂与腿的协同合力，对敌人的脖颈形成挤压［见图 11-14(d)］。

动作要求：双手或单手与大

(2) Twisting Technique

1) Triangle Twist

Action instruction: The defender is positioned in a closed defense position, tightly wrapping their feet around the enemy's waist. When the enemy uses boxing to attack, [see Figure 11-14(a)] the defender seizes the opportunity to grab the enemy's left wrist and push it towards their abdomen [see Figure 11-14(b)]. Subsequently, quickly open the locking feet, step the right foot from the left side of the body to above the left shoulder [see Figure 11-14(c)], and quickly buckle the feet. At this time, the athlete's feet form a diamond shape and wrap around the opponent; Immediately, straighten your hips and abdomen, and use the center of your body to quickly pull back and force your opponent to bend forward [see Figure 11-14(d)].

Action requirements: When the athlete's feet are in a

腿共同协作, 牢牢控制敌人上体。
收腿压腿, 双手向下搂压敌人头
部, 要协同用力, 一气呵成。

diamond shape and entangled with the opponent, they should straighten their hips and waist upwards, and use the center of their body to force the enemy to bend forward. Afterwards, use both hands or one hand to work together with the thighs to firmly control the opponent's upper body. Close the legs and press the legs, hold down the enemy's head with both hands, and work together to subdue the opponent. We need to work together and achieve success in one go.

(a)

(b)

(c)

(d)

图 11-14 三角绞 Triangle twist

2. 断头台

动作说明: 自卫者处在封闭
式防守的下位时, 用双脚紧紧缠
绕对手。面对敌人用双手进攻,
在运用阻挡技术防守的同时, 锁
扣的双脚压腿, 迫使敌人向前俯
身, 控制敌人的躯干 [见图 11-
15(a)]。在控制敌人的基础上, 打

2) Guillotine

Action instruction: The defender is in a closed defense position, tightly wrapping their feet around the opponent's waist [see Figure 11−15(a)]. When the enemy attacks with both hands and uses blocking techniques to defend, the locking feet press down on the legs, forcing the enemy to bend forward and control their torso. On the basis of controlling the opponent, open the locking feet, push the body to the left

开锁扣的双脚，左腿蹬地推动身体向右侧虾行，臀部略后移，身体向右侧拧转［见图 11−15(b)］；左臂快速绕过敌人的脑后，屈肘圈绕其颈部。旋即，上体后躺，左右手形成锁扣，左臂屈肘夹紧，以前臂桡骨为力点勒紧敌人咽喉［见图 11−15(c)］。

with the right leg, slightly move the buttocks back, and twist the body to the right [see Figure 11−15(b)]; immediately, the left arm quickly bypassed the back of the opponent's head, bending the elbow and circling around the opponent's neck; immediately, tilt your upper body backwards, bend your left arm and clamp it tightly, using the radius of your forearm as a point of force to tighten your opponent's throat, and lock your left and right hands tightly; Lock the enemy's waist tightly with both feet again, work together with both hands to pull and pull towards your arms, twist your body to the left, and force the opponent's neck to bend; Push your thighs backwards and press the outer side of your opponent's waist [see Figure 11−15(c)].

动作要求： 自卫者臀部略后移，身体向右侧拧转，为断头台技术提供施展空间。

Action requirements: The defender's buttocks are slightly moved back and their body is twisted to the right, providing space for the guillotine technique to be used.

(a)

(b)

(c)

图 11−15 断头台 Guillotine

第三节
地面解脱

Section 3
Ground Release

当歹徒将自卫者抓住并压在地上时，自卫者必须使用地面解脱技术对付歹徒的抓、锁喉、拳打或刀刺。地面解脱是地面站和擒拿解脱的结合。擒拿解脱技术要求较高，再加之不利的下位地面控制，格斗的难度系数大大提高。尤其是当歹徒身强力壮时，自卫者危险性大大增加，并且脱身机会大大减少。自卫者在被控制于地面下位时应全力相搏，无技术限制，包括踢裆、打脸、挖眼、口咬、抓裆来对付歹徒。

下面介绍的地面解脱被用来对付几种常见的紧急情况。这些技术学起来不难，但在遭到攻击时，能识别歹徒手法，且合理使用应付技术却不易。而快速识别及合理应对是地面战中重要的内容，因为歹徒不会给你时间去考虑其攻击手法是什么及如何对付。因此，所有的解脱技术都应该能够被熟练，自动化地应用。

When a criminal seizes or presses a defender onto the ground, the defender must use ground release techniques to deal with the criminal's grasp, throat locking, punching, or stabbing. Ground release is a combination of ground standing and grappling release. The requirement for capture and release techniques is high, coupled with unfavorable lower ground control, the difficulty coefficient of combat is greatly increased., especially when the criminals are strong and strong, the danger of self-defense greatly increases, and the chances of escape are greatly reduced. Self defenders should fight with all their might when controlled and placed on the ground, without any technical limitations, including kicking the crotch, slapping the face, digging eyes, biting the mouth, and grabbing the crotch to deal with criminals.

The ground release introduced below is used to deal with several common emergency situations. These techniques are not difficult to learn, but it is not easy to identify the techniques of criminals and use them reasonably when attacked. Rapid identification and reasonable response are important aspects of ground combat, as criminals do not give you time to consider what their attack techniques are and how to deal with them. Therefore, all liberation techniques should be able to proficiently apply automation.

一、体侧卡喉解脱

1. Body Side Strangulation Release

动作路线：当敌方从侧面掐住脖颈时［见图 11-16(a)］。两手按压歹徒双臂以缓其力，并防其抽手打脸［见图 11-16(b)］。随

Action instruction: When the enemy pinches the neck from the side [see Figure 11-16(a)]. Press the criminal's arms with both hands to relieve their pressure and prevent them from pulling their hands and hitting their face [see Figure 11-16(b)].

后，左手使用虎爪，抓拿敌人面部［见图 11-16(c)］。当敌方欲后仰躲避攻击时，左手顺着敌方的劲力，快速推其肩膀，同时，左腿蹬地发力［见图 11-16(d)］。

动作应用：此法用于对付歹徒跪在自卫者体侧，以双手卡喉时。

Then, use the tiger's paw with the left hand to grab the enemy's face [see Figure 11-16(c)]. When the enemy wants to lean back and dodge the attack. With the left hand following the enemy's strength, quickly push their shoulder, and at the same time, push their left leg to the ground to exert force [see Figure 11-16(d)].

Action application: This method is used to deal with criminals kneeling on the side of the self-defense person and choking their throat with both hands.

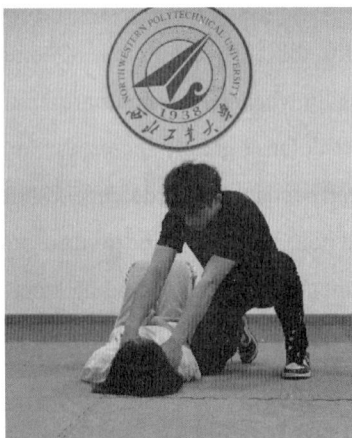

(a)

(b)

(c)

(d)

图 11-16　压肘解脱体侧卡喉　Elbow release with body side entrapment

二、体上卡喉解脱

动作路线： 歹徒上压卡喉时〔见图 11−17(a)〕，双臂猛压歹徒双臂于胸前〔见图 11−17(b)〕。随后，提膝顶击敌人，两手置于敌方的肘关节处，向头顶推歹徒双肘〔见图 11−17(c)〕。

动作应用： 此法用于歹徒压在自卫者身上并以双手卡喉时。

2. Relieve of Strangulation on the Body

Action instruction: The perpetrator presses his throat [see Figure 11−17(a)]., with both arms forcefully striking and pressing the perpetrator's arms in front of his chest [see Figure 11−17(b)], one leg kicking and turning to the side, or pushing the perpetrator's elbows above his head [see Figure 11−17(c)].

Action application: This method is used when the criminal presses on the self-defense person and clamps their throat with both hands.

(a)

(b)

(c)

图 11−17　体上卡喉解脱　Pressure arm rotation to release stuck throat

三、体上压臂解脱法

动作说明： 歹徒上压自卫者双手时［见图 11-18(a)］，自卫者用膝盖快顶并下拉左臂［见图 11-18(b)］，用右臂及全身力量向左推倒歹徒［见图 11-18(c)］。

动作应用： 当歹徒压在身上并压住双手时，自卫者的情况变得十分困难，能应用的技术十分有限。下述的滑臂解脱虽然不能保证次次成功，但可能是实践中唯一的可用技术。

3.Body Pressure Arm Release Method

Action instruction: The assailant presses the defender's both hands upwards [see Figure 11-18(a)], the defender quickly presses and pulls down their left arm with their knees [see Figure 11-18(b)], and uses their right arm and full body strength to push the assailant to the left [see Figure 11-18(c)].

Action application: When a criminal presses on their body and hands, the situation for self-defense becomes very difficult, and the available techniques are very limited. The following sliding arm release may not guarantee repeated success, but it may be the only available technique.

(a)

(b)

(c)

图 11-18　滑臂解脱体上压臂　Sliding arm detachment upper pressure arm

四、体上拳打解脱

动作说明： 歹徒处于完全骑乘位置的上位，一手卡喉一手以拳击脸时［见图 11-19(a)］，自卫者上挡其拳并抓牢其手以防其抽回拳再打［见图 11-19(b)］，左手推其肘使身体向右侧发力，推倒歹徒［见图 11-19(c)］

动作应用： 此法用来对付压在身上并施以乱拳的歹徒。此时自卫者处于绝对劣势之中，常常还会挨上几拳，所能用的技术也十分有限。挡抓压肘则是其中最常用的方法。

4. Physical Fist Release

Action instruction: The criminal presses his throat with one hand and punches his face with the other hand [see Figure 11-19(a)]. The self-defense person blocks his fist and grabs his hand to prevent him from retracting his fist and hitting again [see Figure 11-19(b)]. The left hand pushes his elbow to exert force to the right. and pushes the criminal down [see Figure 11-19(c)].

Action application: This method is used to deal with criminals who are pinned down on their bodies and resort to violent punches. Self defenders are at an absolute disadvantage, often receiving a few punches, and their available skills are also very limited. The most commonly used method is to block, grab, and press the elbow.

(a)

(b)

(c)

图 11-19　挡抓压肘　Shift grab and press elbow

五、体上刀刺解脱

动作说明： 歹徒骑身上欲刺时，格挡歹徒持刀之手［见图 11-20(a)］，用左手猛击其肘［见图 11-20(b)］。

动作应用： 用于对付骑压在身上并以刀相威胁或欲行刺的歹徒，这种情况极其危险，即使自卫者经过专门训练，受伤的概率也很高。

5.Body Stabbing Release

Action instruction: The bandit is about to stab on his body, blocking his knife holding hand [see Figure 11-20(a)], and using his left hand to strike his elbow [see Figure 11-20(b)].

Action application: Used to deal with criminals who are pinned on their bodies and threaten or intend to stab with knives. This situation is extremely dangerous, and even if the self-defender have undergone specialized training, the probability of injury is high.

(a)　　　　　　　　　　(b)

图 11-20　挡抓压肘对刀　Clamping and pressing the elbow to the knife

六、骑背锁喉解脱

动作说明： 歹徒骑背右臂锁喉，自卫者抓住歹徒手臂以缓其力［见图 11-21(a)］，内拉歹徒手臂，右腿蹬地，身体向左侧滚动［见图 11-21(b)］，击其裆［见图 11-21(c)］，齿咬其臂［见图 11-21(c)］。

动作应用： 此法用于歹徒骑在背上并以其臂锁喉时。该情景中能用的技术也极其有限。

6. Riding Back and Locking Throat Release

Action instruction: The criminal rides on his back and locks his throat with his right arm. The self-defense fighter grabs the criminal's arm to slow down his strength [see Figure 11-21(a)], pulls the criminal's arm inward, kicks his left leg onto the ground, rolls his body to the right [see Figure 11-21(b)], hits his crotch [see Figure 11-21(c)], and bites his arm with teeth [see Figure 11-21(c)].

Action application: This method is extremely limited for criminals who ride on their backs and lock their throats with their arms.

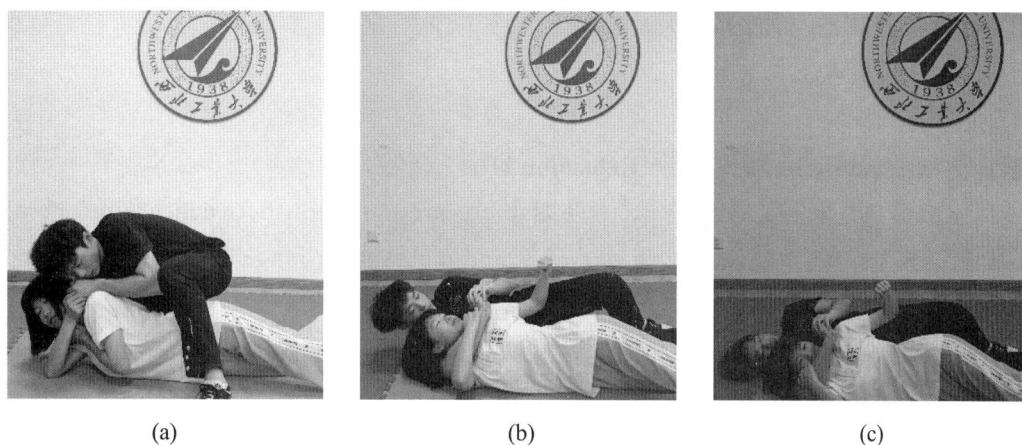

(a)　　　　　　　　　　　(b)　　　　　　　　　　　(c)

图 11-21　抱腰解脱　Waist hugging releas

第四节
地面战格斗策略

Section 4
Ground Combat Fighting Strategies

研究表明，在街头格斗中倒地的一方失败的概率为 59%。为此，在现实场景中，若被歹徒摔倒在地，应尽快站起，重新回到站立位，避免长时间陷入地面缠斗中。

被敌方摔倒，且处于被压制的下位，其危险系数要远远大于站立格斗，首先要秉持技术应用无限制的原则，使用膝盖顶裆、戳眼、牙咬等手段。另外，若陷入地面格斗中，应尽量避免以下情况：第一，处于平躺位置，即在背部完全着地的情况下被敌方骑在身上的躯干位置；第二，被敌人将手伸进腋下位置，进行反锁；第三，被敌方的两腿夹住肋部。总之，处于下位时，应尽量搂抱

Research shows that the probability of failure for the person who is knocked to the ground in a street fight is 59%. Therefore, in real-life situations, if one is knocked down by an attacker, it is crucial to get up as quickly as possible and return to a standing position to avoid being trapped in prolonged ground fighting.

When knocked down and in a disadvantaged position, the danger level is much higher compared to standing combat. One should first follow the principle of using unlimited techniques, employing tactics such as kneeing to the groin, eye gouging, or biting. Additionally, if engaged in ground combat, the following situations should be avoided as much as possible: Firstly, being pinned on your back with the enemy straddling your torso; secondly, the enemy reaching under your armpit to apply a lock; thirdly, the enemy trapping your ribs with their legs. In a word, when in a bottom position, one should try to hug the enemy to limit their attacking space, or create distance to maintain an open defense.

敌方，压缩其进攻的空间，或拉开距离保持开放式防守。

思考十一

1. 地面格斗技术与近战、远战及摔法是否有联系？

2. 地面近战中位置转换技术的目的是什么？

3. 地面近战中的降伏关节技主要运用于什么情况？

4. 地面解脱与擒拿解脱的关系是什么？

5. 地面战源自于哪里？

Reflection 11

1.Is there a connection between ground combat techniques and melee, long-range combat, and throwing techniques?

2.What is the purpose of position conversion technology in ground close combat?

3. In ground close combat, what are the main situations where the joint technique of subduing is used?

4. What is the relationship between ground liberation and capture liberation?

5. Where is ground combat originated?

第十一章微课视频

第十二章
特殊格斗技术

Chapter 12
Special Fighting Techniques

特殊格斗是指在敌我实力相差悬殊情况下的安全防卫，如对付持管制刀具或人数在两个以上的歹徒。"寡不敌众"、"双拳难敌四手"及"好虎架不住群狼"是对"以寡对众"危险状况的最佳描述，而歹徒若手持枪械或管制刀具则更增加了防身格斗的危险性。徒手对刀的危险在于若无法控制歹徒的持械手，持刀者会疯狂不断地从各个角度刺或砍受害者，直至疲惫。如日本的著名摔跤选手力道山，身高一米八，曾赢得国际摔角冠军腰带。但在夜总会喝酒时与人发生口角，在先出手的情况下，被一刀捅中腹股沟，最后因伤口感染去世。

一项针对西南地区 1 340 例故意伤害案件的特征及相关因素分析结果显示，钝器致伤 732 例（54.6%），锐器致伤 482 例（36.0%），其余工具致伤 10 例（火器 6 例、高低温 3 例、电流 1 例，占 0.7%）[①]。另外一项针对 816 例故意伤害未成年人案件的法医学分析显示致伤物

Special combat refers to security defense in situations where there is a significant difference in strength between the enemy and us, such as dealing with controlled knives or two or more criminals. "Being outnumbered", "two fists are difficult to defeat four hands", and "a good tiger cannot withstand a pack of wolves" are descriptions of the dangerous situation of "being outnumbered against others", while criminals holding firearms or controlled knives further increase the danger of self-defense combat. The danger of unarmed swordsmanship lies in the fact that if the perpetrator's armed hand cannot be controlled, the wielder will frantically stab or chop at the victim from various angles until exhausted. Like the famous Japanese wrestler Lido Shan, who stands 1.8 meters tall and has won the international wrestling championship belt. But while drinking in a nightclub, he had an argument with someone and was stabbed in the groin with a knife before taking the initiative. Eventually, the wound became infected and he passed away.

A study on the characteristics and related factors of 1,340 cases of intentional injury in the Southwest region showed that blunt instruments were responsible for 732 cases (54.6%), sharp instruments caused 482 cases (36.0%), and other tools were involved in 10 cases (firearms 6 cases, high/low temperature 3 cases, electric current 1 case, accounting for 0.7%)[①]. Another forensic analysis of 816 cases involving minors in intentional injury cases showed that blunt

---

① 龙武，胡春梅，李思思，等 . 西南地区 1 340 例故意伤害案件的特征及相关因素分析 [J]. 法医学杂志，2019，35(4):433-436.

中，钝器致伤317例（42.0%），锐器致伤364例（48.2%），火器6例（0.8%）[①]。工具致伤的比例如此之高，自然成为安全防卫学的重要研究和教学内容。尽管多数专家认为学生的技术程度达不到相应的水平，不赞成初学者学习对刀对枪，但还是普遍认为中、高级班应包括对刀与枪的教学内容。笔者认为不仅仅是中、高级班，将对刀、对枪格斗技术列入初级班正式教学内容也是十分必要的。

以寡对众和对枪对刀的格斗情况十分复杂，存在许多不确定因素，没有人有百分之百的把握成功，因而全身而退的概率无法预料。对付此类情况的最好方法是预防，避免将自己置于枪口刀尖上。而一旦遇上，最常用的办法是听歹徒命令不作反抗，寄希望于歹徒放过自己，或设法逃走。迫不得已时，则殊死格斗以求脱身。

instruments caused 317 cases (42.0%), sharp instruments caused 364 cases (48.2%), and firearms were involved in 6 cases (0.8%). The high proportion of injuries caused by tools has naturally become an important topic in the study and teaching of self-defense. Although most experts believe that beginners lack the technical level to handle knives and guns and do not recommend learning knife and gun defense techniques, it is generally agreed that intermediate and advanced classes should include knife and gun defense instruction. The author believes that it is necessary to include knife and gun fighting techniques in the formal curriculum of beginner classes, not only in intermediate and advanced classes.

The situation of fighting with many people and guns to knives is very complex, with many uncertain factors. No one has a 100% chance of success, so the probability of a full body retreat is unpredictable. The best way to deal with such situations is to prevent and avoid placing oneself on the tip of the gun. Once encountered, the most common method is to obey the orders of the criminals and not resist, hoping that the criminals will let themselves go or try to escape. If absolutely necessary, fight to the death in order to escape.

第一节
对付持枪歹徒

Section 1
Dealing with Gunmen

自2021年颁布《关于依法收缴非法枪爆等物品严厉打击涉枪涉爆等违法犯罪的通告》以来，我国通过多项举措打击涉枪违反

Since the issuance of the Notice on Strictly Cracking down on Illegal Crimes Involving Guns and Explosions in accordance with the Law in 2021, China has taken multiple measures to crack down on cases of gun related violations, and

---

① 王威，张世林，张宵，等.816例故意伤害未成年人案件的法医学分析 [J]. 法制博览，2023(12):13-17.

案件,已成为世界上枪爆暴力犯罪发案最低的国家之一,在我国涉枪暴力犯罪虽在2022年已降至最低,但此类危险仍然存在。2023年8月公安部通报的年内全国公安机关打击整治枪爆违法犯罪专项行动效果指出,各地共查破枪爆案件1.3万起,打掉团伙37个,捣毁窝点258个,抓获违法犯罪嫌疑人1.4万人。各地共收缴枪支4.3万支、子弹110万发、炸药25吨、雷管10.3万枚。

一般推荐三种做法应对持枪歹徒。一是听命于歹徒,寄希望于歹徒不会进一步伤害自己。二是立即逃跑以免被歹徒劫到僻静处再下手。三是通过格斗的方式击伤或控制住歹徒以创造逃脱机会。三种办法各有利弊,运用时机也不尽相同,应根据具体的情况做出判断与决策。

一、枪下服从

在枪口下不作任何反抗,完全听命于歹徒的吩咐是人的本能反应。大多数武术或自卫防身教师以及警察也大力推荐此做法,尤其是遭遇抢劫时。大部分人没有经过特殊的训练,容错率较低,稍有不慎就会招来生命的威胁。在以下情况中应服从歹徒保持冷静,等待时机,万万不可轻举妄动。

has become one of the countries with the lowest incidence of gun related violent crimes in the world. Although gun related violent crimes have reached their lowest level in China in 2022, the danger still exists. In August 2023, the Ministry of Public Security reported the results of the special action of the national public security organs to crack down on gun explosion crimes in the year, pointing out that 13,000 cases of gun explosion were investigated and solved, 37 gangs were killed, 258 dens were destroyed, and 14,000 suspect were arrested. A total of 43,000 firearms, 1.1 million bullets, 25 tons of explosives, and 103,000 detonators were confiscated in various regions.

Three methods are generally recommended to deal with armed criminals. The first is to obey the criminals and hope that they will not further harm themselves. The second is to immediately escape to avoid being taken to a secluded place by criminals before taking action. The third is to use combat to injure or control criminals in order to create opportunities for escape. The three methods each have their own advantages and disadvantages, and the timing of application is also different. Judgments and decisions should be made based on specific situations.

1. Gun Obedience

Not resisting at gunpoint and completely obeying the orders of the criminals is the instinctive reaction of most people. Most martial arts or self-defense teachers and police strongly recommend this practice, especially when encountering robbery. Most groups have not undergone special training, and their fault tolerance is low. Any slight mistake can pose a threat to their lives. In the following situations, one should obey the gangster to remain calm and wait for the opportunity. Never act rashly.

（1）当自卫者被紧紧抓住，且被枪口抵住头胸，逃跑或格斗的机会不大，服从成为唯一的选择时。

（2）当歹徒很紧张，自卫者的每个动作都会刺激歹徒引起扣动扳机的危险时。

（3）当歹徒已经开枪射击其他反抗或逃跑的受害者时（如在抢劫银行时）。

（4）当歹徒只为劫钱抢物时。

（5）当歹徒劫持人质，自卫者的逃跑或反抗会引起歹徒杀害人质时。

（6）当自卫者技术不高，或穿戴衣物不适合逃跑时。

服从的好处是不会激怒歹徒及让歹徒感到威胁，使其放松警惕心，原来打算开枪的歹徒也许改变主意，而原来不确定是否要开枪的歹徒也会权衡利弊，避免加重案情。

服从的弊端是歹徒可能诱骗自卫者进入圈套，将受害人捆绑并带至偏僻之地，但歹徒的最终本意依然是杀人灭口时，就没有机会逃跑或反抗的余地了。简言之，服从可能不会带来即时的危险，但可能有延迟的生命危险。为此，服从应有底线，该打该跑时，切不能犹豫，尤其是即将被捆绑并带走时。

① When the defender is tightly grasped and the muzzle is pressed against the head and chest, there is little chance of escape or fighting, and obedience becomes the only choice.

② When the criminal is very nervous, every action of the defender will stimulate the criminal, causing the danger of pulling the trigger.

③ When the criminal has already shot other victims who resist or flee (such as when robbing a bank).

④ When criminals only rob money and property.

⑤ When criminals take hostages, the escape or resistance of self-defenders can cause the criminals to kill the hostages.

⑥ When the defender's skills are not advanced or their clothing is not suitable for escape.

The benefit of obedience is that it will not provoke criminals or make them feel threatened, relax their vigilance, and criminals who originally planned to shoot may change their minds, while criminals who were originally unsure whether to shoot will also weigh the pros and cons to avoid aggravating the case.

The downside of obedience is that criminals may lure self-defense into a trap, bind the victim and take them to a remote place, but the ultimate intention of criminals is still to kill and silence, leaving no room for escape or resistance. In short, obedience may not bring immediate danger, but there may be delayed life-threatening consequences. To this end, obedience should have a bottom line, and one must not hesitate to hit or run, especially when about to be bound and taken away.

二、枪下逃跑

面对枪口时，一般人对转身逃跑持怀疑态度，认为再快也没子弹快。其实逃跑并不像人们想象的那般危险。除一般的无差别行凶外，大部分歹徒不愿在公共场合开枪杀人，部分歹徒的最终目的是吓唬受害者，逼迫其就范。另外，即使歹徒开枪也不一定每次都能击中，即便击中了也不一定打到要害部位。有关枪口下逃跑成败的概率，唯一的研究来自美国侦探（前警察）比登本德。他在1991—1992年在电视上作过几次讲演，后来出了一盘录像资料《街头防身巧计》。根据他的研究，在枪口下逃跑而实际上被严重射伤或打死的概率仅为2%，而逃脱或受轻伤的概率则达到98%。如果此研究属实，则逃跑应是枪口下安全自卫的最佳选择。

一般推荐在下列情况下采用逃跑战术。第一，自卫者在公共场合或接近于公共场合，歹徒不想开枪而引人注意。第二，逃跑时身边有障碍物阻挡子弹或歹徒视线。第三，当歹徒迫使自卫者随其去僻静之处时。第四，自卫者离歹徒稍远且穿着又适合于逃跑时。逃跑并躲避枪弹的策略是跑折线、突然变向、弯腰和多利用障碍物。

逃跑的优点是自卫者能立即

2. Run at the Gun Point

Faced with the gun point, most people hold a skeptical attitude towards turning around and running away, believing that no matter how fast it is, bullets are not as fast. Actually, running away is not as dangerous as people imagine. Apart from ordinary indiscriminate violence, most criminals are unwilling to shoot and kill in public, and there are also many who originally wanted to scare the victims and force them to obediently comply. Moreover, even if the criminal shoots, they may not always be able to hit, and even if they do, they may not necessarily hit the crucial area. The only study on the probability of success or failure in escaping at the muzzle comes from American detective (former police officer). Biden Bender. He gave several speeches on television from 1991 to 1992, and later released a video titled "Street Self-defender Tactics". According to his research, the probability of escaping from the muzzle and actually being seriously shot or killed is only 2%, while the probability of escaping or being lightly injured reaches 98%. If this study is indeed true, then escape should be the best choice for safe self-defense at gunpoint.

It is generally recommended to use escape tactics in the following situations. The first is that the self-defender are in public or close to public places, and the criminals do not want to shoot and attract attention. The second is that there are obstacles around the bullet or criminal's line of sight when running away. The third is when criminals force self-defender to go with them to secluded places. The fourth is when the self-defender are slightly away from the criminals and dressed appropriately for escape. The strategy for escaping and avoiding bullets is to run a zigzag, suddenly change direction, bend over, and make more use of obstacles.

The advantage of escaping is that the self-defense

脱离险境而又不需搏斗。但缺点是逃跑可能会激怒歹徒而使其开火，并且逃跑也受其他因素，如奔跑能力、穿着、环境及与歹徒的距离等因素制约。一旦在平坦地段，人跑的速度还是不如子弹。总的来说，逃跑不会引发眼前的危险，但可能影响最终的安全。

person can immediately escape danger without the need for combat. But the disadvantage is that running away may provoke the criminal and open fire, and running away is also constrained by other factors such as running ability, clothing, environment, and distance from the criminal. Once in flat terrain, people still run slower than bullets. Overall, running away may not pose immediate danger, but it may affect ultimate security.

三、枪下格斗

3. Gun Fight

格斗是绝大多数人都不愿采用的手段，因为格斗可能会激怒歹徒或威胁歹徒的安全，迫使歹徒开火。如自卫者技术差，则成功率不高且危险性增大，而且一旦动手便是你死我活，没有退路，枪下格斗必是破釜沉舟，惊险万分。但与逃跑和服从相比，格斗会给自卫者一些主动权，控制和扭转局势，而不是任凭歹徒摆布与宰割。

Fighting is a means that the vast majority of people do not want to use, as it may anger or threaten the security of criminals, forcing them to open fire. If the self-defender's skills are poor, the success rate is not high and the danger increases. Moreover, once they take action, they will fight to the death with no way out. Gun to gun combat is undoubtedly a dangerous and thrilling battle. But compared to fleeing and obeying, fighting gives self-defenders some initiative to control and turn the situation around, rather than letting criminals manipulate and exploit them.

在过去的案例中，自卫者在于持枪歹徒对抗中既有成功的案例，也有失败的情况。一般认为，在下列的情况下应果断选择格斗。第一，当歹徒企图将自卫者牢牢捆绑，使其彻底失去反抗能力时。第二，自卫者判断当前形势极其危险时。第三，机会较好时，如歹徒走神，或歹徒看起来不那么熟练，或不太强壮，而自卫者的技术相对熟练时。第四，当歹徒已射杀其他受害者，来不及调转枪口，不奋力反扑就要被射杀时。

In past cases, there have been both successful and unsuccessful cases of self-defense against armed criminals. It is generally believed that fighting should be chosen decisively in the following situations. Firstly, when the criminals attempt to firmly bind the self-defense, rendering them completely incapable of resistance. Secondly, when the self-defender determine that the current situation is extremely dangerous. Thirdly, when the opportunity is good, such as when the criminal is distracted, or the criminal appears less skilled or not very strong, while the self-defense person's skills are relatively proficient. Fourthly, when the perpetrator has already shot other victims and there is no time to turn the gun, they will be shot if they do not fight back vigorously.

笔者曾于 1996 和 1997 年对 174 名美国大学生作过枪口格斗逃生的实验研究。实验使用压力式水枪（其效果与手枪相似）。结果发现，如果枪手在自卫者每次开始反抗格斗时马上开枪，或自卫者被枪顶在胸口或背后时，击中的概率是 58%。自卫者在两米之外开始反抗格斗时，平均被击中的概率升至 95%。且受试者个体差别很大，8% 的人每次都被击中，而 3% 的人每次都成功地将枪手控制住。决定个人差异的因素包括敌我双方的技术、反应、身体素质。因为这项研究是在模拟情况下，而不是在实际情况下完成，且用的又是水枪，所以双方的心理反应和格斗结果与实际情况会有所差别。由于无法真枪实弹地进行真实实验，因此，在应用实验数据时宜谨慎。

枪口格斗适用于一臂之内的距离。如此，自卫者一伸手就可抓住歹徒的持枪手。实验表明，若自卫者的速度很快，则可避开第一枪，但必须在避开第一枪后，迅速控制歹徒持枪的手以防第二枪。若歹徒较远，则走为上策。最危险的距离是 2 ～ 6 m，这是自卫者想格斗又够不着，想跑却容易被击中的最危险距离。

对持枪歹徒的格斗有多种方法，但各种教科书中及拳术中所教技术都没有经过实验。人们偏

The researcher of this course conducted experimental studies on Gun fighting escape on 174 American college students in 1996 and 1997. The experiment used a pressure water gun (which has a similar effect to a handgun). As a result, it was found that if the gunman fired immediately every time the defender began to resist the fight, and the defender was hit by the gun in the chest or behind, the probability of being hit was 58%. The probability of being hit increases to 95% when self-defense fighters start fighting from two meters away, which is the average number. Moreover, there were significant individual differences among the participants, with 8% being hit every time and 3% successfully controlling the gunman every time. The factors that determine personal differences include the skills, reactions, and physical fitness of both the enemy and ourselves. Because this study was conducted in a simulated scenario rather than in actual situations, and a water gun was used, the psychological reactions and fighting results of both parties may differ from the actual situation. Due to the inability to conduct real experiments with live ammunition, caution should be exercised when applying experimental data.

The gun point combat is suitable for a distance within one arm, so that the self-defender can grab the gunman of the criminal as soon as they reach out. Experiments have shown that if the defender's speed is fast, they can avoid the first shot, but they must quickly control the gunman's hand to prevent a second shot after avoiding the first shot. If the criminal is far away, it is best to go. The most dangerous distance is between two to six meters, which is the most dangerous distance for self-defense fighters who want to fight but cannot reach, and who want to run but are easily hit.

There are various methods for fighting armed criminals, but the techniques taught in various textbooks and boxing have not been experimented with. People prefer capture techniques

爱擒拿技术是因为容易控制对方的持枪手。一般枪口搏斗的过程有三步，第一步是将歹徒持枪手击开并将自己身体闪开；第二步是靠近歹徒控制其持枪手以防止其抽枪再射；第三是用踢打擒拿或咬撞击伤或制服歹徒。这一部分介绍在三种情况下的格斗技术，也是上述实验所用技术。

（一）枪口指胸或腹时

动作说明：歹徒持枪对准自卫者胸腹时［见图 12-1(a)］，自卫者左手迅速推开持枪手，同时身体侧后转身闪开枪口［见图 12-1(b)］。上步贴近歹徒，右手抓住歹徒的腕关节，并向上用力，左手向下按压，形成反关节的同时，向后回带［见图 12-1(c)］。

（二）枪口指背时

动作说明：歹徒枪口抵住背后时［见图 12-2(a)］，快速转身躲开枪口的同时，手臂后击打开枪口［见图 12-2(b)］。贴近歹徒身体，将持枪手压在两人身体之

because they can easily control the opponent's gunman. The general process of muzzle combat involves three steps. The first step is to shoot the gunman away and dodge oneself; The second step is to approach the criminal and control their gunman to prevent them from drawing a gun and then shooting again; The third is to use kicking, catching, biting, hitting, or subduing criminals. This section introduces combat techniques in three different situations, which are also the techniques used in the above experiments.

(1)When the Gun Points to the Chest or Abdomen

Action instruction: The criminal aimed the gun at the chest and abdomen of the self-defense soldier [see Figure 12-1(a)], and the self-defense soldier quickly pushed the gunman away with his left hand. At the same time, he turned back and dodged the muzzle [see Figure 12-1(b)] Step closer to the criminal, grab the criminal's wrist joint with your right hand, and apply force upwards while pressing down with your left hand to form a reverse joint while retracting backwards [see Figure 12-1(c)].

(2) Gun Point at Back

Action instruction: The perpetrator presses the muzzle against the back [see Figure 12-2(a)], quickly turns around to avoid the muzzle, and at the same time, hits the arm back to open the muzzle [see Figure 12-2(b)], gets close to the perpetrator's body, presses the gunman

(a)

(b)

(c)

图 12-1 推闪击肘法 Pushing flash elbow method

间，并把歹徒持枪手与其身体锁
抱在一起［见图 12-2(c)］，如歹
徒用左手持枪，则转身后将其持
枪手顶高，然后以膝顶裆［见图
12-2(d)］。

between the two bodies, and locks the perpetrator and his
body together [see Figure 12-2(c)] If the perpetrator holds
the gun with his left hand, the action after turning around is
to lift the gunman up, and then use his knee to support his
crotch [see Figure 12-2(d)].

(a)

(b)

(c)

(d)

图 12-2 闪抱法 Flash hug method

（三）枪口指头时

动作说明：歹徒以枪口指头时［见图 12-3(a)］，自卫者迅速低头并以手向上推枪口［见图 12-3(b)］，上步抓住持枪手臂［见图 12-3(c)］，双手锁其臂，上步以肩扛肘［见图 12-3(d)］。

(3)When Pointed at Head

Action instruction: The thug uses the muzzle finger [see Figure 12-3(a)], the self-defense person quickly lowers their head and pushes the muzzle upwards with their hand [see Figure 12-3(b)], steps up to grab the gun's arm [see Figure 12-3(c)], locks their arms with both hands, and steps up to shoulder the elbow [see Figure 12-3(d)].

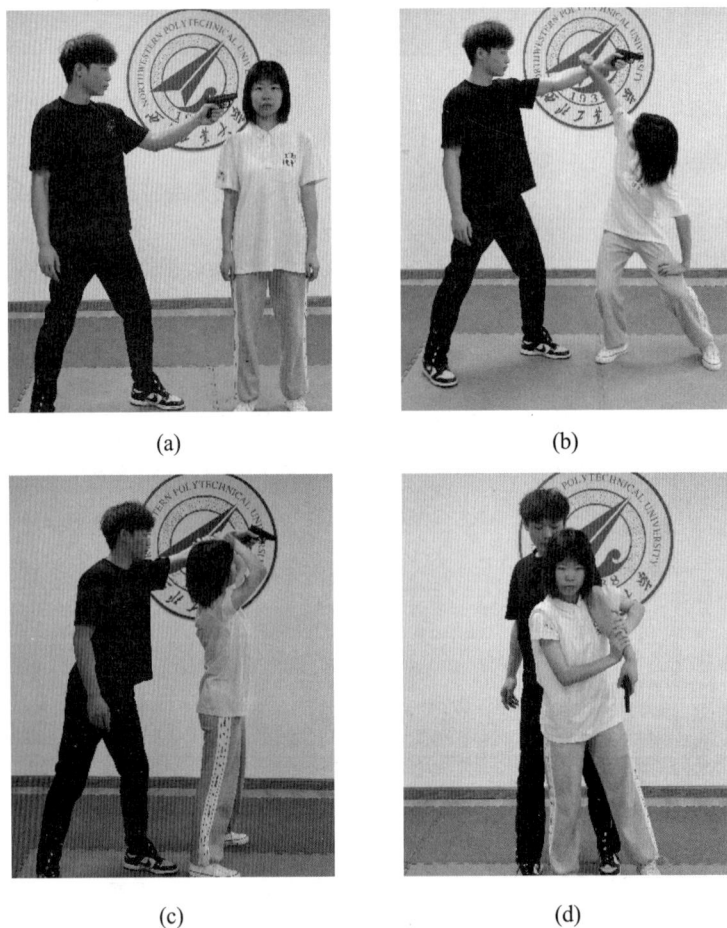

(a)

(b)

(c)

(d)

图 12-3　闪避击肘法　Dodge elbow strike method

枪口格斗要注意以下几点：第一，假意表现服从之意，以麻痹歹徒，使其松懈；第二，格挡动作应似闪电般快速，以避开第一枪；第三，贴近歹徒，以手及身体

There are several points to pay attention to in muzzle combat. The first is to show obedience, to numb the criminals and make them relax. Secondly, the blocking action should be as fast as lightning to avoid the first shot. Thirdly, get close to the perpetrator and use your hands and body to control the

控制住歹徒的持枪手，不给其抽枪的空间，然后制服歹徒。

gunman, without giving them space to draw a gun, and then subdue the perpetrator.

第二节
对付持刀歹徒

Section 2
Dealing with Knife Armed Perpetrators

刀尖上的安全自卫与枪口下的安全自卫有些类似，自卫者所面临的最大难题是因摸不清歹徒的意图而拿不定主意。服从怕失去最后的机会，想格斗又怕受伤。专家们认为对付持刀歹徒的注意事项与对付持枪歹徒相似。第一还是应服从以避免伤害并寻找逃脱机会。第二是逃跑以脱离险境。第三是徒手或使用其他器械与歹徒格斗。

The security self-defense on the tip of the knife is somewhat similar to the security self-defense under the muzzle of the gun. The biggest challenge faced by self-defenders is not being able to understand the intentions of the criminals and make up their minds. Obedience and fear of losing the last chance, wanting to fight but afraid of getting hurt. Experts believe that dealing with knife wielding criminals is similar to dealing with gun wielding criminals. The first is to obey to avoid harm and seek waiting opportunities. The second is to escape from danger. The third is to fight the criminals with bare hands or other equipment.

一、刀下服从

1. To Obey under the Knife

当歹徒紧紧抓住自卫者且刀尖对准其胸口、使其无法逃跑又无法格斗时，或当自卫者自知技术或力量都占下风时，或当歹徒明确表明只要钱财时，自卫者应采用服从的战术。此时应期望歹徒获得钱财钱就离开，而不会进一步伤人；或等待有利时机逃跑或格斗。选择服从应随时注意歹徒的举动，随时准备逃跑或格斗。最好能与歹徒保持一定的距离。

目前虽未有关于刀尖下服从

When the criminal tightly grasps the defender and points his knife at his chest, unable to escape or engage in combat, when the defender knows that his skills or strength are at a disadvantage, or when the criminal clearly states that he only needs money, the defender should adopt a tactic of obedience. Expect the criminals to leave as soon as they receive money, without further harm or waiting for favorable opportunities to escape or engage in combat. But when obeying, one should pay attention to the actions of the criminals and be ready to flee or fight at any time. It's best to maintain a certain distance from the criminals.

At present, there is no research on the effect of obedience

的效果研究，但多数相关案例表明，在遭遇此类案件，尤其是在遭遇抢劫时，服从歹徒的生存效果较好。

on the tip of the knife, but most relevant cases indicate that obedience is particularly effective in obeying criminals during robbery.

二、刀下逃跑

不管武艺多高，在遇上持刀歹徒时首先要跑，除非是无路可逃。逃跑的好处是能迅速摆脱险境，而且持刀歹徒不能像持枪歹徒那样从背后射击，因此安全程度相对较高。另外，歹徒一般也不愿或不敢公然在大街上持刀追人。但逃跑也会受一些因素限制，如是否有路可逃、跑速及耐力如何，等等。

在刀尖上逃跑的机会有以下几种。一是歹徒尚未开始攻击时，自卫者转身就跑。二是离公共场合较近时。三是歹徒胁迫自卫者去僻静之处。四是自卫者的技术经验不足，没有把握。五是自卫者穿着适宜。在逃跑时亦应作好随时回身格斗的准备。

三、刀下格斗

与对付持枪歹徒相似，以格斗对付持刀歹徒有一定机会夺得主动权、控制并扭转局势。但也容易激怒歹徒，使其全力攻击自卫者；并且对方一旦动手，自卫

2. Escape under the Knife

No matter how skilled the martial arts are, when encountering a knife wielding criminal, the first thing to do is to run, unless there is no way to escape. The advantage of escaping is that it can quickly escape danger, and criminals cannot shoot from behind like they do with a gun, so the security level is higher. In addition, most criminals are unwilling or afraid to openly pursue people with knives on the street. But escape is also limited by some factors, such as whether there is a way to escape, running speed and endurance, and so on.

There are several opportunities to escape on the tip of the knife. One is that before the criminals start attacking, the defenders turn around and run. The second is when it is close to public places. The third is when criminals coerce self-defenders to seek refuge in a quiet place. Fourthly, when the self-defender lack sufficient technical experience and are unsure. The fifth is when the self-defender wear appropriate clothing. Be prepared to turn back and engage in combat at any time while running away.

3. Knife Fighting

Similar to dealing with armed robbers, using combat to deal with armed robbers has a certain opportunity to seize the initiative, control and turn the situation around, but it is easy to anger and threaten the robbers, making them fully attack the self-defense, and once they take action, the self-defense has no

者便无退路可言。在其他招数都不灵的情况下，格斗便成为唯一的手段。尤其是在歹徒铁了心要置自卫者于死地时，或迫其去僻静处而自卫者又无法逃跑时，或自卫者技术力量占优势时。

歹徒持刀威胁大致有几种可能。一是遭歹徒锁喉并以刀尖相对，二是歹徒尚未抓住自卫者便乱刀捅来，三是歹徒未抓住自卫者但以刀尖指向其胸腹或背。自卫者格斗的方式亦应随之变化。

笔者在 1997 至 2000 年间对 582 名美国大学生作了关于在刀尖下格斗的研究。实验过程接近真实搏斗，由持刀者使用橡皮刀尽力去刺到自卫者。实验的结果表明，当刀尖抵在胸前，自卫者先动手格斗时，受伤的概率为 52%。但当距离两米左右，持刀者先挥刀攻击时，则自卫者的受伤率增至 80%，而且遭遇男子攻击（84%）与女子攻击（78%）同样危险。80% 的受伤率表明空手对刀确实危险。然而如果自卫者使用一件秋衣来挡住刀锋时，则受伤率降至 65%，而当自卫者用椅子及棍子来对刀时，受伤率分别降至 54% 及 44%，而且大部分刀伤都在手臂。

way out. In situations where other techniques are ineffective, fighting becomes the only means. Especially when the criminal is determined to kill the defender, or when they are forced to seek refuge in a quiet place and the defender cannot escape, or when the defender's technical strength is superior.

There are several possible threats from criminals wielding knives. One is being locked in the throat by the perpetrator and facing each other with the tip of a knife; the other is being stabbed by the perpetrator before they have caught the defender; and the third is being pointed at the chest, abdomen, or back with the tip of a knife when the perpetrator has not caught the defender. The way self-defense fighters engage in combat should also change accordingly.

The researcher conducted a study on 582 American college students fighting on the tip of a knife between 1997 and 2000. The experimental process is close to real combat, and the wielder uses a rubber knife to try their best to stab the self-defense person. The results of the experiment showed that when the tip of the knife was pressed against the chest, the self-defense fighter had a 52% chance of being injured when fighting first. But when the wielder of the knife attacks first at a distance of about two meters, the risk of injury to the self-defense increases to 80%, and it is equally dangerous when attacked by a man (84%). and a woman (78%). 80% of the injury rate indicates that hand to hand combat is indeed dangerous. However, if a defender uses an autumn coat to block the blade, the injury rate drops to 65%. However, when a defender uses a chair and a stick to strike, the injury rate drops to 54% and 44%, respectively, and most of the knife injuries are in the arm.

（一）远战对短刀

远战对短刀相对安全一些，且进可攻退可守。一般要求宁退勿进，距离保持在三臂以上最好。远战对短刀应遵循以下原则。第一，保持移动。保持距离使歹徒之刀够不到目标。第二，少用拳而多用掌以侧挡来刀，并准备抓其手臂。尽管手有时会受伤，要害部位却得到保护。第三，抓住时机，以腿攻击歹徒之膝或踢歹徒持刀之手。第四，随时使用任何可以抓到的武器，寻找机会逃跑。下面是远战对短刀的基本技术。

动作说明：首先格斗势准备并保持移动，拉开距离［见图 12-4(a)］，有机会立即逃脱。若歹徒不断逼近，则寻找机会使用手掌从外侧拍打持刀手臂外侧，改变轨迹的同时快速使用短踹技术击打其膝部，并继续拉开距离［见图 12-4(b)］。

(1) Long Distance Battle Against Short Sword

Long distance combat is relatively safer against short swords, and they can advance, attack, retreat, and defend. Generally, it is required to retreat rather than close, and it is best to maintain a distance of three arms or more. Long distance combat should follow the following principles when dealing with short knives. The first is to keep moving. Keep a distance so that the criminal's knife cannot reach the target. The second is to use less fist and more palm to block the knife from the side, and prepare to grab its arm. Although hands can sometimes be injured, vital parts are protected. The third is to seize the opportunity to attack the criminal's knee with legs or kick the criminal's hand with a knife. The fourth is to use any weapon that can be caught at any time and find opportunities to escape. The following are the basic techniques for long-range combat against short knives.

Action instruction: First, maintain the fighting posture and keep moving, open the distance [see Figure 12-4(a)], and have the opportunity to escape immediately. If the criminal keeps approaching, look for an opportunity to use the palm to pat the outer side of the knife holding arm from the outside, change the trajectory, and quickly use short kick technique to hit the knee, and continue to open the distance [see Figure 12-4(b)].

(a)　　　　　　　　　　(b)

图 12-4　远战对短刀　Long distance combat against short knives

（二）擒拿对短刀

以擒拿对刀，技术适宜，但很难应用。主要问题是在格斗中很难抓住歹徒的持刀手臂。另外在歹徒有备时，也很难拿住其关节。因此，除非不得已，多数人，尤其是初学者，应尽量少用。擒拿对短刀有两种基本手法，即锁肘和卷腕。

动作说明： 歹徒进刀时抓住其持刀手臂，锁住其肘或打断其肘（见图 12-5）；抓住歹徒持刀手，卷腕使其松开刀柄（见图 12-6）。

(2) Capturing the Short Knife

The technique of using a grappling knife is suitable, but it is difficult to apply. The main problem is that it is difficult to grasp the wielding arm of the criminal during combat. Moreover, it is difficult to grasp the joints of the criminals when they are prepared. Therefore, unless absolutely necessary, most people, especially beginners, should use it as little as possible. There are two basic techniques for capturing short knives, namely locking the elbow and curling the wrist .

Action instruction: When the criminal enters the knife, grab the arm holding the knife, lock its elbow or break its elbow (Figure 12-5); seize the culprit holding the knife and roll his wrist to release the handle (Figure 12-6).

图 12-5　锁肘对短刀　Locking elbow to short knife

图 12-6　卷腕对短刀　Wrist roll short knife

（三）器械对短刀

前面所列研究结果已表明使用椅子、棍子，甚至衣服都可以减少对刀格斗的受伤概率。但实战中身边不一定恰好有此类器械，自卫者应灵活利用一切潜在自卫器械来减少伤害，如书背、沙发坐垫、脸盆、水桶、球拍等等。下面介绍的三种器械为对刀实验证明确实有用，包括秋衣对

(3) Instrument to Short Knife

The research results listed earlier have shown that using chairs, sticks, and even clothing can reduce the likelihood of injury in knife fights. But in actual combat, it is not necessarily necessary to have these equipment at hand. Self defenders should flexibly use all equipment to reduce damage, such as backpacks, sofa cushions, washbasins, buckets, rackets, and so on. The three instruments introduced below have been proven to be effective in knife alignment experiments, including autumn clothes knife alignment (see Figure 12-7), chair knife

260 · 大学生安全防卫学双语教程 Bilingual Course on Security and Defense for College Students

刀（见图 12-7）、椅子对刀（见图 12-8）及扫帚把对刀（见图 12-9）。

动作说明：秋衣对刀时，抓住衣服两肩拉紧，两手上下置衣服于体前［见图 12-7(a)］。当刀刺来时侧挡刀锋，马上回到体前［见图 12-7(b)］；椅子对刀时，举椅以椅腿对敌，避免被歹徒抓到椅腿，当歹徒试图抓椅时，可举椅猛击、或后退、或侧踹其膝。扫帚对刀时，持扫帚把对准敌头［见图 12-9(a)］。随后猛刺其头［见图 12-9(b)］、腹或裆，歹徒欲抓时，后撤回棍或侧踹其膝。

alignment (see Figure 12-8), and broomstick knife alignment (see Figure 12-9).

Action instruction: When autumn clothes are paired with knives, grab the clothes by the shoulders and tighten them, and place the clothes in front of the body with both hands up and down [see Figure 12-7(a)]. When the knife stabs, block the blade on the side and immediately return to the front of the body [see Figure 12-7(b)]; When the chair is facing a knife, lift the chair with the chair legs to avoid being caught by the criminals. When the criminals try to grab the chair, they can lift the chair and forcefully strike, retreat, or kick the knee. When aligning the broom with the knife, hold the broomstick and aim it at the enemy's head [see Figure 12-9(a)]. Then he fiercely stabbed his head, abdomen or crotch, and when the criminal wanted to catch him, he withdrew his stick or kicked his knee sideways [see Figure 12-9(b)].

(a)   (b)

图 12-7　秋衣对刀　Autumn clothes with knives

图 12-8　椅子对刀　Chair knife alignment

(a)   (b)

图 12-9　扫帚对刀　Broom handle knife alignment

（四）对付菜刀

菜刀是中国歹徒常用之凶器，对付菜刀也非常危险。目前对菜刀的实验尚未完成，因而受伤概率尚无定论。从一般经验来讲，用器械对付菜刀，如椅子等，效果应当较好。如空手对菜刀，则适用远战，自卫者应拉开距离，以保安全。除非是在无法控制安全距离时，否则应越远越好，尽量远离歹徒抢刀的空间。

动作说明：面对持刀歹徒时，先选择后撤［见图 12-10(a)］，选择时机，以双手抓敌持刀手［见图 12-10(b)］。随后，以膝顶其裆［见图 12-10(c)］，并锁住歹徒肘关节［见图 12-10(d)］。

(4) Dealing with Kitchen Knives

The kitchen knife is a commonly used weapon by Chinese criminals, and dealing with it is also very dangerous. At present, the experiment on the kitchen knife has not been completed, so the probability of injury is still uncertain. From general experience, using tools to deal with kitchen knives, such as chairs, should be more effective. If facing the kitchen knife empty handed, it is suitable for long-distance combat to widen the distance and ensure security. Unless it is impossible to control the safe distance, the closer the better, and try to minimize the space for criminals to swing their knives.

Action instruction: When facing a knife wielding criminal, first choose to retreat [see Figure 12-10(a)], choose the timing, grab the enemy's knife wielding hand with both hands [see Figure 12-10(b)], then use your knees to push against his crotch [see Figure 12-10(c)], and lock the criminal's elbow joint [see Figure 12-10(d)].

(a)   (b)

(c)　　　　　　　　　　　　　　　(d)

图 12-10　空手对菜刀　Empty handed pair of kitchen knives

第三节
以少对多

Section 3
Few vs. Many

　　集中优势兵力打歼灭战此原则正在广泛地被各国的歹徒们运用，以攻击平民百姓。街头流氓或游民自发组成的犯罪同伙，常常以多数之众来对付受害者一人，使得受害者面对群匪束手无策。这些犯罪团伙抢劫、入室行窃、偷盗、拐卖妇女儿童、欺行霸市，遇上此类事件，受害者常常是自认倒霉。全国未成年犯抽样调查结果显示，团伙犯罪的占84.7%，除"聚众斗殴"是100%团伙犯罪之外，"抢劫"的团伙犯罪比例高达93.6%[①]。

　　面对以少对多的情况，主要策略应是以退为主，或者转身逃走，或向歹徒妥协周旋后悄悄退

　　The principle of concentrating superior forces in annihilation warfare is widely used by criminals from various countries to attack civilians. Criminal accomplices spontaneously formed by street thugs or vagrants often deal with the victim in large numbers, leaving the victim helpless in the face of a group of bandits. These criminal gangs engage in robbery, burglary, theft, trafficking of women and children, and bullying the market. When faced with such incidents, the victims often feel unlucky. The results of the national sampling survey of juvenile delinquents show that 84.7% of juvenile delinquents in the country commit gang crimes. Except for "gathering and fighting" which is 100% of gang crimes, the proportion of "robbery" gang crimes is as high as 93.6%.

　　In the face of a few to many situation, the main strategy should be to retreat, either turn around and escape, or compromise with the criminals and quietly withdraw. If

① 郭强. 未成年人抢劫犯罪的研究 [J]. 重庆电子工程职业学院学报 ,2017,26(4):28-31.

出。若歹徒要劫持自卫者或伤害自卫者，则格斗就不可避免了。

一、逃跑脱身

有些拳术教科书或功夫电影中常可见到一位武林高手奋战群敌、挨个将围攻者打倒的场景。但现实情况往往是，众歹徒一拥而上，抱身、拉腿、扯臂、搂腰、锁喉，自卫者应接不暇，顾此失彼。正所谓两拳难敌四手，个人的力量终究是有限的。为此，在遭遇人数为两人及以上的歹徒攻击时，应尽量脱身跑掉，不要逞强好战。不论是在动手前或格斗中，一有机会就应走为上策，将危险抛在身后。

二、妥协待机

在面对众歹徒攻击时，应采用妥协服从的策略。尤其是当歹徒只是为了抢劫而不想杀人、或自卫者无人相助、或无处可逃时，妥协服从可防止歹徒使用更严重的暴力。为防万一，在妥协时，也应随时准备逃跑、或格斗、或打跑结合。

三、格斗应对

格斗会激怒歹徒，使其更加疯狂，所以不到万不得已的时候

the criminals want to hijack or harm the self-defender, fighting is inevitable.

1. Escape

In some martial arts textbooks or movies, it is common to see a martial arts master fighting against a group of enemies, one by one knocking down the besiegers. This is just a cinematic technique. In reality, when a group of criminals attack a person, they often rush forward, hugging, pulling their legs, arms, waist, and throat together. Even the best martial arts masters find it difficult to use their skills when their hands, feet, and waist are hugged. Therefore, most martial arts experts and self-defense teachers believe that when facing attacks from two or more criminals, they should try to escape as much as possible and avoid being too aggressive, whether before or during combat, It is best to take action whenever there is an opportunity and leave danger behind.

2. Compromise Standby

When facing attacks from a group of criminals, a strategy of compromise and obedience should be adopted. Especially when criminals only want to rob and do not want to kill, or when there is no one to help self-defense, or when there is nowhere to escape. Compromise and obedience can prevent criminals from using more severe violence. To be on the safe side, when compromising, one should also be prepared to run away, engage in combat, or combine running and fighting at any time.

3. Fighting Response

Fighting can anger criminals and make them even crazier, so don't use this strategy unless absolutely necessary.

不要利用这一策略。但格斗对歹徒也能产生一定威慑力，并使自卫者获得一定程度的控制权。

以少打多的格斗方式主要以远战为主，结合其他方式，如近战。应尽量避免使用摔技、擒拿或解脱格斗技术，如此会增加被控制的可能性，减少逃跑的概率。以少对多的格斗原则包括下列：第一，不断移动以避免对方接近或形成包围圈；第二，打跑结合，有逃跑机会就跑，没逃跑机会就打，以创造逃跑机会；第三，使用任何可能的武器以增强战斗力；第四，诈一方。而战另一方，总是面对一人、对付一人。一般来讲，若自卫者采取防守势作战、积极移动，两个歹徒一般很难抓得住。如果可移动范围太小，而易被歹徒前后夹击或形成包围时，应果断攻击其中较弱的歹徒，以求破其围攻或合围。两军相逢勇者胜，在遭夹击时舍命攻击较弱的歹徒，常常会使对方害怕而杀出一条血路。图 12-11 显示自卫者利用移动，一次只对一个歹徒的战法。

动作说明：遭到两歹徒夹击时［见图 12-11(a)］，随时注意两个歹徒，始终保持前后移动，保持两个歹徒在同侧一条线上［见图 12-11(b)］。作战一方在该歹徒后退或被击倒时［见图 12-11(c)］

But fighting can also have a certain deterrent effect on criminals and gain a certain degree of control.

The fighting style of fighting less and more mainly focuses on long-range combat, combined with other methods such as close combat. Try to avoid using throwing techniques, grappling, or freestyle fighting techniques, as this can lead to being grabbed by the opponent's hands, feet, or body and unable to escape or engage in combat. The principle of few to many combat includes the following: firstly, constantly moving to avoid the opponent approaching or forming a encirclement; The second is a combination of fighting and running, running whenever there is a chance to escape, and fighting when there is no chance to escape, in order to create an escape opportunity; The third is to use any possible weapon to enhance combat effectiveness. The fourth is to deceive one side and fight the other, always facing one person and dealing with one person. Generally speaking, if a defender takes defensive measures and actively moves, it is difficult for two criminals to catch them. If the movable range is too small and is easily sandwiched or surrounded by criminals, one should decisively attack the weaker criminals in order to break through their encirclement or encirclement. When two armies meet, the brave win. When caught in a pincer attack, they sacrifice their lives to attack weaker criminals, often causing the other party to fear and cut off a bloody path. Figure 12-11 shows the self-defense fighter's strategy of using movement to target only one criminal at a time.

Action instruction: When being sandwiched between two criminals [Figure 12-11(a)], one side of the battle quickly moves to the other side to deal with the other criminal as the criminal retreats [as shown in Figure 12-11(b)], while paying attention to both criminals and always keeping them moving forward and backward [as shown in Figure 12-11(c)] using

迅速到另一边对付另一歹徒 [见图 12–11(d)]。

movement, keep both criminals on the same side and on the same line [Figure 12–11(d)].

(a)

(b)

(c)

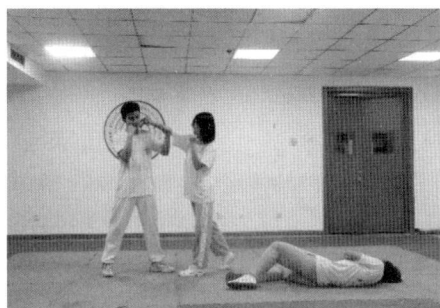

(d)

图 12–11　防夹击　Anti pinch

第四节
提高特殊格斗技术

Section 4
Improving Special Fighting Techniques

特殊格斗对自卫者的技术动作质量、速度与灵活性、勇敢精神等方面的要求都相当高。在学习训练中，要针对性提高各方面能力。在模拟实战训练中，多与不同对手较量增加实战经验，不断提高信心与胆量。另外，不断学习新技术也可增强自卫者在实战中的技术运用能力。中国武术中

Special combat requires a high level of skill, speed, flexibility, and bravery from self-defenders. In learning and training, it is necessary to improve various abilities in a targeted manner. In simulated combat training, compete more with different opponents to gain practical experience and continuously improve confidence and courage. In addition, continuous learning of new technologies can also enhance the technical application ability of self-defenders in practical combat. Capturing in Chinese martial arts,

的擒拿。日本的柔术与合气道、军警的格斗训练及保镖训练等都可帮助提高特殊格斗能力。

Japanese jujutsu and aikido, military and police combat training, and bodyguard training can all help improve special combat abilities.

思考十二

1. 特殊格斗的定义是什么？

2. 特殊格斗技术中面对持枪歹徒，我们应怎么做？

3. 特殊格斗中面对持刀歹徒，我们应怎么做？

4. 面对以少对多的情况，我们应如何应对？

5. 服从、格斗以及逃跑策略的应用场景有哪些？

Reflection 12

1. What is the definition of special combat?

2.What should we do when facing armed criminals in special combat techniques?

3.What should we do when facing knife wielding criminals in special combat?

4.How should we respond to the situation of less versus more?

5.What are the application scenarios for obedience, fighting, and escape strategies?

附录：
16 学时安全自卫学选修课教案参考

Appendix:
Reference for 16 Lessons of Elective Course on Security and Self-defense

第一课

Lesson 1

一、教学内容

I. Teaching content

1. 学习安全自卫防身基础理论。

2. 探讨犯罪方式与趋势及罪犯离我们有多远。

3. 学习格斗技术须知及必须遵循的原则。

4. 学习远距离格斗技术。

5. 进行恢复体力练习及专项素质练习。

1. Learn basic theoretical part of security and self-defense.

2. Discuss crime patterns and trends, and how far away criminals are from us.

3. Learn combat techniques and the principles that must be followed.

4. Learn long-distance combat techniques.

5. Rehabilitation exercises and specialized quality exercises.

二、本课任务

II. The task of the class

介绍安全教育自卫防身课的必要性。

The necessity of introducing security education and self-defense courses.

三、教学重点

III. Teaching focus

进行安全意识教育。

Security awareness education.

四、教学内容与组织教法

IV. Teaching content and organizational teaching methods

（一）准备部分

1. 集合整队，检查出勤情况。

(I) Preparation section

1. Gather the team and check attendance.

2. 小常识简介。头痛关联的主要穴位：百会、太阳、印堂、风池、合谷。

3. 介绍大学生进行安全自卫防身教育的必要性。增强预防意识，防患于未然。谨记：三十六计，跑为上策，智斗为中策，格斗为下策。

4. 讲解格斗技术须知及必须遵循的原则。

A. 增强自信心。

B. 提高身体素质。

C. 掌握学习和应用格斗技术必须遵循的原则：①全面的技术准备；②连续格斗；③综合技术与应用；④标准技术实用化；⑤技术应用无限制；⑥先下手为强；⑦攻守平衡；⑧格斗技术与思维；⑨速度优于力量。

增强自信，提高身体素质，以应对歹徒的不确定性攻击。其攻击方式很难预料，而且手段会很残忍，这一切都是自卫者所控制不了的。为了提高自卫格斗胜利的概率，在训练上要做好各方面的准备，在格斗技术的运用上也要随机应变。（尽量不佩戴易造成损伤的物品，如手机、钥匙、笔、眼镜等；常修剪指甲；虚心学习技术方法，杜绝好胜斗气，注重礼节，点到即止）。

5. 组织学生做关节操。

6. 进行双人游戏：追逐打背。

2. Introduction to common knowledge: The main acupoints for headaches are Baihui, Taiyang, Yintang, Fengchi, and Hegu.

3. Introduce the necessity of conducting security and self-defense education for college students. Enhance prevention awareness, prevent problems before they occur, and remember the thirty-six strategies. Running is the best strategy, intellectual combat is the middle strategy, and fighting is the bottom strategy.

4. Explain the combat techniques and the principles that must be followed.

A. Enhance self-confidence.

B. Improve physical fitness.

C. Harness the principles that must be followed in learning and applying combat techniques: Comprehensive technical preparation; Continuous fighting; Integrated technology and application; Practicalization of standard technology; Unlimited application of technology; The first move is the strongest; Offensive and defensive balance; Fighting techniques and thinking; Speed is better than strength.

Learning combat skills requires enhancing self-confidence and improving physical fitness, as criminals can undergo endless changes when committing crimes. Its attack method is difficult to predict, and the means will be very cruel, all of which are beyond the control of self-defense. In order to increase the chances of winning in self-defense combat, self-defenders need to be well prepared in all aspects of training and adapt to the application of combat techniques (Try not to wear items that are prone to damage, such as mobile phones, keys, pens, glasses, etc.; trim your nails regularly; learn technical methods, eliminate competitive spirit, pay attention to etiquette, and stop when needed).

5. Joint exercises.

6. Two player game: Chasing and Backfighting.

（二）基本部分

1.学习远距离格斗技术。

A.学习基本格斗姿势与移动技术。

自卫者利用脚步的移动与歹徒保持至少两臂长的距离，运用远踢、近打来攻击歹徒并防范歹徒的攻击。

（1）学习拳击里的基本格斗姿势与移动技术。

（2）学习基本格斗姿势与移动技术。与歹徒保持至少两臂长的距离。两脚间距如肩宽，重心偏于前脚掌。两膝稍弯。身体半右转，两肩向内拢。下颌略后收，两眼注视敌人眼睛。左拳约同下巴高，置于敌我之间，主要护头。右手在胸前，主要护上体及裆。

快速的脚步移动，可使防卫者与歹徒保持安全距离，进可抓住对方空当进攻，退可避开对方抓打。移动包括前、后、左、右四个方向。前移主要用于出拳出腿攻击对方，后移主要避开歹徒的抓、打、踢，左右移动则是用来躲避对方的快速前冲。移动的基本方法是向哪个方向移动，哪只脚先动，而另一只脚快速跟进，移动后依然保持原来姿势。有时移动不止一两步，但基本方法一样。如向后移动，后脚先撤，前脚跟随后撤。向左移动时，左脚先动，

(Ⅱ) Basic parts

1. Learn long-distance combat techniques.

A. Learn basic combat postures and movement techniques.

Self-defenders use the movement of their feet to maintain a distance of at least two arms from the criminals, and use far and near kicks to attack the criminals and prevent their attacks.

(1) Learn the basic fighting postures and movement techniques in boxing.

(2) Learn basic fighting postures and mobile techniques. Maintain a distance of at least two arms from the criminal. Both feet should be shoulder wide, with the center of gravity leaning towards the forefoot. Bend both knees slightly. Turn your body half to the right and bring your shoulders inward. Lower your jaw slightly back and gaze into the enemy's eyes. The left fist is about the same height as the chin, placed between the enemy and us, mainly protecting the head. The right hand is on the chest, mainly protecting the upper body and crotch.

Fast footwork can keep the defender at a safe distance from the criminals, advance to seize the opponent's empty space for attack, and retreat to avoid the opponent's capture and attack. Movement includes four directions: front, back, left, and right. Forward movement is mainly used to punch and kick the opponent, backward movement is mainly used to avoid the criminal's grabbing, hitting, and kicking, and left and right movement is used to avoid the opponent's rapid forward charge. The basic method of movement is to move in which direction, which foot moves first, while the other foot quickly follows and maintains its original position after moving. Sometimes it takes more than one or two steps to move, but the basic method is the same. If moving backwards, the hind foot should retreat first, and the front foot should follow and

右脚跟随向左。

B. 学习远战进攻技术。

主动进攻常可扭转局势, 转守为攻, 最好的防卫就是进攻。进攻技术包括拳击和腿击。在每次出腿后, 如未打中目标, 则应马上回原位, 以防对方还击, 并准备下次进攻。如打中目标则乘对方慌乱之际连续进攻。

1) 学习拳击的左右直拳、勾拳。

前手直拳。此拳击出极快, 且离歹徒近, 主要用来击打对方头部, 或用来引诱歹徒护头, 乘机用另一只手击其下腹。快速向右转体, 左肩前送发力, 左臂前伸击打歹徒鼻梁。

后手重拳。此拳极重, 主要用来打击歹徒肋部或下腹。若歹徒个子小, 亦可用来击头。快速向左转身, 右脚也左转, 右臂前送发力, 右臂前伸击歹徒下腹。

勾拳。此拳力量近似于前手直拳, 主要用来避开歹徒的双手并从侧击其耳部。这里只介绍右手勾拳。快速左转身, 右臂向前发力, 右手绕开歹徒前手, 从侧面击其左耳或太阳穴。

流程:

（1）讲解、示范。

（2）学生体会动作, 集体

retreat. When moving to the left, the left foot moves first and the right foot follows to the left.

B. Learn long-range offensive techniques.

Proactive attack can often turn the situation around, turning defense into attack, and the best defense is attack. Offensive techniques include boxing or leg strikes. If the target is not hit, immediately return to the original position to prevent the opponent from retaliating and prepare for the next attack. If the target is hit, take advantage of the opponent's panic to continuously attack.

1) Learn the left and right straight punches and hook punches in boxing.

Front hand straight punch. This boxing is extremely fast and close to the criminal. It is mainly used to hit the opponent's head, or to lure the criminal to protect their head, and to use the other hand to hit the lower abdomen during the opportunity. Quickly turn to the right, apply force in front of the left shoulder, and extend the left arm forward to hit the criminal's nose bridge.

A heavy punch in the back. This fist is extremely heavy and mainly used to strike the ribs or lower abdomen of criminals. If the criminal is small, it can also be used to hit the head. Quickly turn left, also turn left with your right foot, apply force with your right arm forward, and extend your right arm forward to hit the perpetrator's lower abdomen.

Hook Fist. This fist is similar in strength to the front hand straight fist, mainly used to avoid the hands of criminals and strike their ears from the side. Here we will only introduce the right hand hook fist. Quickly turn left, exert force with your right arm forward, and use your right hand to bypass the perpetrator's front hand and strike his left ear or temple from the side.

Procedure:

(1) Explanation and demonstration.

(2) Students experience movements and practice

练习。

（3）分组练习两人一组，一人用拳击套，另一人拿手靶。

2）学习前、侧、后踹，前、侧踢的综合技术。

前踹。这是一种力量较大的踢腿技术，主要攻击歹徒裆、腹或膝以使其丧失进攻能力或后退躲避。前后脚都可用。向左转体，面向歹徒，右膝前提。右脚前伸，用脚跟踹其下腹，脚尖向上。

侧踹。侧踹与前踹相似，只是上脚尖向右，并用脚跟及脚外侧攻击目标。侧踹主要用来攻击歹徒膝关节。水平高者亦可高踹，踢腹或头。前腿向侧提膝，脚尖向右，前蹬用脚外侧踹膝。

后踹。与前踹相近，只是脚尖向下，用来攻击后面的歹徒腹部。两腿均可运用。后腿提膝，脚尖向下，后伸腿以脚跟攻击敌腹。

前踢。这是一种快速踢腿技术，主要以脚面为武器正面攻击歹徒裆部或持刀的手，两脚皆可运用。前提膝，脚尖向下；小腿快速向前弹出，用脚面踢裆部。

侧踢。这是从侧面攻其膝关节或肋部的技术。向侧方提膝；小腿弹出，踢歹徒膝外侧。

流程：

（1）讲解、示范。

collectively.

(3) Group practice with two people, one using a boxing ring and the other holding a target.

2) Learn the comprehensive techniques of front, side, and back kicking, as well as front and side kicking.

Front kick. It is a powerful kicking technique that mainly attacks the crotch, abdomen, or knees of criminals to make them lose their attacking ability or retreat and avoid. Both front and rear feet are available. Turn left, facing the criminal, with your right knee in front. Extend your right foot forward and kick its lower abdomen with your heel, with your toes pointing upwards.

Side kick. Side kick is similar to front kick, with only the tip of the foot pointing to the right and attacking the target with the heel and outer side of the foot. Side kick is mainly used to attack the knee joints of criminals. Those with high skills can also kick high, kick the abdomen or head. Lift the front leg to the side of the knee, toes to the right, and kick the knee with the outside of the foot.

Back kick. Similar to the forward kick, but with the toes pointing downwards. It is used to attack the abdomen of the criminal behind, both legs are subject to use. Lift the hind legs to the knees, with the toes pointing downwards. Extend your legs and attack the enemy's abdomen with your heels.

Front kick. It is a fast kicking technique that mainly uses the foot as a weapon to directly attack the crotch or hand holding a knife of a criminal, and can bc uscd with both feet. Assuming knees and toes facing downwards. Quickly pop your calves forward and kick the crotch with your foot.

Side kick. It is to attack the knee joint or ribs from the side. Lift the knee to the side. Pop out your calves and kick the outside of the criminal's knee.

Procedure:

(1) Explanation and demonstration

（2）学生体会动作，集体练习踹时首先练习向下踩，脚跟用力。

（3）分两组练习，一组练习，另一组帮助改进动作。

3）介绍转身踹组合拳。

转身踹。这是一种大力踢腿技术，它与后踹相似，只是前踹加上一个转身动作。可假装逃走，当歹徒扑上来时乘其不备攻击裆腹。以前腿为轴，顺时针转身，背向歹徒。提膝后伸腿，踢歹徒腹部。

组合拳一般是两个或三个动作的组合，简单、实用、易学。先用前直拳打脸，接着用后手重拳打肋；先用侧踹踢膝再转身踢攻下腹；先用前手勾拳打脸，再转身踢击下腹；等等。如，远打的简单组合为前腿侧踹歹徒膝关节，前手直拳击歹徒脸部，后手重拳击歹徒肋部。

C. 学习远战防守技术。

防守的速度永远跟不上进攻的速度，防一个部位，往往会暴露另一个部位。自卫者用前手直拳打击或佯打歹徒脸部，歹徒必然会去躲或防，这时自卫者用后手重拳打肋或起腿踹膝，则往往能够奏效。

1）防拳击：格挡、躲闪。

防身格斗中，自卫者不仅要会攻击歹徒，也要会在歹徒攻击

(2) Students experience movements and practice kicking together — first practice stepping down and exerting force on their heels.

(3) Practice in two groups, one group practicing and the other helping to improve the movements.

3) Introduction: Turn around kick, turn around kick.

Turn around and kick. It is a powerful kicking technique that is similar to a backkick, except for a forward kick with a turning motion. You can pretend to escape and take advantage of the situation to attack crotch when the criminals come forward. With legs on the axis, you can turn clockwise to turn your back towards the criminal. Lift your knees and extend your legs, kicking the perpetrator in the abdomen.

Combination boxing is generally a combination of two or three movements, simple, practical, and easy to learn. First use a front straight punch to hit the face, then use a back heavy punch to hit the ribs; First kick the knee with a side kick, then turn around and kick the lower abdomen; First, use the front hand to hook the fist in the face, then turn around and kick the lower abdomen, and so on.For example, a simple combination of far play:Kick the criminal's knee joint with the front leg. Punch the criminal's face with the front hand straight. The thug punched heavily in the ribs with his hind hand.

C. Learn long-range defensive techniques.

The speed of defense can never keep up with the speed of attack. Defending one part often exposes another part. The self-defense person strikes or feints the face of the criminal with a straight punch from the front hand, and the criminal will inevitably go to hide or defend. At this time, the self-defense person uses a heavy punch from the back hand to hit the ribs or kick the knee, which often works.

1) Anti boxing: blocking and dodging.

In self-defense combat, the defender should not only be able to attack criminals, but also be able to dodge or block

时躲或挡。防身格斗的攻守转换应频繁，攻中有防，防中有攻。自卫者要熟悉并灵活转换这两种架势。

格挡是对付歹徒出拳的最简单、最容易的办法。安全起见，自卫者可将歹徒之手向侧稍作格挡，使其无法击中目标，但格挡动作要小。挡后手臂立即回原位。最重要的一点是在格挡之后，要迅速退出歹徒的有效攻击距离或立即反攻。

双手护头及上体，顺其来势自然格挡来拳，迅速侧击歹徒手臂使其偏离目标。

躲是防拳击的中高级技巧，其目的是使自己的身体成运动状态，使歹徒找不到出拳目标或打不中。

躲闪技巧有三种：后闪、下闪和侧闪。

上体迅速后仰，双手保护脸。屈膝弯腰下闪对手直拳。左腿稍向左移，上体向左倾，侧闪重拳。

流程：

（1）讲解、示范。

（2）学生体会动作，集体练习。

（3）分组练习两人一组，一攻一防，听口令攻防互换。

them when they attack. The offensive and defensive transitions in self-defense combat are frequent, with defense in attack and attack in defense. Self defenders need to be familiar with and flexibly switch between these two roles.

Blocking is the simplest and easiest way to deal with criminals punching. For security reasons, self-defender can block the attacker's hand to the side to prevent them from hitting the target, but the blocking action should be small. Immediately return the arm to its original position after blocking. The most important thing is to quickly exit the effective attack range of the criminal or immediately counterattack after blocking.

Protect your head and upper body with both hands, and naturally block the punches in the direction of the attack. Quickly flank the criminal's arm to deflect it from the target.

Hiding is a mid to high level technique for preventing punches, aimed at keeping one's body in a state of motion so that criminals cannot find the target or hit.

There are three types of dodge techniques: backward, downward, and sideways.

Quickly tilt your upper body back and protect your face with both hands. Bend your knees and bend down to dodge your opponent's straight punch. Move your left leg slightly to the left, tilt your upper body to the left, and dodge a heavy punch on the side.

Procedure：

(1) Explanation and demonstration.

(2) Students experience movements and practice collectively.

(3) Group practice with two people, one attacking and one defending, switching attacks and defenses by listening to commands.

2）防踢腿：后撤、挡踢腿。

后撤——用腿踢防歹徒的最简单、最安全的方法是后撤一两步，从而避开歹徒的有效打击距离。

挡踢——当歹徒起脚很快，来不及撤步或无处可退时，则宜用格挡技术。提前膝以小腿外侧挡敌腿。保持腿挡姿势，向后跳一步。

流程：

（1）讲解、示范。

（2）学生体会动作，集体练习。

（3）分组练习两人一组，一攻一防，听口令攻防互换。

（4）两人一组利用手靶及拳击套进行对练。教师随时帮助学生改进动作。要求学生在双人对练过程中掌握好动作幅度，点到即止，控制好自己的情绪，不说脏话，要互相帮助，互相谅解，防止伤害事故的发生。

（5）要不断交换攻防对手，适应各种不同情况下的攻防人。

2. 恢复体力练习及专项素质练习：①折返跑；②腰腹肌；③推小车；④组合跳跃练习。

3. 自然灾害的预防与应对案例分析。

4. 放松练习。

（三）结束部分

1. 集体放松活动。

2) Anti kick: retreat and block the kick.

Retreat—The simplest and safest way to prevent criminals from kicking with their legs is to retreat one or two steps to avoid the effective range of the criminals.

Blocking Kick—When a criminal starts quickly and there is no time to retreat or nowhere to retreat, blocking technique should be used. Advance the knee to block the enemy's leg with the outer side of the calf. Maintain a leg blocking position and take a step back.

Procedure：

(1) Explanation and demonstration.

(2) Students experience movements and practice collectively.

(3) Group practice with two people, one attacking and one defending. Follow the command to switch between attacking and defending.

(4) Pair up and practice using hand targets and boxing sets. Teachers are always available to help students improve and enhance their movements.Students are required to master the range of movements during the practice of pairs, from start to finish, control their emotions, avoid using foul language, help and understand each other, and prevent accidents from happening.

(5) To constantly exchange offensive and defensive opponents and adapt to different situations of offensive and defensive personnel.

2. Rehabilitation exercises and specialized quality exercises. Turnback running; Lumbar and abdominal muscles; Push the trolley; Combination jump practice.

3. Case analysis of natural disaster prevention and response.

4. Relax and practice.

(Ⅲ) End section

1. Collective relaxation activities.

2. 讲评本次课。

3. 课外作业为复习本次课所讲技术内容，并要求寻找一个案例。

4. 针对本次课的内容，请学生在课上提问题。

2. Evaluate this class.

3. The homework is to review the technical content taught in this class and prepare a case study.

4. Regarding the content of this class, please ask students questions during class.

第二课

Lesson 2

一、教学内容

I. Teaching content

1. 了解智力防范暴力犯罪—自卫防身—格斗的危险应对程序。

2. 讲解远距离格斗的策略，提高远距离格斗能力。

3. 学习近距离格斗技术。

4. 案例分析。

5. 学习远距离格斗防守技术。

6. 进行素质及专项素质练习。

1. Learn about the coping mechanism of Intellectual Prevention of Violent Crimes – Self-defender – Fighting.

2. Explain the strategies for long-distance combat and improve the ability to engage in long-distance combat.

3. Learn close range combat techniques.

4. Case analysis.

5. Defense techniques in long-distance combat.

6. Quality and specialized quality exercises.

二、本课任务

II. The task of the class

了解遇到危险的处理程序：智力防范暴力犯罪—自卫防身—格斗。

Understanding the handling procedures for encountering danger: Intellectual prevention of violent crimes – Self-defender – Fighting.

三、教学重点

III. Teaching focus

帮助学生掌握远距离格斗的策略，提高远距离格斗能力。

Strategies for long-range combat to enhance long-range combat abilities.

四、教学内容与组织教法

（一）准备部分

A. 集合整队，检查出勤情况。

B. 小常识简介：合谷、内外关、足三里的作用。

C. 理论讲解气质的形成：行为语言，肢体语言，矫正站、坐、行等各种身体姿态。

D. 讲解智力防范暴力犯罪—自卫防身—格斗。

智力防范暴力犯罪：a. 培养安全的生活方式与习惯；b. 万勿树敌；c. 远离是非之地；d. 避开是非时间；e. 武装到牙齿（—自卫防身—格斗）。

预防暴力犯罪的主要原则包括以下几点。

1. 树立自卫防身的意识与观念。有了这种观念，人们才能够对自己成为受害者的可能性有所警觉，从而处处留心，并积极着手学习本领准备对敌。

2. 培养安全的个人生活方式与习惯——保镖模式（保镖都有处处留心安全的职业习惯）。远离不安全的生活习惯和方式，如夜间独自散步、经常与不三不四的人有联系、出门不锁门窗等等。

3. 万勿树敌——好人模式（好人很少遭人恨）。树敌极易引发仇恨犯罪，而仇恨是歹徒作案

IV. Teaching content and organizational teaching methods

(I) Preparation section

A. Gather the team and check attendance.

B. Introduction to Common Sense: The functions of Hegu, Neiwaiguan, and Zusanli.

C. Theoretical explanation of the formation of temperament: (behavioral language, body language, correction of various body postures such as standing, sitting, and walking).

D. Intellectual Prevention of Violent Crime – Self-defender – Fighting.

Intellectually prevent violent crimes, a. cultivate a safe lifestyle and habits, b. never make enemies, c. stay away from right and wrong places, d. avoid right and wrong time, e. arm to the teeth (– Self-defense – Fighting).

The main principles for preventing violent crimes include the following ones.

1. Establish awareness and concepts of self-defense and self-defense. With this mindset, people can be alert to the possibility of becoming victims, pay attention everywhere, and actively learn skills to prepare for the enemy.

2. Cultivate a safe lifestyle and habits for individuals — the bodyguard mode (bodyguards have a professional habit of paying attention to security everywhere). There are various unsafe habits and ways of living, such as liking to take a walk alone at night, often having contact with people who are indecisive, not locking doors and windows when going out, and so on.

3. Never make enemies — Good person mode (good people are rarely hated). Making enemies can easily trigger hate crimes, and hatred is one of the important motivations

的重要动机之一。树敌会将受害者置于非常危险的境地，因为受害者在明处，而歹徒则在暗处，受害者是无法设防的，也是防不胜防的。一旦歹徒铁了心要攻击受害者，受害者便极难逃脱。在日常生活中，树敌非常容易，而且人们往往感觉不到，如参与剑拔弩张的争执、待人太恶、欺辱别人、欺骗别人、整人、虐待妻子，等等。虽然树敌不会每次都遭到报复，但树敌过多终究是危险之举，"多行不义必自毙"。

4. 远离是非之地——河狸模式（河狸都把巢建在最安全之处）。歹徒作案总要挑选一个适合作案的地点。一旦远离这些地点，成为受害者的机会就会大大减少。一般来说，是非之地包括僻静无人处、帮派活动地区、贩毒地区及涉及大量现金的地方，如银行。

5. 避开是非时间——候鸟模式（气候是候鸟迁移的信号）。避开歹徒作案的最佳时机会大大减小成为受害者的可能性。在黑暗的地方、受害者独自一人、受害者松懈而无准备、在危险地区等，都是歹徒易于作案的时机。应尽量避开。

6. 武装到牙齿——刺猬模式（很少有动物去攻击浑身带刺的刺猬）。受害者的软弱性是引发歹徒作案的重要因素。歹徒选择弱者是因为他们有信心让受害

for criminals to commit crimes. Making enemies can put the victim in a very dangerous situation, as the victim is in the open while the perpetrator is in the dark. It is impossible to defend and also impossible to defend against. Once the perpetrator is determined to attack the victim, it is extremely difficult for the victim to escape. In daily life, it is very easy to make enemies, and people often do not feel it, such as participating in heated arguments, treating others too badly, bullying others, deceiving others, manipulating others, abusing wives, and so on. Although making enemies does not always lead to retaliation, making too many enemies is ultimately a dangerous move, and if one does more wrong, they will die on their own.

4. Stay away from the land of right and wrong — beaver mode (beavers build their nests in the safest places). Criminals always choose a suitable location for committing crimes. Once away from these locations, the chances of becoming a victim will be greatly reduced. Generally speaking, trouble spots include quiet and uninhabited areas, gang activity areas, drug trafficking areas, and places that involve a large amount of cash, such as banks.

5. Avoid right and wrong time — migratory patterns (climate is a signal of migratory birds). The best time to avoid criminals committing crimes greatly reduces the likelihood of becoming victims. In dark places, alone, relaxed and unprepared, focused on doing other things, or in dangerous areas, it is a good time for criminals to commit crimes and should be avoided as much as possible.

6. Armed to Teeth — hedgehog mode (few animals attack hedgehogs with thorns all over their bodies). The weakness of the victim is an important factor that triggers the criminal's motive for committing the crime. The criminals choose the weak because they have the confidence to make the

者服服帖帖地听任摆布，因此他们可在最短的时间内作案并溜掉。他们感到安全，因为弱者不会反抗。而全副武装起来的对手则不然，首先会给歹徒一个下马威——"别来惹我，否则没好果子吃。"很少有歹徒愿意去碰全副武装的对手。刺猬模式有多种实施办法，如在家装上防盗门和报警装置，走路时手中拿一防身物品作武器，等等。

7. 隐而不露——变色龙模式（变色龙把自己隐藏在周围环境中，不让对手发现目标）。不炫耀自己的财富，歹徒便不会去抢你。

8. 马上行动——武士模式（动手不动口）。任何防范暴力犯罪的策略与方法，不管多么好，你不用它，它对你就毫无用处。所学的策略与方法应长期坚持练习才能达到预防效果。

进行课堂提问。

主要提问上次课的教学内容，并了解学生学习的感受，同时提醒学生注意安全。

讲解远距离格斗的策略及如何提高"远战"能力。

自卫者格斗成功与否不仅取决于技术好坏，也取决于策略的应用。远距离格斗技术有进攻型策略和防守型策略。

1. 进攻型策略。

这是一种以攻为守的策略。自卫者不是消极等待对方进攻，

victims obedient and at their mercy, so they can commit crimes and escape in the shortest possible time. They also feel safe because the weak will not resist. On the other hand, opponents who are fully armed will give the criminals a warning — don't provoke me, otherwise there will be no good fruit to eat. Few criminals are willing to touch fully armed opponents. There are various implementation methods for the hedgehog mode, such as installing anti-theft doors and alarm devices at home, holding an object as a weapon while walking, and so on.

7. Hidden but Not Exposed — chameleon Mode (Chameleon hides itself in the surrounding environment to prevent opponents from discovering its target). If you don't show off your wealth, criminals won't go and rob you.

8. Take immediate action — samurai mode (hands-on, silent). Any strategy and method for preventing violent crime, no matter how good it may be, is of no use to you if you don't use it. Long term practice of the strategies and methods learned can achieve preventive effects.

Classroom questioning.

This part is mainly about the teaching content of the last class, and also to understand the students' learning experience. Remind students to pay attention to security.

Explain the strategies for long-distance combat and improve long-range combat capabilities.

The success of self-defense combat depends not only on the quality of technology, but also on the application of strategies. Long range combat techniques include offensive and defensive strategies.

1. Offensive strategy.

This is a strategy of taking offense as defense. Self defenders are not passively waiting for the other party to

而是主动攻击，击伤歹徒或迫使歹徒远离以保护自身安全。当自卫者不得不击伤歹徒才能保护自己时，或在身材上不占绝对优势时，实施进攻策略可用以下几种方式。

（1）使用脱身技巧蒙蔽歹徒，待其松懈时发起强攻。

（2）使用各种假动作或组合拳连续攻击歹徒。

（3）摆出一副不要命的架势，即使挨上一两拳也照样猛攻不误。拳王泰森的取胜策略就在于此。

2. 防守型策略。

这是一种避其锋芒、以逸待劳的格斗策略。当歹徒十分强壮凶猛，或手中持刀，或急于抓住自卫者以求速战速决，或自卫者对主动攻击缺乏技术或信心时，自卫者应考虑应用这种策略。其主要目的是不断移动以保持安全距离。应用这一策略要遵循以下几点。

（1）保持移动，保持距离。

（2）节省体力，不轻易出拳出腿。

（3）如果歹徒节节进逼而无法后退时，则应以重踹逼退对方。

（4）留心环境，以求利用武器或地形。

（5）游击战术，打了就跑。见机会就打，打不着马上撤回防卫，准备与歹徒长时间对峙。

attack, but actively attacking, injuring or forcing criminals to stay away to protect their own security. When self-defenders have to injure criminals in order to protect themselves, or when they do not have an absolute advantage in the size of the criminals, the following methods can be used to implement offensive strategies.

(1) Use escape techniques to deceive criminals and launch a strong attack when they relax.

(2) Use various fake actions or combination punches to continuously attack criminals.

(3) Put on a fearless posture, and even if you get a punch or two, you can still attack fiercely without fail. The winning strategy of boxing champion Tyson lies in this.

2. Defensive strategy.

This is a combat strategy of avoiding sharpness and waiting for fatigue. When criminals are very strong and fierce, either holding knives in their hands, or eager to catch the defender for quick action, or when the defender lacks technology or confidence in active attack, the defender should consider applying this strategy. Its main purpose is to continuously move to maintain a safe distance. The application of this strategy should follow the following points.

(1) Keep moving, keep the distance.

(2) Save energy and avoid punching or kicking easily.

(3) If the criminals are constantly advancing and unable to retreat, they should use a heavy kick to force the other party back.

(4) Pay attention to the environment in order to utilize weapons or terrain.

(5) Guerrilla tactics, run away as soon as you hit. Take the opportunity to fight, immediately withdraw and prepare for defense if unable to do so, and prepare for a prolonged confrontation with the criminals.

两种策略各有优缺点，进攻型有声势、积极主动，但易消耗体力，并在主动进攻时由于太靠近歹徒而导致危险性增大。防守型灵活机动、节省体力，但在移动范围受限制时则危险性增大。两种策略的成功率依赖于具体格斗情况和自卫者的技术水平。但一般来讲，防守型较适合初学者。

3. 提高远战能力的方法。

只学会了本节的格斗技术还远远满足不了实战的要求，还应不断练习使这些技术达到自动化和精细化以适应实战情况。提高远战能力有三种途径。

（1）提高各项技术的质量，其中包括速度、力量、准确性、时机、判断、变化及在模拟情况下的运用。

（2）把远战技术与其他格斗方式紧密结合起来。实际格斗没有定式，因为格斗方式转化非常快，自卫者应具备从远距离格斗转变到近距离格斗的能力。在练习时就要着重对这一转换的训练。

（3）通过专修某一门武术而使远距离格斗能力向高深发展。本次课介绍的都是基本技术，欲学中高级技术，应选择一两门着重远距离格斗的武术，如空手道、跆拳道、拳击、截拳道、泰拳，还有中国的南拳、北腿及散手等。

Both strategies have their own advantages and disadvantages. The offensive type is aggressive and proactive, but it can easily consume physical energy and increase the danger due to being too close to the criminals during the active attack. Defensive and agile, saving energy, but increasing danger when the range of movement is limited. The success rate of the two strategies depends on the specific combat situation and the technical level of the defender. But generally speaking, defensive style is more suitable for beginners.

3. Methods to improve long-range combat capability.

Learning only the fighting techniques in this section is far from meeting the requirements of practical combat. It is necessary to continuously practice these techniques to achieve automation and refinement to adapt to real-world situations. There are three ways to improve long-range combat capabilities.

The first is to improve the quality of various technologies, including speed, strength, accuracy, timing, judgment, variation, and application in simulation situations.

The second is to closely integrate long-range combat techniques with other combat methods. There is no fixed pattern in actual combat, as the modes of combat change very quickly. Self defenders should have the ability to transition from long-distance combat to close range combat. When practicing, it is important to focus on the training of this transformation.

The third is to develop long-range combat skills to a higher level by specializing in a particular martial arts. This section introduces basic techniques. If you want to learn intermediate to advanced techniques, you should choose one or two martial arts that focus on long-distance combat, such as karate, taekwondo, boxing, Jeet Kune do, Muay Thai, and Chinese Southern Fist, Northern Leg, and Sanda.

E. 活动各关节，双人拉韧带（矫正站、坐、行各种身体姿态）。

1. 推手练习先慢后快。

2. 抓肩练习。

3. 打膝练习。

4. 双人练习——上—退—上。

（二）基本部分

A. 复习远距离格斗技术。

1. 拳击练习（腿对腿、踢打拳）注意安全。

2. 复习拳，腿进攻组合练习及一对一练习。

3. 集体复习左右直拳，勾拳，前、侧、后踹，前、侧踢。

4. 全体分为四组进行分组练习（互相观看动作改进提高）。

组合动作练习——侧踹、左上直拳、右下直拳、前踹、转身后踹。

B. 学习近距离格斗技术。

这种格斗方式主要应用于歹徒离自卫者不足一臂距离时。其主要技术包括用肘、臂、短拳、头撞来打击歹徒，并防备歹徒应用这些技术反击。近战对自卫者来说危险性较大，容易被打、被抓，受伤的机率大幅增加。另外，自卫者在近战中没有时间去思考，攻守亦不分明，是一种"打成一团"的格斗方式。

1. 学习近战姿势——近战是打成一团的格斗，应注意保护自身的重要部位。

近战格斗的基本姿势类似于

E. Move joints and pull ligaments for both individuals (correcting various body postures such as standing, sitting, and walking).

1. Push hands practice slowly and then quickly.

2. Shoulder grabbing practice.

3. Knee hitting practice.

4. Two person practice — up – back – up.

(Ⅱ) Basic parts

A. Review long-distance combat techniques.

1. Boxing practice with leg to leg kicks and punches, pay attention to security.

2. Review Fist, Leg Attack Combination Practice, and One on One Practice.

3. Collective review of left and right straight punches, hook punches, front, side, back kicks, front and side kicks.

4. Divide into four groups for practice (observe each other's movements to improve and improve).

Combination exercise — side kick, top left straight punch, bottom right straight punch, front kick, turn back kick.

B. Learn close range combat techniques.

This fighting method is mainly used when the criminal is less than an arm's distance from the defender. Its main techniques include using elbows, arms, short fists, and head butts to strike criminals and prevent them from using these techniques to counterattack. Close combat poses a greater risk to self-defender, making them vulnerable to being attacked or caught, and greatly increasing their chances of injury. In addition, self-defense fighters do not have time to think about it in close combat, and their attacks and defenses are not clear. It is a form of "forming a group" combat.

1. Learn melee posture — melee is a form of fighting in a ball, paying attention to protecting important parts of oneself.

The basic posture of melee combat is similar to that of

远战的姿势，但身体缩得更紧，两臂亦靠近身体，两手主要护头，是防卫与进攻的综合姿势。

头胸内缩，两手护头，前腿略内扣护裆。

流程：

（1）讲解、示范。

（2）学生原地体会动作，集体练习。

2.学习近战进攻技术。

膝撞、肘撞、短拳、头撞、短踢腿。

膝撞——膝是近战中力量最大的一种武器，主要用来攻击对方裆部及下腹，若击中，会给歹徒以重创。用力抓住歹徒双肩，以防其逃脱。提膝快速击撞歹徒裆部。

肘撞——肘也是近战中威力强大的武器，因而武术中有"宁挨十拳，不挨一肘"之说。肘撞主要是用来打击歹徒的头、肋及下腹。两肘皆可使用，可击前击后，打高打低。

（1）前横肘——此技术主要用来打击歹徒头部，尤其是歹徒身材不高时。向左转体的同时，用肘（靠前臂部分）打击歹徒头部。

（2）前刺肘——此技术主要用来打击歹徒喉、肋及腹部，尤其是当歹徒身材较高时。重心下降，后腿前蹬，后手顶住前手加力，用肘尖撞击歹徒肋部。

long-range combat, but with a tighter body, arms also close to the body, and hands mainly protecting the head. It is a comprehensive posture for defense and attack.

Shrink the head and chest, protect the head with both hands, and slightly buckle the front legs to protect the crotch.

Procedure：

(1) Explanation and demonstration.

(2) Students experience movements in place and practice collectively.

2. Learn melee attack techniques.

Elbow bump, knee bump, short punch, front and back crossbow, front and back thrust elbow, shoulder bump, head bump, short kick leg.

Knee bump — The knee is the most powerful weapon in close combat, mainly used to attack the opponent's crotch and lower abdomen. If hit, it will cause serious damage to the perpetrator. Grab the criminal's shoulders tightly to prevent him from escaping. Quickly hit the perpetrator's crotch with a knee lift.

Elbow collision — Elbow is also a powerful weapon in close combat, so there is a saying in the martial arts world that "it is better to receive ten punches than one elbow.". Elbow bump is mainly used to strike the head, ribs, and lower abdomen of criminals. Both elbows can be used, with the ability to hit forward and backward, high and low.

(1) Front elbow — This technique is mainly used to strike the head of criminals, especially when they are not tall. While turning to the left, hit the culprit's head with the elbow (on the forearm).

(2) front elbow thrusts — This technique is mainly used to strike the throat, ribs, and abdomen of criminals, especially when they are taller. Lower the center of gravity, push forward with the hind legs, apply force with the hind hands against the front hands, and hit the suspect's ribs with the tip of the elbow.

（3）后横肘——此技术主要用来打击背后之敌，尤其是当对手身材不高时。身体左转，同时用肘（靠上臂部分）打击歹徒头部。

（4）后刺肘——此技术主要用来打击背后之敌，尤其是歹徒身材较高时，其打击部位是肋、腹及裆。身体左转，后挥上臂以肘击歹徒肋部。

短拳——短拳与勾拳相近，只是出拳动作小、距离短，且时时护住头。短拳有下列三种方式。

（1）上短拳——与勾拳动作极相似，目的是绕过歹徒双手而打击其耳后或太阳穴。身体左转，拳心向下，打击歹徒耳根。

（2）下短拳——下短拳主要用来打击对手肋部或腹部。蹬地，左转迅速出拳打击歹徒肋部，手心向上。

（3）冲天炮——冲天炮主要用来打对方下巴，从歹徒两手之间的空当进拳。基本动作如下短拳，拳面向上击打歹徒下巴。

头撞——头撞主要用来在近距离打击歹徒鼻梁或下巴。可分为前撞和后撞两种。

（1）前撞——抓住歹徒使其不能脱逃或格挡，用前额撞击歹徒鼻梁。

（2）后撞——迅速向后仰身、仰头，以后脑勺撞歹徒鼻梁。

短踢腿——短踢腿是利用歹徒着重保护上体时打击其膝或胫

(3) back elbow — This technique is mainly used to strike enemies behind, especially when the opponent is not tall. Turn left and hit the perpetrator's head with the elbow (on the upper arm).

(4) Elbow stabbing — This technique is mainly used to strike enemies behind, especially when the perpetrator is of a tall stature, the striking areas are the ribs, abdomen, and crotch. Turn left and swing your upper arm to elbow the perpetrator in the ribs.

Short Fist — Short Fist is similar to hook Fist, but with small punches, short distances, and always protecting the head. There are three ways to use short fists.

(1) Upper Short Fist — Similar to the hook fist movement, the purpose is to bypass the criminal's hands and strike behind their ears or temples. Turn left, punch downwards, and strike the thug's ear.

(2) Lower short punches — The short punches are mainly used to strike the opponent's ribs or abdomen. Kick off the ground, turn left and quickly punch the perpetrator's ribs, palm up.

(3) Rocket — Rocket are mainly used to hit the opponent's chin, punching from the empty space between the hands of the criminal. Basic movement as short punch, facing up and hitting the perpetrator's chin.

Head bump — Head bump is mainly used to strike the nose bridge or chin of criminals at closc range. It can be divided into two types: front collision and rear collision.

(1) Front collision — Grasp the criminal to prevent them from escaping or blocking, and use the forehead to hit the criminal's nose bridge.

(2) rear collision — Quickly lean back, head up, and hit the criminal's nose bridge with the back of the head.

Short kick — Short kick is a kicking technique used

骨的一种踢法。此法出腿隐蔽，极易击中歹徒并造成一定的伤害。快提后腿，脚尖勾起，猛踹敌膝。

流程：

（1）讲解、示范。

（2）学生原地体会动作，集体练习。

（3）全体分为四组一对一站立，一人练习，另一人帮助改进动作。

（4）两人一组利用手靶及拳击套进行对练。教师随时帮助学生改进提高动作。

C. 介绍近战防守技术，格挡后退、格挡反击、下闪进身摔。

在近战中歹徒亦有可能应用上述技术，发起攻击。自卫者可应用下面三种方式来对抗歹徒的进攻。

1. 格挡后退——自卫者用臂或腿格挡来拳或臂肘，然后猛推对方使自己后退至安全距离，此法对新手比较适合，因为它相对比较安全。迅速格挡来拳触手后猛推对方。迅速退回以远距离格斗。

2. 格挡反击——当自卫者无处可退，或想还击歹徒以扭转局势时，可用此法。这是一种积极的防御方法。快挡对手来拳，将歹徒手挡住，使其不能连击，并抓对方手臂，用膝猛顶歹徒

by criminals to strike their knees or shins while focusing on protecting their upper body. This method conceals the legs and is extremely easy to hit criminals and cause certain damage. Quickly lift your hind legs, raise your toes, and fiercely kick the enemy's knee.

Procedure：

(1) Explanation and demonstration.

(2) Students experience movements in place and practice collectively.

(3) Divide into four groups and stand one-on-one, with one person practicing and the other helping to improve their movements.

(4) Pair up and practice using hand targets and boxing sets. Teachers are always available to help students improve and enhance their movements.

C. Introduce close combat defense techniques, including blocking retreat, blocking counterattack, and diving into the body to fall.

In close combat, criminals may also use the aforementioned techniques to launch attacks. Self defenders can use the following three methods to counter the attack of criminals.

1. Blocking and retreating — Self defenders use their arms or legs to block punches or elbows, and then forcefully push the opponent to retreat to a safe distance. This method is more suitable for beginners because it is relatively safe. Quickly block the opponent's fist tentacles and push them fiercely. Quickly retreat to engage in long-distance combat.

2. Blocking counterattack — This method can be used when the defender has nowhere to retreat or wants to counterattack the criminals to turn the situation around. This is a proactive defense method. Quickly block the opponent's punch, block the attacker's hand to prevent continuous attacks, and grab the opponent's arm, forcefully thrusting the attacker's

裆部。

3. 下闪进身摔——此击以软对硬，使对手失去平衡而不能再进攻。下闪躲避开歹徒抓打，迅速进身搂住歹徒双腿，同时隐蔽好头部，手拉的同时肩顶，摔倒对方。

下次课学习掌握提高以上这些内容。

流程：

（1）讲解、示范。

（2）学生原地体会动作，集体练习。

D. 素质及专项素质练习

1. 耐力练习。

2. 腰腹肌练习。

3. 上肢力量练习。

E. 案例分析讨论——遭遇偷盗的应对策略。

（三）结束部分

1. 组织集体放松活动。

2. 讲评本次课，表扬案例分析有特色、有见解的同学。

3. 布置课外作业复习本次课内容。

crotch with your knee.

3. Diving into the body and throwing — This strike is soft against hard, causing the opponent to lose balance and unable to attack again. Flash down to avoid being caught and beaten by the criminal, quickly get in and embrace the criminal's legs, while concealing the head. While pulling with your hands, push your shoulders and fall over the other person.

Learn and improve the above content in the next class.

Procedure：

(1) Explanation and demonstration.

(2) Students experience movements in place and practice collectively.

D. Quality and specialized quality exercises.

1. Endurance.

2. Waist and abdominal muscles.

3. Upper limb strength exercises.

E. Case analysis discussion — strategies for dealing with theft.

(Ⅲ) End section

1. Collective relaxation activities.

2. Evaluate this class and encourage and praise students who have unique and insightful case studies.

3. Review the content of this lesson for extracurricular assignments.

第三课

Lesson 3

一、教学内容

Ⅰ. Teaching content

1. 预防暴力犯罪的主要策略与方法。

1. Main strategies and methods for preventing violent crimes.

2. 复习远距离进攻防守技术。

3. 考核单人技术（踢打拳）。

4. 进行素质及专项素质练习。

二、本课任务

掌握预防暴力犯罪的主要策略与方法。

三、教学重点

考核单人技术（踢打拳）。

四、教学内容与组织教法

（一）准备部分

A. 集合整队，检查出勤情况。

B. 小常识简介：受伤后的临时处理。

C. 考核单人技术（踢打拳）。

踢打拳考核要求两人一组，一攻一防，远战踢打拳——近战泰拳膝肘也可加防抓破抓保持平衡，摔技及反摔技。

评分标准：

1. 技术部分（满分 60 分）。

第一次考试双人技术（踢打拳）（满分 10 分）

第二次考试双人对练（地面解脱 5 项技术）（满分 10 分）

第三次考试多攻一（解脱 14 项技术）（满分 30 分）

2. Review long-range offensive and defensive techniques.

3. Assess individual skills (kicking and boxing).

4. Quality and specialized quality exercises.

II. The task of the class

The main strategies and methods for preventing violent crimes.

III. Teaching focus

Assessing individual skills (kicking and boxing).

IV. Teaching content and organizational teaching methods

(I) Preparation section

A. Gather the team and check attendance.

B. Introduction to common sense: Temporary treatment after injury.

C. Assessing individual skills (kicking and boxing).

Kick boxing assessment requires two people to work in a group, one attacking and one defending. Kick boxing in distance combat — in close combat, Thai boxing can also add defensive grabbing and breaking grabbing to maintain balance, as well as throwing and counter throwing techniques.

Scoring criteria:

1. Technical part (Full score of 60 points).

First-time exam of double skills (kicking and boxing) (Full score of 10 points)

Second-time exam pairs practice (5 ground release techniques) (Full score of 10 points)

Third-time exam requires one extra attack (freeing 14 techniques) (Full score of 30 points)

评分标准：

优秀：判断准确，反应速度快，时机掌握得好，力点准确，动作连贯，变化合理，干净利落。

良好：精神饱满，动作力点准确，方法合理。

及格：独立完成动作，动作基本正确。

不及格：不能独立完成动作，方法不合理。

2. 个人记录成绩。

Criteria:

Excellent: Accurate judgment, fast reaction speed, good timing control, accurate force points, and coherent movements, reasonable and clean changes.

Good: Full of energy, accurate movement points, and reasonable methods.

Pass: Independently complete the action, with basic accuracy.

Failed: Unable to complete actions independently, with unreasonable methods.

2. Personal record scores.

第一次考试 The first exam	（满分 10 分） （Full score of 10）	你的得分： Your score is：
第二次考试 The second exam	（满分 10 分） （Full score of 10）	你的得分： Your score is：
第三次考试 The third exam	（满分 30 分） （Full score of 30）	你的得分： Your score is：
课上作业 Classwork	（满分 5 分） （Full score of 5）	你的得分： Your score is：
课上作业 Classwork	（满分 5 分） （Full score of 5）	你的得分： Your score is：
案例分析（家庭作业） Case Analysis (Homework)	（满分 10 分） （Full score of 10）	你的得分： Your score is：
理论考试 Knowledge test	（满分 10 分） （Full score of 10）	你的得分： Your score is：
学习态度 Learning attitude	（满分 20 分） （Full score of 20）	你的得分： Your score is：
总　计 Total	（满分 100 分） （Full score of 100）	你的得分： Your score is：

D. 案例分析——火灾现场如何逃生。

1. 911 火灾——如何从 90 多层大楼逃生。

2. 芝加哥 35 层大楼 12 层起火后为何 22 层死亡人数最多（6 人熏死，180 多人重伤）。

D. Case Study — How to Escape from a Fire Scene.

1. 911 Fire — How to escape from a 90-story building.

2. After the fire broke out on the 12th floor of a 35 story building in Chicago, the death toll was highest on the 22nd floor (6 people smoked to death, more than 180 people were seriously injured).

3. 2003 年春节福建省居民楼的火灾（10 人死亡）。

4. 2003 年春节哈尔滨饭店的火灾。

5. 2003 年内蒙古呼和浩特市青城公园湖面——冰面救人。

（二）基本部分

A. 复习上两次课学习内容。

1. 拳击——左右直拳、勾拳、短拳（上下短拳、冲天炮）、短踢腿。

2. 踢——前、侧踢。

3. 踹——前、侧、后踹。

4. 肘撞——前后横肘、后刺肘、横刺肘。

5. 肩撞、膝顶、头前后撞。

6. 防守——防拳击：格挡、躲闪。防踢腿：后撤、挡踢腿。

流程：

（1）学生听口令集体复习动作。

（2）全体分为四组一对一站立，一人听口令练习，另一人帮助改进动作。

（3）分组练习两人一组，一攻一防，听口令攻防互换。

（4）分组进行表演练习（全体分为四组：一组表演，另外三组观摩）。

B. 素质及专项素质练习。

1. 耐力练习。

2. 腰腹肌练习。

3. Fire in residential buildings in Fujian Province during the 2003 Spring Festival (10 deaths).

4. Fire at Harbin Hotel during the 2003 Spring Festival.

5. In 2003, the lake surface of Qingcheng Park in Hohhot, Inner Mongolia - saving lives on ice.

(Ⅱ) Basic parts

A. Review the content learned in the previous two classes.

1. Boxing — Left and Right Straight Fist, Hook Fist, Short Fist (Up and Down Short Fist, Rocket) Short Kick

2. Leg extension — front and side kicks.

3. Kick — front, side, back kick.

4. Elbow collision — front and rear transverse elbows, back stabbing elbows, and transverse stabbing elbows.

5. Shoulder impact, knee top impact, and head to back impact.

6. Defense — Anti boxing: blocking and dodging. Anti kick: retreat, blocking kick.

Procedure：

(1) Students listen to commands and collectively review actions.

(2) Divide into four groups and stand one-on-one, with one person practicing by listening to commands and the other helping to improve their movements.

(3) Group practice with two people, one attacking and one defending, switching attacks and defenses by listening to commands.

(4) Group performance exercises (all divided into four groups: one group performs, and the other three groups observe).

B. Quality and specialized quality exercises.

1. Endurance.

2. Lumbar and abdominal muscles.

3. 四肢力量练习。

C、预防暴力犯罪的主要策略与方法。

预防犯罪的策略与方法可以有多种分类方法，掌握后可让学生了解现实生活中的犯罪情况。

1. 家。

家是人们的避风港，只有在家里，人们才感到安全、舒适、自由、无拘无束。但你的家也是歹徒犯罪的重要的地点之一，因此，人们应尽力把家装备得更安全。

策略一：择安而居。

在买房或租房时，首先应考虑的是安全程度如何。例如，一所住房离上班地点很近，但靠近不良帮派活动地区；而另一所住房则处于安全地区，但离上班地点较远，你会选哪一个呢？

策略二：将住处装备成堡垒。

有一项研究调查了几百名在监狱服刑的盗窃抢劫犯，发现他们在作案时最怕的一是狗（狗又能叫又能咬），二是警铃，三是房主人，四是警察。

策略三：切勿树大招风。

这一策略帮助学生应用各种方法以减少歹徒对其住处的注意力，从而避免被歹徒选为攻击的目标。尤其是女性，不应把自己独居的信息留在留言机里。出远门应留下一盏灯及打开收音机，并且托人每天把信取走，这样就会给外人一种家里有人的印象。

3. Limb Strength Exercise.

C. The main strategies and methods for preventing violent crimes.

There are various classification methods for crime prevention strategies and methods, allowing students to understand the crime situation in real life

1. Home.

Home is a safe haven for people, and only at home can people feel safe, comfortable, free, and unrestrained. But your home is also one of the important locations for criminals to commit crimes, so people should try their best to equip their homes more safely.

Strategy 1: Choose a safe place to live.

When buying or renting a house, the first thing to consider is the level of security. For example, if a house is close to the workplace but close to the gang activity area, and another house is in a safe area but far from the workplace, which one would you choose?

Strategy 2: Equip the residence as a fortress.

A study investigated hundreds of burglars and robbers serving sentences in prison and found that their biggest fear of committing crimes was dogs (dogs can bark and bite), alarm bells, homeowners, and police officers.

Strategy 3: Do not make a big tree catch the wind.

This strategy hclps students apply various methods to reduce the attention of criminals to their residence, thereby avoiding being selected as the target of attack by criminals. Especially for women, they should not leave their information about living alone in the message machine. Leaving a light and turning on the radio when going on a long trip, and having someone pick up the letter every day, will give outsiders the impression of having someone at home. It's best if the lights

灯与收音机能与定时器联上最好。门窗锁好，窗帘拉上以使歹徒不知室内底细。

策略四：处处小心以免置自己于受害者的地位。

与邻里处好关系，不要因一点小事争吵。"千金买屋，万金买邻。"女性则要避免归家过晚，如不得已时请别人送你到家。如果发现门窗被撬，不要急于进去查点损失，歹徒有可能还在里面，应马上叫警察来处理。

策略五：切勿引狼入室。

不要随便把自己的电话或住处给陌生人，也不要请上门推销员入座，如果煤气或上下水管修理人员要上门服务，不要单独陪他们，最好找个朋友一起。

2. 工作单位。

工作单位是大多数人每天度过 8 小时的地方，也是歹徒作案的场所之一。凶杀、抢劫、强奸及伤害案等等都曾在工作单位发生过，而且愈演愈烈。预防工作单位的犯罪有几条基本策略。

策略一：找一份安全的工作。

很多工作都有遭歹徒攻击的危险性，如上夜班、在危险地区（贩毒或帮派横行地段等）上班或路过这些地方，经手大量钱财（如银行、珠宝店）的工作，或常与危险的人打交道的工作（如警察、缉毒人员）。如果你认为自己

and radio can be connected to the timer. Lock the doors and windows, and pull the curtains to keep the criminals unaware of the interior details.

Strategy 4: Be careful everywhere to avoid putting yourself in the position of a victim.

Maintain good relationships with neighbors and avoid arguing over trivial matters. A thousand dollars buy a house, ten thousand dollars buy a neighbor. Women should avoid returning home too late, and if necessary, ask someone to take you home. If you find that doors and windows have been pried, don't rush in to investigate the damage. The criminals may still be inside, and you should immediately call the police to handle it.

Strategy 5: Do not lead wolves into the house.

Do not casually give your phone number or residence to strangers, and do not invite door-to-door salespeople to take their seats. If gas or water pipe repair personnel need door-to-door service, do not accompany them alone. It is best to find a friend to accompany them.

2. Work unit.

The workplace is where most people spend eight hours a day for decades, and it is also one of the places where criminals commit crimes. Cases of murder, robbery, rape, and injury have all occurred in the workplace and have escalated. There are several basic strategies for preventing crime in the workplace.

Strategy 1: Find a secure job.

Many jobs are at risk of being attacked by criminals, such as night shifts, working in dangerous areas (such as drug trafficking or gang infested areas), or passing through these places, handling large amounts of money (such as banks, jewelry stores), or working with dangerous people (such as police, drug enforcement agencies). If you believe that your personal security is above all else, then you should

的人身安全高于一切，那么就应找一个安全的工作。

策略二：保持警觉性。

留心身边的人和事。例如，解雇人员会引起报复，同事与上司之间的冲突也可能在特定情况下变成暴力犯罪。留心这些事情你就不会成为替罪羊。

策略三：应交友，不要处处树敌。

与他人处好关系是安全自卫的一个重要原则，要学会控制自己的脾气，用平和的方式解决冲突。

3. 校园。

校园的安全程度随学校不同而不同。

策略一：留心自己所在的场所。

在学校里要注意自己身处的环境，应了解学校的不安全因素并且避开这些因素。

策略二：留心交往的人。

在大学或中学，学生之间的交往很自由，很频繁，但由于这个年龄的学生思想尚不成熟，又缺乏处理事情的经验，因而强奸、伤害罪特别多。

策略三：控制脾气。

大学、中学的学生常常火气十足，易动怒、易争吵，很容易伤害对方而留下被报复的祸根。

4. 街头。

凶杀、抢劫等是街头常常发生的暴力犯罪。

find a safe job.

Strategy 2: Maintain vigilance.

Pay attention to the people and things around you. For example, dismissing employees can lead to retaliation, and conflicts between colleagues and superiors may also turn into violent crimes in specific circumstances. Pay attention to these things and you won't become a scapegoat.

Strategy 3: Make friends, don't make enemies everywhere.

Maintaining good relationships with colleagues or customers is an important principle of security and self-defense. It is important to learn to control one's temper and resolve conflicts in a peaceful manner.

3. Campus.

The level of security on campus varies depending on the school.

Strategy 1: Pay attention to your location.

In school, one should pay attention to the environment they are in, understand the unsafe factors in the school, and avoid these factors.

Strategy 2: Pay attention to the people you interact with.

In college or high school, students interact freely and frequently with each other, but due to their immature thinking and lack of experience in handling things, there are particularly many crimes of rape and injury.

Strategy 3: Control your temper.

College and high school students are often very angry, easily angered, and prone to arguments, which can easily harm each other and leave behind the root of retaliation.

4. Street.

Murder, robbery, and other violent crimes often occur on the streets.

策略一：注意地段与时间，尽量不要在黑夜出门或路过一些不安全地段。

策略二：做好自卫准备。

如果感觉所去的地方不安全，要事先做好准备，衣着鞋子应不影响逃脱，准备好自卫武器。

策略三：保持距离。

在不安全的地方行走，要注意不要随便与人搭话，当有人故意找话接近你时尤其要小心。

策略四：保持警觉。

在街头打电话时，说话要简短，并且要留意身前身后的情况。

5. 公共交通工具。

公共交通工具也是抢劫、凶杀常见的犯罪场所，乘出租车、地铁、公共汽车或电梯时，都可能遭到歹徒袭击。人们在这些地方如同在街头一样比较容易被攻击。因为没有堡垒可躲，因此，应特别小心，尤其是在天黑后或人少时。

策略一：乘公共汽车或地铁时，要注意在安全地点上下车。

策略二：乘坐出租车时，首先要选大公司的车，并且驾驶员不要让人看起来感到不安。要让驾驶员感觉到你的朋友知道你搭了他的车，这样他就不敢轻举妄动以免被人追查。

策略三：在乘电梯时，如果人少而又发现同乘者不怀好意时，不要和他一起进去，他若硬

Strategy 1: Choose a location and time, and try not to go out in the dark or pass through unsafe areas.

Strategy 2: Be prepared.

If you feel that the place you are going to is not safe, be prepared in advance, dress and shoes should not affect your escape, and prepare self-defense weapons.

Strategy Three: Maintain Distance

When walking in unsafe places, be careful not to casually talk to others, especially when someone intentionally approaches you.

Strategy 4: Stay alert.

When making phone calls on the street, speak briefly and pay attention to the situation in front and behind you.

5. Taking the bus.

The public transportation system is also a crime scene for robbery and murder. When taking a taxi, subway, bus or elevator, one may be attacked by criminals. People are more vulnerable to attacks in these places, just like on the streets. Because there are no fortresses to hide from, special caution should be taken, especially after dark or when there are few people.

Strategy 1: When taking a bus or subway, be careful to get on and off at a safe location.

Strategy 2: When taking a taxi, first choose a car from a large company, and the driver should not appear uneasy. Make the driver feel like your friend knows you've taken his car, so he doesn't dare to act recklessly to avoid being pursued.

Strategy 3: When taking the elevator, if there are few people and you find that your fellow passengers are not good intentions, do not go in with them. If they insist on going in,

要进去，你就出来。

6. 娱乐与锻炼场所。

娱乐与锻炼给人们带来快乐，但前去娱乐或运动时亦可能带来危险，因为人们在玩的时候常常会忘记自己的安全。人们为娱乐或锻炼所去的场所如饭店、影院、聚会场所、健身俱乐部、球场等都有可能发生暴力性犯罪。

策略一：注意时间与地点的安全性。

要娱乐或锻炼时，去一家安全场所，即使价钱贵一些，路远一些也值得。

策略二：保持警觉。

即使是在安全场所，也要保持适当的警觉性，以防突发事件。

策略三：少招惹是非。

出门在外，不要惹麻烦。惹人恨而遭报复非常容易。一句话、一个手势、一个眼神，都可能会惹怒他人。

7. 旅游。

旅游使人快乐，但也带来危险。人们在旅游时对当地情况不熟。携带大量现金，并常常因玩得高兴而放松警觉，常常成为犯罪的目标。人们在旅游时设防十分必要。

策略一：旅游区要安全。

出去玩时要找安全的场所和安全的旅馆。

策略二：保持警觉。

旅游与上街、开车或娱乐锻

you should come out.

6. Entertainment and Exercise.

Entertainment and exercise bring happiness to people, but going for entertainment or exercise can also bring danger because people often forget their security while playing. Places where people go for entertainment or exercise, such as restaurants, cinemas, gatherings, fitness clubs, sports fields, etc., can all potentially lead to violent crimes.

Strategy 1: Security of time and place.

When it comes to entertainment or exercise, it's worth going to a safe place, even if it's more expensive and the distance is longer.

Strategy 2: Stay alert.

Even in safe places, it is important to maintain appropriate vigilance to prevent unexpected events.

Strategy 3: Avoid provoking right and wrong.

When going out, don't cause trouble. It is very easy to provoke hatred and seek revenge. A word, gesture, or gaze can all anger others.

7. Tourism.

Tourism brings happiness, but it also brings danger. People are not familiar with the local situation when traveling abroad. Carrying a large amount of cash and often relaxing their vigilance due to having fun, often becomes a target of crime. It is necessary for people to set up defenses when traveling.

Strategy 1: Tourist areas should be safe.

When going out to play, find a safe place and a safe hotel.

Strategy 2: Stay alert.

Traveling, like going on the street, driving, or exercising,

炼一样，要随时留心周围的人和事，远离有嫌疑的陌生人，带上各种防身工具以防万一。

（三）结束部分

1. 集体放松活动。

2. 讲评本次课。

3. 布置课外作业复习所学内容及设计案例分析。

4. 提醒体委组织学生送还器材。

requires constant attention to the people and things around you, staying away from suspected strangers, and bringing various self-defense tools as a precaution.

(III) End section

1. Collective relaxation activities.

2. Evaluate this class.

3. Review the learned content and design case analysis for extracurricular assignments.

4. Remind the sports committee to organize students to return equipment.

第四课

Lesson 4

一、教学内容

Ⅰ. Teaching content

1. 复习远距离进攻防守技术。

2. 复习近距离进攻防守技术。

3. 学习摔法格斗（保护性倒地）。

4. 学习抓臂解脱技术，介绍抱腰解脱技术。

5. 素质及专项素质练习。

1. Review long-range offensive and defensive techniques.

2. Review close range offensive and defensive techniques.

3. Learn how to throw and fight (protective fall).

4. Learn the arm grabbing release technique and introduce the waist hugging release technique.

5. Quality and specialized quality exercises.

二、本课任务

Ⅱ. The task of the class

学习摔法格斗、解脱技术。

Learn techniques for throwing, fighting, and liberation.

三、教学重点

Ⅲ. Teaching focus

近距离攻防技术运用。

Application of Close Range Attack and Defense

Techniques.

四、教学内容与组织教法

（一）准备部分

A. 集合整队，报告人数。

B. 课堂提问，提醒学生注意安全。

C. 小常识简介：冬天里如何防御疾病。

D. 活动各关节，拉韧带。

E. 双人游戏：打膝打臂、推拉移动

（二）基本部分

A. 复习远距离进攻防守技术。

1. 集体复习直拳、勾拳，侧、前、后踹，侧、前踢的综合技术（转身踢、转身踹）。

2. 集体复习防守——防拳击：格挡、躲闪，防踢腿：后撤、挡踢腿。

3. 10 ～ 15 min 分组练习两人一组不用拳套手靶，一攻一防，听口令攻防互换（互不相让，谁有机会就进攻）。

4. 两人一组用手靶拳套打，拿手靶的学生不断变换方位，给进攻者进攻的机会。

B. 复习近距离进攻防守技术。

1. 集体复习肘撞，膝顶，短拳，前、后横肘，前、后刺肘，肩

IV. Teaching content and organizational teaching methods

(I) Preparation section

A. Gather the team and report the number of people.

B. Classroom questioning to remind students to pay attention to security.

C. Introduction to common sense: How to defend against diseases in winter.

D. Move joints and pull ligaments.

E. Two player games: Knee and Arm Hits and Push Pull Movement.

(II) Basic parts

A. Review long-range offensive and defensive techniques

1. Collective review of the comprehensive techniques of straight punches, hook punches, side, front, back kicks, and side, front kicks (turn around kick, turn around kick).

2. Collective Review Defense - Anti Boxing: Blocking, Dodging, Anti Kicking: Backing, Blocking Kicks.

3. 10–15 minutes of group practice where two people work together without using fists or hand targets, attacking and defending each other. Follow the command to switch between attacking and defending (no compromise, whoever has the opportunity will attack).

4. Two people work together to use hand target fists to hit, while the student with the hand target constantly changes direction, giving the attacker an opportunity to attack.

B. Review close range offensive and defensive techniques.

1. Collective review of elbow bump, knee top, short fist, front and back crossbow, front and back thrust elbow, shoulder

撞，头前、后撞，短踢腿。

2. 利用以上所学内容一对一攻防实战练习。

（1）格挡后退。

（2）格挡反击。

（3）格挡后贴身摔。

流程：

（1）讲解、示范。

（2）学生原地体会动作，集体练习。

（3）全体分为四组一对一站立，一人练习，另一人帮助改进动作。

（4）分组练习两人一组，一攻一防，听口令攻防互换。

要求：

（1）人追逐手靶打，拿手靶人随时移动（练习进攻者寻找打击目标）。

（2）人打靶挡（练习防守者的反应速度，提高击打能力和抗击打能力）。

近战的策略。

（1）自卫者应尽量避开对方的有效打击距离，退到安全距离以作远战。这种策略虽不易击伤歹徒，却保护了自己的安全。

（2）若没有机会退避，则自卫者应积极出击，主动进攻。连续使用各种技术，膝、肘、拳、脚、头、肩齐上，将歹徒置于被动挨打的地步。

（3）自卫者亦可使用其他技

bump, head front and back bump, short kick leg

2. Use the above learned content for one-on-one attack and defense practical exercises.

(1) Block reverse.

(2) Block counterattack.

(3) Lose to body fall after 3 blocks.

Procedure:

(1) Explanation and demonstration.

(2) Students experience movements in place and practice collectively.

(3) Divide into four groups and stand one-on-one, with one person practicing and the other helping to improve their movements.

(4) Group practice with two people, one attacking and one defending, switching attacks and defenses by listening to commands.

Requirements:

(1) People chase hand targets, and the skilled target person moves at any time (practicing attackers searching for hitting targets).

(2) Targeting and blocking (practicing the defender's reaction speed to improve their hitting and resistance abilities).

The strategy of close combat.

(1) Self-defenders should try to avoid the effective strike distance of the opponent and retreat to a safe distance for long-range combat. Although this strategy is not easy to harm criminals, it protects one's own security.

(2) If there is no opportunity to retreat, the self-defender should actively launch an attack. Continuously using various techniques, knee, elbow, fist, foot, head, and shoulder level, to put the criminal in a passive position of being beaten.

(3) Self-defenders can also use other techniques such as

术，如挖眼、齿咬来击退歹徒。

C. 学习摔法格斗（保护性倒地）。

前、后、侧倒地技术，前、后滚翻技术。

1. 摔法格斗。

当歹徒企图抓住或已经抓住自卫者并试图将其摔倒在地时，自卫者应使用以下几种方式：防抓或解脱歹徒手抓，保持身体平衡，保护性倒地，摔倒歹徒及对付歹徒的进攻摔技。

此种格斗方式相对不如远战及近战安全。因为一般情况下，歹徒都强壮些，当他们抓住自卫者时，歹徒往往在力量上占优势。在滚打混战中，自卫者亦没有时间和机会去想主意。另外，此种格斗方式最耗体力，自卫者可能在几分钟就精疲力竭。因此，不宜久战，最好是用一两招击退歹徒，退回准备远战。

2. 保护性倒地。

倒地技术主要用来在歹徒企图摔到自卫者时，自卫者保护自己以避免受伤并能进行地面格斗。

（1）后倒。

此技主要用来在向后倒时保护头和脊柱。一脚在后，后倒时如摇椅一样缓冲。下颌内收低头，双手侧击地以缓冲。

eye gouging and biting to repel criminals.

C. Learn how to throw and fight (protective fall).

Front, rear, and side tipping techniques, as well as front and rear rolling techniques.

1. Throwing fighting.

When a criminal attempts to catch or has already caught a self-defense person and attempts to fall them to the ground, the self-defense person should use the following methods: preventing or releasing the criminal's grip, maintaining body balance, protective falling to the ground, falling down the criminal, and attacking and throwing techniques to deal with the criminal.

This type of fighting method is relatively less safe than long-range and melee combat. Because in general, criminals are stronger, and when they catch defenders, they often have an advantage in power. In the melee of rolling and fighting, the defenders also have no time or opportunity to come up with ideas. In addition, this type of combat is the most physically demanding, and self-defenders may become exhausted in just a few minutes. Therefore, it is not advisable to fight for a long time. It is best to use one or two moves to repel the criminals and prepare for a long battle.

2. Protective fall to the ground.

The technique of falling to the ground is mainly used to protect oneself from injury when a criminal attempts to fall onto a defender and able to engage in ground combat.

(1) Backward tilt.

This technique is mainly used to protect the head and spine when falling backwards. With one foot in the back, it cushions like a rocking chair when leaning backwards. Lower your head and lower your jaw inward, and use both hands to hit the ground sideways to cushion.

（2）前倒。

此技主要用来在向前摔倒时保护头与胸部。一腿前迈以缓冲，两掌与前臂触地，使头与身体保持紧绷不触地。

（3）侧倒。

此技主要用来避免侧面摔倒时的伤害。但侧倒比前倒、后倒安全得多。

歹徒向侧推倒自卫者。身体右侧着地，缩颈使头不触地，右手拍地缓冲。

（4）前滚翻。

这项技术主要在自卫者快速前跃而无法做前倒技术时使用，另外在被歹徒抓牢的情况下，自卫者亦可使用此技术解脱。歹徒踢（或推）自卫者，

自卫者失去平衡，向前倾倒。双手着地，头向下、向后钻，身体缩成一团，以肩着地完成滚翻。迅速起身以接后面的动作。

（5）后滚翻。

这是在自卫者快速后跌，因冲力太大而无法使用后倒地技术避免伤害时使用。后倾时一脚置于后，跌倒动作如后倒地技术，两手触地滚过肩膀，迅速起身准备迎战。

流程：

（1）讲解、示范。

（2）学生体会动作，集体听口令练习，要求学生地面反击后，以最快速度离开格斗现场（快速

(2) Forward inversion.

This technique is mainly used to protect the head and chest when falling forward. Step forward with one leg to cushion, touch the palms and forearms to the ground, keeping the head and body taut and not touching the ground.

(3) Side inversion.

This technique is mainly used to avoid injury when falling from the side. But tilting sideways is much safer than tilting forward or backward.

The gangster pushed down the defender to the side. Land on the right side of the body, shrink your neck to keep your head off the ground, and pat the ground with your right hand to cushion.

(4) Front roll over.

This technology is mainly used when the self-defense person quickly jumps forward and is unable to perform forward fall techniques. In addition, in the case of being caught by criminals, the self-defense person can also use this technology to escape. Gangsters kick (or push) self-defender,

The defender loses balance and tilts forward. Hands on the ground, head down and backward, body contracted into a ball, complete the roll with shoulders on the ground. Quickly get up to take on the following actions.

(5) Rear roll over.

This is used when the defender falls quickly and cannot use the fall back technique to avoid injury due to the strong impact. When leaning backwards, place one foot in the back and perform a fall technique like falling backwards. Roll your hands over your shoulders and quickly get up to prepare for the fight.

Procedure:

(1) Explanation and demonstration.

(2) Students will experience the movements and practice listening to commands collectively. After counterattacking on the ground, students are required to leave the fighting scene at

滚动 2 个 360° 后迅速站起，看最后在垫子上的是哪位同学。)

（3）分组练习。一人练习，另一人帮助改进动作。

（4）分组练习。两人一组，一攻一防，加外力的保护性倒地，听口令攻防互换。

D. 学习防抓破抓及保持平衡。

1. 学习防抓技术。

主要用来挡开歹徒双手，同时迅速闪开以免被歹徒抓住。当歹徒伸手过来时，向右击挡歹徒右手，左脚向左移动一步，右脚迅速跟上，保持格斗姿势。

2. 学习破抓技术。

主要用在被歹徒抓住双肩时横撞其肘，以迫使对方松手。向右转体，以前臂或上臂击歹徒之肘，同时左脚向左闪一步，右腿快跟以保持格斗姿势。

流程：

（1）讲解、示范。

（2）学生体会动作。

（3）分组练习。两人一组，一攻一防，听口令攻防互换。

3. 学习保持平衡技术。

主要用于在歹徒企图摔倒自卫者时，自卫者用来保持平衡并伺机用近战格斗技术或摔技来反击或解脱。当被歹徒抓住欲摔时，自卫者亦抓住歹徒并随之移动以保持平衡并伺机反击。当歹

the fastest speed (quickly roll two 360 degrees and stand up to see which student is on the mat at the end)

(3) Group practice. One person practices and the other helps improve the movements.

(4) Group practice. Pair up with two people, one for attack and one for defense. Use external force to protect the ground and switch attack and defense according to commands.

D. Learn how to prevent and maintain balance through grasping and breaking.

1. Learn anti scratch techniques.

Mainly used to block the hands of criminals and quickly dodge to avoid being caught by them. When the criminal reached out, hit the right hand to block the criminal's right hand, move the left foot one step to the left, and quickly follow with the right foot to maintain a fighting posture.

2. Learn breakthrough techniques.

Mainly used when being grabbed by criminals on their shoulders and hitting their elbows horizontally to force them to let go. Turn to the right and strike the culprit's elbow with your forearm or upper arm, while taking a step to the left with your left foot and keeping your right leg fast to maintain a fighting position.

Procedure:

(1) Explain and demonstrate.

(2) Students experience movements.

(3) Group practice. Pair up with two people, one for attack and one for defense, and switch attack and defense according to the command.

3. Learn techniques for maintaining balance.

These techniques are mainly used to maintain balance and use melee combat techniques or throwing techniques to counterattack or release when criminals attempt to fall down self-defense defenders. When caught by a criminal and about to fall, the defender also catches the criminal and moves along to maintain balance and wait for an opportunity to

徒向侧猛抢，自卫者脚步跟不上时，即应跳起，随后落地，身体便能找回平衡。

流程：

（1）讲解、示范。

（2）学生体会动作，集体练习。

（3）分组练习。两人一组，一攻一防，听口令攻防互换。

E. 素质及专项素质练习。

a. 耐力；b. 腰腹肌；c. 四肢力量练习

F. 案例分析。

1. 北大邱庆丰的死（如何脱离犯罪的时间、地点，连设6个"假如"说明问题）。

2. 从女研究生在校园被强奸——教学生如何处理和应付突然发生的问题。

3. 女研究生在假期回家的途中被18岁村姑骗卖给农民当媳妇。

4. 清华大学宿舍里的投毒案。

通过对案例进行分析帮助学生学会在生活中面对问题冷静处理，不激化矛盾，较好地解决。

（三）结束部分

1. 集体放松活动。

2. 讲评本次课。

3. 布置课外作业，复习所学内容及案例分析。

counterattack. When the criminal swung fiercely to the side and the defender couldn't keep up, he should jump up and then land, and his body can find balance.

Procedure:

(1) Explain and demonstrate.

(2) Students experience movements and practice collectively.

(3) Group practice. Pair up with two people, one for attack and one for defense, and switch attack and defense according to the command.

E. Quality and specialized quality exercises.

a. Endurance; b. Waist and abdominal muscles; c. Limb strength exercises

F. Case analysis.

1. The Death of Qiu Qingfeng from Peking University (How to break away from the time and place of crime, set 6 "if's to illustrate the topic).

2. From female graduate students being raped on campus — teaching students how to deal with and cope with sudden problems.

3. A female graduate student was scammed by an 18-year-old village girl to sell to a farmer as her daughter-in-law on her way home during the holiday.

4. The poisoning case in the dormitory of Tsinghua University.

By analyzing case studies, we aim to achieve a calm and effective resolution of problems that arise during the student's learning period, without exacerbating conflicts.

(III) End section

1. Collective relaxation activities.

2. Evaluate this class.

3. Review the learned content and analyze case studies for extracurricular assignments.

第五课

Lesson 5

一、教学内容

1. 增强自信提高安全意识和防卫能力，察觉危险，掌握脱身巧计及应用。

2. 讲解摔技的运用策略及如何提高。

3. 复习各种倒地滚翻摔技及反摔技。

4. 复习远、近战攻防技术学习防抓、破抓及保持平衡。

5. 学习地面格斗技术。

二、本课任务

增强自信提高安全意识和防卫能力。

三、教学重点

及时察觉危险，善用脱身巧计，提高各种自卫能力。

四、教学内容与组织教法

（一）准备部分

A. 集合整队，报告人数。

B. 小常识简介：动作技能的形成过程。

C. 课堂提问提醒学生注意安全。

I. Teaching content

1. Enhance confidence, enhance security awareness and defense ability, detect danger, use escape strategies and applications.

2. Explain the application strategies of throwing techniques and how to improve them.

3. Review various tumble and backfall techniques.

4. Review long-range and melee attack and defense techniques, learn how to defend, break through, and maintain balance.

5. Learn ground combat techniques.

II. The task of the class

Enhance confidence, enhance security awareness and defense capabilities.

III. Teaching focus

Promptly detect danger, make good use of escape strategies, and improve various self-defense abilities.

IV. Teaching content and organizational teaching methods

(I) Preparation section

A. Gather the team and report the number of people.

B. Introduction to Common Sense: The Formation Process of Action Skills.

C. Classroom questioning reminds students to pay attention to security.

D. 对学生进行人格教育。

1. 培养学生的团队精神。

2. 培养学生的演讲能力。

3. 培养学生的创造性思维。

E. 讲解摔技的运用策略及如何提高。

1. 运用策略。

这一格斗方式的运用策略并不复杂，第一，自卫者要尽量避免被歹徒抓牢。第二，在被歹徒抓住时要首先摆脱其抓。如抓脸、别肘、膝撞、口咬等等，都是摆脱歹徒抓的办法。第三，自卫者在相持（如抓牢对手以保持平衡）时，可应用各种技术，如踢、打、抓、拿等技术。第四，此类技术应用起来不如远打及近战格斗安全系数高，应尽量少用，除非在不得已的情况下。

2. 如何提高。

提高摔技的步骤与远战近战格斗方式相同，首先是提高改进动作质量，然后是提高与其他格斗方式的综合运用能力，融合几种武术亦能帮助提高摔技，其中包括摔跤、柔道、合气道及柔术等。

F. 活动各关节，拉韧带练习

双人拉韧带做准备活动。

G. 游戏：单腿斗鸡。

练习腿部力量和保持平衡的能力。

（二）基本部分

A. 复习远近距离进攻和防守、防抓破抓保持平衡。

D. Provide personality education to students.

1. Cultivate students' team spirit.

2. Cultivate students' speech skills.

3. Cultivate students' creative thinking.

E. Explain the application strategies of throwing techniques and how to improve them.

1. The applied strategies.

The applied strategy of this fighting method is not complicated. Firstly, self-defender should try to avoid being caught by criminals. Secondly, when caught by criminals, one must first get rid of their grasp. Scratching the face, avoiding elbows, knee bumps, biting, and so on are all ways to get rid of the criminal's grasp. Thirdly, self-defense fighters can apply various techniques such as kicking, hitting, grabbing, and holding when engaging in a stalemate (such as holding onto opponents to maintain balance). Fourthly, the application of such technologies is not as safe as long-range and close combat, and should be used as little as possible, unless absolutely necessary.

2. How to improve throwing skills.

The steps to improve throwing skills are the same as those for long-distance and close combat. Firstly, improve the quality of the movements, and then enhance the comprehensive application ability with other combat methods. Integrating several martial arts can also help improve throwing skills, including wrestling, Judo, Aikido, and Jujutsu.

F. Exercise by moving joints and pulling ligaments.

Two people pulling ligaments for preparation activities

G. Game: Single Legged Cock Fighting.

Practice leg strength and balance skills.

(II) Basic parts

A. Review the balance between attacking and defending at close and far distances, as well as defending, grasping,

（1）集体单个动作练习。

（2）一对一攻防实战练习，复习格斗技术熟练提高攻防能力。

B. 复习各种倒地滚翻、摔技及反摔技。

（1）听口令集体练习做各种倒地滚翻。

（2）男女生混合编组练习，提醒学生注意安全。

C. 脱身巧计。

1. 察觉危险。

脑子里有了自卫防身这根弦，人们就容易保持警觉并随时留心各种危险信号，这样可以在歹徒动手之前就设计脱身。自卫者所要留心的危险信号包括自己所处的地点、时间及歹徒（或嫌疑人）的一言一行。身处僻静之处或黑暗之时，人们首先应该提高警惕，而歹徒的言行更是直接的危险信号。

歹徒在作案前或作案时的行为可能有：盯住受害者，尾随；接近受害者，碰撞受害者或抓住受害者；拖受害者去僻静之处，将受害者摔倒在地或用凶器逼住受害者；歹徒在攻击时也可能使用一些字眼，如"不要动，动了就捅死你""把钱包给我""脱衣服""进车去"等。

从歹徒的言行，人们有时可以猜出歹徒行凶的动机及目的，

breaking, and grasping.

(1) Collective individual action practice.

(2) Practice one-on-one offensive and defensive exercises, review combat skills, and improve offensive and defensive abilities.

B. Review various tumble, fall, and backfall techniques.

(1) Listen to commands and practice various tumbles collectively.

(2) Male and female mixed group practice, reminding students to pay attention to security.

C. A clever escape strategy.

1. Sensing danger.

With the string of self-defense in their minds, people can easily remain vigilant and constantly pay attention to various danger signals, so that they can design a escape before the criminals take action. The dangerous signals that a self-defense person should pay attention to include their location, time, and the words and actions of the criminal (or suspect). When in a secluded or dark place, people should first be vigilant, and the words and actions of criminals arc direct signals of danger.

The behavior of criminals before or during the crime may include: stare at the victim and following them; approach the victim, collide with the victim, or capture the victim; drag the victim to a sccluded place, drop the victim to the ground or use a weapon to force the victim; criminals may also use some words during attacks, such as "don't move, I'll stab you if I move", "give me your wallet", "take off your clothes", "get in the car", and so on.

From the words and actions of criminals, people can sometimes guess the motive and purpose of their actions, and

因而有针对性地应付，或跑或战或和。例如，歹徒的目的是抢钱包，那么他得到钱后就可能不会进一步杀害受害者，这就是"花钱消灾"。如果歹徒强迫受害者脱衣服，其目的可能是强奸，如果歹徒令受害者随他去别处，则受害者就更应该小心了，因为在别处，歹徒更可以随心所欲地处置受害者。

与歹徒冲突时，想做出一个正确的决策并非易事，一是对歹徒的底细、目的、动机不了解，二是没有时间考虑。这时受害者的大脑就好像一架高速运移的计算机，把所有的信息在一瞬间整合分析并做出决定。这些信息是决策必备的一些因素，其中包括歹徒的动机与目的（杀人、强奸、抢劫或伤害），什么对受害者最重要（保钱财、保命、保尊严、保身体），敌我力量对比（身材、技术、武器），胜算的概率及所采取的策略（跑、打或谈判）。在与歹徒冲突时，安全脱身的概率是很难预测的，受害者往往是碰运气。一般来说，受害者所采用的策略大多是他们所熟悉的，那些经过训练自动化反应出来的技术。因此，人们应该把自卫防身的策略与技术磨练得出神入化，这样才能在遭到歹徒袭击时不用考虑就能自如地应用。

therefore respond with targeted measures, such as running, fighting, or making peace. For example, if the purpose of a criminal is to grab a wallet, then he may not further kill the victim after receiving the money, which is called "spending money to alleviate the disaster". If the perpetrator forces the victim to undress, the purpose may be rape. If the perpetrator asks the victim to follow him elsewhere, the victim should be even more careful because elsewhere, the perpetrator can handle the victim as he pleases.

It is not easy to make the right decision when in conflict with a criminal. Firstly, one does not understand the criminal's background, purpose, and motivation, and secondly, there is no time to consider. At this point, the victim's brain is like a high-speed computer, organizing and analyzing all the information in an instant to make decisions. These pieces of information are essential factors for decision-making, including the motive and purpose of the perpetrator (murder, rape, robbery, or injury), what is most important to the victim (protecting money, life, dignity, and body), the comparison of enemy and friendly forces (physique, skills, weapons), the probability of victory, and the strategies adopted (running, fighting, or negotiating). The probability of escaping safely during conflicts with criminals is difficult to predict, and victims often take chances. Generally speaking, the strategies adopted by victims are mostly techniques that they are familiar with, which have been trained and automated to react to. Therefore, people should hone their self-defense strategies and techniques to perfection, so that they can easily apply them without considering being attacked by criminals.

2. 脱身巧计及应用（走为上策、舌战、服从、吓唬、失去吸引力、装疯卖傻）。

a. 走为上策——兔子模式 b. 舌战——推销员模式 c. 服从——病人模式 d. 吓唬——吠犬模式 e. 失去吸引力——黄鼠狼模式 f. 装疯卖傻——小丑模式

3. 地面格斗。

地面格斗是自卫防身的一种必不可少的格斗形式，很多案例表明，自卫者（尤其是女子）往往在几秒钟内就会被歹徒摔倒在地，尤其是在遭到突然袭击时，若被摔倒或击倒，自卫者马上处于劣势，而歹徒仍会继续进攻，直至自卫者完全丧失反抗能力。此时，自卫者安全脱离险境的机会大为减少。因此此种格斗技术应只在不得已时才使用，极少主动应用。

被摔倒在地并不是说自卫者已经一败涂地，如果能正确运用所学的倒地技术，并使用各种地面格斗技术，自卫者仍有脱离险境的机会。地面格斗有两种方式：一种是散打，另一种是解脱。

1）学习地面散打。

地面散打的运用时机是在自卫者虽已倒地、但还未被抓住或压住时，自卫者可应用各种远距离格斗中的技术，如防抓、踢打等。

地面散打的基本方法包括以下几个步骤（防抓与踢打）：

2. Escape strategies and applications (taking action as the best strategy, engaging in verbal battles, obeying, intimidating, losing attractiveness, and pretending to be crazy and foolish).

a. The best strategy is to go — Rabbit Mode   b. Tongue Battle — Salesman Mode   c. Obedience — Patient Mode d. Scare — Barking Dog Mode   e. Losing Attraction — Weasel Mode   f. Playing Mad and Foolish — Joker Mode

3. Ground fighting.

Ground combat is an essential form of self-defense and self-defense. Many cases have shown that defenders (especially women) often fall to the ground within seconds by criminals, especially in the event of a sudden attack. If they fall or are knocked down, the defender is immediately at a disadvantage, and the criminals will continue to attack until the defender completely loses their resistance. So, the chances of self-defense safely escaping danger are greatly reduced, and this fighting technique is only used when necessary and rarely actively applied.

Falling to the ground does not mean that the defender has been completely defeated. If they can correctly apply their learned falling techniques and use various ground combat techniques, the defender still has a chance to escape danger. There are two ways to fight on the ground: one is free combat, and the other is liberation.

1) Learning ground sanda.

The timing for the use of ground combat is when the defender has fallen to the ground but has not yet been caught or suppressed. The defender can apply various techniques in long-distance combat, such as grappling and kicking.

The basic methods of ground Sanda include the following steps (Prevent scratching and kick):

（1）踢打或推开歹徒以防其抓或打。

（2）滚出歹徒的抓打范围。

（3）摆出地面格斗架势，以脚对准歹徒，并用两臂支撑随其转动。

（4）当歹徒靠近时，猛击其膝或裆。

（5）当其后退时迅速起身进行远距离格斗。

流程：

（1）讲解、示范。

（2）学生体会动作。

（3）分组练习。两人一组，一攻一防，攻防互换。

2）学习地面解脱技术。

这些技术是自卫者用来在地面对付歹徒抓、锁喉或压在身上殴打时使用。地面解脱比起地面散打来其难度大大增加，而脱身机会要少，尤其是在歹徒十分强壮有力的时候。自卫者在地面解脱时需要用全部力量，使用各种方法，如踢打、挖眼、掏裆及咬等以求脱身。由于在地面遭遇歹徒攻击的情况不同，因此解脱技术也随之变化。单个解脱技术学起来十分容易，但识别歹徒进攻方式并能正确使用各种解脱办法却十分不容易。必须反复练习每个解脱技术，要对歹徒的攻击手法快速做出反应，以使自己的反应及技术都达到自动化，方能有效解脱。歹徒不会给你时间去想该

(1) Kick or push away criminals to prevent them from catching or hitting.

(2) Get out of the criminal's reach.

(3) Put on a ground combat posture, aim your feet at the criminal, and use your arms to support and rotate with them.

(4) When the criminal approaches, strike them hard on the knee or crotch.

(5) Quickly stand up and engage in long-distance combat when retreating.

Procedure:

(1) Explain and demonstrate.

(2) Students experience movements.

(3) Group practice. Pair up with two people, one for attack and one for defense, and switch between attack and defense.

2) Learn ground release techniques.

These techniques are used by self-defender to deal with criminals on the ground, such as catching, locking their throats, or pressing them onto their bodies for physical assault. Ground liberation is much more difficult than ground fighting, and there are fewer opportunities to escape, especially when the criminals are very strong and powerful. Self defenders need to use all their strength and various methods, such as kicking, gouging, digging, and biting, to escape on the ground. Due to different situations of being attacked by criminals on the ground, the release techniques have also changed accordingly. Learning individual liberation techniques is very easy, but identifying the attacking methods of criminals and being able to use various liberation methods correctly is not easy. It is necessary to repeatedly practice each liberation technique and quickly respond to the attacking techniques of the criminals, in order to achieve automation of one's own reactions and techniques, in order to be effectively liberated. The criminals won't give you time to think about which technique to use.

用哪种技术。

a. 体侧锁喉解脱法：压肘解脱法。

此技术是当歹徒跪于体侧锁喉时，自卫者所采用的保护及解脱办法。

歹徒体侧锁喉时，用右手压其两臂以缓其力，右手抓住其腕，左手猛击其肘，迫使歹徒松手，不然必伤其肘，向相反方向滚动，自卫者亦可先抓其眼，再使用以上技术。

流程：

（1）讲解、示范。

（2）学生体会动作。

（3）分组练习。两人一组，一攻一防，攻防互换。

b. 压臂锁喉解脱法：压臂转体解脱法和拉摔解脱法。

（1）压臂转体解脱法。

此项技术是在自卫者被歹徒坐在身上并锁喉时所采用的解脱手法。歹徒跪坐在自卫者身上时用此法解脱比较有效。歹徒上压锁喉，自卫者两臂紧压歹徒两臂于胸前，一脚蹬地向侧转体，将歹徒摔倒在体侧的地上，自卫者亦可攻击歹徒双眼，结合以上技术解脱。

（2）拉摔解脱法。

此技术主要用在当歹徒坐在自卫者身上锁喉，尤其是蹲坐在其身上锁喉时的解脱。两手抓

a. Body side lock throat release method: elbow pressure release method.

This technique is a protective and liberating method used by self-defense when criminals kneel on their sides and lock their throats.

When the criminal locks his throat on the side, he presses his arms with his right hand to slow down his force, grabs his wrist with his right hand, and fiercely hits his elbow with his left hand to force the criminal to let go. Otherwise, he will hurt his elbow and roll in the opposite direction. Self defenders can also grab his eyes first before using the above techniques.

Procedure:

(1) Explain and demonstrate.

(2) Students experience movements.

(3) Group practice. Pair up with two people, one for attack and one for defense, and switch between attack and defense.

b. Arm pressure lock throat release method: Arm pressure rotation release method and pull drop release method.

(1) Arm pressure rotation release method.

This technology is a release technique used when a self-defense person is sitting on their body and locked in their throat by a criminal. This method is more effective when criminals kneel on self-defender. The perpetrator locked their throat with pressure, and the self-defense officer tightly pressed their arms against their chest. With onc foot, they turned sideways and threw the perpetrator to the ground on their side. The self-defense officer could also attack the perpetrator's eyes and use the above techniques to relieve the situation.

(2) Pull and drop release method.

This technology is mainly used for the release of criminals who sit on self-defense guards and lock their throats, especially when squatting on them. Grasp the assailant's

牢歹徒腋下，两手向头上方猛推对方，同时一脚蹬地，一腿猛撞以增加臂部合力，将歹徒从头上摔出。

流程：

（1）讲解、示范。

（2）学生体会动作。

（3）分组练习。两人一组，一攻一防，攻防互换。

c. 上压按臂解脱法：滑臂侧推解脱法。

当被歹徒坐在身上并压住双手时，自卫者处在极为困难的劣势中，所能应用的技术十分有限。滑臂侧推解脱法虽不能次次成功，但却比较容易解脱或创造其他机会。歹徒上压自卫者双臂，自卫者下拉右臂，右臂及全身全力向左推，将歹徒掀翻在地。

流程：

（1）讲解、示范。

（2）学生体会动作。

（3）分组练习。两人一组，一攻一防，攻防互换。

d. 上压拳击解脱法：挡抓推解脱法。

当自卫者处在绝对劣势中时，常常会挨上几拳，甚至有时还难以脱身。此法主要用来对付压在身上并施以乱拳的歹徒。歹徒上压锁喉，并欲击昏自卫者，自卫者应双手挡住其拳并抓牢，

armpits with both hands, vigorously push the other person above their head with both hands, while kicking the ground with one foot and slamming the other leg to increase arm force, and throw the assailant off their head.

Procedure:

(1) Explain and demonstrate.

(2) Students experience movements.

(3) Group practice. Pair up with two people, one for attack and one for defense, and switch between attack and defense.

c. Upward pressure arm release method: sliding arm side push release method.

When the assailant sits on their body and presses their hands, the defender is in an extremely difficult disadvantage, and the technology they can apply is very limited. The sliding arm lateral push release method may not be successful repeatedly, but it is relatively easy to release or create other opportunities. The criminal pressed the self-defense officer's arms upwards, and the self-defense officer pulled down his right arm. He pushed his right arm and body all the way to the left, flipping the criminal to the ground.

Procedure:

(1) Explain and demonstrate.

(2) Students experience movements.

(3) Group practice. Pair up with two people, one for attack and one for defense, and switch between attack and defense.

d. Upward Pressure Boxing Release Method: Block Grab Push Release Method.

Self defenders are at an absolute disadvantage, often receiving a few punches and sometimes even struggling to escape. This method is mainly used to deal with criminals who are pressed on their bodies and use violent punches. The criminal locked his throat and attempted to knock the self-defense victim unconscious. The self-defense victim covered his fist with both

以防其抽回再打，左手抽出迅速推击歹徒右肘，将歹徒向右侧推倒。

hands and grabbed it tightly to prevent him from retracting and hitting again. He quickly pushed the criminal's right elbow with his left hand and pushed him to the right.

流程：

（1）讲解、示范。

（2）学生体会动作。

（3）分组练习。两人一组，一攻一防，攻防互换。

（三）结束部分

1. 集体放松活动。

2. 讲评本次课。

3. 提醒体委组织学生送还器材。

4. 布置课外作业，复习所学内容。

Procedure:

(1) Explain and demonstrate.

(2) Students experience movements.

(3) Group practice. Pair up with two people, one for attack and one for defense, and switch between attack and defense.

(III) End section

1. Collective relaxation activities.

2. Evaluate this class.

3. Remind the sports committee to organize students to return equipment.

4. Review the learned content for extracurricular assignments.

第六课

Lesson 6

一、教学内容

全面复习多攻一考试套路（可按五人一组进行）。

I. Teaching content

Comprehensive review of the multi attack exam routine (can be conducted in groups of five people).

二、本课任务

复习所学技术。

II. The task of the class

Review learned techniques.

三、教学重点

安全第一，动作点到即止。

III. Teaching focus

Security first, do not go too far.

四、教学内容与组织教法

（一）准备部分

A. 班体委集合整队，向老师报告人数，交案例分析。

B. 常识性简介：考试期间应该如何健身（8 减 1 大于 8 的道理）。

C. 讲解以少对多的自卫防身。

a. 逃跑脱身；b. 使用巧计；c. 格斗。

以少对多的自卫防身。

歹徒常常结伴作案以增加其成功率。而自卫者面对团伙歹徒时则是寡不敌众处境危险。以少胜多自卫防身的办法一般有三种：跑掉以脱离危险；服从以避免伤害并寻找脱身时机；打跑结合。

1. 逃跑脱身。

歹徒攻击大都是一拥而上，拉身拖腿抱腰锁喉齐上，武林高手也难对付。因此，大多数专家都认为在遇上两个以上歹徒攻击时，应尽量脱身逃跑，不管是在歹徒动手前或动手中。

2. 使用巧计。

有时歹徒聚众攻击并非为了杀人。因此，在这种情况下，使用一些巧计则可能安全脱身。但在有些情况下并非如此，冷血歹徒一般没有同情心，因此在使用巧计一定要做好跑与打的准备。

IV. Teaching content and organizational teaching methods

(I) Preparation section

A. The class sports committee will gather and form a team, report the number of people to the teacher, and submit a case analysis.

B. Common sense introduction: How to exercise during exams(The reason why 8-1 is greater than 8)

C. Explain the use of few to many self-defense measures

a. escaped and escaped; b. uses clever tactics and; c. fights.

To defend oneself with a few to many self-defense measures.

Gangsters often gang up to increase their success rate. When faced with gang criminals, self-defenders are in a precarious situation and outnumbered. There are generally three ways to defend oneself with less than more: run away to escape danger; obey to avoid harm and seek opportunities to escape; combining driving and running.

1. Escape and escape.

Most of the gangsters attack in a rush, pulling themselves, dragging their legs, hugging their waist, and locking their throats together. Even the best martial arts experts are difficult to deal with. Therefore, most experts believe that when encountering attacks from two or more criminals, one should try to escape as much as possible, whether before or with the hands of the criminals.

2. Use clever strategies.

Sometimes criminals gather to attack not for the purpose of killing. Therefore, in this situation, using some clever tricks may lead to a safe escape. But in some cases, this is not the case. Cold blooded criminals generally lack empathy, so when using clever tactics, they must be prepared to run and fight.

3. 格斗。

格斗虽会激怒歹徒，但同时也可能会警告歹徒，并对控制形势有一定的主动权。格斗方式基本上以远战为主，以避免被歹徒抓住而无法施展。基本原则与做法有三：第一，不断移动以避免对方接近；第二，诈一方而战一方，总是在对付一个人，并置歹徒之同伴于其背后，使二人成一直线；第三，打跑结合，没有机会跑就打，有机会逃就跑；第四，使用任何器械以增强战斗力。

（二）基本部分

全面复习：

a. 徒手解脱 14 项技术；b. 地面解脱 5 项技术；c. 远、近距离格斗和摔法格斗。

考试要求：

1. 每人 1.5 ～ 2 min 的考试时间全程摄像。

2. 多攻一解脱技术主要考核解脱技术。

3. 四人进攻一人防守，各种动作交替使用进行防守反击，考核临场应用能力。

（三）结束部分

1. 集体放松活动。

2. 讲评本次课。

3. 布置课外作业，复习所学内容。

3. Fighting.

Although fighting may anger criminals, it may also warn them and give them some initiative in controlling the situation. The fighting style is mainly based on long-range combat to avoid being caught by criminals and unable to perform. There are three basic principles and methods: first, keep moving to avoid the other party getting close; Secondly, deceiving one side while fighting the other, always dealing with one person and placing accomplices of criminals behind their backs, making the two people in a straight line; Thirdly, combine running and fighting, fight when there is no chance to run, and run when there is a chance to escape; Fourthly, use any equipment to enhance combat effectiveness.

(II) Basic parts

Comprehensive Review:

a. 14 techniques for manual release; b. 5 ground release technologies; c. Long and close range combat and throwing combat.

Exam requirements:

1. Each person should have one and a half to two minutes of exam time, with full camera coverage.

2. Multi attack and one release technique mainly assesses the release technique.

3. Four people attacking and one person defending, using various movements alternately to defend and counterattack, assessing on-site application ability.

(III) End section

1. Collective relaxation activities.

2. Evaluate this class.

3. Review the learned content for extracurricular assignments.

第七课

Lesson 7

一、教学内容

I. Teaching content

1. 复习各种格斗、解脱技术及提高综合实用技术。

2. 学习特殊格斗技术。

3. 简介刀尖上的安全自卫防身。

4. 介绍考试要求。

1. Review various combat and liberation techniques and improve comprehensive practical skills.

2. Learn special combat techniques.

3. Introduction to Security Self-defender on the Blade.

4. Introduce the exam requirements.

二、本课任务

II. The task of the class

掌握特殊技术的运用。

Application of special technologies.

三、教学重点

III. Teaching focus

习得安全脱身的意识。

Awareness of safe escape.

四、教学内容与组织教法

IV. Teaching content and organizational teaching methods

（一）准备部分

1. 集合整队，向老师报告人数。

2. 课堂提问，提醒学生注意安全。

3. 进行准备活动（两名学生合作带准备活动）。

（二）基本部分

A. 复习各种格斗、解脱技术及提高实用技术。

1. 利用所学各种格斗及解脱法一对一攻防实战练习。

（I）Preparation section

1. Gather the team and report the number of people to the teacher

2. Classroom questioning to remind students to pay attention to security

3. Preparation activities (two students working together to lead the preparation activities).

（II）Basic parts

A. Review various combat and liberation techniques and improve practical skills.

1. Practice one-on-one attack and defense using various combat and liberation techniques learned.

a. 分项练习；b. 组合动作练习；c. 四攻一练习，提高技术应用能力。

2. 复习抓臂解脱格斗技术。

a. 复习上下抓臂解脱法（上抓臂：砍拇指法、抓脸解脱法、扭臂解脱法。下抓臂：转体解脱法、锁肘解脱法）。

b. 复习后扭臂解脱法（肘击接后跌法、前滚解脱法、后端、转身撞裆解脱法）。

3. 复习抱腰解脱技术。

a. 复习背后不抓臂抱腰解脱技术（横肘加绊摔解脱法、抓腿摔解脱法、卷摔解脱法）。

b. 复习背后抓臂抱腰解脱技术（击裆加绊摔解脱法、卷摔解脱法）。

c. 前抱腰解脱技术（前抱腰未锁臂抠眼解脱法、前抱腰锁臂撞档解脱法）。

4. 复习锁喉解脱技术。

a. 复习前锁喉解脱技术（断肘解脱法、顶膝加锁肘解脱法、兔子蹬鹰解脱法）。

b. 复习后锁喉解脱技术（抓打摔解脱法、下砸接打摔解脱法）。

5. 复习抓发解脱技术。

a. 复习前抓发解脱法技术（抓踢锁肘解脱法）。

b. 复习后抓发解脱法技术（转身顶档解脱法、倒踢解脱法）。

a. Itemized exercise; b. Combination action practice; c. Four attacks and one practice to improve technical application ability.

2. Review the techniques of grab arm release combat.

a. Review the upper and lower arm release method (Upper arm grabbing: Thumb chopping technique, face grabbing release technique, arm twisting release technique. Lower Grab Arm: Twist Release Method, Elbow Lock Release Method).

b. Twist arm release method after review (Elbow strike followed by fall, forward roll release, backward kick, turn around and hit the crotch release).

3. Review waist hugging release techniques.

a. Review the technique of not grabbing the arm behind the back and embracing the waist for release (Cross elbow and trip release method, leg grab release method, and roll release method).

b. Review the technique of grabbing the arm and embracing the waist behind the back for release (Crotch hitting and tripping release method, rolling release method).

c. Front Waist Release Technique (Front waist unlocking arm eye picking release method, front waist locking arm collision release method).

4. Review the technique of locking and releasing the throat.

a. Review the technique of locking and releasing the throat before review (Elbow Release Method, Knee Top Locking Elbow Release Method, Rabbit Eagle Kicking Release Method).

b. Review of Throat Locking and Relieving Techniques (Grasping, hitting, and falling release methods).

5. Review of hair-grabbing escape techniques.

a. Review of front hair-grabbing escape techniques (hair grab, kick, elbow lock escape).

b. Review of rear hair-grabbing escape techniques (turn-and-block escape, back kick escape).

6. 复习其他解脱技术。

a. 复习夹头解脱法技术（掏档揣膝解脱法、绊跌解脱法）。

b. 复习后架臂解脱法技术——卷摔解脱法。

B、复习地面散打、地面解脱、擒拿格斗技术。

1. 集体复习摔技。

2. 一攻一对练抓摔、破抓摔技术。

3. 一攻一对练拿腕、拿肘技术，破拿腕、破拿肘技术。

C. 学习特殊格斗技术。

特殊格斗一般指如何应付敌我力量相差比较悬殊情况下的自卫防身，如对付两个以上的歹徒，或对付持刀持枪的歹徒。

D. 简介刀尖下的安全自卫防身。

刀尖下的安全自卫防身最大的难题是拿主意。因为对刀太危险，连警察及武术高手都害怕。因此一般都宁愿不战而退。刀尖下的自卫有几种办法：第一，服从歹徒以避免伤害或寻找机会；第二，逃跑以脱离险境；第三，徒手或使用其他器械搏斗。

1. 逃走。

多数武术教师都告诫学生，不管其武艺多高，在遇上持刀歹徒时应首先逃走，除非是无路可逃。逃跑的好处是自卫者能迅速

6. Review other liberation techniques.

a. Review the technique of chuck release. Pulling out the gear and lifting the knee release method, tripping release method.

b. Review of the technique of arm release after revision — roll and fall release method)

B. Review techniques for ground sanda, ground release, and grappling and fighting.

1. Collective review of throwing techniques.

2. One-on-one practice, grab and drop, break grab and drop techniques.

3. One-on-one attacks, practicing wrist and elbow techniques, breaking wrist and elbow techniques.

C. Learn special combat techniques.

Special combat generally refers to self-defense and self-defense in situations where there is a significant difference in strength between the enemy and ourselves, such as dealing with two or more criminals, or dealing with criminals holding knives and guns.

D. Introduction to Security and Self-defender on the Blade.

The biggest challenge in self-defense and security on the tip of the knife is making decisions. Because dealing with knives is too dangerous, even police officers and martial arts experts are afraid. Therefore, people generally prefer to retreat without fighting. There are several ways to defend oneself on the tip of the knife: firstly, obey the criminals to avoid harm or seek opportunities; secondly, escape to escape danger; thirdly, fight with bare hands or other instruments.

1. Escape.

Most martial arts teachers warn students that no matter how skilled they are, they should first escape when encountering a knife wielding criminal, unless there is no way to escape. The advantage of escaping is that the self-defense

脱离险境，而且歹徒不可能像用枪那样可以从背后射击。而且多数歹徒不愿在大街上持刀追人。在刀尖上的逃跑机会有几种：第一，当歹徒尚未开始攻击时，转身就逃；第二，向离公共场合较近时向人多的地方逃；第三，歹徒强迫自卫者去僻静处时找准时机逃跑；第四，自卫者奔跑能力强又穿着适合时；第五，自卫者对付刀没有经验或没有把握时。逃跑的各种办法前文已经介绍过。自卫者在逃跑时亦应随时准备搏斗。

2. 使用巧计。

使用巧计也可能使歹徒改变主意或拖延其进攻以寻找其他办法。使用巧计的好处是不易激怒歹徒，使其不会使用更残酷的手段。若歹徒无意取命，得到所要的东西后就不会伤害受害者。但如果歹徒想取命，则什么巧计也没有用。自卫者在使用巧计时要保持安全距离并随时准备搏斗。

3. 格斗。

a. 远战对刀；b. 擒拿对刀；c. 器械对刀（椅子、衣服、扫帚、书包）

格斗虽容易激怒歹徒并不留后路，但自卫者亦可有一些主动权来控制局势。在其他策略都不灵的情况下，格斗便成为唯一的生存手段。有关在刀尖上搏斗的生存概率尚无研究结果参考。作者曾于 1997 年对美国男、女大学

person can quickly escape danger, and the criminal cannot shoot from behind like with a gun. And most criminals are unwilling to pursue people with knives on the street. There are several opportunities to escape at the tip of the knife: firstly, when the criminal has not yet started attacking, turn around and run away; secondly, when close to public places, flee to crowded places; thirdly, when criminals force self-defenders to go to secluded places; fourthly, when the self-defense person has strong running ability and is suitable for wearing; fifthly, when the self-defender have no experience or confidence in dealing with knives. The various methods of escape have been introduced earlier. Self-defenders should also be prepared to fight at all times when fleeing.

2. Use clever strategies.

The use of cunning tactics may also cause criminals to change their minds or delay their attack in search of other ways. The advantage of using cunning tactics is that it is not easy to provoke criminals, preventing them from using more cruel means. If the criminals have no intention of taking their lives, they will not harm the victims after obtaining what they want. But if the criminals want to take their lives, no clever tricks are of usc. Self defenders need to maintain a safe distance and be ready to fight at any time when using a smart timer.

3. Fighting.

a. Long distance combat with knives; b. Capture with knives; c. Equipment with knives (chairs, clothes, brooms, backpacks)

Although fighting can easily provoke criminals without leaving a way out, self-defense individuals can also have some initiative to control the situation. In situations where other strategies are ineffective, fighting becomes the only means of survival. There is no research reference on the survival probability of fighting on the tip of the knife. The author conducted a simulation experiment with American male and

生做过模拟试验，试验过程近似于真实搏斗，但使用的是橡皮刀。在自卫者每次反抗时，持刀者都尽力捅到自卫者。在10次实验中，自卫者受伤的概率达92%，其中54%的伤在头、颈、胸、腹部，有38%的伤在手、腿上。其中所有的人都被刺中5次以上，有50%的受害者每次反抗皆被刺中，这是徒手对刀的试验结果。而当自卫者使用椅子对刀时，则刺中率大大减少，并且大部分伤都在手臂上。

　　歹徒持刀威胁时大致有几种可能。第一种情况是歹徒锁自卫者之喉，并以刀相对，这是最危险的情况，自卫者应考虑暂时服从并随时准备抓住歹徒的持刀手。第二种情况是歹徒未抓住自卫者，但自卫者距刀尖只一步左右，自卫者可抽身而逃或快速击开刀子，并实施攻击或后撤以远战。第三种情况是双方距离几米远，自卫者暂时安全。格斗方式可用远战、擒拿或使用器具。

　　1）远战对刀。

　　远战比较安全，因为进可攻，退可守。不过一般是宁退勿进。远战的基本原则和方法有几项：第一是保持移动，保持距离。第二是少用拳而是将手置于身前一侧挡来刀，尽管有时候手会受伤，但要害部位却得以保护。第三是

female college students in 1997, which was similar to real combat but used a rubber knife. Every time the defender resists, the wielder tries their best to stab the defender. In ten experiments, the probability of self-defense injuries reached 92%, of which 54% were in the head, neck, chest, and abdomen, and 38% were in the hands and legs. All of them were stabbed more than 5 times, and 50% of the victims were stabbed every time they resisted. This is the result of the unarmed knife to knife experiment. When self-defender use chairs to engage with knives, the stabbing rate is greatly reduced, and most of the injuries are in the arms.

There are several possible ways for a criminal to threaten with a knife: the first scenario is for the criminal to lock the defender's throat and face each other with a knife, which is the most dangerous situation. The defender should consider temporarily obeying and being ready to catch the criminal's wielder at any time. The second scenario is when the perpetrator fails to catch the defender, but the defender is only about one step away from the tip of the knife. The defender can escape or quickly open the knife, and carry out an attack or retreat to engage in long-range combat. The third scenario is that both sides are a few meters away, and the self-defender are temporarily safe. Fighting methods can include long-range combat, capture, or the use of equipment.

1) Long distance battle with swords.

Long distance combat is safer because advancing allows for attack and retreating allows for defense. However, it is generally better to retreat than to advance. There are several basic principles and methods for long-range warfare: the first is to keep moving and maintain distance. The second is to use fewer punches and instead place your hand on the side in front of you to block the knife. Although sometimes your hand

随时抓住机会逃跑。保持距离及移动，双手置于身前，抓住机会击伤歹徒之膝。

流程：

（1）讲解、示范。

（2）一攻一对练。

（3）擒拿对刀。

擒拿对刀技术虽好，但极难应用，主要的问题是很难抓住歹徒持刀的手而自己又不受伤。另外，在歹徒有准备时也很难将其拿住。因此，对多数人来说，尤其是新手，应尽量少用，除非再无别的技术可用。擒拿对刀基本上有两种手法：锁肘及卷腕。

面对持刀歹徒，歹徒进刀时将其持刀手抓住，踢裆、锁肘，制服歹徒。歹徒刀刺时，抓住持刀手，卷腕，拧倒歹徒。

流程：

（1）讲解、示范。

（2）一攻一对练。

3）上压刀刺解脱法——抓推解脱法。

此法主要用于对付骑在身上并以刀相胁或欲行刺的歹徒。此种情况极其危险，即使自卫者受过训练，受伤的概率也极大。歹徒欲刺自卫者，自卫者格挡并抓住歹徒持刀的手，腾出左手猛击其肘，将歹徒推翻于体侧，自卫

may be injured, the crucial parts are protected. The third is to seize the opportunity to escape at any time. Maintain distance and movement, place both hands in front of you, seize the opportunity to injure the perpetrator's knee.

Procedure:

(1) Explanation and demonstration.

(2) One-on-one practice.

(3) Capturing and wielding knives.

Although the technique of catching and wielding knives is good, it is extremely difficult to apply. The main problem is that it is difficult to grasp the hand of the criminal holding the knife without getting injured. Moreover, it is also difficult to capture the criminals when they are prepared. Therefore, for most people, especially beginners, they should use it as little as possible unless there are no other technologies available. There are basically two techniques for catching and wielding knives: locking the elbow and curling the wrist.

Faced with a knife wielding criminal, the criminal grabbed the knife wielding hand, kicked the crotch, locked the elbow, and subdued the criminal as they advanced. When the criminal stabbed, he grabbed the wielder, rolled his wrist, and twisted the criminal down.

Procedure:

(1) Explanation and demonstration.

(2) One-on-one practice.

3）Upward pressure knife stabbing release method — Grasping and pushing release method.

This method is mainly used to deal with criminals who ride on their bodies and threaten or intend to assassinate with knives. This situation is extremely dangerous, and even if the self-defender have been trained, the chances of injury are extremely high. The criminal intends to stab the self-defense, but the self-defense person blocks and grabs the criminal's hand holding the knife, freeing up his left hand to strike the

者也可猛咬其手以夺下刀。

流程：

（1）讲解、示范。

（2）一攻一对练。

4）器械对刀。

作者所做研究表明，使用椅子可在很大程度上减少对刀格斗受伤的概率。但在实战中不一定手边恰好有椅子，此时其他器械亦可以使用。这里主要介绍三种器械对刀方法：椅子对刀、扫帚把对刀及衣服对刀。其他物品如书包、沙发垫、脸盆、水桶等都可以使用。

举椅以封刀路，当歹徒欲抓椅时，可后退，亦可猛力前撞。持扫帚把对准歹徒，乘歹徒不备猛击其腹，歹徒欲抓时则猛踹其膝，用衣服缠手以利于远战格挡，两手拽衣服以侧挡刀路等。

特殊格斗技术对自卫者技术的质量要求甚高，技术越精则格斗时危险越少。此外，通过模拟实战训练和与不同对手较量来增加实战经验则更为重要，有实战经验才有信心与胆量。另外，不断学习新技术亦可增加自卫者临战运用技术的能力。中国擒拿、日本柔术及合气道、军警的格斗训练及保镖训练都可帮助提高特殊技术格斗。

E、简介考试（讲解考试方法及要求）：多攻一。

elbow and overturn the criminal to the side of his body. The self-defense person can also bite his hand to take the knife.

Procedure:

(1) Explanation and demonstration.

(2) One-on-one practice.

4) Instrument knife alignment.

The author's research indicates that using chairs can greatly reduce the likelihood of injury in knife fighting. But in actual combat, it is not necessarily necessary to have a chair at hand, and other equipment can also be used. Here we mainly introduce three methods of instrument knife alignment: chair knife alignment, broomstick knife alignment, and clothing knife alignment. Other items such as backpacks, sofa cushions, washbasins, buckets, etc. can all be used.

Raise the chair to block the path of the knife. When the criminal wants to grab the chair, they can either retreat or forcefully collide forward. Aim the broomstick at the criminal, take advantage of the criminal's unpreparedness and strike him in the abdomen. When the criminal wants to catch him, kick him in the knee, wrap his hands with clothes to block the distance, and pull his clothes with both hands to block the path of the knife.

Special combat techniques require high quality of self-defense skills, and the more advanced the technique, the less dangerous the combat is. In addition, it is more important to increase practical experience through simulated combat training and competition with different opponents. Only with practical experience can one have confidence and courage. In addition, continuous learning of new technologies can also enhance the self-defender's ability to apply technology in combat. Chinese grappling, Japanese jujutsu and aikido, military and police combat training, and bodyguard training can all help improve special skills in combat.

E. Introduction Exam (explaining Exam Methods and requirements): Multiple-to-one attacks.

1. 每人 1 ～ 1.5 min 的考试时间，全程摄像。

2. 多攻一解脱技术主要考核解脱技术。

3. 四人进攻一人防卫，各种动作交替使用进行自卫。

（三）结束部分

1. 集体放松活动。

2. 讲评本次课。

3. 布置课外作业，复习所学内容。

1. Each person will have an exam time of one minute to one and a half minutes, and the entire process will be filmed.

2. Multiple-to-one attack and one release technique mainly assesses the release technique.

3. Four people attacking and one person defending, using various actions alternately for self-defense.

(Ⅲ) End section

1. Collective relaxation activities.

2. Evaluate this class.

3. Review the learned content for extracurricular assignments.

第八课

Lesson 8

一、教学内容

1. 全面复习考试内容。

2. 考试。

3. 总结本学期课程，对学生提出临别希望和赠言。

4. 问卷调查，让每位学生对本门课提出自己的意见和建议。

Ⅰ. Teaching content

1. Comprehensive review of exam routines.

2. Examination.

3. Summarize the courses of this semester and offer farewell wishes and gifts to students.

4. Conduct a questionnaire survey and ask each student to provide their own opinions and suggestions on this course!

二、木课任务

综合考核学生自卫能力。

Ⅱ. The task of the class

Comprehensive assessment of self-defense ability.

三、教学重点

考试。

Ⅲ. Teaching focus

examination.

四、教学内容与组织教法

（一）准备部分

A. 班体委集合整队，向老师报告人数。

B. 讲解考试的方法和要求。

C. 提醒学生注意安全。

D. 鼓励学生自告奋勇带领全班做准备活动简介枪口下的自卫防身。

（二）基本部分

A. 全面复习。

1. 远距离格斗技术。

2. 近距离格斗技术。

3. 摔法格斗。

4. 地面格斗技术。

5. 擒拿格斗技术。

6. 解脱格斗技术。

a. 抓臂解脱法；b. 抱腰解脱法；c. 锁喉解脱法；d. 抓发解脱法；e. 其他解脱法

7. 特殊格斗技术。

a. 刀尖上的自卫防身；b. 以少对多的自卫防身。

8. 综合技术。

a. 两人一组一对一复习动作；b. 分组多攻一复习准备考试

B. 介绍枪口下的自卫防身。

任何人面对枪口时都会胆寒，即使是受过专门训练的警察或武术行家也会如此。因为不知道歹徒到底想干什么，所以安全逃生

IV. Teaching content and organizational teaching methods

(I) Preparation section

A. The class sports committee gathered to form a team and reported the number of people to the teacher.

B. Explain the methods and requirements of the exam. Explain how to improve special combat techniques.

C. Classroom questioning reminds students to pay attention to security.

D. Students report bravely leading the whole class to prepare for an activity introduction on self-defense under the muzzle of a gun.

(II) Basic parts

A. Comprehensive review.

1. Long range fighting technology.

2. Close range combat techniques.

3. Throwing Fighting.

4. Ground fighting techniques.

5. Capturing and Fighting Techniques.

6. Liberation Fighting Techniques.

a. Arm grabbing release method; b. Waist hugging release method; c. Throat locking release method; d. Hair grabbing release method; e. Other release methods

7. Special Fighting Techniques.

a. Self-defender on the tip of the knife; b. Use few to many self-defense measures.

8. Comprehensive Technology.

a. One-on-one to review actions; b. multiple-to-one review, preparation for the exam.

B. Introduce self-defense under the muzzle of a gun.

Anyone will feel a chill when facing the muzzle, even trained police officers or martial arts experts will do so. Because we don't know what the criminals really want to do, the possibility of safe escape cannot be determined, and there

的可能性无法知道，没有哪种办法能保证自己百分之百的安全。

面对枪口的防身，专家们推荐三种做法。第一种是服从于歹徒以期歹徒不会进一步伤害自己。第二种是立即逃跑以免被歹徒带到僻静之处再下手。第三种是格斗以控制住歹徒或创造逃跑的机会。这三种方法各有利弊，运用时机亦不相同。

（1）服从。

面对枪口不做任何反抗，听从于歹徒的命令是大多数人都会做出的选择，很多自卫防身教师也大力推荐这种办法。然而，没有具体数字可以说听命于歹徒的逃生成功率到底有多少。人们采取这种办法基本上是基于常识或个别案例，但案例两种结果都有。有些人听命于歹徒，结果保住了性命，有些人则没有那么幸运，在做了歹徒所要求的一切后仍然被枪杀。

（2）逃跑。

大多数人对在枪口下逃生都抱怀疑态度，他们认为这样一来歹徒会发怒而开枪。其实并不然，有的歹徒可能会发怒开枪，而有的则不愿在公开场合开枪，也有的本来就是想吓唬受害者。另外，即使歹徒开枪也不一定每次都能击中，而且即便击中也不一定是要害部位。

is no way to ensure one's 100% security.

Faced with self-defense at the muzzle, experts recommend three methods: the first is to obey the criminals in order to prevent them from further harming themselves. The second option is to immediately escape to avoid being taken to a secluded place by the criminals before taking action. The third type is fighting to control criminals or create opportunities for escape. These three methods each have their own advantages and disadvantages, and the timing of application is also different.

(1) Obey.

Facing the muzzle without any resistance and obeying the orders of criminals is a choice that most people will make, and many self-defense teachers also strongly recommend this method. However, there is no specific number to say what the success rate of escaping under the command of criminals is. People adopt this approach mainly based on common sense or individual cases, but both cases have different outcomes. Some people obey the orders of the criminals and save their lives, while others are not so lucky and are still shot after doing everything the criminals demand.

(2) Escape.

Most people have a skeptical attitude towards escaping under the gun, believing that the criminals will get angry and shoot. In fact, it's not the case. Some criminals may get angry and shoot, while others are unwilling to shoot in public, and some are just trying to scare the victims. Furthermore, even if the perpetrator fires, they may not always be able to hit, and even if they do, they may not necessarily hit the critical area.

（3）格斗。

格斗是大多数人都不愿采用的手段。因为格斗会激怒歹徒，或威胁歹徒的安全，因此而迫使其开枪。如果自卫者技术不高，则成功的概率不大，而且一旦动手便无退路。但格斗会给自卫者一些主动权去控制局势，而不是听任于歹徒摆布、宰割。

枪口下的格斗适合于一臂之内的近距离，自卫者伸手就能抓住歹徒持枪手。一般来说，若自卫者反应和动作速度很快，都可以避开歹徒的第一枪，但必须在避开第一枪后迅速控制歹徒持枪手以防其射出第二枪。

若歹徒较远，还是走为上计。最难的是敌我相距5～6 m，打又太远，逃又太近，容易被击中。以下几种机会较适合于自卫者使用格斗技术：第一是当不动手就要被打死时；第二是当歹徒走神或放松时；第三是距离近能够着，自卫者又受过一定训练时。

枪口搏斗，方法多样，但大部分却没有经过试验。人们喜欢使用擒拿技术，因为若能控制住歹徒持枪手，自卫者就安全多了。一般枪口搏斗的过程有三步：

第一步是身体快闪，同时将歹徒持枪手击开；

第二步是迅速控制歹徒持枪的手臂，以防歹徒抽枪再射；

(3) Fighting.

Fighting is a means that most people are unwilling to adopt. Because fighting can anger or threaten the security of criminals, it forces them to shoot. If the defender's skills are not high, the chances of success are not high, and once they take action, there is no way out. But fighting gives defenders some initiative to control the situation, rather than being manipulated or slaughtered by criminals.

The combat under the muzzle is suitable for close range within one arm, and the defender can reach out and catch the gunman holding the gun. Generally speaking, if self-defender react and move quickly, they can avoid the first shot of the criminal, but they must quickly control the gunman to prevent them from firing a second shot after avoiding the first shot.

If the criminal is far away, it is still better to go. The most difficult thing is that the distance between us and the enemy is 5-6 meters. If we hit too far, we cannot reach it, and if we escape too close, we are easily hit. The following opportunities are more suitable for self-defense fighters to use combat techniques: first, when they are about to be killed without using their hands; The second is when the criminals are distracted or relaxed; The third is when the defender has received certain training and is close enough to reach.

Gunfight involves various methods, but most of them have not been tested. People like to use capture techniques because if they can control the criminals and gunmen, the self-defense will be much safer. The general process of muzzle combat involves three steps:

The first step is to quickly flash your body and shoot the gunman away at the same time;

The second step is to quickly control the arm of the criminal holding the gun to prevent the criminal from drawing

第三步是用摔、踢、拿、打、击伤或制服歹徒。

面对歹徒以不同形式以枪抵住自卫者头部或心脏的情况，应采用以下格斗方式防卫。歹徒正面单手用枪抵住自卫者头部时（右手持枪），自卫者双手急速上举并向前移动，左转身用左右手臂先后抓住歹徒持枪手臂及手腕同时右手折叠其手腕，也可咬其手臂、反关节击肘，也可以顺势侧抱歹徒手臂，自卫者左右膝可以前后攻击歹徒的裆部，此时的体位歹徒无法还击。

歹徒双手正面用枪抵住自卫者头部，自卫者双手急速上举并向前移动抓住歹徒持枪双手手腕，同时身体下降重心上步用膝击档。

歹徒单、双手背面用枪抵住自卫者头部，自卫者双手急速上举并向后移动，首先判断歹徒用的是单手还是双手，然后快速后转身下面的动作基本上和正面相同。

歹徒用枪抵住自卫者后背，急速右转身用手臂格挡开枪械，并快速靠紧歹徒身体，以使其没空抽回枪，使用锁肘技术，转身下压歹徒手臂，将歹徒按压在地上。

a gun and then shooting again;

The third step is to throw, kick, grab, hit, injure or subdue the criminal.

Faced with various forms and scenarios where the perpetrator puts a pistol to the defender's head or heart, the following combat techniques should be used to defend themselves. When the perpetrator uses one hand to hold the gun against the head of the defender (with the right hand holding the gun), the defender quickly raises and moves forward with both hands, turns left and grabs the perpetrator's arm and wrist with both arms, while folding the wrist with the right hand. The perpetrator can also bite the arm, hit the elbow with the back joint, or hug the perpetrator's arm sideways. The defender's left and right knees can attack the perpetrator's crotch back and forth, but the perpetrator cannot retaliate in this position.

The perpetrator pressed the gun against the defender's head with both hands in front, and the defender quickly raised and moved his hands forward to grab the wrist of the perpetrator's gun holding hands. At the same time, he lowered his body and took a step forward, hitting the block with his knees.

The perpetrator used a gun to hold the defender's head with one or both hands on the back. The defender quickly raised and moved his hands back, first determining whether the perpetrator was using one or both hands, and then quickly turned around. The movements below were basically the same as those in front.

The criminal pressed his gun against the defender's back, quickly turned right to block the firearm with his arm grid, and quickly leaned against the criminal's body to prevent him from withdrawing the gun. Using elbow locking technique, he turned around and pressed down on the criminal's arm, pressing him to the ground.

流程：

（1）讲解、示范。

（2）学生体会动作，两人一组，一攻一防，攻防互换。

枪口格斗需要注意：

第一，自卫者不要露出任何想反抗的迹象；

第二，突然急速格挡以避开第一枪；

第三，手臂粘住歹徒手臂并抓牢，以避免第二枪，然后再制服歹徒。

C. 考试：多攻一（讲解考试方法及要求）。

1. 以组为单位，每人1～1.5 min 的考试时间，全程摄像。

2. 多攻一解脱技术主要考核解脱技术：a. 徒手解脱；14 项技术；b. 地面解脱 5 项技术；c. 徒手对刀解脱；d. 徒手对枪解脱；e. 远、近距离格斗和摔法格斗。

D. 总结本学期课程，对学生提出临别希望和赠言。

1. 希望同学们一生平安健康。

2. 在今后的学习、工作、生活中无论遇到什么样的困难和问题，希望同学们冷静对待，处理好身边的一些小的问题，不让各种矛盾极化。

3. 学会与不同年龄、不同级别、不同层次的人进行沟通。

4. 先学做人，后学做事，全

Procedure：

(1) Explanation and demonstration.

(2) Students experience movements, work in pairs, one attack and one defense, and switch between attack and defense.

Gun fighting requires attention to:

Firstly, defenders should not show any signs of resistance;

Secondly, suddenly quickly block to avoid the first shot;

Thirdly, stick your arm to the criminal's arm and grab it firmly to avoid a second shot, then subdue the criminal.

C. Exam: Multiple-to-one attack (explain the exam methods and requirements).

1. On a group by group basis, each person will have an exam time of one minute to one and a half minutes, with full video footage of the entire process.

2. Multi attack and one release technique mainly assesses the release technique. a. 14 techniques for manual release; b. 5 ground release technologies; c. Freehand knife release; d. releases the gun with bare hands; e. Long range, close range combat, and throwing combat.

D. Summarize the courses of this semester and offer farewell wishes and gifts to students.

1. I hope that students will have a safe and healthy life.

2. In future learning, work, and life, no matter what difficulties and problems you encounter, I hope that students can handle them calmly, handle some small problems around them well, and not let various contradictions polarize.

3. Learn to communicate with people of different ages, levels, and levels.

4. Learn to be a good person first, then learn to do things,

面提高个人能力、素质、气质。

and comprehensively improve personal abilities, qualities, and temperament.

5. 掌握特殊情况下的逃生能力——智斗与格斗。

5. Escape ability in special situations — Smart combat and Fighting.

E. 每位学生对本门课提出自己的意见和建议。

E. Each student provides their own opinions and suggestions for this course.

（三）结束部分

(Ⅲ) End section

1. 小结安全自卫防身课程学习情况。

1. Summary of the learning situation of security and self-defense courses.

2. 让学生留下联系方式和电子邮件地址，以便接收学习视频和照片。

2. Ask students to leave their contact information and email address for receiving videos and photos.

参 考 文 献
References

[1]　杨波. 犯罪心理学 [M]. 北京：高等教育出版社，2015.

[2]　杨海，郑伟民. 大学生公共安全教育 [M]. 北京：高等教育出版社，2021.

[3]　李俊峰，张成明. 综合格斗教程 [M]. 北京：北京体育大学出版社，2019.

[4]　全国体育院校教材委员会. 中国武术教程：下册 [M]. 北京：人民体育出版社，2003.

[5]　《运动解剖学》编写组. 运动解剖学 [M]. 北京：北京体育大学出版社，2013.

[6]　张锐. 拒绝伤害：安全教育与自卫防身 [M]. 北京：北京大学出版社，2020.

[7]　龚兵. 大学生安全教育的发展历程与时代价值 [J]. 黑龙江高教研究，2015(9):72-75.

[8]　郑晓江. 生命困顿与生命教育 [J]. 南昌大学学报（人文社会科学版），2012,43(2):48-54.

[9]　罗斌. 自我防卫术技击应用研究 [J]. 体育文化导刊，2015(12):79-83.

[10]　ALEXANDER J, ALLAN D R, RHODES D D. Cryotherapy in sport: a warm reception for the translation of evidence into applied practice[J]. Research in sports medicine，2022, 30(4): 458-461.

[11]　万国华，宋军，杨小勇，等. 大学生课外运动损伤的影响因素 [J]. 体育学刊，2013, 20(1): 88-92.

[12]　曾国际，郭夕语，邵璐，等. 软组织运动损伤处理原则的发展概述 [J]. 按摩与康复医学，2022,13(6):54-56.

[13]　何庆，黄煜.2020 AHA 心肺复苏指南解读：二　成人基础和高级生命支持：上 [J]. 心血管病学进展，2020,41(12):1333-1337.

[14]　浦鹏飞，冯德富. 溺水与急救 [J]. 中国医药导报，2007(25):133-134.

[15]　汤家全，刘建锋.88 例已破故意杀人案的回顾性分析 [J]. 法医学杂志，2016, 32(2):119-122.

[16]　尹明灿，李晓明. 故意杀人罪实证研究：以 493 例故意杀人罪案例为视角 [J]. 中国刑事法杂志，2009(6):105-115.

[17]王威，张世林，张宵，等.816 例故意伤害未成年人案件的法医学分析 [J].法制博览，2023(12):13-17.

[18]　史振，曹文江. 重新犯罪的原因分析及对策研究 [J]. 法制与社会，2016(34):280-282.

[19]　林亚刚. 暴力犯罪的内涵与外延 [J]. 现代法学，2001(6):138-142.

[20] 龙武 , 胡春梅 , 李思思 , 等 . 西南地区 1 340 例故意伤害案件的特征及相关因素分析 [J].
　　 法医学杂志 , 2019, 35(4): 433−436.

[21] 马洁 , 薛顶峰 . 天津市青少年故意伤害行为调查分析 [J]. 中国慢性病预防与控制 , 2014,
　　 22(6):679−682.

[22] 陈朝 . 婚恋型故意杀人及故意伤害犯罪研究 [D]. 南昌 : 江西财经大学 , 2023.

[23] 邹溪海 , 薛枫艳 . "两抢一盗" 的预防和对策 : 以东莞 1 095 份问卷调查分析为视界 [J]. 法
　　 治论坛 , 2008(2):221−231.

[24] 黄靖 . 未成年人犯罪特点、原因、变化趋势及对策 : 以某县级市未成年犯罪案件调查为基
　　 础 [J]. 青少年研究 (山东省团校学报), 2014(5):48−51.

[25] 熊秋红 . 最高检首批刑事抗诉指导性案例评析 [J]. 中国检察官 , 2023(18):18−22.

[26] 邵嘉 . 论强奸犯罪的成因及防范对策 : 基于河南省 100 起样本分析 [J]. 商丘师范学院学报 ,
　　 2023, 39(10):86−92.

[27] 张应立 , 戴晶晶 . 盗窃犯罪被害问题实证研究 : 以宁波市北仑区为例 [J]. 公安学刊 (浙江
　　 警察学院学报), 2021(2):86−95.

[28] 陈舒琦 , 任延涛 . "杀猪盘" 网络诈骗的心理诱导机制及预防对策 [J]. 广西警察学院学报 ,
　　 2022, 35(4):86−93.

[29] 邱晓妍 . 网络诈骗犯罪特点及其预防 : 以交友诱导赌博投资为例 [J]. 广州市公安管理干部
　　 学院学报 , 2019, 29(3):18−23.

[30] 李欣 . 暴力犯罪心理成因及防治研究 [D]. 长春 : 吉林大学 , 2014.